TELLING TALES ON CAESAR

Telling Tales on Caesar

Roman Stories from Phaedrus

JOHN HENDERSON

OXFORD
UNIVERSITY PRESS

OXFORD
UNIVERSITY PRESS

Great Clarendon Street, Oxford, OX2 6DP
Oxford University Press is a department of the University of Oxford.
It furthers the University's objective of excellence in research, scholarship,
and education by publishing worldwide in

Oxford New York

Athens Auckland Bangkok Bogotá Buenos Aires Cape Town
Chennai Dar es Salaam Delhi Florence Hong Kong Istanbul Karachi
Kolkata Kuala Lumpur Madrid Melbourne Mexico City Mumbai
Nairobi Paris São Paulo Shanghai Singapore Taipei Tokyo Toronto Warsaw
and associated companies in Berlin Ibadan

Oxford is a registered trade mark of Oxford University Press
in the UK and certain other countries

Published in the United States
by Oxford University Press Inc., New York

British Library Cataloguing in Publication Data

Data applied for

ISBN 0-19-924095-7

Library of Congress Cataloging in Publication Data

Data applied for

1 3 5 7 9 10 8 6 4 2

Typeset in Imprint
by Regent Typesetting, London
Printed in Great Britain
on acid-free paper by
Biddles Ltd, Guildford and King's Lynn

PREFACE

Let me let you into a very small secret. Hardly anyone at all is aware that the stories retold in this book exist. It's not just that not many people ever sit down and read Phaedrus on purpose, though that is perfectly true, but when his stuff does get looked at, it is for some point of Latin idiom from a reference in a work of (you got it) reference; or it is because someone who is, for some reason, on the hunt for a particular Aesopic fable, either has drawn a blank in the Greek collections and must resort to Phaedrus' version, or else (more scrupulous moments, these) is checking out one that turns up in Phaedrus *as well as* in Greek. This is no way to see what this Roman writer has to offer, let alone what he is up to.

The dozen or so stories I shall be looking at will be compact fictions that crept upon Phaedrus as he took liberties with the *Fabulae*. Maybe he meant from the first to let these extraneous excursions beyond Aesop grow on him, or rather his readers; or maybe the select but star-studded Roman cast of characters smuggled their own way in among all the wolves and foxes, the lions and apes, the kite and . . . (not forgotten) the frogs. Teachers long ago called time on poor Phaedrus, even as a way of getting started on the Latin language, let alone somewhere you could begin to think about what's what; and Latin Literature looks the other way. Ancient Historians simply haven't known what they've been missing, or, until recently, that they've been missing it—'anecdotal history' has only recently ceased to be a contradiction in terms. No, I'm not here telling tales on Classics. And I'm certainly not 'telling tales', either.

Just a few words about myself for you to grin and bear. I'll own up to one thing: I've been keeping these juicy chunks of ancient storytelling to myself for far, far longer than merits either credit or crediting. I've known all along that inconsequential anecdotes are up to more than showcasing frivolity; they flex the imagination. And to construe the Roman imaginary has to be the challenge, the whole point, of 'cultural history'. So, no, the throw-away lines of these *fabulae* aren't exactly pinnacles of human achievement; but (as we have needed to learn) if you want to know a culture, then study what it throws away. If this reads all too like a 'moral', here's what Bahaudin Naqshband replied, when someone said to him:

'You relate stories, but you do not tell us how to understand them.'
'How would you like it if the man from whom you bought fruit consumed it before your very eyes, leaving you only the skin?'
(Idries Shah (1974) 137)

To be plain, this book segues my doctoral thesis, *Anecdote and Satire in Phaedrus*. It has been a pleasure to work with the team again – Hilary O'Shea, her readers, Tom Chandler, and, especially, Georga Godwin – and I hope they realise the difference they make.

CONTENTS

LIST OF ILLUSTRATIONS

1*a*. Tiberius: Detail of seated portrait statue.
From Caere. Marble (body perhaps re-used from Gaius).
Mid first century CE. Height (from head to abdomen)
1.42 m. Musei Vaticani, Rome (inv. 9961). Photo:
Felbermeyer, DAIR 35.960. With permission.

1*b*. Flunkey: Detail of a Roman mosaic pavement, showing
preparations for a banquet.
From Carthage. Marble, limestone, glass. Late second
century CE. Height 2.25 m. Acquired in 1891. The Louvre,
Paris (MA1796). With permission.

2*a*. Freedman: Detail of a funerary plaque for various freed-
men, from Rome.
White marble. Late first century BCE–early first century CE.
Height 0.74, length (overall) 1.85, depth 0.30 m. Restor-
ations include the nose. Bought at auction from the
Lansdowne Collection in 1930. Ny Carlsberg Glyptotek,
Copenhagen (inv. 2799). With permission.

2*b*. Augustus: Head of Augustus found at Meroe, south
Sudan, in 1910.
Bronze. *c*. 27–25 BCE. Height 0.44 m. BM (inv. 1911). The
story goes that the head was ripped from a statue and
buried by tribesmen under the steps of a temple of victory,
which carried pictures of bound captives: thus entry was
over the prisoners' bodies and the head of the emperor.
Eyes inset: the whites are alabaster, the irises a yellow-
black stone, the pupils glass in a bronze ring. Photo: Nigel
Cassidy, from a cast in the Museum of Classical
Archaeology, Cambridge. By permission of the Curator.

3*a*. Phaedrus (?): Funerary relief.
Carrara Marble. First century CE. Dimensions: 0.50 × 0.36
× 0.23 m. Privately owned, in Zurich. Photo: from Helga

INTRODUCTION

The stories in this book come from a source close to the palace in the formative decades of the Roman Empire. Phaedrus was a freedman of Augustus who put *Aesop's Fables* into five books of Latin verse in the reign of Tiberius. (The sparse and tantalizing biographical evidence is examined in Chapter 3.) He included a fair number of stories and anecdotes on everyday life situations and topics, and as he went on, he expanded the range to include, as well as assorted satirical bits and pieces, several distinctive 'Roman tales'.

These include cameos for the first pair of emperors: *Augustus*, who appears as the wise 'Solomon': only the Emperor can clear up a domestic murder mystery (Chapter 2); and *Tiberius*, who sees through the fawning that pursues him even along his garden path (Chapter 1). Their forerunner *Pompey* the Great stars as the buddy general fooled by a soldier's camp appearance (Chapter 5). In the theatre, a star musician called *Prince* (Latin, *Princeps*) milks applause meant for the first Emperor (Chapter 4). In Greece, one predecessor of the Caesars, the dictator *Demetrius*, eats his words to flatter the great thespian *Menander* (Chapter 6). In the land of fiction, it takes an archetypal *King* to suss out a quack *Doctor* (Chapter 7) . . .

Along the way, *Phaedrus* picks his own moment to tell us what fables are for, and why *he* is writing them: he hints at his own persecution by the villainous would-be Caesar *Sejanus*; outlines what sort of readership he'd like to get; what we're to make of his project; and sends himself up (Chapter 3).

Finally, the overall spread of the *Fabulae* adds up to a storehouse of 'Aesopic' ideas, not least on power, power-politics, and the downtrodden have-nots of our corner of the universe. Apes, Lions, Foxes, Logs all serve up *Emperors* to think with; they are ways to probe, prod, and ponder kingship (Chapter 8).

Are all of us, then, astute readers? Are we, then, being told that *we* are, precisely . . . helpless . . . slaves? And is this Roman stuff a spot of light reading? Or is 'Aesop in verse' a cosy corner specially provided for toying with risky ideas? And *compilation*, now: is a collection, an anthology, the surest way to decommission and disarm the *vox populi* (word on the street)? Does *Phaedrus* at bottom teach how to muzzle the awkward cuss he could have been? Something along the lines of: 'Put stories in cold storage, and see what is in store for them'? . . . Whatever else we may decide, the fabulist is 'Romanizing' *all* the tales he tells—not just because he puts them into Latin, but by his choice of material, by his editorial framing, by his *montage* of the collection (as the design of a controlling 'author', and a 'poet', at that: Chapter 3). Turn this round, and you'll see that this mock-empire of narratives authorizes a distinctive take on Rome and Roman cognition. In my book, Phaedrus puts in (its) place storytelling within Roman literary discourse.

The genre of the Aesopic fable, the freedman author, and his tales involving perspectives from below, as well as on high, take readers for a rare, in many ways unique, excursion into the wider world of imperial Rome, beyond the senatorial/court élite. You can look at each story from *both* perspectives—in fact, you *must* to-and-fro between the two—peek inside the gilded cage, and safari through the human menagerie at large. The dual illustrations that head each chapter are meant to bring out, and keep before you, the bifocal hermeneutics written into any (acidic, non-saccharine) discourse on power: the top-down vista side-by-side with the underlings' eyeful. The reason that these perspectives are mutually constitutive is that 'looking up to' and 'looking down on' are inseparably and incessantly trained on each other. Maybe royals in the coach know they can never know how (supercilious) they look from the kerb; perhaps the mob of burghers can only suspect that inferiors are there for a supremo to despise and disregard ('humiliate' and 'humble' share their derivation, from Latin *humus*, 'ground').

Without, I hope, giving away twice too many secrets and half the plots, this paragraph and the next will sketch in the skirmishes ahead in terms of this two-way street between throne and gutter. First, the book's look at the imperial animal: we explore the private grounds of Caesar's summer palace; join the public gallery in court at the capital for a sensational murder trial and a ruling from Caesar; glimpse the toppling of Caesar's henchman in the waves that rippled through the royal retinue; we then drop by Rome's national theatre, for patriotic choruses of 'God save Caesar, God help Rome' (Chapters 1–4). Heading off to the frontier, we catch the greatest general in the world in full view of his invincible legions, displaying his command of the common touch (Chapter 5). Over in Athens (and back in time), an invading prince paddles his own Canute through a flood of expert Greek kow-towing, and finds a winning quip for their local Shakespeare (Chapter 6). From here on, we shall be in Story Land: just about anywhere in fiction (or, for that matter, non-fiction), the head of state calls the body politic to heel (and—maybe—health: Chapter 7); ultimately, though, in the stark world according to Aesop, we'll find that rulers of all shapes and sizes—rulers as such—have their people for breakfast. Either on the sly, or else making no bones about it: their people deserve all they get (Chapter 8).

Second time around, let's skim the stories for rougher trade. Plumb the depths, and scrape the barrel. Here is the way of Phaedrus' world: *servants* run palaces, those nests of seduction and infernal terrorism—favourite underlings worm their way up through the undergrowth, and favoured vipers in the bosom wreak havoc in the bedroom (Chapters 1–2). Raw savages from the back of beyond already infiltrate the classical library and profane the haunts of the Muses; they even sniff around high politics—and you're reading one of them (Chapter 3). Off at the theatre, an unsung hero gets one of those embarrassing tribute sessions of special recognition by the industry: we get the low-down on *all* adulation (Chapter 4). A trooper traps his officers—he is lowest of the low, and yet he scales the heights: so what do *they* know about the men? (Chapter 5). In a truly civilized world, a fabulous creative writer could face down any tinpot Napoleon (Chapter 6). Cobblers! The lives and soles of the community are in their hands! Downtrodden heels! (Chapter 7). For a finale, take a look at us all—grilled monkeys and mangled doves, frightened frogs and torn lambkins. Be sad and stay mad—*and vice versa* (Chapter 8). Something like this is what Rome makes of Aesop; and what 'Aesop' can get said about Rome.

What happens, then, if you set your Rome watch by Phaedrus? The Latin writer does not drop his Greek fore-runner and supplier of material; but he does play off his own

stake in the business against the mythic prototype. Phaedrus
sows a row of hints that narrator and audience are both exposing themselves in playing this game. If Aesop came back to
haunt Rome—where would you expect to find him, and how
would he ply his trade—of cheek, nous, street cred.? Suppose
'*Phaedrus*' is our answer—another slave; but a slave who is a
member of the divine household of the rulers of the planet, at
the core of the cosmopolis . . . Could we pin him down, if we
wanted to? Is it daft to hail the mask of 'Aesop' as the best-
protected code-name that an imperial mole could want—just
the ticket for leaking stories of *doxa* (common opinion, gossip,
commonsense) from the palace, and back again? Or, if
Phaedrus just doodles blithe banality—what does that bubble
look like when blown-up Rome-size, in the eye of the purple
and gold tiger? These are the questions that matter.

Written in just about the easiest classical Latin verse there is,
these are zippy colloquial texts, making clear points and presenting thoughtful dilemmas. (Chapter 8 will even dip into
medieval Latinity.) The poems are glad to be brief, they are
readily mastered, and they lead readers along many different
avenues right into the grain of social life at Rome, as well as
into informal thinking about the rule of the Caesars. This anecdotal 'cultural history' tells tales of vanity and hypocrisy,
parades wits and foibles, performs a literary diversion, outlines
a humour for imperial Rome. Yes: *humour*. At the same time, in
their off-beat way the *themes* of the stories also link up with hot
topics in current scholarship—the construction of the Emperor;
theatricality in Roman public life; declamation as a site for
mythologizing Romanness; masculinity in ancient gender
codes; patronage for poets under autocracy—and they also
profile an agenda of focuses and anxieties, of predilections and
preoccupations, for an imperial people learning to orient itself
between two eternities: achieved world conquest, and future
domination of the Caesars.

In looking to beef up *Aesop* and find a niche in Latin
literature, Phaedrus looked for (I would say 'found') amusing
tales that would speak of the ways of the world with no less
sagacity, and with added specificity. While his fate was to be
garbled into the medieval *Aesops* from which the nurseries and
belles lettres of modern Europe and the West in large measure

learned their fables, and to become for centuries the archetypal Beginners' text for induction to Latinity in school, this odd author's bid for acclamation as a (minor) poet, through stretching his range to include his string of Roman stories, is still waiting for its moment. Have these telling tales of Phaedrus been biding their time for now?

In order to extract all possible fruit from Aesop's fables, one cannot stop simply at the letter; it is necessary to penetrate into the spirit of the fable, where one can imbibe of beautiful lessons. (Abbé Bellegarde, *Les Fables d'Ésope* le Phrygien (1709), *Préf.*, in Noel (1975) 103)

PRAEFANDA:
HOW TELLING TALES ON CAESAR
WORKS

This book does its level best to accommodate all sorts of reader. The format is for each chapter to tackle one story, announced with twin illustrations: first come the Latin text and an English translation, then follows an introductory essay of analysis; finally, a 'slo'mo' commentary works through the lines of the poem, exploring literary, social, and cultural topics in detail. (Chapter 4 smuggles in a second tale (in fact, a tail); Chapter 8 moves away from 'anecdotes' to open up consideration of four 'fables' on kingship, before craning to survey the whole Aesopic take on monarchy, autocracy, and empire.)

1. *Illustrations* include some bogus, *but actual*, identifications: the data are provided in the *List of illustrations*.

2. *Text* for Phaedrus is largely a question of how far we trust one fragile manuscript in the case of verse written without too much pretension to greatness, in a conversationally relaxed metre which allows plenty of options for resolution; and written, too, in a colloquial, sometimes idiomatic but generally plain, Latin, with subject matter that often moves outside usual parameters. Where my text differs from the standard modern editions, information will be found at the relevant point in the *Endnotes*. Details of all the *sigla* (abbreviations) used to identify the *textus fontes* (manuscripts and quotations) will be found at the head of the *References*, along with a key for other abbreviations. (Chapters 5 and 8 explain how we know many of Phaedrus' *fabulae* only at second remove—with engrossing challenges in both medieval and Renaissance transmission.)

3. *Translation* is mine, for both stories and citations in Greek or Latin.

4. *Introductory Analysis* gives an accessible response to each story.

5. *Commentary* on successive sections of each story pursues issues more intensively, in tougher terms—cultural, historical, narratological, whatever.

6. *Endnotes* provide scholarly documentation primarily for the use of professional classicists. But I hope these notes have curiosity value, and more, for anyone who dares consult them: they deliberately reach way back through the modern past of Classics, bridging centuries. If you like, this is my homage to formative Oxford years spent in the spellbinding Bodleian Library; but that is not why they are here. They add up to a sort of 'fable'—and the 'moral' goes something like this: the challenge represented by the study of Antiquity has two sides— to key in Classics with our contemporary intellectual environment, and *vice versa*; but also to learn from our predecessors, whose work is not just (staggeringly) prodigious in bulk, but regularly tuned in to sharp and serious critical debate, however much its opacities require translation and explication before it can speak to us. When anyone dips into Classics, they are connecting with the original worldwide web of applied thinking.

Note: Dates are CE unless otherwise indicated.
Caveat: Modern fictions will be cited from time to time as if on all fours with ancient texts. I am out to make a point about 'anecdotal history'.

1(a)

1(b)

I

We Are Not Amused: *Tiberius Caesar* and the Flunkey (2. 5)

Est ardalionum quaedam Romae natio,
trepide concursans, occupata in otio,
gratis anhelans, multa agendo nihil agens,
sibi molesta et aliis odiosissima:
hanc emendare, si tamen possum, uolo   5
uera fabella. pretium est operae attendere:
   Caesar Tiberius cum petens Neapolim
in Misenensem uillam uenisset suam
quae monte summo posita Luculli manu
prospectat Siculum et respicit Tuscum mare,   10
ex alticinctis unus atriensibus
cui tunica ab umeris linteo Pelusio
erat destricta cirris dependentibus,
perambulante laeta domino uiridia,
alueolo coepit ligneo conspargere   15
humum aestuantem, come officium iactitans
—sed deridetur. inde notis flexibus
praecurrit alium in xystum, sedans puluerem:
agnoscit hominem Caesar remque intellegit.   19
'Heus' inquit dominus. ille enimuero adsilit   21
donationis alacer certae gaudio.
   tum sic iocata est tanta maiestas ducis:
'Non multum egisti et opera nequiquam perit.
multo maioris alapae mecum ueneunt.'   25

There is one particular tribe of muckers in Rome,
they dash to and fro in a tizzy, tied up in free time,
hustling for free; lots ado but nothing doing, they're
a drag for themselves and for others loathsome as can be . . .
This is the lot I mean, if only I'm up to it, to put straight   5
with the help of a true story. It's well worth a good listen:
   The Emperor Tiberius, Naples bound,
once reached his villa at Misenum.

Stuck bang on the summit by the hand of Lucullus, this
looks out over the Sicilian sea with a view behind of the
    Etruscan.   10
There was one of the doormen all tucked right up to *there*,
his tunic drawn taut away from the shoulder by one of those
Pelusian linen belts, woollen tufts dangling down from the
    hem.
As master comes taking a turn through his exuberant
    shrubberies,
this fellow starts spraying the steaming ground   15
from a wooden scoop, flaunting *such* a considerate service
—but he's laughed away. Next, off he hurries on ahead, an
    expert on ways round,
into another promenade, and stills the dust there.   18
The Emperor recognizes the man, and realizes what's what.
'Hey' calls master. Abracadabra, he jumps to it,   21
looking lively, for the thrill of a sureWre hand-out.
    Then His Mighty Majesty quipped,
'You've got nowhere fast, your labour's lost.
Liberty-taking costs much more where I'm involved.'   25

The Emperor Tiberius's witticism on the topic of flattery was
most likely Phaedrus' maiden first-hand contribution to his
collection. At any rate, this story *proclaims* its departure from
his Greek stock of fables. The first book promised 'polished
versification of Aesop's amusing fictions'; the introduction to
book 2 flagged a new phase: 'If I choose to insert some material,
I'd like you, dear reader, to take it in good part' (1. *Prol.*; 2 *Prol.*
9 f.). When Caesar bursts on the scene—after Cat just terrorized
both her neighbours, Eagle and Sow (2. 4)—the narrator gives
him both a special build-up, with six action-packed lines of preliminaries, and a special status, star of 'the *true* story' (v. 6). The
Roman anecdotes to come will follow this lead, with relatively
elaborate *montage*; but only here will we run into that storyteller's favourite self-promotion, the 'promise of factuality'.
And here the question of 'truth' *glares* out at the reader. It just
had to be the Emperor who first pushed himself onto the stage,
now that the Roman planet pivoted round the dictatorship.
With him Tiberius brought the inescapable issue of *historical*
veracity.

Of course all spinners of yarn pretend at will that their true stories deserve our attention; but they don't always expect to be believed. So one response to the story is to discount Phaedrus' responsibility for the concoction of the tale, and to suppose he gleaned it from oral circulation, presumably in Rome, hungry for celebratory lore featuring the Royal Family under Tiberius' depressed régime.[1] Then we are dealing with a contemporary anecdote that provides an interesting insight into Tiberius' standing among his people. We could feed this in to our file of hints from elsewhere that suggest that 'la vieille roche' won his subjects' respect sufficiently for traces of a favourable impression to weather the storm of *inuidia* (resentment) among the senatorial élite.[2]

But we can't be sure when the story was committed to Phaedrus' *senarii* (iambic verse, relatively loose, and conversational in feel). For Tiberius *Caesar* made sure that that stayed his proper title when he was in charge, turning down one bright courtier's suggestion after another for relabelling him up-market.[3] And when he was gone, the next régime, crazy Caligula's hothouse of narcissism, let him keep his precious name. No senator stepped forward to attest Tiberius' ascension from the pyre to join his divine father, deified Augustus, among the gods. Instead, 'the consuls and others orchestrated in advance by Caligula' had the will read out and set aside as 'of unsound mind' (Dio, *Roman History* 59. 1. 2). Tiberius Caesar died human and stayed dead, thereby setting a precedent: not every ruler of Rome need follow Augustus' lead.

No external evidence gives much of a handle on Phaedrus' dates, and internally, as we shall see (Ch. 3), we can only align the present tale with the coming allusion in the proem to book 3 to his tangling with Sejanus, Tiberius' aide and, ultimately (in 31 CE), victim. So a *floruit* (approximate heyday) is all we can manage: 'after 14' (since Augustus is divinized in 3. 10: Ch. 2); and, for books 3 and following: 'post-31'. The argument that Tiberius was alive when (at least) book 2 was published is circumstantial: could Phaedrus help knowing where the Emperor died? If he knew, could he have managed *not* to mention that his story takes place where Tiberius spent his last hours? Thus we date the poem before 37. But as we turn to pondering how long we might guess Phaedrus took over

producing each book of fables and at what sort of interval, in the
effort to fix book 2 to an appropriate date before book 3, we
must not make the mistake of thinking that its writer himself
had no eye on his historicality.[4] We could even say that this is
what he wants 'Phaedrus' to mean: the only thing he'll tell us
about himself must, after all, be our earliest reference to what
was to become the perennial classic example of history's lesson
of mutability—meteoric Sejanus! As we try to decide when 2. 5
was written, and come up with 'sometime between 14 and 37',
we'll find ourselves caught in the hermeneutic circle that places
the anecdote in the story of Tiberius' reign so as to fit the way
we (mean to) read them both. We'll know that Phaedrus, his
readers, and his rulers were all well aware that the accession of
Tiberius in his mid-fifties meant on the one hand that no one
should count on a long reign in prospect, and on the other that
the second Caesar *might* last another twenty years—or even
outdo the first.

The closer we allow ourselves to come to the Sejanus, and
post-Sejanus, years under Tiberius, the more tightly the story
will bind itself to his astounding *secessus* (retreat, virtual exile,
holiday) which saw the Caesar absent himself from his capital
for the entire last decade of his reign. In 26, nobody, and that
probably includes the Emperor, knew he would never set foot
in Rome again; as time went on, and to all appearances Sejanus
more or less took over running the world, only then to be eliminated in his most spectacular fall, and *still* Tiberius was always
somewhere else, the riddle must have become increasingly
salient, until in the final years there can have been no more
insistent a subject for speculation than what this present absence
was spelling for the future, and not least for the dynastic succession. What was Tiberius, what *can* he have been, thinking of?
What was in his mind—when there was, and he would pick out,
no single obvious convincing heir; when Rome had so far only
managed one faltering uneasy misfire of a succession; when his
own unchoreographed improvisational shambles of a take on
imperatorial exsequies and consecration, and on coronation and
inauguration, had thrown up precedents for establishing ceremonial constitutional ritual proprieties which he was himself
relentlessly ruling out for imitation by his successor? Overall,
too, was Tiberius' whole model for playing Caesar so idio-

syncratic, so bound into the psychopathology of the incumbent, so invested in self-subordination to the lengthy felicity of his beatified predecessor's paradigm, that his own tenure was universally recognized as predestined for elision from any future administration? What *was* 'Tiberius' going to mean? Everything? Nothing? There was no one anywhere who wouldn't have loved a clue.[5]

But if we decided to freeze the anecdote to Tiberius' early years in power, we should be looking at a story that homes in on the special style of self-presentation that he brought to his rule; a glimpse behind the scenes, away from public protocol and formalities of state, a chance to catch Tiberius going walkabout 'at home', and see how his bearing in private squares with, explains, encapsulates his profile as monarch. If the dramatic date envisaged for the narrative is 'early Tiberius', *c*.15–19 or early 20s CE, then the composition and publication dates could already imply a dimension of retrospection. As the gap to be reckoned between these dates lengthens, the story acquires an ever-lengthening shadow of explanatory significance, once it settles into offering an 'aetiology' for Tiberius' reign, pointing his subjects back to where he was coming from, when his blankly baffling behaviour as monarch had originated in less extravagant prototypes. At the same time, layers of nostalgia accrete, as the appalling reign of terror of the 30s progressively cut the ties with recognizable normality.

In the other direction, too, Phaedrus could scarcely help seeing that telling tales on Caesar called for thinking *ahead*. If it seemed sensible to showcase the Emperor at time of writing, prudence should have demanded that it was going to stay that way in whatever eventuality might lie in times to come. Now recall that we have no idea of Phaedrus' own dates: 'The Old Woman and her Empty Wine-Jar' (3. 1) *might* mean to tell us he was past his own sell-by date by book 3, as 'Old Hound and Hunter' (5. 10) hints, apparently, for book 5; but, as we have said, this might not help us very much for books 1 and 2; in any case, how many people ever bet how much against their own prolongevity, let alone their writings? So whereas everything that happened, and was likely to happen, under Tiberius, or for that matter under any dynastic successors of Augustus, argued that there would never be cause to regret positively celebrating the divine memory of *Divus Augustus* (Ch. 2), the anticipated future standing of Tiberius' memory might readily be felt precarious, not to say under threat. In reading the story, we shall therefore want to take into consideration that it might *mean* to leave the door open, though not necessarily demonstrably so, for interpretation as loyalist, as neutral, as satirical, or as damning.

Even if the tale seems deliberately chosen and produced to be tame in *any* event, this only brings into focus its (elusive?) author: what is it for an imperial freedman to turn writer? Does it matter what gets written into a bunch of Aesopic drolleries? Did it matter *only* if its author was a member of the palace staff or retinue? And only if its palace was being run by a paranoid terrorist Chief of Police like Sejanus, running menacing rings of suspicion and entrapment around victims, whether they ranked as predictably exposed to attack, or were randomly selected to accentuate panoptic arbitrariness? One obligation that comes with the role of 'Aesop' is the provision of a 'moral', whether prefixed to the fable or appended (*promythium* or *epimythium*), and with it, a cue for interpretive activity on the part of the reader: inferring a position from which the writer speaks is intrinsic to the transaction, so 'authoriality' is necessarily crucial (authority and authorship): Phaedrus' self-presentation, direct or oblique, is bound for close scrutiny.

The thinking we entertain for our reception of the anecdote is built into the story we give of its writing, for this is how tales deliver us to the theatre of history. We shall return to this business of the peril that might, or might putatively, attach to Aesopian fables of power under Tiberius in Chapter 3. For now, we turn to the 'truth' of Phaedrus' story, with the thought that any readership will relate teller to tale, and wonder: did the freedman witness this incident personally? If he did not, then was he not suggesting all the same that he has privileged insider's information, about the detail and local colour, the milieu and the *mores*? We could otherwise only presume that we are supposed to know that *this* 'freedman of Augustus' never worked for *Tiberius*.[6] And negotiating these questions is a reminder that the idea of a freedman turned fabulist may not be easy to reconcile with the imperial agent turned Aesop. As we make the acquaintance of the story's attendant, too fly for his

own good, we are bound to wonder how far he might be from
his narrator, and perhaps his creator—and how close. All we
know or need to know of Phaedrus is precisely that he once was
a palace-slave, but now is a free man: as Tiberius' flunkey fails
to elicit his freedom, we'll be wondering, when Phaedrus
passed that way, did he succeed because he avoided the
flunkey's errors, or because he had *Augustus* to charm? (Ch. 3)

At the general level of content, we can pick out plenty of
corroborative material for Phaedrus' cameo *Tiberius*. We are
told he took a strict line on manumission: 'he was so totally
equitable and impartial that when the people once wanted a
certain dancer set free, he reserved approval for the owner's
consent and receipt of the price'; in fact, he 'scarcely ever went
to the games in case he would be petitioned for something,
especially after he was obliged to manumit—buy the freedom
of—Actius the comic actor'. They say 'he but rarely allowed his
veterans their discharge, in the hope that they'd die in service,
and save him the pay-outs', and he was always careful (stingy)
with money, public or otherwise. Back in his earlier *secessus*
(retreat), out of the way on Rhodes when not part of Augustus'
plans, he had liked 'walking about freely, to mix with people—
Greeklings—virtually on equal footing', and tried to stay 'really
approachable and affable' (to senators) after his elevation.
Indeed, we hear on all sides, what he really hated was flattery:
'he bitterly rebuked people who called his undertakings
"divine" and himself "master", hence public speaking was a
limited and slippery business under a ruler who feared liberty
but loathed adulation.'

This was the recipe for his famously sociopathic contrariness,
what made him impossible to read or even second-guess, and
(you could say) his master tactic for cowing others without
crudely throwing his weight around: 'in the habit of confusing
jokes with jobs (*ludibria seriis permiscere solitus*), he thanked the
senators for their kindness', then leniently forgave Togonius'
offer of an armed bodyguard of senators, but was merciless to
Gallio, who had proposed a privilege for the praetorians, and
dispatched him into immediate exile, with worse to come, 'and
this was the reward he got for his well-rehearsed flattery'.
Everything this Caesar said always escaped secure reception;
you just knew it was ominous and meant no good, so his sense

of humour was a particularly lethal cocktail: soon after his accession, 'someone had whispered in a corpse's ear, at the funeral procession, and told people he was sending Augustus the news that his bequests were still unpaid; Tiberius had him executed instantly, so that—as he said in mockery at his expense—he could be his own messenger'. Egyptian pretty-boys cut no ice with him either: 'Back then, Helikon won no privilege, in as much as Tiberius thoroughly loathed adolescent *bons mots*.'[7]

Whatever we may think of Late Tiberius' alleged debaucheries in the 'privacy' of his *secessus* to the villa-complex on the island of Capri (Suetonius, *Life of Tiberius* 43), biographers ancient and modern all present a distinctive combination of self-insulation, hatred of flattery, and twistedly logical vindictiveness (ibid. 60):

A few days after he got to Capri, a fisherman unexpectedly offered him a giant mullet when he was in private (*sibi secretum petenti*), so he ordered his face scrubbed with the fish: he was scared because he had crept up to him from the rear of the island over rough and trackless terrain (*per aspera et deuia erepsisset ad se*). Now, when the man said in the middle of his punishment how thankful he was that he hadn't offered a lobster, a monster he'd caught, as well, he ordered his face to be sliced up with the lobster too.

As we set Phaedrus' tale in this company, we can feel how crucial such vignettes were, for getting somewhere towards embodying the special charisma and miasma of a world dictator, and (no less) for installing inscrutability as a primal trope. The Caesars all lived, and made all their satellites and subjects live, by their wit(s).[8] One conclusion from reading the anecdote may well be that it acts out the resistance to explication which is proper to all tales of the quintessential *impossibility* of omnipotence: we may well see exactly how it would be in the servant's shoes; but struggle to read his master's voice. Given that Tiberius was preordained fall-guy to the sainted Augustus' memory, stories about him were always going to be variants on the aetiology of corruption by absolute power; predicated on a teleology of descent into a finale of horror, they sketch an abyss in the soul to stigmatize the fouling of social relations, even pitying the *person* monstrified by unlimited vulnerability to his flaws.[9] But suppose we turn the spotlight on the servant—give Tiberius a back-seat and turn the heat off him, for once? Then the tale tells us an inside story about the palace household, in its own right an increasingly emergent locus of power in the Roman world, a by-product of Caesarian despotism urgently requiring comprehension on the part of everyone—and just as insistently impenetrable and oppressively baffling to them all.

If the strong-man adjutant Sejanus modelled one new style of access to clout, bypassing the traditional echelons of genealogical and plutocratic oligarchy, then the imperial slave-turned-chamberlain, trusted adviser and diplomat, eventually king-maker and *éminence* behind every throne, was the other outrageous upstart in post-senatorial Rome. The *liberti* (freed slaves) who ran *this domus* (household) would run the world, as their duties stretched to provision of a skeleton 'alternative' bureaucracy for the World State: because they were social ciphers but personal creations and intimates of the Emperor, these Greeklings soon took over the reins at the palace, as effectively as if the aliens had shipped Alexandria to the West . . . This was the coming story of political reality in the first dynasty, heading for sensational episodes in the bizarre courts of Claudius and Nero—or should we say, rather, of Narcissus and Pallas, their lesser satellites Anicetus, Euodus, Graptus, and the rest? From this point of view, Phaedrus' story gives an ironic twist to the freedmen's success-story—which he himself seems to attest.

It looks as though our Tiberius is stemming the tide, of ex-slaves 'greecing' their way to the top: in which case, our tale could portray a rearguard action staving off at least the grossest Pharaonic tendencies of post-Augustan Rome? Or at any rate we get a privileged shot of the *kind of process* which accounted for the new dispensation? The palace-grounds were where individuals could get close to Caesar; the strictly and emphatically vertical relationships within a household ensured that here all the ruler's dealings were those of an owner with his property; in the absence of civic standing and civil courtesies, only the discourse of adulation was open to his associates. Surely the young father-to-be of Claudius Etruscus, born in Asia Minor around the year dot and rising from Tiberius' servants to join Gaius' retinue, Claudius' and Nero's administrations, and, as a grand equestrian, Vespasian's kitchen cabinet, must once have been just such a twinkle in the corner of Tiberius' eye? One miracle certainly happened to a slave called—in Greek—'Miracle', through fall-out around Tiberius (Josephus, *Jewish archives* 18. 193 f.):

One hot dusty day, a slave of Gaius, one *Thaumastos*, was carrying a jug of water when princeling Agrippa, just on the point of managing to get himself arrested for high treason against Tiberius, begged a swig, and promised him, 'If the matter of this service of yours turns out for the good, when I escape these bonds I shall not lose time in securing freedom for you from Gaius, for not decreasing respect toward me at all in serving me as a prisoner from the respect you showed me in my former condition.' And he told him no lie in saying this, but did indeed repay him. For later, as king, he received Thaumastos from Gaius, now Caesar, and immediately set him free. He even made him steward of his estate . . . and, after outliving them both, Thaumastos died in old age, still holding this honoured position.

So a word one morning in the royal ear, a jape in the flower beds, *could* be the making of any varlet of a valet. But Tiberius was by repute the toughest nut to crack, and as Caesar even stood for that:

The most daring thing [Gallus] did was . . . to tell the story of the teacher of rhetoric at Rhodes who had refused Tiberius' modest application to join his classes, on the ground that there was no vacancy at present, saying that he must come back in seven days . . . On his recent accession to the monarchy, when the same impertinent fellow arrived to pay his respects to the new divinity, . . . with a wit only equalled by his clemency [Tiberius] told him that he had no vacancies at present in his corps of flatterers and that he must come back in seven *years*.[10]

Getting noticed was the game; the objective was to *oblige* the master. Strictly speaking, no master could owe his slave anything; but an 'obliging' owner was going to have a fonder self-image and a nicer (perhaps longer) life. And any *paterfamilias* positively *needed* recruits to help keep the show on the road. Of course any slave that attracted attention for trying it on could pay for miscalculation: if ingratiation was an art form, playing carried a high tariff. If a moment's whim could transform serf to fief—still (o best beloved) no one's going to forget that lobster in a hurry!

As we reflect on the story from this angle, wondering what *did* earn preferment from *what sort of* Caesar, we're facing criteria for success and failure in this still relatively novel, and arbitrarily volatile, Rome. In drawing our (own) conclusions, just as we need not confine thoughts to the particular individual of the story's circumstantial setting, so we can brood beyond the literal ranks of petty tyrants among the palace staff, to reflect on the dynamics of Caesarism—and so back to *Tiberius*, again. And Phaedrus' puny poem on the sidelines also gives us a mighty push in the direction of applying the story to Roman society at large: his introduction shoves us into the streets of cosmopolis, to explore the seething circulation of power in the greatest concentration of humanity the world had ever supported. When the *dux* (Leader) speaks, his voice commands everyone everywhere. Even a muttered remark down the garden path reverberates his almighty 'NO!' clean across country, not just from the coast back to the city, but throughout the imperial world. A Caesar, the subjects of Caesar—they never walk alone. Stories follow them off limits, track them down side by side—partners in crime all the more obviously caught in the act when tales tell of their separation.

A closer look at the poem will show how this 'Roman' anecdote is extended and distended until it befits a quip from 'His Mighty Majesty'. An elaborate raconteur's come-on works up a barrage of clichés from the satirical store of denigration of the urban jungle, instead of the formulaic and peremptory *promythium* of fable; then a generous scene-setting and thumbnail character-sketch embellish the poem along the way.[11] At the same time, the opening cue retains its pertinence to the end, contrasting the jackpot pay-off for close-reading the tale with the colossal waste of energies that demands the parable for cure: the flunkey will have wasted his time, *if* 'we' have not. Even if suckers who have fallen for the rat-race *are* nailed here, there is surely an irritant provocation somewhere along the way—a whiff of the put-on, where anticlimax and bathos await mugs who take a 'true story' to heart? The sign of a telling tale, no doubt, is that it exploits *anecdotal* open-endedness and multi-directionality, to guy readers as well as its more obvious targets?[12]

vv. 1–6

Phaedrus' strictures directed against the busybody, working
frantically in the web of the client system, and caught in it, too,
make for a back-handed tribute to the baffling, thrilling,
Dickensian dementia of booming metropolis:

> Nothing is understood to be so effectual as scouring nowhere in a
> violent hurry, in short, as taking cabs and going about. London has
> become a gigantic Circumlocution Office, or Circum-motion Office.[13]

We are treated to a pompous moralist's opening: 'There is one
particular tribe . . .', where *natio* is a characteristic term in
censorious invective.[14] And drag in a choice bit of city-slang,
ardalio (mucker), for its first use in Latin literature, a typically
bastardized Graecism: derivation from Greek ἄρδα (dirt) is con-
firmed by the gloss ἄρδαλος· ὁ μὴ καθαρῶς ζῶν ('ardalos: someone who lives unclean'); and the termination -*io* is a common
word-formation for vigorous denigratory colloquialism
(ἀρδάλιον, too, was a chamber pot). This rare instance of stylistic
slumming is repeated only in Martial, who first sets up a clash
between the 'pretty, pretty, pretty—but nugatory' performer
who is just 'a great big *mucker*' (*Epigrams* 2. 7), and later
lampoons an old hustler (4. 78):

> You rush round all over Town and there's never a sedan
>   that you don't bring your indefatigable dawn 'Salutations'
>
> Let young men do this by all means; a greater blemish, Mr Black,
>   there absolutely is none, than a *mucker* of an old man.

Elsewhere we find just a juvenile graffito, answering 'Perrarius
you're a thief' further up the same column buried at Pompeii:
'Aephebus you're a *mucker*' (*CIL.* 4. 4765). Conceivably *ardalio*
relates to the spattering of mud which a client, clad in his
laundered toga, was bound to pick up as he raced to make his
morning calls on the grandees; but stigmatizing a busybody as
'dirt' would be the classic mechanism for abjection, picking on
agents of change as threatening, pollutant, 'matter out of
place'.[15] Four feverish verses mime hyperactivity, starting with
the rhyme (*ardalio-num* ~) . . . *natio* | ~ . . . *otio* |, before lever-
ing three patterned pairs of compact clichés through vv. 2–4.
These appositional phrases drum up a breeze, with the superla-

tive six-syllable *odiosissima* for finale. Just as *we* had to 'palpi-tate' through the 'scurrying', so we must 'gasp and pant' our way through verbiage—and for why?—as Phaedrus' string of present participles (*concursans* | ... *anhelans* | ... *agens* ||) piles up 'many items' but 'to no purpose' (*multa* ... *nihil*). This amounts to a warning to take cover: all this bustle says that *something*'s soon going to hit the fan. 'Meaninglessness' is always a promising start for telling tales, which also waste(s) time, more or less hyperactively.

We have here a capital case of Rome writing down Rome, just the stuff Seneca's moral essays would soon do to death (*On peace of mind* 12):

The dashing to and fro (*concursatio*) must be cut to the bone—the sort that the majority among human beings do as they roam right over houses, theatres, and market-places: they obtrude themselves on other people's business, forever hard to tell from people with work to get done (*alienis se negotiis offerunt, semper aliquid agentibus similes*).

This 'scurrying' was how society worked at Rome, but satirists liked to brand it dysfunctional: 'that lot who dash in all direc-tions, disturbing themselves and others' (Seneca, *On life is short* 14. 3, *isti qui per officia discursant, qui se aliosque inquietent*). 'Tied up in free time' was a commonplace oxymoron in this rhetoric, and jingling knots of the 'much ado, but nothing doing' type belong here too; alongside unpleasantness 'to self and to others'.[16]

Now we're all fired up, the narrator plays winsome. He has a worthy target; the best intentions; our approval. This is a lesson, a scolding, not scurrility or frivolity. Hence the false modesty of 'if only I'm up to it'.[17] But we recognize perfectly well that 'a true story' parades *fiction* in store—along with what-ever truth*s* they may bring. *Vera fabella* carries a certain degree of verbal tension, since the word *fabula* spells make-believe; but in this collection of *Fabulae*, the all-important wor(l)d 'Rome' has already led us out of the realm of Aesop. So, yes, 'This story is all so true, I undertake, | As is—the book of Lancelot de Lake', but its fictional bullets are nonetheless lobbed at reality.[18] Thus, although we (muckers) may or may not feel we need 'putting straight', we all know to pin back our ears when the storyteller signals ready to begin, with the alliterative formula *pretium est operae*; but none of us can guess that the story will turn out to be about 'not much doing' (*non multum egisti*), and about 'what efforts *aren't* well worth while': *opera . . . perit* (v. 24).[19]

vv. 7–17

To hit us hard, the Latin piles up the components of the story into a single, twisting, winding, complex, and perhaps devious, ensemble of a sentence: 'la phrase monstre' (vv. 7–17).[20] Caesar Tiberius, for a start, must reappear as 'master' when he touches down in an absolute ablative (v. 14). This is, then, not just any master out for a stroll in his grounds; but Tiberius at Misenum. No doubt the scene-setting just pads, amplifies, glamorizes. But is it, all the same, 'well worth a good listen'? Let's see.

'Naples bound' means heading in the opposite direction from Roman busy-ness, into the arms of Greek ease. We catch the Emperor dropping into his villa as a stopover, en route from *ardaliones* to *secessus*. Just the halfway house for the meeting of two worlds, and a parting shot from the exit.[21] We happen to know the 'splendid villa on the promontory of Misenum' pretty well, if only at second hand. Master strategist Marius built it as a castle-cum-paradise; Sulla's daughter Cornelia acquired the property by proscription and sold it to L. Licinius Lucullus, at huge profit. Quite how it reached Tiberius is not known, but he was to end his last journey there on 16 March 37. Much later, we like to think, Odoacer retired the last Emperor of the West, Romulus Augustulus, here in 476.[22] It was the epicure's suggestive name that stuck, the archetypal retiring Roman, who put his feet up, stocked his lake and built (no doubt) with black 'Lucullan marble' veneer, letting Rome go hang. So our story scenario is defensible space, overdetermined for rest and respite from lowering society.[23]

The vivid phrasing erases Marius' foundation, and flippantly pictures a giant Lucullus playing toy chateaux, and 'sticking' the villa 'bang on the summit' by poetic licence or ignorance. For this component of the location fits the Monte di Procida, but that is bare of ruins, and hardly on the Capo. The *point* is to cue that monstrous blot on the landscape of the Late Republic, the private castle with its parasitic absentee billionnaire: 'citadels stuck upon summits', 'edifices stuck upon summits for panoptic prospect over land and sea'.[24] Or rather, *the* point is 'like property, like owner'. We are meant to dig it, Tiberius Caesar was *also* 'stuck on the summit', top man on the Roman totem-pole. The story's stakes could not get any higher: when we join the Emperor in his lair, we get mighty close to the hot seat. Now for the Misenum vista. This is an imperial vantage-point, an Olympian view of Italy, *Roman* Italy, Italy from a Roman perspective, and so by reflex the exact shot for palace-watchers to keep in their sights: normally geographers and cartographers opposed *Hadriaticum* to *Tuscum*, *Siculum* to *Ionium*, but from the capital *Tuscum* would mean the waters north of Ostia-Portus, and it would hardly stretch a point to call coastal stretches off Campania and Lucania 'Sicilian'; on the world stage, it would be as the base responsible, since Augustus took over, for housing the Home Fleet that the Punta di Miseno 'looks out over the *Sicilian* sea'.[25] This prominent headland is where we have been brought, if it needs saying, to gauge the 'outlook' for the planet—at the geophysical 'point' of inter-section between 'hindsight' and 'prospect'. See where Rome is headed from where it has come; and, via the retrospect, triangu-late where it will all lead.

Time to meet dummy. Emperor and slave, *one on one*. The attendant gets his own loving send-up of an entrée, measured up to master in a mouthful of long words and exotic insignia. First, *ex alticinctis unus atriensibus* makes him an Emperor Among Door-Men.[26] Stuck bang on a summit of his own, this specimen of humanity is what the *uilla* is coming to. The gate-keeper stands in, if not up, for the estate; this heavenly creature belongs aloft in the clouds of Misenum, riding high as his dissolute hem-line. The *tunica* 'as usually worn fell over the belt in a loose blouse which thus conceals the girdle', and, back in the good old days, the loins were girded up for hard work. But imperial Rome was going to swoon at toy-boy *mignons* dolled up in garish livery by the decadent: 'How studiously they tuck up the tunics on their roué pets!' (Seneca, *On life is short* 12: *tunicas succingunt*). Workers (i.e., as Empire entailed, slaves) needed the arms free, but here the taut exposure of shoulders and profile is sensual. To get closer to the element of satire, this sexy servant is going to perform his routine for our benefit, as he did for Tiberius: he is the parody worker who turns the daily grind into cabaret bump and grind. In the eternal playground of Roman opulence, only style wars are left to fight, and household economy must pivot on photogenic impact: 'a footman tucked up with a belt (*succinctus cingulo*): green with cherry!' (Petronius, *Satyrica* 28. 8) Phaedrus even makes us peer and read the designer label: 'one of those Pelusian linen belts'. 'When dining, Caligula would have servants tucked up with a belt stand now by the back of his couch, now at his feet' (Suetonius, *Life of Gaius* 26: *succinctos linteo*). If this pet is worth what he's wearing, he's a gold-mine. Egypt produced the finest linen; and fine slaves, if it's lingeried slaves you wanted. As for pulsating Pelusium, much of the trade must have passed through the entrepôt, but 'Pelusian' was a leading brand in its own right (Pliny, *Natural History* 19. 14). Again, however, the intent is more metaphoric than euphoric. This mug is being stitched up with too much material for his own good, he is as outlandish as his description makes him, othered and orientalized as the invert from the land of eunuchs, harems, and Cleopatras. Is this what Augustus brought back from Egypt in his train? Does Pharaoh translate to Latin as *Caesar*?

Still worse to come, the storyteller wets our lips with a pendant: 'woollen tufts dangling down'. These probably belong to the belt, not the tunic (the ends of which are tucked up beneath the belt). But to be sure, you'd have to look real close, and risk us wondering how you got to be an expert. *Something* curly is a-dangling down below that belt, and just how high was that tunic tucked up? This intimate waist-line fussiness is, in short, a provocation for the reader: *de-stricta* ~ *de-pendentibus* makes for a peepshow of paradox, taut but dangling, like this flashy *soupçon* of sordid overwriting. So hot a property is a temptation for anyone who would, in Tiberius' shoes, be making for Neapolitan shade to put their feet up in Ptolemaic, sorry: Capitol, style. Surely cutesy page-boys in Nilotic costume are *just* what made a Roman holiday . . . (So the founding father of Art History, J. J. Winckelmann, mused, when he pictured dream-boat Antinous's day-job in Hadrian's retinue by reference to Phaedrus' *atriensis*.)[27]

We rejoin Caesar, not the grim Tiberius dreaded in senatorial history, but unbuttoned off-duty and glad of it. I don't
myself suppose Phaedrus either knew the Misenum lay-out, or
thought we'd worry about it. The villa is provided with lavish
walks because they are half the point. The daily constitutional
was an article of faith: 'the spaces in the middle which are out-
doors between the porticoes are thought to require adorning
with greenery because open-air walks have important health-
properties' (Vitruvius, *On architecture* 5. 98. 5, *adornanda
uiridibus uidentur quod hypaethroe ambulationes habent magnam
salubritatem*).[28] What we are being told here is that 'master's
happiness' is in the balance; that he was looking to immerse
himself in the 'healthy growth' of his garden, give himself a
thorough dousing in its medicine, by 'going the whole distance'
until he had got the city out of his creaking old bones (*perambulante laeta . . . uiridia*).[29] Woe betide anything or anyone that
interfered with the idyll, any reminder of back in Rome, not
ahead in Naples. Shades of Arcadian self-fashioning back in
retreat on Rhodes, where a heavy-handed Tiberius *must* have
enthused (if only life, an Emperor's life, could be like this):[30]

there are a number of walks through these groves, some shady, others
planted with roses . . . Having passed through these winding alleys,
which are indeed so seductive that I can spend hours in their delight,
you come upon a straight walk, which breaks off into a number of
others, bordered by little box hedges.

Right on cue, the dumb-show at the core of the tale—its
central image. *Coepit* ('starts') gets the story *going*, for sure, but
actually triggers the false move, as in many (of the) *Fabulae*, the
initiative that provokes repressive retaliation: 'Just stop it,
then.' An *alueolus* was multi-purpose wickerwork (*nassiterna*
being Latin for 'watering-can'). Stilling of the dust by spraying
was a real chore, and part of the *housework*. In the grounds and
garden, this is literally taking things too far.[31] The '(precious?)
little scoop(-let)' makes for a mock-quotidian moment of
effrontery when it's brought up against *this* 'master', for this is
Caesar. In the intensive *iactitans*, sense that this lad's over-
doing things; pushing his luck. The 'steaming soil' would be
nice cool, and no one was going to hose down the streets and
hurly burly of *Rome*, even for Tiberius; but no slave should

claim recognition as 'considerate', posing as if he is a patron's devoted client offering respectful 'service' (*officium*); and even the *implication* that this was by way of a 'good turn (deserving another)' could land this flunkey in a lot worse than hot water.[32] He gets what he has coming: *de-ridetur*. Yes, without risking making a sound, he makes master laugh, 'laughter at his expense', but a laugh's a laugh, and putting master in a good humour is half the game. And Tiberius is meant to see this *is* a game? In which he gets to notice that a piece of the equipment has its wits about it, enough to improvise a special reception for the unexpected arrival at the motel, and stage a light-hearted stunt—antics from the garden-furniture, with added wit. But yes, this is, did he but realize it, getting off lightly, with wordless scorn, as aloof master jogs on and past, above noticing this hypertrophic under-gardener from Babylon. Yet more important, *we* are strongly advised, 'derision' is topicalized for the anecdote. Yes, we line up behind Tiberius and behind (him) Phaedrus, to mock the afflicted, join in the satire against the 'muckers'. But can Phaedrus know any better than his former self, this palace-slave, what a jeer from the self-imprisoned solipsist Tiberius may spell? Inscrutable, but ominous silence: just how close a call was this?

vv. 17–22

The rhythm of the story is now set. Tortuous build-up, punctured by one word, one wordless under-reaction, or indeed non-reaction: *deridetur*. Round two will repeat the pantomime, in précis, to be finally deflated by a double whammy of verbal response, and put-down, from His Majesty. As the story stokes up for the kill, Phaedrus makes his usual neat job, too, of pouring out verbal coolant of his own. Vivid touches make the 'encore' structure, the need to repeat the servant's jape, pull its weight in nuancing the story, as well as setting up the final confrontation for all its out loud—negativity.

First, *notis flexibus* is an expressive phrase that marks the thinking of both narrator and butt. Together they move on 'next, from here' (*inde*), as 'experts on ways round', circumventing dull repetition so as to entertain with a fresh variation.

Presumably the servant doesn't thrash through the bushes, but short-circuits the labyrinth of alternative routes intertwined through the topiary. For the 'promenade', second time around, Phaedrus trots out just the word for it, prominently Greek jargon for the lifestyle customized for theory-aware tycoons, to optimize exystence: the *xyst*, a walkway 'kept trimmed' for keeping in trim, was a 'walking-ground with alleys sheltered by shrubs and pleached hedges'. An essential perquisite of the Roman Good Life, you might associate this (circum)ambience with any dour throw-back of an aristocrat sooner than Tiberius. But all this is specially rigged, to be the last place on earth where Tiberius might seek solitude. For the thing is impossible—there is no escape from the luxury of your own dietetics. The story fashions an *aporia* (impasse), or *adynaton* (impossibility), going to extraordinary lengths to extract master from his routine habitat, precisely to expose him to predators, even behind the deepest curtain of security. With him he takes his milieu, as sure as callisthenics follows anywhere a jogger jogs. Seclusion *prompts* intrusion.

Indeed the interior design of the estate now traps its latest Lucullus: it diagrams applied thinking into the terrain as surely as any urban system of avenues and junctions such as post-Augustan Rome, which generate, in *their* turn, the mess of short-cuts, radial routes, flyovers and bypasses that makes the concrete, or marble, jungle such wearing bewilderment. Have the world at your disposal, and you can take a break from the human rodent-race any time you please; but inevitably you walk straight up the garden path, and into your own predictability. Rome boasted a 'tribe' of *ardaliones*; but it only takes one fly-boy-day *atriensis* to block a *xyst*. Special knowledge, of the going, promises a glimpse of power, to go with it, and this threatens to equalize master and slave, as 'devious cunning' (*notis flexibus*) fabricates a lookalike relationship of a client's considerateness (*come officium*). This is how to get ahead of the game, get in first, the only way to beat the xystem: *praecurrit*. But this will stir Tiberius to show *his* grip, draw himself up to some of his real stature, and torpedo his wideboy's fast track: flunkey has run on ahead of himself, over-extended his reach, jumped the track: *praecurrit*.[33]

In the process, the tale fixates on the schematic gesture of 'stilling the dust'. And this is what we're here to home on. No garden can be free of dust; it comes with the soil. No imperial secretariat, not all the nozzles of a gendarmerie, intelligence corps, or security police, could spray all the dirt out of Caesar's way; it was what made Rome go round (and round). The mock-obeisance play-acting mimes every administration's dream, the clean-air environment of a settled society lulled into post-political somnolence. As the 'tribe of muckers' multiplies to an infinity of Particle Men, all clamouring for sedation, pressure of sheer numbers turns the screw on the one-man state. Monarchs must go it alone—would-be solitary, actually isolated, flying solo, and in sole charge . . . of themselves (auto-cracy). They *make* the rest of the cosmos dirt.

No wonder Caesar spots his man, 'and realizes what's what'. It takes one to know one. Phaedrus flexes his muscle, too, with a perfectly constructed verse. The hermeneutically loaded chiasmus ('A-B-C-B^1-A^1') *agnoscit hominem Caesar remque intellegit* is spot on, installing the Emperor at the centre of the plot (the plot to impress him). As he moves to crush the insect, his omniscience is simultaneously *ad hominem* and *ad rem*. He's been here before, he 'recognizes' the instance, *because* he has mastered the pattern. He knows the pattern, because this is the inner logic of Caesarism. Whatever the politesse, despotism dynamically simplifies sociality into a vertical pyramid of asymmetrical power-relationships in the ratio 1:0 (*Caesar remque = Caesarem*). Because this one person is out of place, we all matter: we clog up his circuit, muck on the line. So the *story-teller's* point is this: what do *we* (little Caesars) suppose there is to know in this story? If Tiberius took it all in at a stroke, how far can we follow him? 'Hey', calls the king of kings—we'd best jump to it.[34]

This is exactly what the frenetic fall guy is doing, upping the tempo from *iactitans* through *praecurrit* to *adsilit*. One grunt from master, and the wind-up toy has eyes like saucers: the snappy writing squeezes in nice touches of vulgarity (*donatio*) and colloquialism (*certa*, 'in the bag'). And simulates the convoluted hopes spinning vainly round the dupe's noddle, with contorted word-order, parodic dissonance (*-cer cer-*), and compacted double-subordination (*alacer . . . gaudio . . . donationis*, an idiomatic objective genitive). Here is what the 'man['s . . .] thing' amounts to—instant mis-recognition of 'what's what' (*alacer certae* is the response to, and corresponds with, *agnoscit . . . . -que intellegit*).

v v . 2 3 – 5

And this is what all Tiberius' subjects were doomed to, whether 'muckers' or not, monkeys working for the Organ-Grinder. Who now dons his flamboyant 'Bigger-than-Everything-Ness' self, ready to pulverize the mote in his eye. 'The Leader'— *Caesar Tiberius*, then *domino*, *Caesar*, and ultimately *tanta maies-tas ducis*, reaches into his own Circumlocution Office, and imposes respect.[35]

Not much longer to go, so not a moment to lose; or the *story's* labour is lost. One line from Emperor Phaedrus to tell us so. To flatten the flunkey, and risk the reader to the muckers' ranks: as remarked, *non multum egisti* flays the proem's *multa agendo nihil agens*; but *opera nequiquam perit* flogs *pretium est operae*, and by *this* end of the tale, the reader's 'attention' has fused with the flunkey's 'alacrity'. Specifically, his would-be 'service rendered' (*officium*) collapses to 'stint required' (*opera*), and takes our 'in-put' (*opera*) for Phaedrus' 'profit' (*pretium*). The storyteller knows perfectly well that we're all looking for the pay-off: just as *donationis . . . gaudio* flags up our moment of pleasure, courtesy of Aesop–Tiberius' 'quip' (*iocata est tanta . . .*), so the 'financial' note latent in *perit* (go for nothing) will be cashed out in its banal correlative, the anecdote's last word, *ueneunt* (fetch a price). This is the way—'Whassinitforme?'—that Romans discuss sociality, too: 'Just because this favour must not be sold, that doesn't mean it should go for nothing' (Quintilian, *Training of the orator* 12. 7. 12, *non enim, quia uenire hoc beneficium non oportet, oportet perire*). Good listeners like us are going to have to count the cost, as well as the flea-bite.

The punchline has beaten the scribes, derailed all-too-easily by *uenire*, 'be sold', and by two lovely colloquial touches, the chest-tapping *mecum* (so easily projecting forward into a *uenire*, to come ('come (with me)' . . .), and *maioris* (sc. *pretii*) for *pluris*. But, as we have said, there's no earthly point in our pretending we have all the angles covered, either. As Livia told Tiberius,

' "I've never liked your jokes. I don't understand them, but there's always been a cruel streak in your idea of humour".'[36] These *alapae* may be a resounding 'slap in the face' for all of us who aren't familiar with the lower reaches of social life at Rome, its rude ways and its crude says. Classical literature doesn't often bring us, *ardaliones* or upper crust, this far round the houses and down the track. We know that *alapa* names the sound of a slapped cheek; for manumission, one homely practice was to revolve the lucky slave, presumably to lose his bearings (= *uertigo*: e.g. Persius, *Satire* 5. 78), and/or to give him a more-or-less friendly sock in the jaw, an unofficial, informal, but apparently far-from outlandish or outmoded ceremony, even if it is most explicitly attested in an ancient Commentary, and Dictionary entry: 'Every time they used to manumit slaves, they punched them slap-happy and led them around to confirm they were free' (Schol. Persius, loc. cit. = Isidore, *Etymologies* 9. 4. 88, *quotiens manumittebant eos alapa percussos circumagebant et liberos confirmabant*). They and we are then left to speculate about the moral: was the blow felt to be 'apotropaic', forestalling hybris? Was this conclusive punchuation, 'the slaves' last drubbing' (Basil, *Homily on the sacred baptism* 3, *MPG* 31. 429)? If you ask me, it was also to remind the slave that 'freedom' was no leveller. Whatever rationalization we plump for, the likelihood that the *alapa* on occasion weakened to a *handshake* should give us pause. Our telling story tells us all about the options for masters and slaves; but it *reflects* on citizens and on Caesars, and regales us with ideas about *that*.[37]

Now that we know what Tiberius' *words* (ought to) mean, we are left with his 'joke'. From Bentley's stimulus ((1726) note ad loc.), J. S. Reid proposed a *double entendre* between the primary sense 'Much greater services are needed to win a slave his liberty', and 'A slave must commit much greater faults before he earns a cuffing'. This is just the point where the story opens onto imperial history. Royalty is systemically vulnerable to problems περὶ δυσωπίας—'the embarrassment that threatens the mighty when forced to deny, overlook, ignore, anyhow *deal with* a(n unwelcome) request'. The endlessly admirable Plutarch wrote an inevitable essay on this. His advice? 'You meet a pest who gets his hooks in you and clings on: don't be embarrassed, chop though his grasp, and soldier on with the job in hand' (4. 530 f.). And here is one of *his* telling tales: 'A Cynic once asking him for a drachma, old King Antigonus said, "Such a gift's not regal"; and when he came back with, "So gimme a talent", he replied, "Such a take's not Cynic" ' (7. 531 f.). We saw Tiberius shrug off this endemic nuisance of power, and yet we saw it stick, in the stories we began from. No one should suppose that the web of Augustan legislation henceforth codifying and regulating manumission in pagan Rome could dent optimism or deter desperation.[38] For this is the net set to trap a Caesar, and with him the entire population of the World State, so far as it impacts on his vicinity.

Here, no one stays clean.
Now, where's that lobster?[39]

2(a)   2(b)

2

The Only Good Caesar . . .:
Divus Augustus and the Case
of the Widow and the Wicked
Freedman (3. 10)

Periculosum est credere et non credere;
utriusque exemplum breuiter exponam rei:
Hippolytus obiit quia nouercae creditum est,
Cassandrae quia non creditum ruit Ilium.
ergo exploranda est ueritas multum prius   5
quam stulta praue iudicet sententia.
sed fabulosam ne uetustatem eleues
narrabo tibi memoria quod factum est mea:
    maritus quidam cum diligeret coniugem
togamque puram iam pararet filio,   10
seductus in secretum a liberto est suo,
sperante heredem suffici se proximum,
qui cum de puero multa mentitus foret
et plura de flagitiis castae mulieris,
adiecit id quod sentiebat maxime   15
doliturum amanti, uentitare adulterum
stuproque turpi pollui famam domus.
    incensus ille falso uxoris crimine
simulauit iter ad uillam clamque in oppido
subsedit: deinde noctu subito ianuam   20
intrauit, recta cubiculum uxoris petens
in quo dormire mater natum iusserat,
aetatem adultam seruans diligentius.
dum quaerunt lumen, dum concursant familia,
irae furentis impetum non sustinens   25
ad lectum accedit, temptat in tenebris caput.
ut sentit tonsum gladio pectus transigit,
nihil respiciens dum dolorem uindicet.
lucerna allata simul aspexit filium

sanctamque uxorem dormientem cubiculo   30
sopita primo quae nil somno senserat,
repraesentauit in se poenam facinoris
et ferro incubuit quod credulitas strinxerat.
  accusatores postularunt mulierem
Romamque pertraxerunt ad Centumuiros.   35
maligna insontem deprimit suspicio
quod bona possideat. stant patroni fortiter
causam tuentes innocentis feminae.
  A DIVO AVGVSTO TUNC PETIERUNT IVDICES
ut adiuuaret iurisiurandi fidem   40
quod ipsos error implicuisset criminis,
qui postquam tenebras dispulit calumniae
certumque fontem ueritatis repperit:
'Luat', inquit, 'poenas causa libertus mali,
namque orbam nato simul et priuatam uiro   45
miserandam potius quam damnandam existimo.
quodsi delata perscrutatus crimina
paterfamilias esset, si mendacium
subtiliter limasset, a radicibus
non euertisset scelere funesto domum.'   50
  Nil spernat auris nec tamen credat statim
quandoquidem et illi peccant quos minime putes
et qui non peccant impugnantur fraudibus.
  hoc admonere simplices etiam potest
opinione alterius ne quid ponderent,   55
ambitio namque dissidens mortalium
aut gratiae subscribit aut odio suo.
erit ille notus quem per te cognoueris.
  haec exsecutus sum propterea pluribus
breuitate nimia quoniam quosdam offendimus.   60

Both trust and distrust are full of pitfalls.
I'll give you a prime case of each. It won't take long:
Hippolytus came to grief because his stepmother was
      trusted;
Cassandra wasn't trusted, and Troy came tumbling down.
The moral is, the truth must be thoroughly investigated
      before   5
a stupid conviction delivers a criminal verdict.
But in case you make light of ancient myth,
I'll now tell you the tale of something that happened in my
      ken:

There once was a husband loved his wife.
He was just getting ready the plain robe of adulthood for his
    son,   10
when one day he was taken into a corner by a freedman of his.
This character had hopes of being put into the will as new
    nearest heir.
When he'd told a pack of lies about the boy,
and a longer list still on the scandalous doings of his—in fact
    chaste—wife,
he then proceeded to add what he saw would cause   15
the doting husband most heartbreak of all. Another man was
    coming round
and the fair name of the house was getting stained by ugly
    adultery.
    The husband blazed at the imaginary crimes laid at his
    wife's door,
faked a trip to his farmstead but secretly lay low
in town. Then after dark he suddenly stepped in   20
the door, making a beeline for his wife's bedroom.
Now she, like the mother she was, had told her son to sleep
    in here,
sparing no pains in keeping safe his now full-developed
    maturity.
While the staff are getting a light and scurrying round,
the man fails to check the surge of crazed rage,   25
and up to the bedside he goes, gropes for a head in the pitch
    dark.
When he feels one with hair close-cropped, he thrusts his
    sword through the ribs,
reckless of all else but revenge for the pain.
A lamp arrived and the moment he set eye on his son,
and his wife sleeping innocently there in her room,   30
— in fact so deep in the slumber of first sleep that nothing
    had penetrated her
dreams—he paid on the spot the penalty for the terrible
    thing he had done.
Fell on the sword which credulity had made him draw.
    A string of accusers indicted the woman
and had her marched off to Rome and the High Court of the
    Hundred Judges.   35

Spiteful suspicion tells heavily against the innocent,
since she's the one who now owns the estate. Her protectors
    stand firm in courageous defence of the blameless lady.
**AT THIS POINT, THE GODHEAD AUGUSTUS
    WAS PETITIONED**
by the panel of judges, to rescue the honour of their oath,   40
since the vagaries of the indictment had them tied up in
    knots.
He first blew away the murk of vindictive slander,
and found the certain key to the truth. Next came his
    judgement:
'The freedman caused the mess. Let him receive the knocks.
Indeed this woman who has lost her son and been denied her
    husband in the same instant   45
we consider to merit our sympathy, certainly not our
    condemnation.
Now. Had the father in this house gone over the crimes
    informed against the others
with some thoroughness, if he had used his wits
and run over the fabrication with a fine-toothed comb, then
    he would not have torn
his house up by the roots with his heinous death-dealing.' 50
    The ear must spurn nothing, but must not instantly trust,
    either.
For, as you can see, those you would least suppose do go
    wrong too,
and, as well, people who don't go wrong get victimized in a
    frame-up.
    All this can serve as warning to the less devious among us
    as well.
They mustn't measure things by their neighbour's
    yardstick.   55
You know, greed for incompatible goals conscripts mankind
for complaisance, or else for their animosity.
The person you know will always be someone you have got
    to know *yourself.*
    I'll tell you why I dwelt on this poem at extra length—
It's because I've put out some people by too much brevity. 60

Tart Tiberius Caesar imposed himself on his tale, and on its telling. Next up, Augustus the God serves us a great pudding of a poem. The story is sandwiched between an aggressive warm-up and multilayered complex of *epimythia*, which together— believe it or not—amount to all but *one third* of this, the longest extant *fabula* in Phaedrus. In the process, the meta-narrative dimensions of the plot are foregrounded, as we are led, through the narrator's interpretative function, into the story as itself a scene of interpretation, and then run into a sequence of reflexive positions from which to evaluate both narrative and narration.

Readers are brought into the reckoning by the framing of the piece as a Roman event 'from recent memory' of the reign of Augustus (v. 8). The introduction insists that this is Roman, and that it is Roman 'myth', beggaring Greek myth by comparison, and portentously presaging a double-barrelled intrigue. Two diametrically opposed lessons will be resolved in(to) one cross-fire, of 'believing *and* non-believing' (or 'trust and distrust': *credere et non credere*, v. 1). At stake is the ruin of a loving family triangle, and the Emperor must be called in to vindicate civic structure, and save the City, as poisonous talk of adultery infects an exemplary *domus*. Sense, if not sweetness, and light are restored when divine wisdom lays bare 'what the butler did';[1] courtesy of Augustus, and his freedman Phaedrus, the villainy is pinned to the freedman in the fable.

As the tale uncurls to its inexorable dénouement, we find that its role as a pre-eminently collectable item for the newly self-promoting and loquacious fabulist announced in the extended preface to book 3 (Ch. 3) takes over. For its outermost ring picks up on the 'brevity' and otherwise of the performance (v. 2), to show (at once) how there's no pleasing some people, and no laying down the law without giving offence (vv. 59–60). One thought we are left to ponder is that a story which warns us to listen but not to believe other people, and their stories, 'right away', is courting *longueurs*, or looks suspiciously like it (v. 51). There may be a fine line between nugatory lack of substance and dragging out a formulaic routine; but are we prepared to devote 'plenty of research' to deciding which side we're on? (vv. 5 f.)

In which case, you could well stand condemned of agreeing (with your storyteller) that pious homage to the Emperor

unerringly capsizes into bathos. But Rome may still come out
ahead on the deal. For Phaedrus is doing a spot of Empire State
building here, in telling this tale out of court; his fiction is itself
part of the business of consecrating Augustus; and learning to
love a dead Caesar, or finding a use for one, is no sideshow, in
the reign of Tiberius. *Divus Augustus* is, it cannot be over-
emphasized, the eternal prototype. Mythologized through the
four decades and upwards of his reign, he was then forever
being returned to centre-stage in the rhetoric, mentality,
imagery of Tiberius' own quarter of a century of rule—as 'son
of the god', but himself obstinately and permanently mortal
(Ch. 1). No theorist of theirs worth their salt would look
forward to a future Caesar set fair to outlast the founder; and no
subject of the day could have believed that Caesars would come
and go for two centuries before a single one of them lasted
longer than *Tiberius*. But Tiberian Rome set the style for keeping Augustus present in whatever lives the Empire might
support, with legendary lore as well as official hagiography. If
apotheosis played a multitude of roles at the capital and in the
provinces, these could not immediately be excogitated or
grasped, let alone codified and sanctioned; but this business was
instantly urgent, an insistently pressing need.

Trust me or not—it would take *plenty* of 'believing and dis-
believing' before anything like a conventional line could be
found for negotiating and disseminating a more or less stable
régime, idiom, propriety for the emperor as god, among the
many cultures, politics, and religions of Rome. It would take
until kingdom come.

There is, accordingly, an instructive lesson laid down
when the ex-dictator butts into our adaptation of Aesop,
memorialized as the incarnation of wisdom, Roman-style. To
turn the thing round, we are handed this soup of a composition,
with its soap of a storyboard, as an occasion for the imag(in)ing
of a paradigm Emperor. The verities of Roman ideology and
affect make for a spongy old melodrama, but they posit a link-
age between 'Solomon'-in-Latin and the domestic apparatus of
decent society wherever. Put Phaedrus' mini-tragedy in with all
the clutter of headline crime and sensational fiction of early
imperial Rome, and it emerges starkly how the positioning of
wedlock as the hub for social cohesion and intelligibility targets

wifely purity as the crucial site of subversion and vindication of the culture.

Over the wife's body, the patriarchal system played poachers and gamekeepers, by turns uxorious and misogynist, so that marriage *was* the mythology, it modelled social modelling as such, serving as 'the structure that maintains the Structure, or System'.[2] In particular, adultery—'by bringing the wrong things together in the wrong places (or the wrong people in the wrong beds)'[3]—was the blind-spot where society was risked to crisis. Basic categories for construing the world, not least of them love/hate, and most certainly trust (and distrust), got thrashed out over and over again in variations and mutations of those banal family romances, those cliché family tragedies, that hog so much attention in the mundane exchanges that create the fabric of our private lives together.[4]

Narratives of marital deadlock such as ours highlight, not so much the potential to interrogate, pressurize, and de-naturalize the fix of traditional roles and values (as potentially or for real in the hype and hustle of a radical novel), but rather the identification of routes for the rescue, revenge and recovery of the social contract. The attribution of stable gender, sexual, conjugal, parental roles in positioning individuals within asymmetrical power-relationships of control, responsibility, care, pleasure, is incessantly reasserted by stories knotted into eventual closure, so that the shuffle of perils, sins, riddles, predicaments functions as provocation for triumphant acclamation of right, justice, sense, and wisdom.[5]

Divus Augustus is, in this perspective, the genie who watches over the narrativity of Rome, authorizing stories of due process in congratulatory celebration of the culture of 'leg*alism* . . . and the *idea* of law, in its purest (because imaginary) form'.[6] His correlative is the *matrona* he saves from the venom of infamy, the god come to override the fragility of his mortal analogue, the *paterfamilias*. Omniscient, omnipotent, he shields sanctity, here to show what counts. The wife privileges her son's vulnerability; her priority is to preserve and protect him from harm, love ranged against out-of-place lust, premature, unprescribed (v. 23). The tale, of course, prioritizes, as it fixates on, or fetishizes, mother love. But it also gears this into beatification of the civil process at *Rome* (v. 35). Replicated, amplified, enshrined in the sacrosanctity of the jurors' oath to deliver Truth (v. 40), the wife's goodness is publicly risked to malevolent incrimination, just as it had been privately maligned to her loving, so credulous, so vulnerable, husband (vv. 35 f., 13 f.). She *is* 'the good name of the house', so 'the house falls', as it stood, 'by the husband's polluting death-dealing' over her innocence (vv. 17, 50). Yes, Augustus is found a useful job, to exorcise the spectre of adultery.

We could think of it this way:

The unfaithful wife is, in social terms, a self-cancelling figure, one from whom society would prefer to withhold recognition so that it would be possible to say that socially and categorially the adulterous woman does not exist. Yet physically and creaturely she manifestly does, so she becomes a paradoxical presence of negativity within the social structure, her virtual non-being offering a constant implicit threat to the being of society.[7]

As the tale is told, the verdict of Augustus is clearly marked out as the operator of myth, a transcendent Word of the Father that needs no whodunnit sleuthing or ratiocination to detect the criminal. No, this is society imaged as deflecting evil from itself, reflected back onto its bogeyman, dispelled with a stereotype. No Caesar could live up to such a billing in the here and now; but Augustus' name would not cease to stand for the dispensation he had inaugurated, so long as such tales continued to be told.

The recognition of adultery as a legitimate focus for surveillance and punishment by the state did indeed retain its Augustan label, in the form of a complex of stipulations centred on the *Lex Iulia de adulteriis coercendis* (*c*.17 BCE), when the monarchic régime projected itself as an all-out crusade for monological meaning, set above the rights of fathers and husbands, as 'the ultimate *paterfamilias*, the whole state had become his household' invaded every corner of every Roman home, and climbed into, under, every bed.[8] Read against the grain, so as to tell tales on Caesar, Phaedrus' story even stakes out the downside of the criminalization of adulterous liaisons by pointing to the incubation it provided for the proliferation of calumny, gold-digging, and mischief-making.

Personal relations were put at the mercy, not merely of *mis*-representation, but of *representation*, since cases taken to court must be conducted in an atmosphere of suspicion, with recourse only to the oratory of psychopathological probability and the eloquence of testimony to character. Feel how panoptic supervision from watchgod Augustus provides vital underpinning for the system it put in place, and partakes in the perpetuity of the law and life of Romanness. The 'post-Augustan' topos of adultery on trial did not only sharpen Roman ingenuity and paranoia in law-court and declamation-hall; though that it certainly did, as the logic and dynamics of interpersonal relations were scrutinized, theorized, and melodramatized. But all this activity was laced into the policing of privacy by *the* court, duly marshalled by law but enforceable at any turn by pressure from the palace. Yes, the identification of autocrat with Law was no less close than wife with *domus*; and *that* is the mythologization articulated through the invocation of *Divus Augustus* by, as well as in, Phaedrus' Roman fable.

So no wonder this brew of folklore and fakelore, street-corner gossip and hand-me-down palace leak, makes for syrupy stuff—a golden opportunity for our scribbler in verse to play on our nerves with his tricksy treacly trickle of editorial chivvying. Hard to swallow? Guilty, as charged.

vv. 1–8

Aesop's fables provided teachers of rhetoric with just the stuff for exercises in variation on a theme, and our fabulists offer several prize displays of *dilation*.[9] In storytelling, an initial promise of 'brevity' (v. 2) more often than not promises *extra* length, abusing the usual dynamics governing reception of stories.[10] Phaedrus' collection makes a particular point of waving 'brevity' at us, (not) wanting to waste our precious time on his frivolities, and (so) guying our frivolousness (Ch. 3).[11] The coda (vv. 59–60) will offer up a facetious 'apology' for long-windedness; the preliminaries feint with a brisk pair of mythological *exempla* (vv. 3–4), invoked as by-play to warm up the mammoth anecdote in store. Such gambits were habitual in teaching by illustration: 'Why am I telling tales of Dionysus and Heracles? *That*'s just myth; *that*'s just hero-tales. *I* tell of Socrates . . .' (Maximus of Tyre, *Orations* 32. 8).

We begin with a formulaic gnomic pattern that fits proverbial thought to verse-unit, to make a blunt and businesslike 'text' for our parable.[12] Combining and dove-tailing tales was another ancient Creative Writing exercise, and this is a skit on it.[13] Even so, the move of dismissal of fiction in favour of hard fact is another characteristic opening for a high-profile storyteller: 'Let's quit stories, and focus in on what's closer to us' (Cicero, *On divination* 2. 2); 'Leaving these images, their stories and all, approach a man who lived not in the reign of Kronos, but bang in the middle of this Iron Age race of ours' (Maximus of Tyre, *Orations* 36. 5). We recognize that the dummy-run was to set up the story as just *meant* for us: 'he didn't care for ancient tragedies ('prehistory'), or names famous down the ages, but was about to recount something that occurred in his own memory (*rem sua memoria factam*; 'in our own times'), if we should like to listen' (Petronius, *Satyrica* 110. 8, with Lucian, *Toxaris* 10 in quote-marks).[14] And the sidelined myths do speak to the cueing of the main attraction, not just negatively, as the classic Greek mythological repertoire that Romans grew up on and could dissociate from as old hat foreign fictional nonsense, but positively, as both index of prestige and thematic short-hand: let's pretend that Augustan myth-making bids to emulate and surpass the best of the Greek legacy; and, in all seriousness, let's roll into one mess the distinctive Cassandra, 'the woman nobody believed' (Cicero, *To Atticus* 8. 11. 3), and Hippolytus–Phaedra, the archetype of remarriage as disaster since 'Potiphar's wife'.[15]

We'll see already that the lowly fabulist is taking on the best of high culture, moving his baby 'novella' into the big league of epic and tragedy, for what it's worth envisaging the displacement, on its own terms, of Hellenism from its privileged locus in the formation of Roman culture: *poetry*.[16] He expects his readers to acknowledge the compliment to their knowing the (t)ropes, implied by his allusive off-handedness and *soupçon* of mannered writing.[17] In seeing off Classics, Phaedrus also good as promises us a fea(s)t of storytelling, his very own double bill of domestic double-murder, together with collective doom and obliteration brought down upon the City and Empire. In the event, he and we shall not get another stepmother into bed with the son who is not her son; and we have the surprise package of

Augustus the God waiting in the wings to save *both* the woman everyone should, but no one could, trust, *and* our home, though not hers, namely the City that must not die, Rome.

In the course of the next few lines, we momentarily come to a premature grinding halt, as the pair of exempla is given an *epimythium*, 'The moral is . . .', and formal closure is duly achieved.[18] How far would our budding Roman Aesop dare to go in jazzing up his work? Far enough to serve up a lecture but spare us a tale? He will pretty well do this on a number of occasions apparently from the fourth book onwards, kidding us that one more narrative is on its way soon, but dispensing with it after some satirical reflection or other,[19] and the notion of 'brevity' in overdrive (v. 2) could conceivably have been realized in the shape of two one-line summaries, too well-known to need—. . .?

Disconcerted or not, read on, and find yourself rebuked for jumping to the hasty conclusion that your host has himself jumped to a hasty conclusion. Yes indeed: 'the truth must be *thoroughly* investigated *before* | a stupid conviction delivers a criminal verdict' (vv. 5–6: *multum prius* | *quam*).[20] What kind of judges will we make for the story when it does arrive? What sort of jurors would we have made in the Case of the Widow and the Wicked Freedman?

If truth be told, these shenanigans show how easy it is to switch off, detach, and disregard, a fable moral. We're only being stroked for a second, before we get our claws and teeth into the next tale. 'Exhaustive research into truth' isn't *really* why we've called in at the house of fiction. The most we're likely to allow is that this Phaedrus is coming out of his shell far enough to suggest that we'd best not miss any put-on's he may try. And there's plenty of that to cope with, as the fabulist presumes he can read us like a book, knows full well we have less respect than even he does for antediluvian myth,[21] and banks on our preference for something new, something that happened in true life, something of Phaedrus' own, any old yarn but (please) NO MORE GREEK MYTH!

But 'Editors, like Chinese shopkeepers, must write on their door-lintels, "No cheating here".' (Carlyle (1932) 16) Same goes for storytellers, but we know better: we can tell ourselves that 'both trust and distrust are full of pitfalls', but still we believe a likely story at our peril. So, but me no but's, this story really happened, not so long ago: 'But now mine is a real fact and happened no longer ago than last October . . .' (Busk (1874) 264: a ghost-tale).[22] Why, the narrator 'remembers it happening', he can swear to the fact, and even—the limit case—he *was* that soldier, so the story is not just history, it really is his story, the story of him, and now us.[23] The word 'my' caps the foreplay, and the preamble is done: *mea.* | (v. 8).

But to find out *where* we are, and *that* we are anywhere at all, we shall have to wait till after we've put in *plenty* of reading (v. 35). And which of us is going to take a stab at the truth and get convicted of 'stupidity for delivering the premature verdict' of frivolous prejudice? (v. 6) Can this be *Rome*?

You'd better believe it.

But not too soon.

VV. 9–17

A husband loves a wife to death; a devoted father takes good care of his young son: both veneer and core of this tale are kitted out for a crisis in *purity, Roman-style*.[24] The Othello-like *paterfamilias* is the hub of family, plot, and problematic; for the umpteenth time in fiction, this rock of social order crumbles at his Iago's first push, and we plunge into the crime of passion, filicidal infanticide, suicide in remorse, what people used to do before they had television. Variants abound—not least, we shall find, in a dreadful catalogue of major rivers of the world and their stories preserved among Plutarch's worthy essays (*On rivers*, esp. 20 and 22).[25] But here a relatively uptown ambience is pictured all through, as Phaedrus limbers up for the sequel, where the story goes public so that Law may come into its own, and imperial Rome can reach for its ruler. If the tectonics are perennial—has the coming of electric light shut down more primitive versions of the 'stab in the dark'?[26]—a suite of *topoi* plugs the armature of the anecdote straight into the contemporary Roman ethos of declamatory histrionics.[27]

'A man's enemies are the men of his own house' (Micah 7. 6; *TMI* P365). Iago, the proverbial nigger in the woodpile, is bound to be the ancient 'villein': the trickster 'freedman'.

Defined by his change of social status and category, *libertus* works for further mutability by taking his patron and former master 'aside into a discreet corner' (v. 11). Continuing 'to live in his patron's household and even to perform the same function as he did as a slave',[28] he speaks from the liminal, or interstitial, position of the outside of the inside/inside of the outside, opening a gap, then a rift, in the end a chasm, as he 'seduces' this worthy away from his heart(h). Despite the technical phrase *proximus heres* (v. 12), we need not hear how on earth *libertus* might hope *he* would come into the estate, even if he eliminated the Mrs, somehow got rid of the only son, and himself became 'chief' non-agnatic 'heir'. Rather, 'legacy-hunting' (*captatio*) serves to topicalize the Law, for later on in the tale, and virtually translates as Rome's trademark obsession.[29]

Meantime, the plot sickens, pitting solemnity against slang, 'chaste wife' and 'back-door man' (vv. 14, 16), and upping the stakes with poisonous smears of desecration (v. 17).[30] 'Many lies' lead to 'more', and 'the most wounding' cut of all, as Phaedrus turns the screw (*multa mentitus . . . | et plura . . . | adiecit id quod maxime . . .*, vv. 13–15). Conspicuously, the manoeuvring gets the son playing second fiddle to the real star: the wife (vv. 13 > 14 *vs.* vv. 9 > 10).

vv. 18–33

A bourgeois husband will fake a visit to his country property: 'Anselmo left the house, making the excuse of a visit to that friend of his in the country. He then came back to hide . . .' (Cervantes (1950) 309). Archetypal Unexpected Returns are from the fields worked by the farmer.[31] So too the ambush belongs to the articulated story; in simpler tales the husband merely returns 'from a business-trip' (Pseudo-Plutarch, *On rivers* 22. 1):[32]

Thestios was away from town . . . and after spending sufficient time he returned to his ancestral home. Finding his son Kalydon asleep with his mother and supposing he was an adulterer, he committed infanticide unawares. When he saw with his own eyes the deed he least anticipated, he threw himself into the river Axenos.

It is clear as daylight how our ~~father~~/husband/lover at once abdicates authority: takes the fatal false step, himself joining and springing the villain's 'lying frame-up' and 'dark' disinformation (*simulauit . . . clam . . . subsedit . . . noctu ~ falso . . . crimine*, vv. 19 f. ~ v. 18); and loses control, 'going up in flames' and 'precipitating' disaster (*incensus . . . subito*, vv. 18, 20). So the *domus* is deranged by diabolic lust to kill. But not so fast: this is also the flipside of the *paterfamilias'* love: he 'can't stop himself', for primeval violence is the drive that sanctions *his* social imperative to protect and defend the purity of the Structure (*impetum non sustinens*, v. 25). So this gent must see, and shed, red to stay in role, and act out the normality he stands for. Perhaps we could put it that Power is come to overpower its wielder? At any rate, *night* spells chaos, abyssal abolition of sense; and we shall need, more than the staff to fetch a lamp (vv. 24, 29), The Father to bring back The Light of Reason (vv. 42 f.).

In a well-to-do novella milieu the shared bedroom must be engineered: folktale can have a returning husband take the *baby* born in his absence to be a lover! In the primitive theme the son just shares the family-bed as a matter of course, no comment (Pseudo-Plutarch, *On rivers* 20. 1):[33]

Finding his son Axourtas sleeping with his mother and supposing it was some citizen or other, in jealousy's war-on-wickedness Euphrates drew his sword and slit his throat. When he saw with his own eyes the deed he least anticipated, in too much pain to bear he threw himself into the river of the Medes.

But, as we have seen, the mechanics of our story also allow us to wallow in dutiful righteousness (vv. 22 f.),[34] here transferred onto the ~~beloved~~/wife/mother, in readiness for our sequel. This is the ideal conjugality of Roman nostalgia: 'in the old days, sons were brought up in their mother's arms, on her lap, her pride was good housekeeping and childcare' (Tacitus, *Dialogue on the decline of oratory* 28. 4: *tueri domum et inseruire liberis*, 'supervise the home, and slave so the kids could be free').[35] At the other end of the idiomatic spectrum, the jealous passion of 'this rash and most unfortunate man' (*Othello* 5. 2. 84) takes the melodramatic form of groping for the head on the pillow, risking tone for immediacy:

'Twas the middle of the night . . . when I gently lifted the latch, and entered without making a sound . . . All were asleep. Next I felt my way along the wall and stood beside the bed . . . But then, finding more than one lot of breathing, I felt around, and found a soft and beardless person, cropped short . . . If I'd had a sword, I wouldn't have hesitated, make quite sure of that . . .

But that was salacious comedy, where it belongs, in the whorehouse: Lysias' special courtesan, Ioessa, was sharing her sheets with a colleague, whose head was shaven because of occupational disease, or (to make a point) men set this woman at risk of being taken for a man and—see what comes of it: 'There, laddie, that's the fucker you were crazy jealous of!' (Lucian, *Dialogues of courtesans* 12. 3–5)

Phaedrus' stab in the dark is bad enough, but folklore versions relish their nightmares of gore (Hans Andersen, 'Little Klaus and Big Klaus'):[36]

In came Big Klaus with his axe. He knew where Little Klaus's bed was, and, making straight for it, he hit the dead old grandmother on the forehead, thinking it was Little Klaus. 'Take that!' he said. 'You won't come fooling me any more!'

Our killer 'cashes in his chips' with instant tragic suicide, leaving one poor widow out for the count—dead to the world as she 'sleeps the sleep of the just', while (gentlefolk of the jury) the boy by her side is slaughtered, the servants dash round till a lantern is fetched, and the slayer does the decent thing, bedside hara-kiri. I put it to you, things don't look too good. For her; for 'holy' matrimony.[37] Laddish Roman declaimers would pile in with their own special brand of imaginary gusto (Pseudo-Quintilian, *Minor declamations* 347):

The wife of a husband away abroad learned of his death from rumour. Found to be heiress, she married a young lad and delivered the house as dowry. The husband arrived one night, killed the pair of them. He is charged with slaughter.

Imagine the defendant 'who so loved his wife'—though, yes, 'it *is* hard to bring home to yourself other people's nightmares, but do let's all put ourselves in his shoes'—'. . . well, when I had come into the bedroom and caught my wife lying next to her adulterer, was I supposed to wake them up, and leave it at that?' (ibid. 7, 9, 4).

In a similar case, the prosecution shreds the wife's story (Pseudo-Quintilian, *Major declamations* 1):

A man had a blind son, his designated heir. He brought a stepmother into the home, and demoted his son to a secluded corner of the house. One night he was murdered while sleeping in his room with his wife. Next day he was found with his son's sword stuck in the wound. The wall from his bedroom to his son's was smeared with bloody hand-prints. The blind son and the stepmother accuse each other of the crime.

For the son: 'note that the wife's strongest argument, that he stood to inherit, cuts both ways'; and 'without his father, he has lost everything—now he *does* want his sword, to end his own life!' The nub, though, is this: surely, both the others must have woken up if the blind man was groping around? So (ibid. 2, 4, 6, 9):

See him reach his father's bed and lean over to hear them breathing in their sleep. How will he know where to aim the sword, which of the pair to strike? Will he then feel their faces and limbs, will he explore the quickest route to end someone's life? How deep must be the sleep that couldn't feel all this? You will say 'I didn't feel it'. So you realize how bad your case is, when your only defence is unparalleled and beyond belief: your husband is slain in your arms, just so, and you—'you don't feel *a thing*'?

A more tortuous version of the same menu produces even more sarcasm in the next case up for performance (Pseudo-Quintilian, *Major declamations* 2): for the blind son who swaps accusations with stepmother, of murdering the man of the house, when 'on the very night the son was removed from the will, there was a hubbub in the house, and the servants found master murdered in his bedroom, with his wife lying next to him evidently sound asleep. The blind son was found standing at his own bedroom door. But his bloodied sword *was* under his pillow' (6, 19, 17 f.):

The whole household . . . was on the scene, only the stepmother couldn't be roused, right where all the commotion came from . . . Alarmed and in a rush they break down your door—see how many hands carry lamps over your bed, and at the apparent sight of two dead bodies the chamber is filled with groans and yells . . . Suppose the boy did get to his father's side: he must probe the differences between a couple lying together, feel their faces, remove the duvet, find the place for the blow: isn't he going to wake them up? . . . Let me ask *her*: what sleep is so deep that a killing inches away wouldn't rouse you? . . . See: his blood is spurting all over your arms after his guts have burst . . . Now look some more: the gush of gore is clotting all round your body and you are being gripped tight by the corpse in *rigor mortis*. And *still* you don't wake up?

vv. 34–8

The scene abruptly shifts to the 'highest court in the land', with proper-sounding Roman décor. The suicide must have been a *ciuis Romanus* (citizen of Rome) of some standing, hence automatic transfer to the metropolitan court?[38] Such is life: 'A certain T. Caelius went off to bed after dinner with his two growing sons in the same suite, and in the morning was found dead: no one, slave or free, could be found to attach the suspicion to, so the sons were indicted for parricide' (Cicero *In defence of Roscius of Ameria* 64). But our story homes on Woman, rallying round the 'Genoveva' figure of the persecuted widow.[39]

vv. 39–50

In courtroom and mock-courtroom, sensational crime brings out dirty washing for public scrutiny, but also stimulates debate about what is on our (lurid) minds. The confrontational rhetoric and format of advocacy, whether real or pretend, made Romans formulate and manipulate, explore or discredit, commonplace positions that could be taken up or discarded to suit the brief. These shuffled the stock of truths known elsewhere in the culture, as well as coming up with more or less memorable and reusable gems of their own; but particularly the declaimers' fictional play also made for cracks in the schemata and holed the conceptual equipment of their society, questioning and problematizing norms, stereotypes, structures.[40]

'When the father suspected his son of incest with his mother, took him off into a corner, and tortured him to death, he would not tell the woman what he found out. She prosecutes him

for maltreatment' is the hook for hanging (post-)adolescent
ingenuity on, for stimulating verbal facility; but this is also the
moment that prompts the thoughts, among many, many more,
that 'Rumour is not so important that a mother should be
anxious for her modesty because she loves her son. Indeed, if
you ask me, all mothers love their children as though they have
fallen *in* love with them' and 'No one kills a son because of
hatred; even if despised, no young man is worth so much pain'
. . . (Pseudo-Quintilian, *Major declamations* 18: for the woman;
19: for the man; 18. 10, 19. 5)[41] Consider, too, how everyone is
primed to relive the horrors, drool their way through speculation on illicit desire, fill in the silence of the abused (but how
many times?) child . . .

Declamation tells tales on imperial Rome not least by
concentrating much of its fire on trapping women in sexual
criminality: 'A man with a lovely wife went abroad. A foreign
trader moved into her neighbourhood and three times over
propositioned her for sex, money down; she turned him down.
The trader died and left the lovely woman heir to all his estate,
adding the compliment "I found her chaste". She took the
legacy. Husband returns to accuse her of adultery on suspicion': explicitly a forum, this, for imagining impossible proto-
cols for a matron to live above suspicion (Seneca the Elder,
Legal cases 2. 7). Star of the show, however, was always The
Cuckold wreaking mayhem: whether as the proving-ground for
masculinity, and wreckage of conjugality on the homosocial
rock of loss of face, or as the interface between nature and
control, and juncture between state and domestic spheres.
Just what vengeance was permitted, on adulterer and on
adulteress? Just what was mandatory? On what authority or
imperative, and with what chance of modifying sentiment, let
alone behaviour?[42]

Headline news could be strange as fiction: a Neronian
Tribune of the Plebs, one Octavius Sagitta (aptly named as if
for the boy Augustus once had been, *Octavius*, and for Cupid's
'arrow', *sagitta*!), seduced a wife, but she refused divorce;
allowed one last night of passion, he took a freedman confidant
and a weapon, and stabbed the woman and her maid: *this* loyal
libertus then confessed to the murder—he had taken revenge for
her maltreatment of Sagitta—but in the end the maid recovered

to rescue the truth. The melodramatic poet Lucan, we are told, very soon declaimed the case—for *and* against (Tacitus, *Annals* 13. 44; Vacca, *Life of Lucan*). An equestrian had sworn never to divorce his wife, but Tiberius absolved him from this bind when she was caught in bed with her son-in-law (Suetonius, *Life of Tiberius* 35. 1). A late Tiberian princess was pounced on by informers for having a slave adulterer, and there was no doubt about the outrage: so she skipped defence and brought her life to an end (Tacitus, *Annals* 6. 40. 3). Criminalization under Augustan Law must have glamorized the adultery stakes: had ancient Rome sanctioned/demanded the killing of both parties in hot blood? Did modern Rome now ban such uxoricide and only pardon slaughter outside the ranks of the élite? Was the main effect to spur declaimers to spoof the crusade, as staple post-Augustan entertainment, with Caesar's name written all over it?[43]

In our story, Augustus supervenes on the courtroom scene just as the Caesars did in Roman history. The vignette of *accusatores* pitted against worthy *patroni* (vv. 34, 38) keeps the traditions of stout civic duty going strong;[44] but the Emperor must supplement the apparatus of the Republic, with superhuman wisdom to uphold its honour. In the post-Augustan dispensation, real tribunals could follow the procedure of 'consultation', sending in a 'report' with full documentation. This terminated, if accepted, 'the juror's binding oath' (v. 40: *iusiurandum iudiciale*).[45]

On the other hand, the court was a godsend to a monarch, an arena for the display of Wisdom ~ the power to dictate Truth (= 'ver-dict').[46] He should champion the afflicted and win kudos for clemency: 'Yea the cases of the humble are of grave importance: a weak and lowly thing is a widow, an orphan, an immigrant. For these must the king in the highest be judge, the one who has fastened his rule upon all' (Philo *On the special laws 4* 176: on The Good King). Seneca would teach Nero the way: 'Let one not believe lightly, but sort out the truth, and back up harmlessness' (*On clemency* 1. 20. 1: *ne facile credat, ut uerum excutiat, ut innocentiae faueat*).[47]

Which is to say, Caesar could intervene in any trial, by whim (Suetonius, *Life of Tiberius* 33):

If someone said a defendant was wriggling out of it, Tiberius would suddenly show up and remind the jurors, either from the floor or from the judge's bench, of the laws and their oath, as well as the case they were hearing. (*legum et religionis et noxae*)

A Caesar could exercise, or refrain from exercising, the power of a deity, arbitrarily, outside of any regulation.[48] And expect, extort, congratulation.

Our late (lamented?) Augustus makes his entrance to a double fanfare of (mixed, and faded) metaphors, the 'murk of slander' and the 'source of truth', which are surplus to requirements, but written up into expectant parallelism and complement: *tenebras . . . calumniae ~ fontem ueritatis* and *dispulit ~ repperit* (vv. 42 f.). Declamatory mimesis always means to bring to light dark secrets of Roman hearts and minds: 'Here is a crime shrouded on all sides by the deep darkness of night, and by a thick, thick veil of shadows' (Pseudo-Quintilian, *Major declamations* 18. 7). This is why we have seen so much *blindness* involved, one way or another: 'A father hid away his wife and expensive son, retired into retreat. He came back blinded. He seeks an eye for an eye from the son. Mother claims she did it.' (Calpurnius Flaccus, *Declamation* 9) And so on, and so forth. In short, Phaedrus' 'finish' once more effortlessly directs us to the true source of . . . his story's *cultural power*.

So the Emperor sees that the defendant makes a doubly-deserving special case for royal mercy: 'widowed and deprived of her child in one go' (v. 45).[49] We're not here to wonder—*what sort* of 'certain key to the truth' did this Solomon 'find'? (v. 43: a witness . . .?); we're here to marvel—*what* a blessing, a (good, and dead) Emperor! Taken at face-value, indeed, Augustus doesn't bother to pronounce the accused *innocent*; and his sentencing of the freedman seems to pin the punishment to him all too peremptorily (in the decisive first words, | '*Luat . . . poenas*', v. 44), somewhere short of *guilt*. His attention directs ours, back to the *paterfamilias*, to hand out a spanking: the deceased exercised no judgement (unlike the *Cuiri*, and their supremo—speaking), and that failure (*sc.* to exercise trust/belief properly) destroyed (— the Emperor's last word, v. 50, the keynote, cf. v. 17, *domus* | —) a, or the, *domus* |.

Listen up, and ask: does Phaedrus seize his big chance? Does his Augustus sound divine? He certainly pontificates, spouts pathos worthy of declamation's guardian angel. First he wraps the villain in a half line of damnation: *causa libertus mali*, v. 44. Then neatly balanced lines first mark (with the link-word *simul*) parallelism, in *orbam nato* and *priuatam uiro*, and then intone a thunderous preference: *miserandam* not *damnandam*. The second imperious sentence inflates to double up two versions of the conditional deploring the *paterfamilias'* irresponsibility; to mix four lines, the first three with room for just four words each, with unadventurous-through-dull metaphors; and to showcase an exceptional sequence of majestically long words (*perscrutatus, paterfamilias, subtiliter, limasset, radicibus, euertisset*). If *Divus Augustus* must speak in iambic verse, his freedman could be best placed of anyone to catch the manner?[50]

vv. 51–3

The storyteller takes up where his right royal voice left off, amplifying his original double-barrelled premonitory lesson (v. 1) with more (uselessly blank) proverbial admonition: 'Hold to that commandment of Epicharmus, "Don't believe/trust recklessly"' (Pseudo-Cicero *On running for president* 39: *non temere credere*).[51] 'Hearsay' (*auris*, v. 51) forever loses out to the evidence of your eyes:[52] hear this re-coded, as 'you have got to know yourself' (v. 58). And the usual plonking format of Aesopic morals is not so very far from His ponderous Majesty's style: *et illi peccant quos* ~ *et qui non peccant* (vv. 51 ~ 52: *quandoquidem* lumbers by; the alliteration thumps past, *peccant . . . putes . . . peccant impugnantur*).

vv. 54–8

These lines of padding set us up for the ironic coda. Not that their fabulist would insult his readers as 'simple' (v. 54), and surely they don't need telling, for instance trusting *his* opinion to weight theirs (v. 55), as he preaches about the entire human race and its tell-tale flaws—for all the world like a real historian,[53] not just a ruffian Aesop let loose on Roman anecdotage (vv. 56f.)—before he catches *you* out by turning to address you after all (v. 58). Not that, it turns out, you simply need your fabulist to tell you all or any of this!

By all means, you must make up your own mind; listen to my reading, but size up Phaedrus-Augustus' performance for yourself. Go over the crime with some thoroughness, use your wits and run over the fabrication with a fine-toothed comb. Surely these lines of waffle are more than usually clumsy, halting, flabby?

Either way, the case rests.

vv. 59–60

At last, the editorial blurb. Wouldn't you know it, the tag has been taken at face-value: 'Phèdre était si succinct qu' aucuns l'en ont blâmé. | Ésope en moins de mots s'est encore exprimé . . .' (LaFontaine *Fables* 6. 1. 11 f.). But the ironic apology—with its heavily alliterating connectives (*propterea pluribus* | . . . *quoniam quosdam*)—was loaded by the introduction: the pose is that of a compiler who affects a persona in his work, 'To some people I seem scanty in my comments on the adages, and meagre. . . . I wanted to show them that in the rest of the book I have made an effort to be brief . . .' (Erasmus, on *Adages* 3. 7. 1). The storyteller covers his tracks by going on the offensive, and laying the blame at another's door: 'For there is folke superstycious or capaxe that they may not be contented with fewe words' (Alphonsus, *Miscellaneous fables* 8 in Caxton's *Aesop*), or 'T'en ferais, pour vous plaire, un | ouvrage aussi long que l'Iliade ou l'Odyssée . . .' (LaFontaine 12. 15. 123).

It does hit the spot when our very own *causa libertus mali*, Phaedrus, spreads his inventive and malign lies about the heights of Roman society, and complains, at the death, that he still just can't win. One reason why we see (through) his game with the reading of fables is the generous profile he allowed himself to start this third book (Ch. 3).

Remember: both trust and distrust are full of pitfalls.

Don't forget: the ear must spurn nothing, but must not instantly trust, either.

Must we go on so?

3(b)

3(a)

3
Another Hard Luck Story: *Phaedrus'* Tale (3. *Prologue*)

Phaedri libellos legere si desideras
uaces oportet, Eutyche, a negotiis,
ut liber animus sentiat uim carminis.
'Verum' inquis 'tanti non est ingenium tuum,
momentum ut horae pereat officiis meis.'   5
non ergo causa est manibus id tangi tuis
quod occupatis auribus non conuenit.
fortasse dices 'Aliquae uenient feriae
quae me soluto pectore ad studium uocent'?
legesne, quaeso, potius uiles nenias   10
impendas curam quam rei domesticae,
reddas amicis tempora, uxori uaces,
animum relaxes, otium des corpori,
ut assuetam fortius praestes uicem?
mutandum tibi propositum est et uitae genus   15
intrare si Musarum limen cogitas.
ego, quem Pierio mater enixa est iugo,
in quo Tonanti sancta Mnemosyne Ioui
fecunda nouies artium peperit chorum,
quamuis in ipsa paene natus sim schola   20
curamque habendi penitus corde eraserim
et laude inuicta uitam in hanc incubuerim,
fastidiose tamen in coetum recipior.
quid credis illi accidere, qui magnas opes
exaggerare quaerit omni uigilia,   25
docto labori dulce praeponens lucrum?
    sed iam 'quodcumque fuerit', ut dixit Sinon
ad regem cum Dardaniae perductus foret,
librum exarabo tertium Aesopi stilo,
honori et meritis dedicans illum tuis.   30
quem si leges, laetabor; sin autem minus,
habebunt certe quo se oblectent posteri.
    nunc fabularum cur sit inuentum genus,

breui docebo. seruitus obnoxia,
quia quae uolebat non audebat dicere,   35
affectus proprios in fabellas transtulit
calumniamque fictis elusit iocis.
ego porro illius semitam feci uiam,
et cogitaui plura quam reliquerat,
in calamitatem deligens quaedam meam.   40
quodsi accusator alius Seiano foret,
si testis alius, iudex alius denique,
dignum faterer esse me tantis malis
nec his dolorem delenirem remediis.
suspicione siquis errabit sua   45
et rapiet ad se quod erit commune omnium,
stulte nudabit animi conscientiam.
huic excusatum me uelim nihilominus:
neque enim notare singulos mens est mihi
uerum ipsam uitam et mores hominum ostendere.   50
    rem me professum dicet fors aliquis grauem.
si Phryx Aesopus potuit, Anacharsis Scytha
aeternam famam condere ingenio suo,
ego, litteratae qui sum propior Graeciae,
cur somno inerti deseram patriae decus,   55
Threissa cum gens numeret auctores suos,
Linoque Apollo sit parens, Musa Orpheo,
qui saxa cantu mouit et domuit feras
Hebrique tenuit impetus dulci mora?
ergo hinc abesto, liuor, ne frustra gemas,   60
quoniam mihi sollemnis debetur gloria.
    induxi te ad legendum; sincerum mihi
candore noto reddas iudicium peto.

Phaedrus: The Works, if you're longing to read them,
it's essential, Eutychus, to take time off from commitments,
so that a mind set free can feel the power poetry has.
'But' you say, 'your talent isn't great enough to be worth
a minute of time lost from my obligations.'   5
So then there's no reason why something should get in your
    hands
which doesn't suit preoccupied ears.
Perhaps you'll say, 'Some holiday or another will come along,
and invite me to relax the brain for some study'.
I put it to you: are you *really* going to read twopenny
    nonsense,   10

rather than invest in taking care of homelife,
find time for friends, take time out for the wife,
unwind mentally and give the body a rest,
so you can get through your usual stint more strongly than
 ever?
A change is what you need, of approach and choice of life, 15
if it's crossing the Muses' threshold you're thinking of.
I myself, someone delivered by their mother on the Pierian
 range,
up where Holy *Mémoire* for Thunderer Jove
gave birth in nine-fold pregnancy to the troupe of Arts,
even though I was virtually born right in school, 20
and I have scoured care for possessions from the bottom of
 my heart,
and I have won unbeatable fame from my plunge into this
 life,
still I am received into the fraternity with shudders of
 distaste.
What do you believe becomes of anyone who looks to amass
grand wealth with every waking hour, 25
setting sweet earning before sweated learning?
 But now, 'come what may', as Sinon put it,
when he was brought before the King of Troy,
I shall inscribe all *Book Three* with the pen of Aesop,
dedicating it to respect and recognition for you. 30
If you read it, I'll be glad; but if not,
they'll anyhow have something to enjoy in times to come.
 Now, the reason why the genre of the fable was invented,
will be a brisk lesson from me. The vulnerable Slave,
because he dared not say what he wanted, 35
shifted his own sentiments into fables,
and jollied away incrimination with fictional fun.
I then took his track on further, made it a road,
and thought up more than he'd left behind,
choosing some stuff for my disaster. 40
But if the prosecutor were someone other than Sejanus,
if the witness were someone else, and lastly the judge were
 someone else,
I'd admit to deserving such a bad time,
and wouldn't soften the pain with these remedies.

Phaedri libellos, the first words of the book, seals the grand(iose) opus with the only self-naming included anywhere in the whole corpus; *Eutyche*, v. 2, fetches in the collection's first addressee to match. Kept for later, the only scrap of 'History' in the *Fabulae* will mutter darkly about hard times— '*Sejanus*, calamity, courtroom, pain, suspicion . . .' (vv. 41–5). This triangle of players from (post-)Tiberian Rome puts a hard edge on the timeless nowhere of fables. It supports an insistent account of writer and genre.

First, an ironic plea to the reader to 'find time for Phaedrus' gets written up into a posh sermon to 'rethink life-choice' and qualify for 'admission over the threshold of the Muses': our poet is his own hard lesson, because 'his mother bore Phaedrus on the Pierian ridge' and so he was 'almost born in [the Muses'] school' (vv. 1–20); however, by-play on the subject of the ex-slave Phaedrus' birth later in the poem leads uncomfortably to the concession that this makes him 'Thracian—and proud Thracian', but feral Thracian for all that: *not* likely to command automatic respect for an authority on the weighty theme of 'Life itself, the ways of Humanity' (vv. 50–6).

Along the way, however, a knowing quote from Virgil (the solitary attributed citation in the *Fables*) has wily Phaedrus shrug 'à la Sinon, "*Che sera*"', to cap his opening fanfare and self-profile (v. 27); the matching bravura which later claims for Thracian forerunners 'Apollo's child Linus, Muse's child Orpheus' leads to a final flourish of self-glorification (v. 57): this time readers who don't know their Virgil get no help, but any wannabe gatekeeper of Parnassus dare not miss the reference, through the *Sixth Eclogue*'s poetic song of songs, to the unitary genealogy of poetic song, from Hesiod through Callimachus through Gallus, which Virgil wrote to resonate through the library of Classical poetry.

By running through a double Helicon's worth of recognizable authorial moves, this Aesop in iambics meanwhile shows he belongs in the fold. He lines up behind the inventor of his genre, with a radical aetiology for Fable, before claiming his own credentials as a worthy successor: if a prudent slave might cover protestation with obliquity, this hard-headed palace freedman could well take on the mantle of Aesop as self-proclaimed victim of domineering Sejanus (vv. 33–7, 38–44). If a background of maltreatment sits easily on a lowly fabulist, still he can ape his betters by disclaiming personal malice, as in *bona fide* Verse Satire, and turn finally, like every other Roman Callimachus, to broadcast the poetic 'justice of his triumph over Envy' (vv. 45–50, 60 f.).

The three chief surges of self-promotion in the manifesto are each marked with an emphatic First Person: | *ego, quem . . .*, | *ego illius . . .*, | *ego . . . qui sum . . .* (vv. 17, 38, 54), and they usher in a poet's autoportrait distinctly reverberating with the tales of hard work and hard luck handed to posterity by two of the (recent) all-time greats: Horace, in his rough diamond son-of-a-freedman character, and Ovid, in his genius' deathwish trip to perdition (v. 32, *posteri*).

The blunt and bluff *captatio beneuolentiae* ('pitch for sympathetic reception') that concludes this pivotal mini-essay tells you that this is *exactly* what it has been—a psychagogic effort to 'lead you where the reading starts' (vv. 62 f.). The *point* is to put it, to surrogate reader-in-the-text and to you, that reception of '*Phaedrus: The Works*' cannot be entirely detached from the 'trials' of any persecuted, or constructively paranoid, satirist, yet at the same time belongs in the same company as the best of Rome's literary effulgence, as the nexus of effective submission for 'critical probation' links up with formal dedication to patron. The exit line presses home that 'your *judgement* on Phaedrus' straddles both these scenes (vv. 62 f. ~ 29–32).

Considered as itself a 'fable', the poem has starkly posited literary culture as constitutively liberal, by virtue of its grounding in the exercise of civic liberty, for it presents the dyad of writing-and-reading as an investment of time set over against the ordinary occupations and regular obligations of social 'life' (vv. 15, *uitae*, 22, *uitam*, 50, *ipsam uitam*; v. 5, *officiis*). At bottom, Literature is necessarily dependent on the 'freedom' to devote 'mental space' to its demanding régime, and predicated on the exercise of 'frank honesty' between social equals (vv. 3, *liber animus* ~ 62 f., *sincerum . . . candore*). So we should think on 'The Fable *of Phaedrus*' when it points to slavery's jive as a ruse to elude the power of masters, and glimpses poetry as an up-town equivalent, played between citizens under the nose of imperial power politics.

No doubt this scenario manufactures imaginary heroism

from innocuous shadow-boxing, and this is primarily self-serving posturing from one more poetaster, *exemplum sui* ('an instance of what it is talking about').[6] All the same, there is a telling moral here for post-Augustan Rome, as this compiler contrives to bob and weave his way through the claim to infuse stories with 'personal self-incrimination', past the enigmatic casting of the fables as, somehow, 'these remedies', and on by way of denial of any 'individual animosity' (vv. 35 f.; 44; 49): see what follows once this warm-up pep-talk has made sure to imprint 'suspicion of their own making' on any reader, roundly branding response 'their own guilty conscience' talking (vv. 45, 47).

At the same time, the naming of Roman names in triplicate pushes every reader into second-guessing the writer's 'intent' (v. 49, *mens*) *precisely* in terms of specifics related to individuals: *ego* = Phaedrus, *tu* = Eutychus, and the Third Man [the other] = Sejanus . . .: '*such* a bad time' (v. 43, *tantis malis*). The attempt to plot these relationships has cost more academic energy and occasioned more ingenuity than any other Phaedrian issue. But forewarned is, here, *dis*armed. We are obliged to join in, knowing all the while that we shan't get it right, and that the way we get it wrong will tell tales on ourselves. Reading this poetry will be an invitation to no-win self-condemnation. And it rings true, too—such *is* 'the power poetry has' (vv. 1, 31, 63, *legere* ↔ *leges* ↔ *legendum*; 3, *uim carminis*).

No doubt Phaedrus was doomed to remain always the *Nachdichter* (creative translator-cum-versifier) of his first incarnation (1. *Prol.* 1 f.). But his maxi-prologue's gloss on his work tries hard to rub in how thoroughly any line separating fable from fabulist will be blurred, how many opportunities will be found to feature his own say alongside, as well as through, the stories. He animates the interpretivity in fable until the exchange in reading between reader and text wins recognition for an authorial design in the writing, beyond the minimally-contextualized aspiration for fame to match 'the cleverness that won Aesop a statue in smart Athens, for putting humanity back on the rails' (2. *Prol.* 3, *corrigatur error ut mortalium*). The row of eight 'if's in 3. *Prol.* (vv. 16; 31, 31; 41, 42; 45, 52, 52) are out to condition us to dialogue with the writer, *on his terms*.

So this feedback from Phaedrus does not so much describe as

mobilize fable, as a model for how culture gets shaped, imposed, transmitted. His 'Fable of *The Fabulist*' heaps pedagogy into protest, exercise into exorcism, diversion into subversion. But at the very moment when the frame widens beyond Aesop to include all slavery, every servility, any status vulnerability, so that Fabulation is built into the functional logic and dynamics of asymmetrical power relations, the frame of poetic form, trappings and décor intervenes: leisure, books and Latinity, literary citation, quotes and allusivity . . . Pompous or silly, piquant or knowing, whatever the tonal effect, where can this plug into the apparatus of Rome?

Of the threesome, *L. Aelius Seianus* belongs with the Aesopian freedman and his addressee in a tale told on Caesar, in the sense that they stand against the homoeostatic drag on social mobility represented by aristocratic networks of nobility, and represent the threat of mutability inherent in the new power-lines associated with the revolutionary superimposition of the principate on the old republican system.[7] Sejanus stood for the possibility that a strong-arm bodyguard could ingratiate himself with his boss, get a stranglehold on access to the palace administration, and line himself up for eventual succession: ' "A serving-boy." . . . And now, the second face of the whole world. | The partner of the Empire hath his image | reared equal with Tiberius'.[8] The same world spawned The Greekling Freedman turned minister and imperial chamberlain in virtual charge of a department of the administration. Both figures stand against power through birthright. Both play 'second fiddle' to reach the top. But easy come, easy go: Sejanus became the permanent byword for spectacular demise; and it went with the territory when a row of great imperial freedmen fell just as precipitately, under Gaius, Claudius, and Nero.

Phaedrus wants us to gather from his naming Sejanus in connection with his activities as fabulist, either that he provoked the monster in his hey-day or that his stories reflect on calamity after the fact; or indeed that he maybe never fell foul of him at all, but rather introduces Sejanus as the instant legend, the limit-case of the Roman 'Reichsmarshal' as prosecutor, hostile witness, and hanging judge rolled-into-one for a petty tyrant's show-trial (vv. 40–4). Whichever line we take, Sejanus brings with him perversion of justice, and persecution with the law; a tale told on his superiors, the Caesars. Whatever view we take of his rise and fall, he implicates the Julio-Claudian court in a reign of terror, where informers ruled Rome, and 'treason' emerged as the leading edge of repression: certainly no less far-fetched denunciation than any Aesopic innuendo from Phaedrus received serious consideration in senatorial proceedings of the 20s (Seneca, *Consolation to Marcia* 22. 4):

Sejanus handed over [Cremutius Cordus] to a satellite, enraged on account of one or two all-too-freely expressed remarks he uttered because he couldn't endure that Sejanus was, not being set, but himself climbing, upon our necks: when Sejanus was voted a statue to be erected in Pompey's Theatre, just restored by Tiberius after being gutted by a fire, he exclaimed 'Now the theatre really is ruined'. Cordus promptly starved himself to death, in 25.

And victimization by Sejanus could be a badge of courage to display from late October 31 onward, earned or not (Seneca the Elder, *Advisory speech* 2. 12):

Attalus the Stoic, who 'swapped countries' when trapped by Sejanus, of all the philosophers seen in your time was at once the most subtle and fluent by far.

There was only ever going to be the one and only *Seianus*, but *Eutychus* was one of the commonest slave-names of them all, proclaiming the 'luck' that ruled all unfree lives, and so pushing the question of ~~freedom~~ under autocracy. Shall we canvass a nonentity in a corner, such as *Ti. Claudius Eutychus*, the imperial freedman labelling a cupboard in, and once seen as the owner of, the Augustan villa at Boscotrecase?[9] Possibly we are dealing with a grandee approaching the stature of Caligula's aide Polybius, dignified in 43 by the exiled Seneca with the stirring *Consolation* which 'almost dares coax him to the point of linking up stories and *Fables Ésopiques* with his customary charm, a genre untried by Roman talent' (8. 3: *fabellas quoque et Aesopeos logos, intemptatum Romanis ingeniis opus*).[10] This character attracted such *mots*, or gaffes, as 'A great fortune (= "*Poly-bios*") is a great servitude' (6. 4, *magna seruitus est magna fortuna*), and 'You, though, need change nothing of your ways' (18. 1, *tibi uero nihil ex consuetudine mutandum est tua*).

But was Phaedrus a player in that league, or did he grease up to such likes, grovelling next to Seneca? When he splashes 'free thinking' across his page, and presents his gathering as a dangerous brew of glorified slave's cheek, does he risk *his mots* being (mis)taken for gaffes? (vv. 3, 34–7) When he demands a complete 'change of plan and of life', does *he* put his foot in it? (v. 15, *mutandum tibi propositum est et uitae genus*) Or is it just that whatever pleasantries he might try to lay before the *libertus*, the literary world of compliments and banter was not designed for his kind, who must just have, or grow, thick skins or else lump it? One of the pressure-points of post-Augustan Rome, this—the call to festoon former slaves with the markings of liberal culture. Do we owe Phaedrus' remarkable itemization of the 'duties' that call a regular *hombre* such as Eutychus to this anxiety for accreditation (vv. 11–13)? (On what premises) Does it make sense for Phaedrus' formal dedication to take such risks of causing offence as the swagger that follows it: 'if you read it, I'll be glad; but if not, they'll anyhow have something to enjoy in times to come'? (vv. 29–32) Is this candour between two feisty characters who know to relish and parade freedom between themselves? Or is *Eutychus* a *non*-reader, the best patron a vulgar fabulist could aspire to? Is he a *joke* of a model recipient and critic, the incarnation of the impossibility of a poet's recognition in late Tiberian, or Caligula's, Rome? Is he in any sense a guide for Phaedrus' own standing? Had they shared shackles at an auction? Were they freed side by side, and did one get lucky, while the other scribbled his stories? Here is Phaedrus, coming on as Greekling, ex-slave, (Graeco-) Roman poet, fit to bandy the name of Sejanus: is the very unplaceability of the *libertus* exactly the trademark of his cultural significance?[11] These folk may spell the shape of the future: condescension to them may be exactly the prejudicial fastidiousness Phaedrus warns his readers *off*.

Suppose that this jumped-up hack convinces you that he can play poet on Helicon, that he has better credentials than any 'Roman', so good he can laugh at his own wild origins, in terms any Hellenistic professor and his clone in Italy after Augustus must approve as just the ticket; what then shall we make of his mock(ery of) social politesse? The motley signature of a Phaedrus or a Polybius *could* become more explosive for the cultural agenda than any Seneca . . . So we must weigh up care-

fully the combination of a passport from the Muses, and inti-
macy with the royals: that frivolous optimist the dolled-up
servant of 2. 5 could make himself into that indispensable
viper-in-the-bosom, the freedman of 3. 10; and, given an inch,
he could take over your library, your shelf of poetry, and all the
time you have free. Is this how to make it big in Rome? When
the slaves get to quote Virgil, and become the chattering classes,
is Aesop bound to be where the action is—his lions and apes
alive and kicking, as never before, in the concrete and marble
jungle of cosmopolis?

Control of informers gave 'the Lord Sejanus" one-man
assault on power worldwide grip, so he, or just the thought of
him, could menace charioteers anywhere on earth (as the
daughter of Balthasar threatens Ben-Hur).[12] Those who met
him would tell us, ' "he made my skin crawl and I had to admit
he terrified me" . . .; his eyes had widened, and his face had gone
the colour of milk. . . . Sejanus's name tended to have that effect
on people.'[13] But the real story of these times was not the one-
off fall-guy for a Caesar turned recluse, but the proliferating
undercover army of *liberti* operating outside, and against, the
civic social pyramid. A smart aristocrat such as Messalla
Corvinus hadn't a hope of outwitting them:

A prim little man in a neat lemon tunic [Felix] was picking his way
carefully across the open ground towards me . . . The man-mountain
[Lamprus] gave a negative grunt and came over to stand beside him.
It was like watching a war-ship docking . . . A freedman—'Whose?',
and a seven foot gorilla—'Uh . . . is that thing safe?' . . . 'Oh, well
done! You're quite correct, these are *not* our proper names. . . .
Although it was lucky for you that I came along, wasn't it? And
although Lamprus isn't exactly bright he really is rather splendid.' I
laughed. Puns, now. I was beginning to like Felix, or whoever the hell
he really was: Lamprus is Greek for 'bright' or 'splendid', just as Felix
means lucky . . .
                    [It turns out they work for Gaius]
'Oddly enough, sir, we really are Felix and Lamprus.' I stared at him.
'It's called a double bluff, sir.' . . . [Gaius:] 'We had a terrible time
dragging . . . Lamprus, isn't it? . . . Dragging Lampus away from his
damned library and persuading him to help. These academics are such
stick-in-the-muds, aren't they? And once they decide to write a
treatise they simply will *not* take a holiday!'. 'Uh . . . treatise?' I looked
at the man-mountain in sudden horror. . . . ' "On the Concept of Being

and Non-Being as expressed by the Milesian Philosophers", sire',
Lamprus said. 'And I don't happen to like holidays all that much.'[14]

So we are not going to trust our own instincts too far in placing
Phaedrus in any *particular* company. The best we can do may be
to bundle him in with the teacher, librarian and scholar *liberti*
that dominate the first century of Caesars as outlined in
Suetonius' maddeningly cursory listing *Of teachers*. He cannot
have scaled the heights of M. Verrius Flaccus, freedman tutor
to Augustus' grandsons and 'the most distinguished philo-
logical-antiquarian scholar of Rome after Varro', with a school
on the Palatine and annual salary of 100,000 sesterces;[15] let
alone those of the Spaniard Hyginus, freed by Augustus to be
his librarian, friend to the consular historian Clodius Licinus
and to Ovid, Virgilian commentator, prolific agricultural and
theological writer, antiquarian and biographer.[16] But the strange
story of the freeborn foundling C. Maecenas Melissus, who
preferred to stay Maecenas' property when reclaimed by his
mother, may ring a bell or two: 'swiftly manumitted, he even
got into Augustus' good books', and was made librarian in
the Portico of Octavia; at the age of 59, Melissus started to
compile *Nonsense*, 150 books' worth of it, now entitled *Fun-
house*' (*libellos Ineptiarum, qui nunc Iocorum inscribuntur*),
among other shelf-loads of copy, including a new genre of
Roman comedy.[17] We can throw in, for good measure, a gaggle
of shadowy imperial freedmen in 'the learned professions and
the fine arts'—tutors to princes, such as Octavian's Apollodorus
of Pergamum, or Tiberius' Theodorus of Gadara, procurator of
Sicily, writer on rhetoric, and historian; and librarians like
Antiochus: 'Tiberius Claudius Caesar's freedman charged with
the Latin Library of Palatine Apollo', or Ti. Iulius Pappus:
'superintendent of all Imperial Libraries from Tiberius through
Claudius'.[18]

    Phaedrus, named for his 'brightness' or to make up for his
lack of it, named because someone cared for Plato, or admired
the Professor who taught Atticus' teacher his Epicureanism,[19]
anyhow named by a master 'for luck', just like Eutychus, may
belong somewhere on this spectrum. His other addressees,
Particulo of book 4, and (the conjectural) *Philetus* of book 5 (?),
put him somewhere on the social ladder where we can't follow.

Dropping Sejanus' name may be just his one lunge for reflected 'glory'. Yet, whatever the social heights or depths, it should sink in (if we don't block it out) that this freedman knew *all* about *poetics*. In my book, this is a pay-off for his causerie that is no way to be sniffed at.

And we can't rule out the *possibility* that Phaedrus' Eutychus is, indeed, a key player in telling the tale of the Julio-Claudian Caesars. Could this be Caligula's Charioteer of the Greens, for one—2,000,000 sesterces in his pocket, and the Roman legionnaires forced to navvy, re-vamping his stable-block? In 41, Caligula's assassin, Cassius Chaerea, would jeer in vain at the soldiers, 'Let someone bring me the password from Eutychus', as they installed Claudius, 'How monstrous to get rid of a madman, and then give power to an idiot!'[20]

Feel the difference it would make to Phaedrus' gesture of dedication, sometime in the years after Sejanus' fall (in 31), sometime before or after Tiberius left Rome to his successor, if we could pin it to the Eutychus who got caught up to his neck in the Late Tiberius ructions around the palace on Capri—a story from the run-up to Gaius' accession in 37 which we have met already (Ch. 1: when a drop of water miraculously changed Thaumastos' life; Josephus, *Jewish archives* 18. 168–237):[21]

Out riding, young Gaius and his princeling pal Agrippa were alone— not counting Gaius' charioteer and freedman Eutychus—when Agrippa turned to prayers: 'May Tiberius retire from his position, pronto, and yield to one more deserving in all respects: you'. Later, in 36, Eutychus was caught stealing from Agrippa's wardrobe, took to his heels, and when he fetched up before the urban prefect, declared that he had top secret information for Caesar that related to his personal security, a matter of life-and-death. He was sent to Capri in chains, where Tiberius kept him on ice, in his usual dilatory way. Until Antonia Augusta—who had blown the whistle on Sejanus to Tiberius—weighed in, and for all his dire warnings, obliged the Emperor to examine Eutychus. The freedman spilled the beans, and Macro, the new Sejanus, was ordered to arrest Agrippa on the spot, to the utter disbelief of both. Antonia got Macro to allow him the best conditions for his detention, but there he rotted, without prospect of release. Six months passed, and news of Tiberius' death came, prematurely at first, then for real. After a short delay, for decency, the new Caesar, Gaius, had him released, crowned, and sent off to rule *his* kingdom.

Whatever became of *that* Eutychus? Whether or not he knew
Phaedrus, Phaedrus certainly knew *of* him. His story is a fable,
too: the freedman who (literally) stole his master's clothes. His
tale would be all about borrowed plumes: telling tales on
Caesar, *as* telling tales *to* Caesar, *about* Caesar.

vv. 1–26

Book 1 struck up with a spare seven-line prologue: first words
Aesopus auctor; 'Phaedrus polishes Aesop's material in verse,
his book's tricksy/twin dowry is laughter and a word to the
wise; if anyone should want to carp at talking *trees*, not just talking beasts, remember this is fun with fictive tales.' The next
editorial we have is 2. *Prol.* Its fifteen lines on *Aesopi genus* (v. 1)
exude, or display, confidence that fables win friends for their
stuff, not their authorship, before promising fidelity to old
Aesop's *manner*; while requesting a fair reception for any inser-
tions made for variety's sake. This prologue spills over into its
book's first fable by cutting (pretending to cut) the puffing of
his promised 'brevity', and instead briskly drumming up a
moral: 'heed the following reason why you should [be good]'
(vv. 14 f.); the ensuing story once over, its teller pulls away, to
dub it 'a rare and praiseworthy lesson, absolutely, | *but* [this
isn't how wealth and morality *really* correlate]' (2. 1. 11 f.). So
'editorial + fable + moral' have fused into urbane complexity,
emptying out the story as piety in the sky, and in the process
satirizing the very Theory of Fable—'out to straighten out
people's mistakes | and get them to pitch themselves into hard
work' (2 *Prol.* 3 f.)—that it was supposed to be implementing
without more ado.

Such self-satirizing heralds Phaedrus' characteristic obtru-
sion into his *Fabulae*, as when the first, minimal, story in book 3
is nailed to the epimythium 'The pertinence of this, someone
[anyone?] who knows me will spell out' (3. 1. 7); as again when
seven-verses of raillery at his readers get a fable appended 'so
I'm not thought to have said this without a pay-off' (4. 2. 8);
when a lecturette mocking snooty scorn for the fables turns into
an excuse for some mock-tragic parody (one more *Medea* set-
piece), which never does generate a narrative, but closes all the

same with a regular, and even formulaic, moral (4. 7); and where, as it appears, a rebuke to Envy, for attributing anything that is memorable to Aesop but all the flops to Phaedrus, prompts the re-affirmation that 'good or bad, | Aesop discovered, and I finalized, this work' before peeling away, *sans* fable, to rejoin the 'planned order of the project', so that an 'internal' *editorial* turns out to have been staged as an *interruption* to the compilation of contents (4. 22).

There is much, much more of this badgering of the reader, until what seems to be the final book's only dedication, and epilogue (or epilogue-trait), checks us out in the form of the laconic, enigmatic, epimythium 'Why I wrote this, ʾPhiletusʾ, you see just fine' (5. 10. 10). These japes and antics turn into psychological warfare—what else is the moral 'I'd have passed by this fable in silence, | if the drones hadn't reneged on their solemnly pledged bond'? (3. 13. 16 f.)[22] In all, enough sermonizing lather is worked up to earn Phaedrus the label 'diatribist', and maybe even 'satirist'.[23]

We noticed how the other editorial previous to 3. *Prol.*, namely 2. *Epil.*, began again from *Aesop* (first word), but made a 'fable' *of him*, set in stone by smart Athens to signal life a *carrière ouverte aux talents*; but this was also the place where Phaedrus first steps out himself to take the role of Latin *littérateur*, a hero in the making for *Latium* to challenge *Graecia* (vv. 8 f.). Vicious Envy at once looms, but your stoical fabulist/ well-schooled poet will harden his heart, and take any stick critics can dish out to his *labor*, his *doctus labor* (vv. 8, 15). While the typical length of the stories increases, the (four or five) editorials outstanding after 3. *Prol.* will wind down (3. *Epil.* 1–35; 4. *Prol.* 1–20; 4. *Epil.* 1–9; 5. *Prol.* 1–9—which starts, once more, with *Aesopi nomen*, but breaks off with an *Abbruch* (breaking-off formula) that jumps us into 'a fable on this sort of scheme:'; maybe add 5. 10). They restrict themselves to progressing earlier themes (we shall notice several instances at relevant moments in what follows).

Negotiations with the reader of book 3 begin at once with terms and conditions, a battle of willpower and imposed rules: 'if + longing + necessity' (vv. 1 f.) This will punctuate (structure) the prologue, first when it scales the heights to instal Poetry as the grandest of existences: 'Change is a must + if +

thinking' (vv. 15 f.).[24] To feel free, feel the power, *carmen* (song/ode) is used for the only time in the *Fabulae*, and sure enough, right on cue, out of the azure this burnisher of *Aesop* nerves himself to demand the vocational devotion specially imagined to kick into unprecedented Horatian lyric aspiration (*Odes*, i.e. *Carmina*, 1. 1. 29–32, 35 f.):

> Ivy, the reward of scholar brows . . .
> distances me from the masses, if . . .;
> but if you [= dedicatee Maecenas = reader] catalogue me under
>   Classic Lyric,
> I shall dent a star with my sublimity—the universe my spinning
>   Everest skull.

This remarkable 'Romanmanticism' is only (over-the-)topped by Ovid (not least, we shall find, in his first *envoi* to erotic elegy, *Sex* 1. 15). For his part, Phaedrus means to spell out the tariff on The Poet's Calling by rehearsing an outline autobiography which is tailored to capture the spirit and ideology of the work in prospect; he keeps the high-falutin' mythology of the *Dichterweihe* ('Initiation into Poesie'), but cashes it out in the terms set by mundane life. The effect owes plenty to the persecuted pride of Ovid's *Res Gestae* (Achievements) from exile (*Sadness* 4. 10):

> So you may know who it is you are reading, take heed, posterity . . .
> Sulmo is my homeland . . . My father railed 'Why bother trying
> useless poetry for size? Homer's will set no one up for life.' I did try,
> quitting Helicon (*totoque Helicone relicto*) to write prose . . . As
> Tibullus succeeded Gallus, and Propertius Tibullus, I was fourth
> epigone . . . This is my R. O. A. (*meae acta uitae*) . . . The Muse is my
> comfort (*solacia*) . . . Envy will not win . . . I am in your debt,—
> thanks—o reader, for your fairness and frankness (*iure tibi grates,
> candide lector, ago*).

But this is, just as clearly, combined with the persona and dynamic of Horatian *Sermo* (*Satires* 1. 4; 1. 6; *Letters* 2. 2):

> Is satire a suspect genre of writing? . . . My father taught me self-
> improvement through noting specific negative examples, without
> malice . . .; people dig at me for my ex-slave father, but he gave me
> everything that has recommended me to my dedicatee and Friend
> Maecenas, so while I'm sane I shan't regret this father and so—unlike
> most people who say it's not their fault it's happened that they don't

have freeborn or distinguished parents—I sure wouldn't defend myself that way . . .; I was lucky enough to be reared at Rome and taught how much harm the wrath of Achilles did the Greeks. Athens instilled a bit more technical know-how for telling straight from bent . . . but civil war soon clipped my wings, and one way or another, poetry was the shift I made . . . But you surely don't imagine I can write poetry at Rome in among all the distractions and demands (*inter tot curas totque labores*)—one calling for a signature, another inviting me to hear what he's penned, drop all my obligations (*relictis | omnibus officiis*), someone up this hill, someone up that, and both needing a visit . . . The whole chorus of writers loves the glades . . . We write our own sort of stuff, and 'It's a marvel to behold—a work chiselled by all nine Muses!'

Phaedrus, of course, has *no* father; but, as we saw, he makes great sport with the *tabula rasa* where his origins ought to be, building his (dubious) homeland and (mis)fortune into exactly the design appropriate for the life of an '*Aesopoet*'.[25] In the company of *Eutychus*, that ten-a-penny entertainer's and servant's handle, perhaps an Aunt Sally who can be flattered to deceive, then jeered, got at, and ultimately hooked, as dummy stand-in for dummy readers like us,[26] *Phaedrus* can but come alive as a servile 'Speaking Name', and let us read *his* fortune from it—that double-take story of *Felix* and *Lamprus* all over again: 'PHAEDRUS in Greek . . . signifies *Gay*'.[27] Cicero's friend Clodius *Aesopus* may have been named for showbiz, as Nero's freedman *Phoebus* must have been;[28] but once you put 'reading the text of *Phaedrus*' next to 'taking time off from commitments, to set a mind free' (vv. 1–3), then many an ancient graduate would just *know* you meant to cue the start of that mainstream set text, and favourite book, *Plato*'s *Phaedrus* (227b):

[Ph.] You shall have the answer, Socrates, if you can take the time to listen as you proceed (εἰ σοὶ σχολή).
[S:] Well, wouldn't you reckon I'd make it my business—as Pindar has it, 'set above even work-time' (καὶ ἀσχολίας ὑπέρτερον)—to listen to your exchange with Lysias?

This was, famously, the one occasion when Socrates, would-be versifier of *Aesop* on death row and canonized martyr of free-thinking, is allowed by his apostle-and-ventriloquist to take time out for a trip away from the frenetic mobile phones and car-horns of pulsating Attic busyness; and he relaxes into a stimulating read down among the cicadas. Listening to the *Fables*, however, is no picnic, as we are to learn from the discussion that starts with a first demand, of freedom from mundane obligations—*liber* for *libellos* (vv. 1, 3: 'free' for 'books')—before digging into the nitty-gritty problem of fitting literature into life. Poetry regularly posed as freedom from civic responsibility, but any investment in study, like all other forms of work and leisure, turned then, as they turn now, on complex interplay between freedom and compulsion.[29]

Particularly in the field of public oratory, a normative idiom of *devotion* was in play, so that the high priest of handbook enthusiasts will agree to recommend solitary 'woods and forest' or 'sealed box' hide-out, preferably in the hours of daylight, 'if there's time' (*si uacet*), though 'busy people' (*occupatos*) have to work on into the night, but must insist that 'silent retreat and a mind altogether set free' are the dream-ticket, though rarely an option (*silentium et secessus et undique liber animus*: Quintilian, *Training of the orator* 10. 1. 22–8). Dour didactic poetry also demands serious attention of *its* readers: 'an epic topic, this, and, if it is not conquered by love-and-care, by pain-and-anxiety, an unequal struggle' (Grattius, *Hunting to hounds* 61, *magnum opus et, nisi cura uincitur, impar*). Phaedrus may have in mind the preliminary cowing of *his* addressee by Lucretius (*On the genesis of reality* 1. 50–3):

> *uacuas auris animumque sagacem*
> *semotum a curis adhibe ueram ad rationem,*
> *ne mea dona tibi studio disposta fideli*
> *intellecta prius quam sint contempta relinquas.*

Apply unoccupied ears and a sharp mind
distanced from cares to true rationality,
so that all the offerings I have arrayed for you with zealous devotion
you don't, before they're understood, put them behind you in scorn.

Elsewhere, addressees could expect the very different power-ratio with poets conveyed by cautious plea-bargaining for a modicum of attention in a sliver of spare time: 'You'll read this book through when you've the time' (4. *Prol.* 14, *quartum libellum cum uacaris perleges*); 'Horace's words won't pass through Caesar's overladen ear barring a propitious moment'

(Horace, *Satires* 2. 1. 18 f.); and '. . . *if* you can be delivered to him during time out, *if* you see 100 per cent clemency, *if* his wrath has broken its strength . . .' (Ovid, *Sadness* 1. 1. 93 f.).[30]

But the likes of Eutychus should be so lucky: Phaedrus is on *his* way to the most strained terms of dedication you could wish to read, rivalled only by rebarbative Saturnalian epigram (Martial *Epigrams* 5. 80. 1–5):

> Severus, you can grant and loan me
> not one whole hour, if you're not busy (*si uacabis*),
> while you read and check my nonsense.
> 'It's tough throwing away a holiday.' (*durum est perdere ferias*) I ask
> you to allow and tolerate this loss . . .

The twist here is that to bid the *Emperor* 'You just accept the book, and I'll count that as your reading it' is blatant (excellent) grovelling (Martial 5. 1. 9); whereas Phaedrus' toying with Eutychus, 'read book 3, make my day. But if not, | the future will have fun, whatever' (vv. 31 f.), flips easily into just the sort of inopportune outspokenness that fable is claimed to eliminate: their 'dialogue' *threatens* at once to portray our model First Reader as more of a holier-than-thou snob than a paragon, an inspirational enabler, or even an all-round nice bloke. In short, the dummy that a spikey satirist *needs* (to mimic, interrupt, face down, draw the heat from lovely people like us genial but genuine readers).[31]

This Somebody puts a world of self-importance between Phaedrus and himself (vv. 5 f., *tuis* | ~ *meis* |). And retaliation is instant: 'Hands off work meant for *un*preoccupied ears' says, as a rejoinder, that these delicate *Fables* are for serious folk to unwind over, not for brutes (vv. 6f., *manibus* ~ *auribus*); but will soon come to read as keeping the world at arm's length; and risk pricing these wares out of the market altogether, by serving notice to VIPs as a class that they *can* have no business touching poetry. For the next spat with the unfortunate Eutychus shoves his polite (fobbing off) promise to pack a *Phaedrus Three* for his next holiday, and give him due cerebration,[32] back where it came from, with a sarcastic catalogue of all the obligations that any Eutychus must make it his duty to prefer to cheap nonsense like Phaedrus: if he can't spare time off work, he shouldn't dream of taking time off holiday, either.

Picturing the reader as (conceitedly) conscientious in his cultivation of his extended self might send *us* packing—who *doesn't* feel got at if pressed to say where reading for relaxation is supposed to fit into a satisfactorily full life?[33] But the trade-off is that the poet uses the friction to draw himself up to his own full majesty: ordinary occupations serve as foil to set up his stern vision of the poet's life—nothing short of totally engrossing and constant devotion to The Muses—above all other claims, interests, outlets or responsibilities. Poetry has no time-out, makes no concessions, an extraordinarily high threshold for Antiquity—as rare, and oddly situated, as are portraits of well-adjusted social specimens (Horace *Letters* 2. 2. 131–3):

> . . . *qui uitae seruaret munia recto*
> *more, bonus sane uicinis, amabilis hospes,*
> *comis in uxorem, posset qui ignoscere seruis* . . .

A man who kept life's duties going in upright manner—you know, good to neighbours, popular at parties, nice to the wife, the sort who could go easy on the servants . . .

What could conceivably prompt such a gem? (ibid. 126–40)

I'd rather seem to be a crazy lazy writer (*in-ers*), provided I enjoy my folly, or else don't realize that's what it is . . . A well-known Argive once believed he was listening to a marvellous performance of tragedy when really he was a satisfied bum on seat clapping away in an empty theatre. *For the rest (cetera qui . . .),* he was a man who etc. etc. . . . He cursed his friends when they had him cured of his delusion.

Phaedrus' implied vocation was just as 'Utopian', cf. More's epistolary prologue:

Howbeit my other cares and troubles did leave almost lesse then no leasure. Whiles I doo dayelie bestowe my time aboute lawe matters . . . While I go one waye to see and visite my frende: another waye about myne owne privat affaires. While I spend almost al the day abrode emonges other, and the residue at home among mine owne; I leave to my self, I meane to my booke, no time. For when I am come home, I muste commen with my wife, chatte with my children and talke wyth my servauntes. All the whiche thinges I recken and accompte amonge businesse, forasmuche they muste of necessitie be done: and done muste they nedes be, onelesse a man wyll be straunger in his owne house . . .[34]

Once up on the heights of Parnassus, the writer plays purist bard, scrubbed clean of mundane distractions: turning back to us, who are denied admission to the holy academy, he nags us relentlessly, and if he were not our characterful chum and our amusing jester, his climax of insulting scorn for *real* life could easily get irritating; particularly when he pupates into his idea of a Horatian scold. 'Scouring care for possessions from the bottom of the heart' and 'plunging into this life of unbeatable fame' (vv. 21 f.) is one thing—the fervid talk of entranced artists everywhere—but coming down from the mountain with a big pile of all-out exaggeration to inveigh against people taking the time to read this stuff in between respectable wealth-creation (vv. 24–6) is pretty rich, coming from a Greekling freedman, of all people . . . Surely the finale, 'setting sweet earning before sweated learning', abuses the poet's musical prerogative, with a cat-call for curtain-fall: d*octo* l*abori* mimetically routing d*ulce* l*ucrum*? (v. 26)[35]

Phaedrus' high and mighty elevation of himself to vatic status (vv. 17–23, *ego . . . recipior*) already toppled into send-up. A posh poet would long 'to worship Helicon in the blush of youth, and link arms in the dance of the Muses'; polite flattery would tell him 'it's a marvel! A piece fashioned by all nine Muses!'; a satirist must renounce Helicon and the rest, 'half-in, half-out, of hicksville'; and a respectable vaudeville act would be remembered as 'well-trained and virtually raised by the hand of the Muses, | adorning not long since their lordships' games, | the first to step it out before the people on a Greek stage' . . .[36] On one side, Phaedrus' solemn theogony has 'Mnemosyne bear nine Olympian Muses to Jupiter in the Pieria' of *Hesiod*'s pro- logue (*Theogony* 52–62):

> Μοῦσαι Ὀλυμπιάδες, κοῦραι Διὸς αἰγιόχοιο,
> τὰς ἐν Πιεριῇ Κρονίδῃ τέκε πατρὶ μιγεῖσα,
> Μνημοσύνη, . . .
> ἡ δ᾽ ἔτεκ᾽ ἐννέα κούρας . . .
> ~
> vv. 17–19.[37]

On the other, the tell-tale modifier *paene*, '*virtually* born right in school' (v. 20), tells us that Phaedrus is stretching a point: where others were proverbially 'born in a book', and 'raised in the studio',[38] this character is making a sick purse from his boor's ear of slave ~~origins~~: 'delivered by mother on the Pierian range' (v. 17) underlines that this is orotund spouting from a Greekling; worse, he will go on to sport a 'Thracian' origin (vv. 54–7). Predictably, interminable discussion has ensued: he *could* mean he was literally born 'in Pieria' *and* came 'from Thrace', because Roman Macedonia included Thrace as well as Thessaly; or 'Pieria' is his metaphor for a 'poetic clime', whereas 'Thrace' spells the unpoetic wasteland that life saddled him with, and so calls for special pleading to repair the hard luck story; Phaedrus would be the only imperial freedman we know as from Thrace; was he brought to Rome as a p.o.w. by the conqueror Piso Frugi in 10 BCE—perhaps along with Antipater the epigrammatist?[39]

In context, however, it is more important to register how Phaedrus takes care to mock himself as he interrupts his flaying of Eutychus, Rome, and the rest of us, to step forward into the limelight. What he is pushing at us, hard, is the question of what we should make of the poetic fable. Why does Plato have Socrates putting Aesop into verse on death-row? (*Phaedo* 60d–61c) When Phaedrus told us his game was to 'polish *Aesop* in iambics' (1. *Prol.* 1 f.), what difference did he suppose that the formal change would make? The rest of 3. *Prol.* gives the Roman Aesop's answer, or his parrying of the question, as put to the original Aesop, by his master, in the course of *his Life*: 'Are *you* permitted to enter the Muses' Helicon?' (*Life of Aesop* 36)

VV. 27–32

This short passage draws the opening tirade to a close, marked by the loaded move to break off the chain of thought (*sed iam . . .*, v. 27), presaging return to the initial question of 'reading' (vv. 1, 31), and formal blessing of the addressee as dedicatee (vv. 29 f.). The 'take-it-or-leave-it' terms shoved Eutychus' way cap all the tough talking so far, exposing the compliments of 'respect and recognition' as conditional, and open to cancellation (v. 30). Cryptic citation from Rome's greatest poet's greatest triumph of first-person narration supplies poet Phaedrus with just the verdegris voice he needs: when Virgil has Aeneas tell Dido's court of Troy's Closing Night, bringing on the Greekling Sinon to undo the city with deceit, Aeneas must repeat the fatal lies Sinon told King Priam's people. First promising he 'will confess everything truly, come what may, starting from his Greek origins' (*'Cuncta equidem tibi, rex, fuerit quodcumque, fatebor | uera',* inquit, *'neque me Argolica de gente negabo, | hoc primum',* Aeneid 2. 77–9), Virgil–Aeneas–Sinon went on to claim that the Greeks framed and lynched his innocent friend Palamedes, before turning on his allies. He will be set free by the generous mug Priam: 'Whoever you are, . . . You will be one of us' (vv. 148 f., *'quisquis es . . ., | noster eris'*).

Quite what Sinon's gesture at the future he and his words are bringing to pass might 'mean' has exercised Virgil's readers—his *fuerit quodcumque* has been called 'A notable proof of the almost hopeless obscurity of the Latin language', and Phaedrus' *quodcumque fuerit* lamented as no less obscure than Sinon[40]—but this unfathomability is exactly the point of wheeling him on, both in Troy and the *Aeneid,* and now, once more, in the *Fables*: 'obviously the most important liar in Latin literature'. In terms of the diatribe Phaedrus has brandished in his reader's face, 'che sera' raises the spectre of imminent elimination, drawing attention to its likelihood by parading its repression from direct verbalisation. He deserves something to 'happen' to him, on the spot, or sometime, anyhow: 'whatever the consequences'. But in terms of his dramatization of the workings of Fable, as Phaedrus is about to theorize, the annoyance and prejudice that his appearance amongst us may cause are coded through malign Sinon as the incarnation of the principle of the irresistible power of *powerlessness.* Think of Phaedrus talking to Eutychus' Rome as Sinon cozening Priam's Troy, and see what (be)falls . . .[41]

At the other end of this book, you will find Phaedrus stepping out prominently (| *ego, quondam legi quam . . .,* v. 33) to deliver his only other citation (from Ennius, but *un*attributed). His parting thought is reticently presented as a *sententia* (maxim) on reticence, 'which I read as a child: | "To mutter out loud is taboo for a groundling." | While I have my reason, I'm going to remember that, and remember it well' (3. *Epil.* 34 f.). This, the proceeds of *Phaedrus'* reading, unforgettable as it is unquantifiable, must also be the best gloss there could be on *Reading*

Phaedrus, the subject of 3. *Prol.* Once again, it comes with the mantle of Poet(aster).

VV. 33–50

Into five lines, Phaedrus now squashes the pithiest ancient definition of Fable we have.[42] Testimonia present Aesopic fables as 'fun', or as 'seriocomic' didaxis or admonition; bizarre but true, the only classical company for Phaedrus' analysis as 'Sklavenmoral' (slave counsel) comes from the fourth-century pagan Roman Emperor Julian, writing in Greek.[43] In so far as the Fable attaches to the slave Aesop, we could decide, the simple virtues of brevity, accessibility, translatability, and anonymity do fit the bill;[44] but we are entitled to ask whether the Roman Aesop preaches his theory in practice. The wily fox who uses fable as the weapon of the weak to protest against victimization and violence at the hands of the strong lion or brute wolf is a well-represented theme; but many a sad ape or insolent ass insults the great, and pays for it without enlisting sympathy. If anything, rank is underscored rather than levelled (Ch. 8).[45]

Modern theory has added the notion that this 'simplest kind of poetry forms the basis of all poetry', and, still more radically, that this is the pure stem of philosophy, 'short and dry'.[46] But in the full context of our prologue, *un*excerpted, the point takes up from Sinon's devastating play for sympathy, and leads into poor Phaedrus' pitch for pity after rough justice from Sejanus' Rome: this poet's 'literary' fables scarcely fulfil their claimed original function, though that is latent and might be realized in a suitable context; rather, they are about their potential for being *about that function*. Any page of imperial history will show how strong was the potential for transference and translation from literal servitude to social and political subjection post-Augustus. The correct frame of reference for Phaedrus' writing is therefore within the practice of 'safe criticism' by oblique rhetoric and double-bluff. Sinon, Aesop, and the maxim that openly mutters about 'open muttering' provide a continuum on which to place the secondary utterance of Phaedrus, both as author and as raconteur.[47]

This second panel of the poem next applies its position-statement on Fable, just as the first applied its sublation of Poetry, to Phaedrus (| *ego quem* . . ., v. 17 ~ | *ego* . . ., v. 38). Our 'Aesopoet' has pictured his predecessor at work originating the genre, as in any poetic genealogy.[48] Now he images his own contribution: 'I took his track on further, and made it a road' (v. 38). The contrast between 'track' and 'road' was proverbial; but in this context, it must evoke the imagery of poetics after Callimachus, who had urged: 'tread where the wagons don't | run. Don't drive your chariot along the common tracks of | other people, but use paths | untrodden, even though you'll drive a narrow way', and given notice 'No path | brings me joy, which carries crowds this way and that'. So Phaedrus capsizes this mindset, proud to banalize the bold spirit of Aesop, and advertise that he means to flood the market with formula-*Aesopica*. Perhaps this genre is, like Roman satire, not sure whether it should want to count as 'poetry' at all?[49]

But Phaedrus casually appends to his brag an enigmatic clause which gives his equivalent of the way Aesop had once 'shifted his own sentiments into fables' (v. 36). By (*somehow*) 'choosing some stuff for my disaster' (v. 40), Phaedrus failed, where Aesop succeeded, in 'jollying away incrimination with fictional fun' (v. 37). Did his choice of some of the Fables lead to his demise, or does he choose fables that relate to his demise? Was he another Ovid 'punished for his talent'? (*Sadness* 2. 12) Is he giving himself a free make-over as archetypally suffering satirist? Did Sejanus have him squashed? And are the fables his 'antidote to this pain'? (v. 44, *his . . . remediis*) Who is supposed to be doing or have done what to whom, and when, if anyone, ever . . .?[50]

All of which serves as foil to the point, a surprise when it comes, for Phaedrus moves on to deny any personal animus in his work: 'the disclaimer of malice' is the figleaf every satirist 'openly' carries ready to brandish at all times, however unconvincingly, and it is hard to see how that 'vulnerable Slave', who fabled 'because he dared not say what he wanted' (vv. 34 f.), *can* have 'shifted his own sentiments into fables' (v. 36) without intending to incriminate the neighbourhood bullies in his own particular neck of the woods—however generally the fables were couched, out in the open.[51]

So much cry, little wool: it is now possible to cite this classical author should you ever want to claim, or seem to claim, high-minded moralism—all it will cost you is your street cred, and it will buy pomposity that never quite rings true![52] In the short notice of 1. *Prol*, 'advice on living' (v. 4, *uitam . . . monet*) could strike any reader as acceptably blank formula; but in 3. *Prol.*, with its Phaedrus, Eutychus, Aesop, and now Sejanus, it is impossible to erase the 'suspicion' that this Aesopic satire 'parades Life itself, the ways of Humanity' (v. 50) as a way to get at *somebody*, precisely because it actually *parades* this very *suspicion*, in denial. (*Qui s'excuse, s'accuse.*)[53] In any case, even if a reader of Phaedrus should manage to talk all *ad hominem* pertinence out of the reckoning, there is no way to discount the functioning of 'Fable', anywhere *else* it may arise—along the lines simply but graphically inscribed at the heart of this very poem.

Through the smokescreen canopy of wonky poetics, it should, at any rate, still be clear that this imperial freedman's mini-essay posits a link between 'freedom to think' and 'freedom to cast aspersion', within its own arena of writing and reading, Muses and Memory, Virgil and Sinon, books and courtrooms.[54] This is what matters, *not* whether we are entitled to write Phaedrus into Tiberian history as (e.g.): 'pre-31: the satirist represents Sejanus as accuser prosecutor witness and judge alike. Convicted. Sentence unknown'.[55]

Certainly Sejanus, that one-man assault on power, produced a 'reign of terror' with real enough victims, so that perversely paranoid charges brought some ruin, and more paranoia; the rigged court was not just a proverbial bogey, but a feature of 'life on earth' (élite Roman life, and death).[56] And the fact that once 'Sejanus was dragged by the hook | on show, there was joy unconfined' (Juvenal, *Satires* 10. 66 f., cf. 61–113) did not erase, but rather sealed, forever, the exemplary moral of 'The Fable of Sejanus'. For one thing, ' "Court favourite or not, Sejanus [was] a nobody. We're not talking simple power here, you understand. We're talking family." '[57] Skulking on the paratextual margins, this fabulation of *Phaedri libellos*, of Eutychus and the Roman Aesop, more nobodies without family, narrates the ruses and bruises of the social contestation of power, strung out between palace–populace, and writer–reader, relations.

So, obliquely, The 'Fable of the Prologue' does contrive to tell its pointed, heartfelt, tale on Caesar.

Without so much as muttering his name, once.

vv. 51–61

This surprise passage caps what we have just read, commenting on what was just said: acknowledging that the Big Talk, of a crusade for 'Life itself, the ways of Humanity' (v. 50) *was* indeed a flourish of pomposity that merits immediate satirical deflation. The crescendo from the functional analysis of fabulation, through the self-declaration of the fabulist, rose through alarm set off by mention of Sejanus to such a grandiose climax of authorial glorification that our heads should have been shaking in disbelief. This final section means to return us to where we came in; it sets up the opportunity for a third revelation about where the writer is coming from; and it expropriates our reactions once again to turn us back toward poetics, the reception and power of poetry, in preparation for the *envoi* when it comes up.

For now, words are dubbed onto the lips of 'somebody', continuing the impersonal articulation of the broadside on Fable (vv. 33–50, cf. *si quis*, v. 45 ~ *aliquis*, v. 51); only at the death will your narrator turn again to address 'you' (vv. 62 f.). Apostrophe to personified 'Envy' [your stand-in] bridges between the two planes of utterance (vv. 60 f.). In fact, we shall now see, the whole paragraph essentially jazzes up the ubiquitous paratextual topics of the Roman poet's 'talent' (*ingenio*, v. 53).

The challenge is to say why Phaedrus and Fable are suited, and, at the same time, why the combination should deserve anyone's attention. The writer owes us some claim for 'the power' that *his* 'poetry has', or lacks, or refuses (cf. v. 3). All 'minor' genres of poetry defined themselves so as to promote their wares as attractive, refined, effectual; they were *all* their authors could manage—i.e. the *best* they could produce, and readers could ever wish for! Thus talk of what others 'have managed to achieve' is an oblique way to define the 'ability' of our host (*potuit*, v. 52). He allows that his Big Talk has added up to a bid for 'eternal fame' for himself (*aeternam famam*, v. 53). Now he must talk himself down from the tree, or risk vainglory. For the 'Callimachean' (more or less = Latin) poet's standard move was founded on urbanity's blend of eccentric puffery with self-deprecation (*Aitia Prologue* 1. 1–20, 37 f.):

> The Telchines [malign sorcerers] mutter against my song, I know,
>   ignoramuses, and no friends of the Muse, they,
> [for all sorts of shortcomings . . ., but]
>   nightingales sing sweeter. So
> vanish, the lot of you—deadly tribe of Evil 'I'!
>
>   .   .   .   .
> And don't search for mega decibels from any song
>   created by me: thunder isn't my thing—it belongs to Zeus . . .
> No nemesis threatens me: people the Muses looked upon in infancy
>   without askance obliquity, they never drop once they fade.

Yet a writer who wanted to be liked (sponsored, fêted, read . . .), in short, all writers, required modesty to forbid. Grandiose ambitions must be jettisoned with some version of the disclaimer 'I would if I could, but I can't, so I shan't . . .', which told your 'Eutychus' and, through him, your readers (your Varus, your Maecenas, your Augustus, your Rome),[58] that they were about to receive work from a genius (Horace, *Letters* 2. 1. 232–70):

Alexander the Great liked Choerilus' savage and ill-begotten verses about him (*incultis . . . uersibus et male natis*):
   If you invited his powers of judgement . . . to the world of books, my patch, the gifts of the Muses, you'd swear he was born in the thick smog of the Boeotians.
   Whereas you, Augustus, aren't let down by your judgement, or by investment in your favourite and favoured poets, Virgil and Varius . . .: Horace (*ego*) wouldn't prefer his *Chatter* crawling at ground-level to grand composition of your *Res Gestae*, [vast continents, river systems of the world, castles in the air, *terra incognita*, a planet of imperial *pax Augusta*:]—if my ability stretched as far as my longing. But . . . (*si quantum cuperem possem quoque. sed . . .*)
   [Horace doesn't want to end up, he ends up by saying, writing rubbish to be remaindered and pulped.]

When writers wrote their 'doodles' *down*, as failing to match up to their eminences' majesty, they did *not* expect to be taken at their word, and this is, indeed, 'The Fable of Poetry *as* Self-

Reflexiveness'. More, they *also* propositioned future fame in the reception of the work—by anticipating it. This was done inside-out, by positing scathing hypercriticism, which was to be sent packing with some variant on the ἀπόπεμψις (aversion, curse) of Callimachus' prologue (to *Aitia*, and so to *Collected Works*): 'Vanish, the lot of you—deadly tribe of Evil "I"'. The Master had himself shown how to use the trope as a closural device, in his inimitable Hymn to Self-Reflexivity, to the Power of Poetry, to Apollo (*Hymn to Apollo* 2. 113): 'May Vitriol—you know where Jealousy be—go join 'im! ||'.[59]

So Phaedrus primes himself to step before us as the umpteenth clued-up Hellenistic poet courting Roman pride. Callimachus brought his homeland of Cyrene and his chosen ancestry from its founder Battus into his poetry (not least the *Hymn to Apollo* 2. 65). Poets reflected glory on their origins, both to create a cultural identity for themselves and to capture prestige for their vocation (Propertius, *Elegies* 4. 1. 59f., 63 f.):[60]

> . . . and yet, whatever stream shall stem from this miniature
>   mind, this shall all be at the service of my country (*patriae seruiet*
>   *omne meae*) . . .
> so that Umbria may swell with pride for my books,
>   Umbria, the homeland of the Roman Callimachus.

Phaedrus plays the cards straight and skilful: pitting loyalty to *his* 'country's honour' against 'feeble sloth' (v. 55, *somno inerti . . . patriae decus*) artfully works into his autoportraiture the poet's (etymo-philo-logical) claim that art works because 'art' is *work*, hard work, just as much the opposite of 'in-ertia' as *negotium* is the privative of *otium* (vv. 2 ~ 13).[61] These are grounds for triumphant abjection of Envy (Ovid, *Sex* 1. 15. 1 f., 7, 39 f.):[62]

> *Quid mihi, Liuor edax, ignauos obicis annos,*
>   *ingeniique uocas carmen inertis opus . . .?*
>
> *mihi fama perennis . . .*
>
> *pascitur in uiuis Liuor; post fata quiescit,*
>   *cum suus ex merito quemque tuetur honos.*

> Why, biter Envy, do you smear me with years of sloth,
>   calling song the product of talent with no heart?
> Fame through the years is mine . . .

Envy feeds on the living; after death it rests in peace,
    when the individual's good standing takes care of him according
    to his deserts.

In a bid to press his unique claims for recognition on *Rome*, Phaedrus follows up the more straightforward bid for Latin literary status made in his previous editorial, immediately before our prologue (2. *Epil.* 8–11):

    quodsi labori fauerit Latium meo
    plures habebit quos opponat Graeciae.
    si Liuor obtrectare curam uoluerit,
    non tamen eripiet laudis conscientiam[63]

If Latium favours my hard work,
it will have more people to match up to Greece.
If Envy chooses to denigrate the loving care I take,
still it won't rob me of my knowing the fame I deserve.

A campaign he carries on into book 4: 'I long for no unlettered applause' (4. *Prol.* 20, *illitteratum plausum nec desidero* ~ *desideras*, v. 1, *litteratae*, v. 54) and 'my addressee's name will live on my pages, | so long as kudos shall abide with Latin Literature' (4. *Epil.* 5 f., *chartis nomen uicturum meis,* | *Latinis dum manebit pretium litteris*). Harping on 'Envy' encodes this bid for a place in the poetic firmament.[64] And it suits particularly the put-upon persona of the down-trodden Roman Aesop, too: at the other end of this book, an epilogue of complaint, self-righteousness, pessimism, winds itself up into apoplexy (3. *Epil.* 29–33):

It's hard to contain your mettle
when you just *know* you are squeaky clean
but get squashed by abusive treatment at the hands of guilty
    villains.
'Who are they?', do you ask? They'll be exposed in time.
I, though [have lips well and truly sealed.]

How neatly this undoes the majestic denial of personal vendetta that resonated at the heart of our prologue!

Further unravelling of the poet's mission statement arises from the double-barrelled claim to play Roman Aesop, against 'Greece' and its original fabulist. The jocular logic by which a Greekling beats an outlandish 'Phrygian or Scythian' in literal terms of 'proximity to the Muses' torpedoes itself when Phaedrus lets slip that by 'Pieria', he *meant* 'Thrace', which at first blush would sound as far from culture as . . . Rome itself (vv. 52–6 ~ 17).[65]

But it also sets up a double bracketing of Phaedrus, between the pair of less-than-Greek sages Aesop and Anacharsis, and the pair of less-than-Greek poets Linus and Orpheus. First these famous names cast Aesop *as* a sage, one of a kind with Anacharsis; agreeably enough, they encircle Thracian Phaedrus between the soft Phrygian south and the wild beyond of northern Scythia. Second they dub Phaedrus a poet—a Roman connoisseur who has appreciated Virgil's expertise in Hellenistic poetics, and a composer well able to manipulate the classic imagery for conveying the 'power that poetry has' (v. 3).

This surprise package completes the self-presentation of the author, reacting to 'Telchines' of his own creation, to give himself the occasion to improvise a proud profile, as if in self-defence. If he found 'taste' gave him a hard time before admitting him to poetic circles, he has now handed prejudice the stick of 'Thracian' savagery: his question, 'Why should I give up?—just think of Thracian song in Myth', contains its own answer (along the lines of: ' "You know they refused Jesus too"—"You're not him" ') and puts the poet just where he needs to be if he is to play down-trodden marginalized 'Aesop' (vv. 23 ~ 55–9). Where he belongs, among the no-hoper nobodies from nowhere—'none of 'em could stick a pin in a map and name a fatherland father's'.[66]

Aesop was Phrygian because Phrygia means slaves, means the unclassical margins of Greek culture where status differentials can suffer mischief; when he is not, he is himself Thracian.[67] Anacharsis was just as marginal, put in contact with Aesop, but a sage rather than a slave: 'insulted by an Athenian for being Scythian, he either said, "My homeland is an insult to me—but you are an insult to your country', or else "Yes, by birth, not by character".'[68]

'Not even Orpheus was wise, being Thracian', so 'Why *is* Orpheus a Thracian?'[69] The Roman Aesop's answer has to be: 'Because young Virgil staked his reputation on it' (*Eclogue* 4. 55–7):

non me carminibus uincet nec Thracius Orpheus
nec Linus, huic mater quamuis atque huic pater adsit,
Orphei Calliopea, Lino formosus Apollo.

Thracian Orpheus shall not worst me in song
and no more shall Linus, for all that Orpheus' mother and Linus'
    father lend their aid,
Calliope for the one, lovely Apollo for Linus.

Linus, son of Apollo and Psamathe, died the death in Callimachus (torn apart by shepherd dogs: *Aitia* 1, fr. 26–8). He featured alongside Orpheus in some sort of visionary 'Callimachean' line of descent for poetry, from the source of Hesiod, presented prominently in the (lost) Roman elegy of Gallus: this is adapted by Virgil (at *Eclogue* 6. 64–73, where the genealogy extends to embrace Gallus), and by Propertius (at *Elegies* 2. 13. 3–8).[70] Later pairings of Orpheus with Linus in Latin texts must count as post-Virgilian allusion.[71] Phaedrus plants this godsend to a 'Thracian' wannabe so as to spring on us a flash of poetic writing, on the subject of the irresistible power of poetry. His Orpheus gets a couple of coruscating iambics that hymn his demigod cosmic omnipotence, 'moving' the immovable and 'stopping' the unstoppable (vv. 58 f., *mouit . . . tenuit*). At the same time, Phaedrus slips in the motif of the Thracian bard 'taming wild beasts' (v. 58), so as to indoctrinate, overpower, and seduce *his own readers*.

    This author(ity-figure: cf. *auctores*, v. 56) has set about 'moving' lumpen blockheads *like Eutychus* 'with the power of his song' (v. 3, *sentiat uim carminis*). He has put over his project of civilizing Aesopic fable by promoting it to continue the good work by civilizing Rome, as a 'remedial bid to mollify' brutes *like Sejanus* and 'to alleviate the grief' they cause (v. 44, *dolorem delenirem remediis*). And he has managed to detain busy folk *like ourselves* 'through the entertaining twists and enjoyable turns of his longest composition of all' (v. 59, *dulci mora*).

    Orpheus' paradigmatic success in persuasive coaxing of creation[72] carries the 'Aesopoet' to his yell of ultimate triumph, dismissing Envy with a flea in his ear (v. 60). We know our 'Callimachean' visit to the mansion of the Muses is over, and 'Callimachean' closure at hand: as we have noticed, Phaedrus' self-reflexive Fable on Fable, and Poem on Poetry, apes the master's seal to *his* Song on Song:

'Then leave this place, Envy, . . .' (v. 60)

~

'May Vitriol—you know where Jealousy be—go join 'im! ||'
                              (*Hymn to Apollo* 2. 113).

A small voice might, however, just mutter that the chosen twin icons of Poetry as Emulsifier, Linus and Orpheus, both paid for (underscored) their heroic status by dying the same horrific death, torn apart by feral savagery.[73] And Phaedrus in fact thrusts this thought on us even as he joins his triumph to theirs. For mention of 'Hebrus' as the irresistible *force de nature* successfully resisted by Orpheus' melody (v. 59) takes his poetry to the banks of Virgil's Hebrus, and very likely to Gallus' Hebrus, too, as the scene where Orpheus' passion was played through: Orpheus mourns his lost Eurydice there (*Georgics* 4. 463), and eventually is dismembered by the feral women of Thrace driven wild by his refusal to respond, whereupon the river carries away downstream his head, still singing (ibid. 524). When Ovid matches Virgil by featuring his own sensationally parodic Orpheus as his epic's grandest icon for The Poet (= 'The Fable of Ovid' . . .?), he faithfully and tearfully echoes the detail with an apostrophe to Hebrus, as the head floats downstream, muttering inaudibly on its way across the sea to Lesbos (Ovid, *Metamorphoses* 11. 50–5: 50, *Hebre*).[74]

First extant in Latin poetry at Virgil *Eclogue* 10. 65, in the mouth of Gallus (proclaiming his defeat by/the triumph of Love), Hebrus must have been the scene in Gallus' poetry of 'his Hesiodic-Callimachean meeting with the Muses',[75] and it emerges from juxtaposition of Phaedrus' verses (58–9) with a pair of other shady texts on the same topic that his vignette may owe something to Gallus as well as to Virgil, and to Ovid:

> *qui saxa cantu mouit et domuit feras*
> *Hebrique tenuit impetus dulci mora*

> ~

> *. . . non tantum Oeagrius Hebrum*
> *restantem tenuit ripis siluasque canendo*
>   (pseudo-Virgil, *The Gnat* 117 f.);

> *Orpheus, Calliopae genus,*
> *. . . illius stetit ad modos*
> *torrentis rapidi fragor,*
> *oblitusque sequi fugam*

> *amisit liquor impetum;*
> *et dum fluminibus mora est*
> *defecisse putant Getae*
> *Hebrum Bistones ultimi*
> (pseudo-Seneca, *Hercules on Oeta* 1034–42).

It is possible, too, that Phaedrus' fragment of 'Orphic hymn' owes something to Ovid's tragedy, *Medea*, or perhaps shares with that lost extravaganza further debt to Gallus:

> *qui saxa cantu mouit et domuit feras*
> (vv. 58 f.)
>
> ~
>
> *munus est Orpheus meum*
> *qui saxa cantu mulcet et siluas trahit*
> (Seneca, *Medea* 228 f.)[76]

In Greek poetry, Orpheus worked his artistry on beasts and trees/rocks until Apollonius introduced rivers (*Argonautica* 1. 26 f.); Roman poets often followed his lead: e.g. Propertius (*Elegies* 3. 2. 3 f., *Orphea detinuisse feras et concita dicunt | flumina Threicia sustinuisse lyra*), and Seneca (*Mad Hercules* 572–5, (of Orpheus) *quae siluas et aues saxaque traxerat | ars, quae praebuerat fluminibus moras, | ad cuius sonitum constiterant ferae, | mulcet non solitos uocibus inferos*).[77]

A student of Virgilian poetry could learn to appreciate, and appreciate the learning of, selection of 'Hebrus' for the irresistibly onrushing torrent to be blocked by the impetus of a sweet barrage of song from Orpheus. For it was an item of 'Callimachean' wordlore that 'Hebros is a river of Thrace, getting its <?former?> name from the impact of the flood water' (pseudo-Plutarch, *On rivers* 3. 1: probably deriving from discussion in Callimachus' system of works about rivers); and where ancient commentary could dare accuse Virgil of getting his facts wrong, by writing that 'Harpalyce of Thrace outstrips the Hebrus in flight', when 'that is false—to be sure, it's the most placid of all, even when it swells through the winter' (Servius on *Aeneid* 1. 317, . . . *fuga praeuertitur Hebrum*), we can presume that he is getting his philology right, by including a mythical figure taken from Callimachus within a multifaceted simile founded on Homer, and taking care to associate her with a river whose name evokes in Greek the nimble butting of a *billy-goat* (ἔβρος).[78] Do grand post-Virgilian poets get the onomastic point? Did Seneca, when he wrote: *rapidusque campos fertilis Hebrus secat* ((?) *Phoenician women* 607)? Does Silius: *cursuque fatigant | Hebrum innupta manus*, and (of Orpheus) *cui substitit Hebrus |* (*Carthage epic* 2. 74 f., 3. 618)? Did Phaedrus, the new Linus–Orpheus, the Roman 'Aesopoet'? Did he not?

The negative note in the victorious dismissal of any unresponsive rocks, uncultured beasts or large muddy river-loads of sludge among his readership (= Envy) is itself trumped by one last verse that solemnly claims 'proper dues', which contrives to have the last word of the body of the poem echo, and re-echo: 'glory . . . |' (v. 61; cf. 53, *aeternam famam*).[79]

vv. 62–3

The *Prologue* is sealed with this neat 'couplet' that returns us to the polite world of Roman readers, and wraps up within the chiastic ring between | *induxi* and *peto* || a telling equivocation between address to the named dedicatee (Eutychus) and *envoi* to all prospective readers lined up for the book. A device which is also found in rather grander works.[80] Figuring the reader as dedicatee, first reader, who is asked to prove the final draft before publication of copy, binds the manners of bookish reading-culture to its own playground of judgement and prejudice, frankness and freedom, power and reputation (= Phaedrus)— and so, to the realm of Roman power politics (= Sejanus), and the primal scene of subhuman non-personhood (= Aesop): *iudicium*.[81]

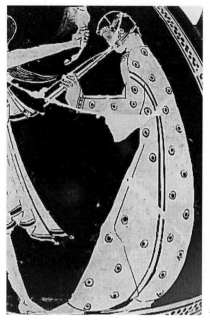

4(a)

A PIG-ULIAR CARD from LONDON.

4(b)

4
L'Acteur-Roi: Piper Prince
Breaks a Leg and Gets a
Good Hand (5. 7)

Vbi uanus animus aura captus friuola
arripuit insolentem sibi fiduciam
facile ad derisum stulta leuitas ducitur:
    Princeps tibicen notior paulo fuit
operam Bathyllo solitus in scaena dare.   5
is forte ludis, non satis memini quibus,
dum pegma rapitur concidit casu graui
nec opinans et sinistram fregit tibiam,
duas cum dextras maluisset perdere.
inter manus sublatus et multum gemens   10
domum refertur.
                    aliquot menses transeunt
ad sanitatem dum uenit curatio.
ut spectatorum molle est et lepidum genus,
desiderari coepit, cuius flatibus
solebat excitari saltantis uigor.   15
    erat facturus ludos quidam nobilis
et incipiebat posse Princeps ingredi:
eum adducit precibus pretio ut tantummodo
ipso ludorum ostenderet sese die.
qui simul aduenit rumor de tibicine   20
fremit in theatro. quidam affirmant mortuum,
quidam in conspectum proditurum sine mora.
aulaeo misso, deuolutis tonitribus
di sunt locuti more translaticio.
tunc chorus ignotum modo reducto canticum   25
insonuit, cuius haec fuit sententia,
'Laetare incolumis Roma saluo principe!'
    in plausus consurrectum est. iactat basia
tibicen, gratulari fautores putat.
equester ordo stultum errorem intellegit   30

magnoque risu canticum repeti iubet.
iteratur illud. homo meus se in pulpito
totum prosternit. plaudit illudens eques;
rogare populus hunc coronam existimat.
    ut uero cuneis notuit res omnibus,   35
Princeps, ligato crure niuea fascia
niueisque tunicis niueis etiam calceis,
superbiens honore diuinae domus,
ab uniuersis capite est protrusus foras.

When an empty head gets caught up by a capricious breeze
and picks up self-assurance above its station,
it doesn't take much to make silly flightiness a laughing-
    stock:
    Prince was a pretty famous piper
who always used to back Bathyllus on stage.   5
It so happens that at some games, I forget quite which,
he takes a heavy fall while the stage rig lifts off:
the result he wasn't expecting, a broken left leg,
when he'd rather go right off his legato!
Chaired off, he's carried home   10
with agonized groans.
                Several months go by
while the treatment gets him back to health.
As audiences are a mawkish, sentimental lot,
he starts being missed, as the one whose playing
had always lifted the dancer's energy.   15
    Some grandee was going to hold a show,
and Prince was just starting to be able to walk again,
so he gets him for a favour and a fat fee to agree
to a walk-on, that's all, on the day of the show.
Once this arrived, rumour about the piper   20
spreads through the theatre like wildfire, some asserting he's
    dead,
others that he'll be coming out into view any minute.
Away with the curtain, out rolled the peals of thunder,
and the gods spoke their lines the way they always have.
Then the choir sang a number that the man now on his
    comeback   25
hadn't heard, the gist of it being,
'Rejoice Rome, you are sound since your prince is safe!'.

All rose as one man, to clap and clap. Prince blows
kiss after kiss—he thinks his fans are congratulating him!
The front rows see his silly mistake, and   30
splitting their sides call for an encore of the number.
A repeat performance, and my lad prostrates himself
full-length on the apron of the stage, everyone in the front
    takes the mickey clapping,
the crowd behind guesses he's after a presentation.
    But when the situation was known to all the blocks,   35
Prince, his leg strapped up in a dazzling bandage,
his suit bedazzling lamé, even his shoes a-dazzle too,
swanking over the honour meant for the Celestial House,
was by one and all . . . shoved right out on his ear.

Prince the Piper was probably paired with another anecdote
about the stage, 5. 5, the joke shifting from audience to performer (or vice versa: see *Appendix*).[1] The stories are distinguished by their settings, 5. 5 anonymous and short on
coordinates, 5. 7 by implication an incident in Augustan Rome
(v. 27) concerning the public debacle of a key musician behind
the metropolitan star *Bathyllus* (v. 5). The kernel, confusion of
the stage-name *Princeps* (v. 4) with the imperial title *princeps*
(v. 27), comes over as 'folklore'. Epigraphic identification of
Princeps by Bücheler presses historicity on us (first century
inscription, in fine big capitals on a grand stone urn, from territory just north of Rome):[2]

L. MINI. TIBICINIS
CASSIA. UXOR
L. CASSI PRINCIPIS TIBICINIS
CAPPAE
(L. MINIUS PIPER'S WIFE,
CASSIA, DAUGHTER
OF L. CASSIUS PRINCEPS PIPER
K)[3]

Most commentators take it the events really happened;[4] but we
could prefer to see the 'Augustan' setting as those 'good old
days' again, as in 3. 10 (Ch. 2), just comfortably placed in the
fading past of anecdotage, where all the best yarns hold court.
Such stories may always trace back to *some* kind of incident.

The stealing of another's thunder has the ring of perennial stage-lore, as in this music hall 'memory':[5]

During the Danny Kaye years [i.e. a generation before, in a lost world] there was an old-timer called Scott Sanders who pushed a knife-grinder around the stage while he sang. One night he finished and as he got into the wings, the applause became terrific. A stage-hand remembers how his face lit up with delight at this sensationally unexpected reception. He turned to give the encore they were obviously demanding. As he came out of the curtains again he realised the sickening truth. Everyone in the audience had his back to the stage, applauding the entrance of Winston Churchill . . .

This because the invitation is to (imagine) a show, any show, where the basic structure of theatre turns back-to-front—and inside-out:[6]

No sooner had we sat down when came the National Anthem, and very strangely. It was being played by Gunner Edgington on a piano from the stage behind vast heavy velvet curtains . . . Colonel Harding started to sing 'Send him victorious, happy' etc. etc. He was joined by a few promotion-seeking officers. At the end, the small band of brave singers were given a tremendous ovation with shouts of encore enriched with farts. Edgington, thinking the applause was for him, appeared grinning through the curtain, a waste of time, as the house lights went off, blacking him out.

On one side, the earnestly scolding *promythium* (vv. 1–3), the historical names, and the long circumstantial account of Princeps' accident which gives an opening for his comeback (vv. 7–25) tempt us to 'swallow' the saga. On the other, 'a tale well told' looks to be the required response: the rest of the material patently builds up a fair old anecdote, with a story-teller's scene-setting o-so-considerate enough to tell us what he can, *and* what he can't, vouch for (v. 6), with a daft verbal joke for a surprise 'aside' (vv. 8–9), plus electric atmospherics of crowd-reaction and participation (vv. 13–15, 20, 30–4, 39), an ironic sketch of showbiz—both behind the scenes (vv. 18–19) and in full swing (vv. 23–4)—, and, to pump up the grand finale, a colourfully sarcastic pen-portrait (vv. 36–38). All of which contributes to the successful *peripeteia* (dénouement), which has the accompanist, suitably devoid of status and as such an ideal victim, come crashing to earth all over again. This time in broken pride, not fractured bones. And, this time, conclusively. You just knew what was going to happen, and it does.[7]

Spare a minute to search out what is at stake in any such feeling of compulsion. I shall get back to my answer to this when I have first tried to spell out 'what' *does* 'happen'. The narrator turns our scorn on the public performer with a dozen insults packed into three verses of introductory moral (vv. 1–3). But his narrative will open the vista to take in a full cast of characters, and a full house. More is going on than stage fright. Up front, the symbiotic relations that a mass audience builds with their idol get the spotlight, rehearsed before us as they turn from loving adoration to contemptuous hate. This not despite the fact, but *because* the incident picks on a bit-player. To get us into dry-eyed focus on the power ratios that are realized in audience reaction, in applause and in disgust, the marginal figure of the piper is dreamed up. Made for the part: he was one of the performing troupe, but in a supporting role; he was not an 'act', but without his music there would be no act. He shadows the soloist pantomime on stage, as against the choir's backing and backgrounded role. We'll see him get caught up in the business of the show, and stand, at one remove, for the whole contraption of show-biz. No, he wasn't the headliner, but he was the regular choice, counted on to lift every performance, Mr Dependable (vv. 4–5). The entire extravaganza was just his hot air, the magic of a reed-player's breath energizing a dancer's muscles to boost him into one more gravity-defying high, to gasps from the crowd (vv. 14–15).

All very well to insult such balletic miracles of levitation as 'a snare of the capricious breeze' (v. 1), but we know these talented people work hard to conjure up their superhuman *aura* and waft charisma to all parts, from pit through circle to gods. Theatre doubles the up-draught, with its stock of props: the stage-crane—hey presto!—whisks people up in the air, before our very eyes (v. 7). Dance, music, song, SFX (special effects), together they make a programme of scripted surprise. Suddenly, the routine shows up what it is made from, when the spell breaks—along with the piper's left leg. He is just an ordinary creature, flattened by a clumsy gadget, who needs carting off home, and six months lay-off to recover: he *has* a (mundane) home, and his (after all ordinary) body can't be hurried (vv. 7–12). Just a servo-mechanism, but flesh as well as bone: see how this accident undoes the role.

But the prolonged absence that makes him missed by habitués is being specially contrived so as to ease the subordinate into a protagonist's shoes. As invalid, the piper is hot property as never before; he is head-hunted, just to put in an appearance, for a personal gig (vv. 18–19). He gets a fat fee and flattery, and, for once in his own right, the prospect of an ovation all to himself; the impresario pays for the spectators to get a *sighting* (for heaven's sake) of a *musician*. This mock-performance, as in our award-ceremony gaucheries, rubs off on theatre proper. When this player is manoeuvred to premiere in his one-off over-exposure, he is made *to act the 'actor'*. In his failure to handle the star treatment, the piper shows how (literally) 'precarious' the celebrity of an idol must be.[8]

Phaedrus plays it so that we see and hear the buzz of an audience living on its nerves, jittery and expectant (vv. 20–1); the performance chimes with them, all claps of manufactured stage-thunder, and prating gods large as life (vv. 23–4). We came here knowing, better than the theatre-goers, that *this* show has an unusual feature, so we wait for its normality to fracture (v. 24). The chorus sings, we listen; the house gets up and cheers (25–8). Music to dance Rome into eternity.

Just one person among so many is in the dark (v. 25). Put on the wrong footing, so he must read the theatre awry, the fall-guy acts up stardom for all a *prima donna* is worth. As he takes his bow, returning his 'love' to the fans with the traditional histrionic show of adoration, we are shown how all tinsel gods live and perish on the knife-edge of their last performance. Close observers in the front rows ham up their role as audience; they extract still more extravagant rigmarole from the posturing invalid, as he humbles himself before the host in thanks for the honour. Now up on the stage, flat-out, getting flattered, and getting flattened!

Hired to parade himself, he is making a spectacle of himself, as he knows they know he knows . . .; but whereas the theatre at large recognizes this as a performance, the turn where the Thesp. milks applause for all he's worth and where he looks for still more exceptional tokens of cult status (and they do not guess him wrong), the cognoscenti now grab the chance to stage a show of their own (within the piper's show within the latest show). For our benefit.[9]

Brushing the pixie-dust off the boards is what we came to watch, to catch: dramaturgy dying on its feet. The whole play-house joins in the fun, until the one and only virtuoso is once more the only one who is in the dark, and in the dock (v. 35). Up in the glare of the lights, this celeb. god of ours is looking sick. He thinks he's in heaven; we see an old crock in angel costume and plaster (vv. 36–8). Our entertainment is complete when the auditorium finally erupts, as one, and pulls Princeps down from his cloud, lower than he could prostrate himself in his mime of overwhelmed gratitude, and out of the theatre. Out of Rome. Out of the poem. OUT. (v. 39, . . . *foras* ||)

Reverberating through the skit have been powerful forces— praise, honour, divinity, affect, expressivity . . . And the pre-carious conditionality of crowd-pleasing comes across, too, just fine. The very absence that made hearts fonder of the hub of the passion pit also left him out of the know. Singled out as the only one in Rome who hadn't heard the latest hit in the rep., he is a stranger to his own stamping-ground. This was plotted so we should see how clowns are for making and break-ing. *Princeps* stands for every artiste that ever believed their own publicity and got ahead of the audience—for every artiste that ever lived! Yes, the sketch cries up applause; by dissecting it.

And throughout, our performing monkey, *Phaedrus*, is enrolling us in *his* fan club. He pulls out the stops to get us to love the hounding of that favourite showman. We must *like* the piper enough to pay him out, and let the storyteller call the tune. But this involves his conscripting us into an uncompro-mising *theatre of social relations*.

We picked on our stooge exactly so we could nail him for the order of the city, in sickness as in health: his music stiffened the dancer's sinews, and that softened the spectator's hearts (vv. 13–14). The collective will make the 'aristocrat' who gave Rome its next show lower himself to elevate Princeps, for the unique curtain-call (v. 16, *nobilis*). At the showdown, solidarity is reinforced when the 'upper echelons' lead the 'groundlings' into a bodily stunt of scapegoating: the theatre maps out the

hierarchized collectivity, 'everyone' in their proper political
'tier', *equester ordo, eques, populus, cuneis . . . omnibus, universis,*
vv. 30–9). We must all join in, too. Send the social nonentity,
this upstart 'extra' framed into understudying the puppet
queen of the footlights, where he belongs: OUT (with Vitriol,
and Envy: Ch. 3).

For he made the biggest mistake of all; dared to put himself
up there with heavenly Rome. He thought that The People,
which *is* Rome, shone out of Pantomime's tights; that the
city would never conga its way into eternity without a libretto.
Who could want to be on his side? The price is steep: the cruel
breakage of our rag-doll's body was exactly orchestrated to
hook us into this lesson in political right-thinking: no, the
prospective happiness of Rome did *not* depend on a pipe(r's)
dream. Squash him, and Rome would dance right past, and not
notice a thing, into forever. For him, for *anyone*, to think otherwise is unimaginable delusion. *That* is what fools the hoi polloi;
their sanguine betters must blow the whistles (jeers, catcalls,
bouncers) and inspire concerted direct action, to vindicate the
sanctity of the community.

So this is what the story showcases: the holy name *Roma*,
embraced in the centre of the one-line summary of the patriotic
hymn which is broadcast again every time Phaedrus' Latin
repeats the choral 'hit', and demands us all to stand up and be
counted as Romans (v. 27). Power magnetizing emotion—the
feel-good factor in political cathexis. Yes, this fable shows
exactly how to control an audience by planting heavy chunks of
cultural capital and symbolic affect at the heart of the action in
your script. Just like Gunner Edgington's 'National Anthem'.

But the story also ties its Roman scene to *Bathyllus*. To
capitalize on this: here is a founding moment enshrined in the
unfolding narrative told about itself by imperial Rome. For this
freedman, the favourite of Augustus' senior aide Maecenas,
along with his rival Pylades, no less an *Augusti libertus* than
Phaedrus, was credited with the introduction of the pantomime
to Rome, just precisely when the first emperor was consoli-
dating the form and language of the 'principate', while taking a
firm grip on social order and behaviour (around 23/22 BCE).
Stamping out mob/popular shows of insubordination, protest,
and displeasure with the governing of the city, in the theatre or

any other venue, went hand in hand with the fading of drama as traditional festival fare, and its replacement by the sensational pyrotechnics of the choir- and orchestra-backed balletics of pantomime. Here is a Roman Myth of Empire, as Augustus would tell us, of his friend's, 'new and far too blatant love affair with the actor Bathyllus, I disapproved of his public displays of affection for him, and had told him so'.[10]

What was the régime of pantomime to signify? The planting of lines in scripts which could be heard as speaking to what was on the citizen body's minds, and the demonstrative appropriation of lines by the audience for the same purpose, would be dampened and discouraged by the paraded muting of the solitary 'actor', in an idiom deprived of mock-social settings and their promise of suggestion. The pantomime's repertoire needed to be familiar, if expressive hoofing and gesticulating was to explore more than the most rudimentary plot lines. Erotic Greek mythology was therefore optimal: picture the Cynic Demetrius, who had sneered at the genre—as all silk and mask, music and sexy vocals—being converted by a special performance of the lay of 'Ares and Aphrodite', unaccompanied, until he had to shout despite himself 'I hear the story you are acting, mate, I don't just see it: you seem to be talking with your *hands!*'[11] Between such performance art stunts and contemporary critique lay as wide a gulf as could be acted out. It would take a Sejanus to find a Roman, indeed anything 'Roman', in this ~~theatre~~.

In this sense, then, Phaedrus is telling another tale on the emperors' Rome. In a word, this is what the Caesars made of Rome: a pantomime. They brought the *populus Romanus* all this huffing of hot air and and puffing of put-on airs. Fans swooning, performers fanatically hyped; in the city where formerly huge assemblies had heard urgent and spirited prosecution of politics before voting the shape of their future. The story mobilizes a fantasia NOW that must be content with inconsequential slapstick: come join in the extrusion of a slaveling hack for a farfetched faux pas! This floorshow is the new reality of the global theme park. High rolling—for show-biz stakes. Passionate—all over vaudeville. Committed—but only to frivolities. This anecdotal Rome is, in short, the Rome of Satire.[12]

There is no call to pin down 'quite which occasion' Phaedrus is memorializing (v. 6), for the simple reason that Bathyllus after Bathyllus would perpetuate the entertainment inaugurated by the original pantomimist, 'Bathyllus § 1'. He had been fetched all the way from steamy Alexandria, so marking Augustus' conquest of Egypt after Actium, and his consequent assumption of the role of cosmocrat. Thereafter, post-Augustan 'theatre' essentially set in this mould, for centuries: Bathyllus gave imperial Rome its sound-track.

And yet, the fable tells us true, the gagging of Roman theatre was *never* secured. Rather, the auditorium became still more crucially than of old *the* place to feature in any portrait of Roman politics in the early Empire. This was where Caesars played for goodwill and satisfaction among 'their' subjects; where enthusiasm could ignite, take tangible form, find a language to express, and conjure, contentment; by the same token, naturally, theatre *still* amplified social unrest and complaint, disaffection and cynicism.

If ~~actors~~ could not speak 'to', or 'with', one another as if sharing a make-believe polity, still pantomimic silence spoke volumes, and in an ever more resonant idiom all its own. The gap between choir and dancer opened up a space for dialogue and disputation. And the audience itself achieved a relatively articulate eloquence for its own repertoire of body talk. Unscripted applause and hissing were, as always, expected to play a prominent part in the dramaturgy of the event; *they* could become a vehicle for partisan intervention or collective comment, as easily as for dumb servility and hypnotized sedation. What I am here sketching are exactly the complex *social semiotics* which power Phaedrus' narrative.

All this, however, is so far to miss the point of the fable. *Bathyllus* does not just cue us to Augustan, so Tiberian, Julio-Claudian, political theatre. Rather, he works *together with Princeps* (whether historical or fictional). Scott Sanders' come-uppance—Winston Churchill—should surely have stopped me playing down, even for a moment, that 'confusion of the stage-name *Princeps* (v. 4) with the imperial title *princeps* (v. 27)'. But maybe we are now in a better position to see what Phaedrus is handing us. The 'Fable of the *Principate*', no less.

Take a good look at Princeps. Our story eased the woodwind into the maestro's ba(thy)llet shoes; once we fix on his parody-performance as the darling of Rome for a day, this animator, indispensable inspiration, and close associate of the supreme soloist brings his own *name* to the role. The product of the synthesis is a devastating caricature of every Caesar. Welcome to the spectacle of *The Princeps'* worst dream come true! Yea, the 'first' *shall* be last . . . The vicious maiming, ridicule, and abjection of the piper undoes charisma, prestige, star quality, in order to show up the humble being that lurks beneath the robes of state. The rituals of mass adoration, its acknowledgement and incitement; the suspense and volatility of public hysteria; the 'actors in the audience' responding with the resplendent '*Acteur-Roi*', trapped in the spotlight glare.[13] The script unravelling . . .

Such is the theatrical world of Caesarian personality-cult. A giant imposture of a hot-air ballet kept aloft by the power of belief alone. By credulity, no safety-net.

Emperor as piper: a Caesar dying a thousand deaths, faced down, by a myriad looking daggers. Tiberius' horror show, Caligula's provocation.

Some ancient history—their news—will make the point. Riots and a strike, escalating into crises of public order, hit the first sets of *ludi* in Tiberius' reign; soon he strengthened the bar against members of the élite appearing on stage, before moving to banish actors, dancers, and their fan-club leaders from Italy (in 23). Phaedrus' story militates against it, but for the next fourteen years, pantomime might even be categorized 'a type of performance which had incurred Imperial disfavour and which must have seemed doomed forever'.[14] As we have seen, Tiberius' response was drastic. He entirely gave up on the scripted, costumed, mannered theatricality of exposure to public gaze, and hid from Rome, on his own, OUT at Capri, in a fish-bowl of his own (Ch. 1).

Fanatical Gaius, *he* recalled the luvvies on his accession (in 37), but then (at some point) had 'a farce writer cremated in the middle of the arena, all for a verseling's ambivalent fun', and (just two years later, in 39) capsized the dynamics of proscenium theatre by erasing the line mutually defining actors and audience, and thereby, at a stroke, collapsed oblique political metaphor into brute reality (Dio, *Roman History* 59. 13. 3 f.):[15]

When the spectators failed to applaud his favourite performers, and taunted him into the bargain, with jeers of 'L-plate Augustulus!', he refused all their requests, provoking them only to further defiance, until he went wild, and had spectators arrested wholesale, and executed.

Absurdist Nero would play the Emperor as love-god rival of the latest Paris. His mad merger of impresario and virtuoso, by quitting the audience and himself mounting the stage, may have rubbed in the stark truth about Rome's leading men and principal boys, but it was an open secret far earlier:[16] after repeated vacillation, or its simulation, over a potential ʾreturnʾ to Rome by Tiberius the recluse, 'he was commonly nicknamed *Callippides* for fun—someone famous in Greek proverb for never advancing a metre'. Which is to say, in graphically telling style, the Prince was always a mime-artist, running on the spot while kidding you he was running his hardest.[17] And Phaedrus' fable surely knows the score, best of all: 'L'acteur règne sur Rome'.[18]

Ultimately, the anecdote pipes up political reflection on *auto-cratic ideology*. When Rome takes its patriotic hymnbook to its heart, and pledges 'national security' to the 'security of the *Princeps*' for the theme of its song (v. 27), it is the first principle of the Principate which is blessing the applause, and gets blessed by it. Watch the story dent and deflate the work of ratification-validation-reaffirmation-valorization which the acclamation represents for the power-structure. First, consensus is forfeit, as the 'act' begins to go wrong; when a universal thumbs-*down* is achieved, the wally in fancy-dress has lost himself to apotheosis fantasy, and must pay for misreading the scene of his own fifteen minutes of fame. If this catastrophe in erotics happens to *Princeps*, if it *can* happen, are we not being invited to visualize it happening to *a princeps*, and ruminate that it is also a possibility? Why else would we bother to reminisce on this oboist? Why else would Phaedrus bother, and bother us?

Take it one step further. What if we work backwards from the debacle, and ask what is the fate of a *princeps* who guesses Rome wrong? Maybe Augustus, Tiberius, and Claudius would all, in the idiosyncratic ways that made them what they were, manage somehow to get their act together, and carry it off till (virtually) the end of their run; the scripts for Gaius and Nero, however, led straight to the mix of megalomania, malignancy, and misprision which our fabulist stigmatizes so earnestly (vv. 1–3). *Princeps* the piper dies a social death, and fades from his(s)tory; Caesars could be killed off far more conclusively, first with swords, then with words (for ever and a day). It stands to reason: read the fable for its mandarin manqué, either in the wake of Caligula's removal from sight, or looking forward to it as a possibility, and this potential will leap from the page.[19]

The upshot must be that Phaedrus' *coup de théâtre* is to hit on a storyline where the sanctimonious formulae bonding Emperor to Rome could be dissolved *in righteous and universal derision*. He can congratulate himself and all his readers, along with the audience in his story, by ventriloquating his chorus to fire off a salvo of: 'Rome, rejoice, secure / inviolate / in one piece' (*laetare incolumis Roma*, v. 27). So say all of us. But, as always with Latin's 'ablative absolute' construction, the qualifying phrase (*saluo principe*) then invites each of us to supply the *modality* ourselves: the refrain may congratulate Rome on her vitally thriving Emperor; but not without raising the spectre of a Rome undone by an *un*safe, or *un*sound, Caesar.[20] And the spectacle we are here to enjoy is, undeniably, the deposition of *our* Prince; *his* unsoundness is to be forcibly *prevented* from undoing Rome. (He is 'kicked out', like the Kings of primeval Rome; v. 39.)

Many of us saw on our screens how the later Roman*ian* Caesar, Ceausescu, 'the minor comedian, the paranoid hero who has fulfilled his ambition to take over the world's great stage for a while with his attacks of arrogance, devastating masquerades, absurd rituals', watched uncomprehendingly as *his* adoring crowd turned against him. Incredulous at first, then non-plussed, dithering, pathetic, and headed straight for lynch-law removal from life.[21] 'Princeps' even tells, not least, on that unholy alliance, even symbiosis, between crowd and fascist power so necessarily theorized for our times:[22]

The appearance of a White Clown (the Fascist) transforms us into similar clowns as soon as we surrender and return the Roman salute in a disciplined fashion.

VV. 1–3

Banging the drum, our censorious host reads us the write-act (a *promythium* twin for 5. 5. 1–3: *Appendix*). The keynote is the promising promise of 'risible stupidity' (v. 3).[23] This crowns a spate of damnations: 'empty head; feeble instability; passive mug; potty pettiness; windfall opportunism; self-centred self-promotion; smug self-satisfaction; push-over; laughing-stock; foolishness; straw-in-the-wind pawn; lamb led to the slaughter' (vv. 1–3).[24]

No uncertain terms to steer us to our target: at all costs, *don't* reflect that your own 'Eutychus' mind isn't exactly bursting (or you wouldn't be keeping these *fabulae* company: Ch. 3); that your host blows pretty gently himself, varying his throw-away material to keep you hooked (softly, softly, catchee monkey: ibid.); that a well-advertised sneer is guaranteed to bring readers flocking in (you can resist a good belly-laugh? As long as it's not on you?: ibid.); that, to bring things to a head, the 'light-heartedness' appropriate when you're dipping into some daft nonsense is the very next thing to its twin—downright 'plonk-ing silliness' (you're too smart to think that fiction wears its intelligence, its gravity, on the sleeve. Specifically, you learned better than that from the fable of Fable: Ch. 3). The target being, *through* the cipher-piper, all the citizens of Rome, their pathologically muted theatre, emotionally stunted fetish-fascism, and farcically crippled politics. *The* target: every Roman salute returned to (make) a tyrant. Being *princeps* need not be 'easy' (and so forth)—so the Fable of Collective Responsibility would have it.

VV. 4–11

Stage-names bespoke good omens and good luck, power and glory, so they were nothing if not good-to-say (= εὔφημα). The cognomen of our artist formerly known as *Princeps*, v. 4, maybe camouflages a primal *slave*-name, for the 'First(-born)'. It was, in any case, an ideological accident just waiting to happen (like the piper's physical and psychic accidents). Think of it/him as a *wor(l)d-game*.[25]

Most musicians were luxury slaves. Pipers were a popular choice for butts, as upstarts and aesthetes, derided for the puffed-out cheeks which made monkeys of them, for their puffed-up *egos*, their lecherous strains, and their silk-clad effeteness; but this badmouthing just underlines how vital the pipe had always been to culture, to celebration: alien to human speech, orgiastic delirium had electrified drama, and now energized dance.[26] Palladium and palace we easily recognize today as powerplants linked by more than shared terminology (The King Lives = Elvis). In Julio-Claudian Rome, there was at least as much crossover between glamour queens and royalty as we know:[27] in the Empress's close companion Mnester's last performance, a silent supplication to Claudius for his life, we can fairly identify the tragic—tragically *real*—counterpart of Princeps' charade. Brilliant acting as ever, but he was executed all the same. (Tacitus, *Annals* 11. 36) Without so much as an encore.

Just how much fame could a piper accrue? We need to be told that he was the genius's constant accompanist (*solitus*, v. 5), if we're to credit even a modicum of fame (*notior paulo*, v. 4)? For the record, we have the name of another member of the Bathyllan entourage: Philonides, his librettist; as well as a little more shadowy personage from his outfit, '*Ms Wise, Bathyllo-scape Productions (Global), Inc., doyenne of the interlude*'. Pipers at least wore no masks, so they *could* be recognized; you could tell one he was in it *for* recognition: 'You love no mean thing—praise, fame, being a celebrity, and known by millions.' For the storyteller, of course, historicity may come a poor second to efficient familiarization of his lead role.[28]

But *Bathyllus*, plausible name-dropping or not, opens the anecdote to history, to Rome and the Caesars: *Cilnius Maecenatis lib*. Maecenas' adoration for his *protégé* was notorious at the time—'You will know, for all Rome knows it, that I am helpless before the actor Bathyllus'—and he remained the type of the dancer for good: thus, a declaimer lists him as *la crème de la crème*, 'If I were in panto, Bathyllus I should be' (capped by Cestius' report, 'If you were a drain, the Main Drain you'd be!', Seneca the Elder, *Legal cases* 3. *Preface* 16). Together with Augustus' Cilician freedman Pylades, he is credited with introducing pantomime to Rome in 22 BCE; what-

ever milestone this may mean to mark, it must be one expression of the political settlement inaugurated in 23 BCE when the
'Principate' was inaugurated, with a kind of presidential role for
Augustus and restoration of the Republic's annual elections
for consuls. Electoral and theatre riots (same People, different
personae) marked the tension masked by ceremonial concord.

The two ring-leaders spanned theatre, entwining tragedy and
comedy, for *'Pylades'* is *the* mute figure beloved of Greek tragic
theatre, always the strong and silent friend by mother-killer
Orestes' side, come hell or high water, and *'Bathyllus'* spells the
ravishing sex-object forever drooled over by all 'Maecenas'
voluptuaries in the classic lyric *songs* of Anacreon. Both names
for song-and-dance men were perpetuated: 'How much care is
taken that no pantomime's name should perish! The house of
Pylades and Bathyllus abides through successors' (Seneca,
Science Quiz 7. 32. 3).[29] Mummery, then, and the flummery of
dynasty.

Anecdotes get under way when 'chance' happening supervenes on 'habitual' routine; this first instalment is interwoven
with the storyteller's play with his dispensation of 'knowledge'
(*solitus / is forte, notior paulo / non satis memini quibus*, vv. 4–6).
Fuzzy autopsy in the form of distant memory indirectly empha-
sizes the storyteller's authority by his years: 'I remember the
thing, I do, ages ago, no, not recent, not a bit of it . . .' (old
Phoenix, Homer, *Iliad* 9. 527). The flourish 'I forget *quite*
which' is also fake-conscientious stage-business from a raconteur's repertoire: 'The years that have gone by, I dunno—five,
is it?, since when . . .' (Lucian, *Lover of lies* 18); 'after some
days, I don't rightly know the exact number . . .', Eustathius
Macrembolita, *Romance of Hysmin and Hysmine* 11. 14); 'He
went and became a monk, I forget in which order . . .; He did
penance . . . at some Church, I forget which . . .' (Busk (1874)
315, 191). Similar sorts of fussing over the delivery beef up our
run of Roman stories (2. 5. 6, 3. 10. 8; contrast 5. 5 in *Appendix*;
it's difficult to know about *App* 10).[30]

Our knowledge of the culture is by implication compli-
mented, in the compression of the account of the disturbance
that opens space for the tale. We *must have* heard, surely, of this
piper; we all know what 'Bathyllus' connotes; 'games—the
stage rig lifts off' (vv. 4–7)—you get the picture. This assured,

and reassuring, host Phaedrus even takes time out for a surprise joke of his own. Blatantly extraneous, surely, to the 'plot': the accident that befalls the 'hero' is a chance fall, and (of course) it comes 'out of the blue', (*concidit casu | necopinans et*, vv. 7–8).[31] The machinery of theatre—that conveyor belt of illusory surprise—was meant to run like clockwork, so the characters are let *down*, this way, and we are set *up* with our narrative, at their expense. At the same time, the narration plays a trick of its own, the same trick, on us, with a surprise aside that whips the ground from beneath *our* feet! The low-down pun between (broken, agonizing) limb and (unscathed, insensate) equipment[32] is at odds with the atmosphere created by the scene-setting; bathos makes us act out the cruelty we mean to show our joke pal. Phaedrus' entrée promised to take *him* down a pegma, or two. And now—what a blow!

The accident on the stage-crane arose when the piper, who actively 'did the business' for the star, became a passive *passenger* (*captus . . . ducitur*, vv. 1–3 ~ *rapitur*, 7). Either this is what matters, and *not* what exactly the chump was doing soaring to heaven as if the limelight was for him; or else Phaedrus isn't taking *quite enough* care of us on flight 5. 7.[33] You might think so, but those on the receiving end of stories are always well-advised to take note when the tale moves from external to interior focalization. How Princeps felt about being in this story—he would rather have stopped being a piper at all ('would prefer to lose/trash his double-pipes', v. 9, tells us as much)—will be as crucial to our entertainment as it was excruciating to the musician.

This time round, his humiliation by theatre makes a hero of him, his abasement is prelude to exaltation, his fame is established indelibly in the hearts and minds of Rome. *This* got him *noticed*. But we've seen it all before, the 'pretty famous' minor celebrity finds himself handed 'all too brief a moment of notoriety' (*paulo notior*, v. 4). The way the casualty departs the stage this time, escorted home like some big-time wheel, sets him up for the total wipe-out we are given to anticipate by Phaedrus' silly pun. Those hands which hold this 'Eddie the Eagle' high now will be used to shove him out of the stage-door, and wipe him and his pipes out of the book (contrast *domum* ~ *foras* ||, vv. 11, 39; and do NOT confuse with *domus*, v. 38).

We only remembered his playing so as to stop him performing; we love him, then tear him, to pieces; then it's oblivion for
him, while we forget the way we *felt* his pain—taken inside his
point of view (*maluisset*, v. 9), as well as hearing his amplified
groans (*multum gemens*, v. 10). But reed-player and play-reader
both must tip-toe through this movie together, we all get caught
up in the 'stupid derision' which *homo* and *populus* act out in
tandem. That's the score.

So Princeps goes before a fall; his accident disrupts the
proscenium separating 'us' spectators from our fall-guy. This
happens in many an anecdote about the theatre, where method
'acting' over-achieves, and spills over into the reality shared
between actor and audience (Lucian, *Dance* 83, an actor over-
does Ajax's madness), or where theatre finds its frame of autonomy from society 'outside' shattered, warped, or forfeit: as
when the hyper-realist emperor Claudius 'used to send straight
to the lions stage carpenters responsible for any flop of the
props, or stage-machine failure' (Suetonius, *Life of Claudius* 34,
si automatum uel pegma uel quid tale parum cessisset . . .).[34] It's
easy to see how life splices clips when the un-Stoical piper gets
to play wounded hero, as 'extras' chair him from the fray (*inter
manus sublatus*, v. 10).[35] To sacrifice *duae dextrae* for real would
outbid the (stagey) folklore of a Mucius Scaevola's symbolic
devotion to Rome of his *uirtus* (manhood)—what two right
hands would be for![36]

VV. 11–15

Time passes = the rift in normality is healing (*dum ~ dum*, vv. 7,
12).[37] But longing for normality *interrupts* the healing. Now a
musician dragged out for ogling must perform out of character,
away from his patch of knowledge (*solebat ~ ignotum modo
reducto*, vv. 15, 25). The story descants on the imagery of
'health', with knowledge and self-knowledge included as part of
that. Watch the sick booby cynosure mistake the body politic
for his left leg: as if Roman sanity could depend on Princeps'
sound (*sanitatem ~ incolumis . . . saluo*, vv. 12, 27).

Pantomime may have depended on its backing, both constitutively and for that extra fillip which liberated the *dancer*'s

shins from gravity, and the auditorium from earthbound mundanity.[38] But Princeps was not a *sine qua non* for *spectatores* (v. 13) in their Quiritane, civic, roles: if they needed a fix of Bathyllus and Bathyllus needed a shot of Princeps, that was the louche sense and sensuality of theatre as a genre of urban life; but as *populus* and *equester ordo*, desire for instruments of pleasure is on no account to be allowed to blur with worship of the Holy Roman Empire (*Roma, honore diuinae domus*, vv. 27, 37).[39] The anecdote risks a glimpse of this chaos, in order to send it packing; or, as I am proposing, so as to show how flimsy any such ordering must be.

vv. 16–27

Phaedrus takes the lid off the promotions business. Performers bartered the use of their bodies to pleasure others, in broad day-light, eroticized for the gaze of society; they lived on deceit.[40] To turn this round, they were catalysts in the chemistry of the public gaze. The spectacle (*spectatorum ~ in conspectum*, vv. 13–22) breaks down 'seeing' into 'seeing as', 'seeing through', 'see-ing red' (*putat, existimat ~ intellegit*, vv. 29, 34; 34). The field of visuality is perpetually criss-crossed by power and knowledge: to this point, the story has handed 'knowledge' over to us in no uncertain terms; with the fissuring announced with 'rumour', the movement into doubt and peril commences, ready for the closure of Roman ranks that arises when empowerment through coalescence in universal 'knowledge' excludes trans-gressive 'ignorance' (*notior paulo ~ notuit ~ ignotum*, vv. 4, 35, 25).

Funny or not, the rival views that split the theatre-buffs will only become intelligible to the very spectators concerned once they profit through the show-down between the superior gaze of their leaders and the inferior perspicacity of their victim. *We* must see/know, without delay, that the apparent equal weight-ing between *quidam* and *quidam*, and their sharing of the single strong, affirmative, verb *adfirmant* (vv. 21–2), represent a false perspective. Because we are always already in a position to affirm that Princeps is *not* dead, but is contracted to appear in a moment and for a moment (and no more than appear).

However, we should also remember later how wrong we must have got all this.

It will come into view, without delay, that Princeps *is* 'dead'; he is going to die before our very eyes, we'll be enjoying, enjoining, and joining in the manhandling he gets, too (*mortuum* further prepares *incolumis . . . salvo*, vv. 21, 27). And, let's affirm it, that is *also* when Princeps will 'be coming out *into view*', at a theatre near you, 'any minute'. That is when *we* shall see/know 'Airhead' (v. 1) in his true colours (*iactat basia, se in pulpito | totum prosternit, superbiens honore*, vv. 29, 32–3, 38).

(And Princeps-Phaedrus' divine comedy will be muttering, nothing you could possibly confirm, 'gossip' about how to view the *princeps* through this namesake mimicry. This, mind, is how fable told us it works—obliquely, through transferred language (Ch. 3). Every single *senarius* now tells us to *hear* Princeps and *princeps* as one, not to *look* for tell-tale signs to tell them apart: remember, *we* are reading—listening to?—a story about *watching a musician . . .*)

We do indeed get 'a grand show from a grandee' (v. 16), where the nobs rustle up fun and games by exhibiting a dunce, and teach the plebs not to forget who is who and what is what (*nobilis ~ eques*, vv. 14, 33). Into the bargain, we buy the power within tales of theatre, mime or not, to tell on Caesar. But/So Phaedrus' summary of the miracle of drama writes it down with heavy sarcasm. At the drop of a stage-curtain, to pretend peals of thunder, centuries of mass delusion get the jaws of the gods working (vv. 23–4). Defamiliarized by straight talking and pressurized by extreme concision, the whole scenario looks as daft as . . . any fable. Again, we readers are flattered we can take the rigmarole as read, we must be at home in Rome, this story is ours, it is for us.[41]

The choir's hit-song (v. 24) may well be an *intermezzo*, unrelated to the drama we just finessed by précis; in any case, learning the *cantica* was a popular pastime.[42] The mini-'quotation' we are given, though it's the 'thought' that counts (*sententia*, v. 26), still manages to *evoke* the 'soteriological good wishes' used at Rome as the all-purpose formula for acclamation of greatness (grandiosity). Such chants themselves crisply squashed royalty and loyalty into one juxtaposition:[43]

Salua Roma, salua patria, saluus est Germanicus

Safe Rome, safe fatherland: safe is Germanicus

(Suetonius, *Life of Gaius* 6)

If the song marked a particular occasion, Phaedrus has not bothered/managed to let us know it (as he announced: v. 6). And if the anecdote depends somehow on the absentee of a few months missing out on a ditty, then it sounds as if we're to think of a song that didn't need any specific context. The summary impression we're given could hardly get more omnivalent: 'We are Imperial Rome, we are!' But suppose we do pick up the best homology on offer, and scent imperial 'return' to Rome as the likely impulse for putting this *canticum* on. Phaedrus' story would have a quizzical ring during the years of Tiberius' 'retirement', on this score. But more important, we would home straight on Princeps' situation, 'just now returned' (*modo reducto*, v. 25), by tuning into the din of imperial 'advent' to Rome (*aduentus, reditus*). Snatches of the schedule of Horace *Odes* 4. 5, for example, will then reverberate through the text of 'Princeps' (vv. 2, 4, 13, 14, 27, 33):[44]

abes iam . . . redi . . . uotis ominibusque . . . sic desideriis icta fidelibus |
quaerit patria Caesarem . . . incolumi Caesare . . . multa prece.

You've been away so long now . . . Do make a come-back . . . with vows and omens (blah-blah-blah) . . . even so, pierced by waves of loyal desire, the fatherland looks for Caesar (la-la-la) while Caesar is safe and sound (rhubarb, rhubarb) with full many a prayer . . .

This thought then sponsors another: the 'return' of Princeps is more pertinent to the ceremonial construction of the *princeps* than I have yet ventured to suggest. What makes anyone ever suppose that they can know what 'take' the crowd is putting on the chant it adopts? When is it ever a simple case of meaning what it says and saying what it means? Read this anecdote as a fable, and there will always be that risk for a *princeps* to be treated as a *Princeps*—Caesar taken for Ceausescu.

VV. 28-34

With the standing ovation, regular marker of personal acclaim, the fatal moment of misprision arrives, and a staccato run of paratactic phrases in the present tense without connectives whizzes us through the crunch moments of misprision, detection, entrapment, and complication (vv. 28–34).[45] Mass reaction to sentiments, casual allusions and hints dropped from the Roman stage had been a recognized outlet expression of public opinion, and bearpit for heckling (Suetonius, *Life of Augustus* 68 and 53):[46]

Octavian once on the day of the games found the whole people first take as an insult against him, and then express their approval with maximum consensus, a line delivered on stage about a Eunuch Priest of the Mother of the Gods playing his tambourine: 'Don't you see the perve beating up with a finger?'

and

Augustus, when as he watched the games the words were delivered in a mime, 'O Master, fair and good!', and one and all leaped up to approve it as describing him, he first nipped such demeaning flattery in the bud with instant wave and frown, then on the following day censured it with the heaviest proclamation he could.

Through these lines, Princeps limps from the wings; by v. 32 he reaches centre-stage. Performers and rulers blew the same kisses to their public.[47] Intensification parts the ways, for a prince would only prostrate himself like a *prima donna* (vv. 32–3) if he had crossed over and joined the show.[48] Bowing and scraping is just what a lowly piper should be doing: only for real. So this is where the paint turns to grease.

A simpler version of Princeps' asinine misunderstanding turns up in fable guise (*AES* 182):

An ass carried the goddess's image around with her on-the-road priests. When crowds prostrated themselves before the statue (προσκύνησις), he supposed they were prostrating themselves before *him*, and all in a flutter swelled with pride. His driver thrashed him.

The moral is: those who trick their way with good things not theirs incur derision among people who know them.

In complex Rome, the plot staggers the upshot, as the audience gets split, first notionally, when the piper thinks it's all his fan club's doing (v. 29), then for real, as sharp eyes and wits in the front rows get ahead of the rest of the audience, as in Lucian, *Dance* 83:

When an actor over-realized Ajax's madness, there were on the one hand the social refuse, people who saw neither the worse nor the better . . ., and on the other the more urbane ones who understood . . . but rather than exposing what was happening by their silence, they drew a veil over the madness of the dancing with their praises, seeing precisely that the goings-on weren't Ajax's doing but a freaked-out dancer's . . . So it was that some marvelled, others mocked, and still others had their suspicions . . . When fans later begged him to dance the same Ajax for them all over again (αἰτούντων γὰρ αὖθις τῶν συστασιωτῶν), this nice guy (ὁ γενναῖος) told the theatre: 'Going mad once is plenty'.

The theatre custom of the 'encore' *encorages* the anecdote into the skulduggery of a cutesy repetition routine (*repeti, iteratur*, vv. 31–2). This calls for some escalation in the writing to match: the 'condescending' storytellers' formula *homo meus*, v. 32, is a tetchy feature of the effort to vary terms at this crucial late stage of this one-man-band narrative. One more by-product is the benighted crowd's notion that Princeps' display of self-abasement means he wants something: in a word, this prince, like all others, is angling for '*a crown*' (v. 34).[49] The interpretations fray and re-double, until everyone gets into line to settle the story's hash; but *this* misprision nails *Princeps* to *princeps* with a clear simplicity that brooks no argument. What is *any* king without a crown? (See Ch. 8 § 5)

As we have noticed, social stratification emphatically framed the theatre as a political arena, only heightened by purges of political expressivity from the stage. Privilege materialises as spatial precedence (προεδρία). Senators up in the orchestra, *equites* in the first fourteen rows; the rest, the *populus*, seated in vertical blocks (*cuneis . . . omnibus*, v. 35). The 'knights' traditionally put their vantage-point to concerted work, mediating between the troupe and the audience at large—or rather, as here, interfering for all they were worth, having fun / keeping Rome sane.[50]

vv. 35–9

A generous caricature sets up the catastrophe, and the dramatic finale takes us, without aftermath, on OUT. Extravagant repetition satirizes—whites out—the peacock's gorgeous display: *niuea . . . niueis . . . niueis*, vv. 36–7. 'White bandaging' wraps together accident victim and high-and-mighty fop; 'white tunics' sound like fussy holiday gear, not the piper's professional costume; 'white shoes' were for women and for stage wear.[51] The 'glory of the household of the gods' refers directly to the treasonous misappropriation of imperial praise (vv. 28–34), but the harlequin's mix of glitter and plaster builds him up to constitute an offence to the Roman gaze, ready for our sudden release into vengeful violence against his personage (v. 39).[52]

Another musician gets the same treatment in an anecdote from [Anon.], *To Herennius* (4. 60):

Enter the guitarist, perfectly dressed, clad in a gilded robe, with a purple cloak embroidered with rainbow hues, plus golden crown . . . Suppose he's stirred up great anticipation in the people with all this stuff, and then suddenly, when silence falls, he then lets out a truly foul voice . . .: the better dolled up and the more eagerly anticipated he has been, the more derided and scorned he is when he is thrown out on his ear.

And the same happens in Lucian (*Against the unschooled* 9 f.):

A vain kitharist decked in purple and gold breaks his strings and sings abominably, so that laughter arose from all the spectators, and the officials staging the games got cross at his nerve, gave him a whipping, and chucked him out of the theatre.

More kings of rock, more Machiavellian fables.

Society ritually drubbing in collective solidarity through unmanning the idols who act up for the treatment.[53]

APPENDIX

It's the Real Thing:
Grunt *Piggy* Grunt (5. 5)

Prauo fauore labi mortales solent
et praeiudicio dum stant erroris sui
ad paenitendum rebus manifestis agi:
    Facturus ludos diues quidam et nobilis
proposito cunctos inuitauit praemio   5
quam quisque posset ut nouitatem ostenderet.
uenere artifices laudis ad certamina
quos inter scurra notus urbano sale
habere dixit se genus spectaculi
quod in theatro numquam prolatum foret.   10
    dispersus rumor ciuitatem concitat,
paulo ante uacua turbam deficiunt loca,
in scaena uero postquam solus constitit
sine apparatu, nullis adiutoribus,
silentium ipsa fecit expectatio.   15
    ille in sinum repente demisit caput
et sic porcelli uocem est imitatus sua
uerum ut subesse pallio contenderent
et excuti iuberent. quo facto simul
nihil est repertum, multis onerant lancibus   20
hominemque plausu prosequuntur maximo.
    hoc uidit fieri rusticus, 'Non mehercules
me uincet' inquit et statim professus est
idem facturum melius se postridie.
    fit turba maior. iam fauor mentes tenet   25
et derisuros non spectaturos scias.
    uterque prodit, scurra degrunnit prior
mouetque plausus et clamores suscitat.
tunc simulans sese uestimentis rusticus
porcellum obtegere—quod faciebat scilicet,   30
sed in priore quia nil compererant latens—
peruellit aurem uero quem celauerat
et cum dolore uocem naturae exprimit.
acclamat populus scurram multo similius
imitatum et cogit rusticum trudi foras.   35
    at ille profert ipsum porcellum e sinu

turpemque aperto pignore errorem probans,
'En hic declarat quales sitis iudices'.

Mankind is forever blundering through wrongheaded
    favouritism.
While they stand by their premature judgements-in-error,
out come the facts, and they're brought to contrition:
    A loaded grandee meaning to hold some games
invited everybody for a promised prize   5
to display any novelty acts they could.
Showmen came along to compete for the fame,
among them a wag well-known for city wit.
He said he had a show of a sort
never before performed in a theatre.   10
    Word gets round, stirs up the whole people.
Seats shortly before unoccupied are now too few for the
    throng.
In fact after he took the stage all alone,
with neither props nor supporting cast,
expectancy brought hush unaided.   15
    The man without warning ducked his head down under
    the fold of his cloak
and did an imitation with his voice of a pig squeal, so well
they all maintained a real one must be beneath the robe
and shouted for it to be given a good shaking-out. This
    done,
nothing at all was found and they at once load him with lots
    of salvers,   20
giving the guy a send-off with the loudest applause possible.
    A bumpkin saw all this going on and said, 'He won't
beat *me*, begorrah!', and promised on the spot
he'd do the same trick the next day, only better.
    The throng gets even bigger this time. By now
    favouritism has their minds in its grip,   25
and you could tell they were there to have a good laugh at
    him, not watch him perform.
    The pair of them step out and the wag does a quick grunt
    first,
pulling in applause and rousing the cheers;
then the bumpkin, pretending he was covering up
a piggy under his cloak—as of course he was,   30

but getting away with it because they hadn't found anything
   in the first performer's case—
well, he gives the ear of the real pig which he had hidden a
   good tweak,
and forces out the voice of Nature with the pain.
The people shout out that the wag's imitation had been
   much more lifelike
and insist that the bumpkin be shoved off the stage.   35
   But he draws the piggy large as life out of his fold,
and proving the shameful mistake by producing his
   conclusive exhibit, declares,
'Look, this fellah clinches what sort of judges you lot are.'

Plutarch's *Party Quiz* (5. 1. 674b–c) asks: 'Why when people
mime rage and pain do we listen to them with pleasure, but
when they're actually in these passions, without any?' He comes
up with the convincing parable of Pork and Prejudice:

. . . because, well, what was the matter with them, what external
stimulus was at work, when they so marvelled at Parmeno's sow that it
became proverbial? Yet, they say, when Parmeno was famous for his
mimicry, other people were jealous and put on rival performances.
People were prejudiced and said 'Great, but nothing to Parmeno's
sow'. Then one of them took a piglet under his arm and stepped out.
When they heard the real noise and responded with 'What's this to
Parmeno's sow?', he released the piglet into the open and proved that
this judgement was all about opinion, not truth.

On this authority, the story has been accepted as the '*Sprich-
wortaition*' (origin-story for a proverb) of this Greek saying:
'Great, but nothing to Parmeno's sow' (*Εὖ μὲν ἀλλ' οὐδὲν πρὸς
τὴν Παρμένοντος ὖν*). An allusion in Plutarch *On listening to poets*
(3. 18c), associates the proverb with a historical setting in the
mid fourth-century BCE:

Just as when we listen to a pig scream and a windlass shriek we get
irritated and vexed, but if someone mimics them credibly, like
Parmeno's sow and Theodorus' windlasses, we enjoy it . . .

The *Parmeno* concerned would be the famous comic actor of
that time.[54] Plutarch, then, puts it over that 'windlass' imitations were part of Theodorus' stock-in-trade, and a 'sow' effort
part of Parmeno's.[55] This seems difficult to pigture, especially

for the tragic stage! Is it perhaps ultimately traceable to critical hyperbole: 'Theodorus could even imitate a *windlass*, and entertain his audience'? In Parmeno's case, we could posit prior existence of the elliptical proverb 'Parmeno's sow'. '*Parmeno*' would always seem right in any context where 'fidelity' is the issue, for it was a 'speaking name', 'Loyal', everywhere tagging and typing faithful slaves, and acquiring some currency as a performer's stage-name.[56]

The late (and unique in *CPG*) explanation of *Appendix of Proverbs* 2. 87 is a curio:

Relates to those who try to mimic but don't pull it off: the artist Parmeno painted a pig and hung it: viewers thought it used its voice.

This encourages the suggestion that Plutarch's account, too, gives a '*pseudaition*' for an older proverbial phrase.

The argument that a story became attached to a proverb which was associated with a historical namesake of the Parmeno in the proverb weakens the idea that Phaedrus ousted Parmeno from his tale.[57] His version shows up some awkwardnesses in Plutarch's;[58] in turn, Plutarch's 'naive' version brings out points of elaboration which Phaedrus (and/or his putative Greek anecdote source) has, not entirely happily, introduced to articulate a realistic but urbane poemette. The setting becomes organized municipal *ludi*, v. 4 (Roman-style?).[59] The audience within the story provides a medium through which to transmit excitement to the reader. Crowd-reaction is made the hinge for presentation in the form of two matching tableaux: 'Seats shortly before unoccupied too few for the throng' grows to 'The throng gets even bigger this time' (*turbam*, v. 12 ~ *turba maior*, vv. 24f.). Most important, antagonism entirely in the Aesopic spirit is introduced by making the victim of crowd bias a lone outsider, the 'bumpkin' (v. 22): for once, Phaedrus doesn't bother to change around the terms for his actors: *scurra*, 8, *ille*, 16, *hominem*, 21, *scurra*, 27, *priore*, 31, *scurram*, 34 ~ *rusticus*, 22, *uterque*, 27, *rusticus*, 29, *rusticus*, 29, *rusticum*, 35, *ille*, 36. But the pigmentation of the 'plot' does get touched up, so that the 'famous act' of Parmeno in Plutarch, vainly attempted by rivals, becomes a novelty 'never seen before in captivity' (v. 10), which only the odd-man-out bumpkin will try. Crude 'under-arm' concealment of the porker is sanitized as 'under his cloak' (*subesse pallio*, v. 18, cf. *in sinum*, 16, *vestimentis* . . . | . . . *obtegere*, 29–30, *e sinu*, 36).[60] And in the process, the story-line grows an extra twist or two that this already curly tale doesn't need.

From Plutarch, Erasmus would append the story to his collection of Proverbs.[61] Scheiber (1966) noticed in the Russian autobiography of Ilja G. Ehrenburg the story passed on by the artiste Aleksandr Jakowlewitech Tairov, as told *him* by 'Coquelin', a famous French artiste (of the late nineteenth century):[62]

An itinerant player at a fair imitated the squealing of a pig. Everyone was delighted and applauded him. Then a peasant from Normandy wagered that he could do as well as the actor. He hid a live piglet under his coat and started pinching it. The piglet squealed, but the audience booed: they did not think the peasant was a good mimic.

This is evidently from *Phèdre*, although the clutter of 'sophistication' has been pared away again.[63] Here the carnival milieu of the fair, with its cultural license to play at mockery of given power categories and hierarchies, exploits the parody human status of the pig, to stick the pretensions of the animal farm.[64]

Read on its own, the *fabula* makes a good point well enough, but as it wears no names, it sports no History. Once we reach 5. 7, however, we are bound to fix on these doublets as a meaningful diptych. 'A grandee meaning to hold some games' kick-starts both tales (v. 4 ~ 5. 7. 16).[65] Announcement of a reputation foreshadows its breaking (8 ~ 4; cf. *App* 15. 5). 'Word gets round, stirs up the whole people' and 'Rumour spreads through the theatre like wild-fire' (11 ~ 20–1). Community is in the spotlight*s* (*ciuitas*, v. 11, varies *turba*, *populus*, 12, 34 ~ *populus*, *cuneis* . . . *omnibus*, *uniuersis*, 34, 35, 38). The tales are hooked together tightest of all at the death: the people 'insist that the bumpkin be shoved off the stage' where Princeps will by one and all be 'shoved right out on his ear' (*cogit* . . . *trudi foras*, 35 ~ *capite est protrusus foras*. ||, 39).[66] In retrospect, the rustic will have already rammed abuse of the poor piper back down our throats. He puts the lie to any reading of 5. 7 that supposes the traffic is all one way, a swinish stampede on the victim of our sense of humour. 'Foolish levity leads to derision' (5. 7. 3) doesn't work so cleanly once we're

obliged to ask 'who gets the last laugh?'. In 5. 5, clever-clogs
urbanity doesn't read its butt's vainglorious misreading of the
words uttered in the theatre; instead, prejudicial urban misreading of wordless theatre takes its turn in the stocks, and the
words uttered turn out to be the custard-pie thrown in the faces
that most resemble *ours*.

In tandem with 5. 7, then, 'Grunt piggy grunt' does
have something to say to Phaedrus' Rome. Perhaps the story
embodies citified self-deprecation; or it practises civilized self-
condemnation? The peasant is always a wild card to play in
literature. But what of our high profile storyteller? (How) Do
these porky pies work as a vehicle for Phaedrus?

This must be the question the story is crying out to get asked.
Just put together in the same breath the Thracian ex-slave and
his Aesopic talking-beast fables, along with the peasant and
his squeaking pig. Then, the multilayered ruse which parades
the product of dissimulated simulation as, simultaneously,
unacknowledgeable *and* self-evident truth, leads straight back
to Fable Theory (Ch. 3). Which sort of piggy can squeal, and
make us think it's Phaedrus' voice? 'Great, but nothing to
Parmeno's sow'? (Huh.)

VV. 1–3

The moral writes grand-ish Latin, and hooks onto the story
perfunctorily, but enough (*favor, errorem*, vv. 37, 25; *rebus
manifestis* responds with *aperto pignore*, 37). Fabulists have to
wield massively panoptic knowledge for milliseconds. This is
why they look daft if they start claiming the stories for themselves, not 'tradition'.[67]

VV. 4–10

The elaboration of a show set up by an impresario for the public
matches this pig of a poem to Princeps'; but such re-scheduling
of simple tales in urban surroundings is always on the cards in
literary versions: thus 'Androclus and the lion' has much
simpler analogues, minus Androclus and amphitheatre.[68] If you

let yourself think about it, then the idea of the show, with the gruntee's invitation for novelty acts, presumably as warm-up, or intermission, stunts on a 'proper' bill, if we're envisaging anything like a city scene, starts to split away from the wager which obliges everyone to 'come back tomorrow' for round § 2, and the story to fall apart. None, some, or much of this may be Phaedrus' doing, rather than his Greek source.[69] If none of this worries you, then the familiar world of Roman show-biz, with its 'urban(e) pepper', can make Latin readers feel at home, and slip easily into the fiction. As we shall see, they walk into the trap set for them . . .[70]

VV. II–I5

This punchy bridge-passage further stokes up eagerness for the 'novelty' promised us in v. 6, and then rarefied in vv. 9–10. You would not be entirely wrong to suppose that the coming impersonation of the jokester's turn by Phaedrus itself required 'silence', while he reads his poem, 'alone and unaided, with no tricksy back-up assistants' (vv. 13–15), to the massed ranks of the expectant public on holiday.[71] All these stories do compete against the rest of the hucksters in the fame business; no rabbits up his sleeve, the Roman Aesop does hawk an unprecedented form of entertainment for our delectation. It does revolve, too, around the same plunges from ambitiously advertised programme down into an amusingly sordid trough, as the grandee's theatre-bill, when its boar delivers his shock for our midden. Phaedrus, too, hogs the airwaves.

VV. I6–2I

The mock-concealment reminds me of the 'Evil-wit' story, where a bird *is* hidden beneath the cloak, to try and fool the Delphic oracle (*AES* 36).[72] There is something fundamentally iconoclastic about magicking up a creature from thin air, then exposing the coup. To lend a voice is a vastly suggestive way to borrow a semblance of power. To throw voices around is a gleefully invasive appropriation of autonomy and identity.

Disrespecters of persons have accordingly cultivated mimicry always and everywhere.[73] It was free, it involved a knack, it was silly, it made people laugh—even when they didn't want to. Not unlike that vocalization of Old MacDonald's farm which is known as Aesopic Fable.

The exchange of 'nothing' for 'loads and lots of salvers' is certainly a telling way to picture a performer's (including a raconteur's) prestidigitation of 'the loudest applause possible' (vv. 20–1). Successful Roman artistes *were* handed silver salvers, though we're not going to believe that people brought along a stack of plates to a showdown, just in case they got impressed when a bet came off this way. Phaedrus' impress...ionistic phrase, however, neatly manages to combine metaphorical 'heaping with prizes', literal 'presenting with heaped prize platters', and symbolic 'honouring with prizes'.[74]

VV. 22–4

Like Coquelin's 'Norman', Phaedrus' bumpkin is a typically 'adoxographical' hero (the inglorious written up): one facing a horde. The wisdom of the soil trounces city wit in stories meant for townspeople.[75] Romans were *supposed* to respect the old ways of the countryside, so readers should feel caught when Phaedrus deserts his joker and sides with the peasant.[76] Naive enough to catch out sophistication, he should serve as a snare for the wary, for we all know at once that barnyard noises are the rustic's province. What do we expect when 'we' take him on at his own game—and he takes 'us' on, at our own games?

VV. 25–6

No longer 'expectation', but 'prejudice' (vv. 15 ~ 26). The wording of v. 26 is not secure,[77] but division between 'watching' and 'deriding' in the spectator-sports of theatre and story-telling always preludes consternation. To look on Aesop, a tale of Phaedrus' told, was to (mis)recognize the mocker for a mock-able old-timer (*quidam . . . Aesopum . . . cum uidisset . . .; quod sensit . . .. derisor potius quam deridendus senex*, 3. 14. 1–4).

VV. 27–35

The ludicrous puerility of (this) fable is summed up in the *ad hoc* and never again reused word *degrunnit*, v. 27, 'does a quick grunt'. In a word, the quintessence of Aesopic versicles.[78] To redouble the applause, the chiasmus | *mouet . . . suscitat* |, v. 28, outdoes *plausu . . . maximo* with the common phrase *plausus et clamores* (vv. 21 ~ 28).[79] The Great Grunt trick must come our way three times: up to a point, the varied phrasing is expert, with a clear original, then a forceful repeat, before the rousing k.o. finishes us, and the oinking, off (*porcelli uocem est imitatus sua ~ degrunnit ~ peruellit aurem . . .. et cum dolore uocem naturae exprimit*, vv. 17, 27, 31–2). But along the way Phaedrus falls into the silly complication that where the *scurra* pretended to conceal a pig, the *rusticus* pretended to do . . . what he was pretending to do. The original turn already gives the game away: 'so well they all maintained a real one must be beneath the robe and shouted for it to be given a good shaking-out. This done, nothing at all was found.' So when the folk in the crowd get their ears well and truly tweaked in the grunt finale, the pretence must become double-bluff: 'pretending he was covering up a piggy under his cloak—as of course he was, but getting away with it because they hadn't found anything in the first performer's case' (vv. 29–31). Symptomatically, the language enacts this over-cooking, with awkward parenthesis, awkward padding, and awkward syntax (vv. 30–1; v. 32; v. 32, *peruellit aurem uero quem celauerat*).[80] A disgruntled and disgruntling pig in a poke: contrast Plutarch and Coquelin.

VV. 36–8

None so deaf as them as won't hear: maybe the actions of Plutarch *Party Quiz* speak louder than Phaedrus' words (plus triumphant waving of the damning confutation).[81] But maybe Phaedrus is obliged to (over-)compensate for the punch-line proverb which is denied him, but motivates Plutarch's whole narrative.[82]

And it's a moot point how to decide what spoils a daft story about how daft stories can be.

Especially when the sty turns out, not one, but two lots of swill on the trot.

'Now I'm a sow most of the time.'[83]

5(a)

5(b)

5

The Price of Fame: *Pompey the Great* and the Queen's Shilling (*App.* 10)

[QUAM DIFFICILE SIT HOMINEM NOSSE][1]

Magni Pompei miles uasti corporis
fracte loquendo et ambulando molliter
famam cinaedi traxerat certissimi.
hic insidiatus nocte iumentis ducis
cum ueste et auro et magno argenti pondere   5
auertit miles.
              factum rumor dissipat,
arguitur miles, rapitur in praetorium.
tum Magnus, 'Quid ais? tune me, commilito,
spoliare es ausus?' ille continuo excreat
sibi in sinistram et sputum digitis dissipat: 10
'Sic, imperator, oculi exstillescant mei,
si uidi aut tetigi'. tum uir animi simplicis
id dedecus castrorum propelli iubet
nec cadere in illum credit tantam audaciam.
   breue tempus intercessit et fidens manu   15
unum e Romanis prouocabat barbarus.
   sibi quisque metuit, primi mussitant duces.
tandem cinaedus habitu sed Mars uiribus
adit sedentem pro tribunali ducem
et uoce molli, 'Licet?' enimuero eici   20
uirum ut in re atroci Magnus stomachans imperat.
   tum quidam senior ex amicis principis,
'Hunc ego committi satius fortunae arbitror,
in quo iactura leuis est, quam fortem uirum,
qui casu uictus temeritatis te arguat'.   25
assensit Magnus et permisit militi
prodire contra.
              qui mirante exercitu

dicto celerius hostis abscidit caput
uictorque rediit. his tunc Pompeius super,
'Corona, miles, equidem te dono libens   30
quia uindicasti laudem Romani imperi
— sed exstillescant oculi sic' inquit 'mei',
turpe illud imitans iusiurandum militis,
'nisi tu abstulisti sarcinas nuper meas.'

[How tough knowing someone is]

A soldier of Pompey the Great, an enormous physical
    specimen
whose squeaky voice and effeminate walk
had saddled him with the name of a dead-cert. fairy,
one night bushwhacks the general's baggage-animals;
along with the finery, the gold and the great haul of silver   5
he rustles the mules.
                      Word spreads round of what he'd
    pulled off,
fingers point at the soldier, off he's frogmarched to camp
    HQ.
The Conqueror now asks him, 'Well, speak up man, have
    you had the nerve, comrade,
to clean me out?' Not a moment lost, the man hawks up
spit into his left hand where he spreads it round with his
    fingers till it's gone,   10
and takes an oath, 'My commander, so may my eyes drip
    away to nothing
if ever I clapped eye or set finger on the stuff'. Then the
    hero, always straight as they come,
orders that disgrace to the camp to be kicked out,
never crediting for a moment that nerve on that scale is in
    his league.
    A short while passed by when a challenge came from some
    barbarian,   15
backing his trusty arm, for a Roman to come out and fight.
    Each individual fears for his own look-out; the foremost
    officers keep quiet as mice,
until finally the man who looked the part of a fairy, but was
    really a tower of might, approaches his C.-in-C. at his
    desk out front of the tribunal

and softly asks 'Permission to proceed?' Well! The
    Conqueror is furious,   20
and orders the man kicked out, what else in view of the grim
    situation?
  At that point one of the more senior members of the
    generalissimo's staff
made a suggestion, 'My own belief is that this man is better
    trusted to Fortune,
as with him there is no serious loss to be incurred, rather
    than some staunch hero,
who might get unlucky and lose, and so bring you under fire
    for foolhardiness'.   25
  The Conqueror nodded and authorized the soldier
to advance to meet the foe.
                    To gasps from the onlooking
    army
he whipped the enemy's head off his shoulders quicker than
    words can say,
and back he trooped in triumph. Then it's Pompey's turn to
    comment,
'It is with the greatest of pleasure, I do assure you, that I
    present you with a crown   30
in recognition of your success in upholding the honour of
    Roman rule.
But', he went on, 'so may my eyes drip away to nothing'
(and he copied that foul oath of the soldier)
'if it wasn't you the other day made off with my baggage.'

This camp yarn of Pompey the Great and the Best-and-Worst
of Privates is preserved for us by the fifteenth century Bishop of
Siponto, Nicolai Perotti, in a collection of *fabulae* made for his
nephew: 32 of Perotti's 157 poems (one written out twice) are
the otherwise lost *Phaedriana* we call the *Appendix Perottina*
(= *App*).[2] The ingredients are thoroughly jumbled, but most of
App probably came from Phaedrus' fifth and last book.[3] Perotti
deliberately streamlined his texts (simplifying, with imperfect
control of metre). In particular, he regularly cut 'morals', turning
their gist into his own 'titles' instead (thus 5. 5. 1–3 became his
title *PRAVO FAVORE SAEPENUMERO HOMINES LABI*;
cf. 1. 14 in Chapter 6). Extraction of the title 'How tough

knowing someone is' from whatever paratextual frame Phaedrus may have provided for *App* 10 has made it tougher to know Phaedrus, and I'm not sure it *is* specially tough to know Perotti.

But the anecdote has tales to tell anyhow: in particular, any performance will bring out its compelling mimetic properties. Both the lively snapshot of the Soldier's camp gait and vocal style, and the rapid-fire dispatch of the barbarian champion, call for animated delivery: we must match 'squeaky voice and effeminate walk' up with 'softly asks "Permission to proceed?" . . . Authorized . . . to advance to meet the foe . . ., he whipped the enemy's head off his shoulders quicker than words can say, and back he trooped in triumph' (vv. 2, 20, 27–9, *fracte loquendo et ambulando molliter ~ uoce molli 'Licet?' . . . permisit . . . prodire contra. . . . hostis abscidit caput | uictorque rediit*). All this, however, is just byplay compared to the imperative built into the text to act out its highlighted speech-act, the soldier's 'foul oath' and Pompey's reduplication of it: '*So* may my eyes drip away to nothing if . . .' (vv. 11, 33, *Sic . . . oculi exstillescant mei | exstillescant oculi sic . . . mei*). Both times, *sic* guarantees that the script will always enact its foul mission, of putting every reader through the thrill of playing Pompey the Great for a second, just so every one of us Pompeys can foul up when we find the role requires us to play Pompey having to play the joker's part. The freedman Phaedrus could particularly relate to this sketch.[4] Our prejudicial stereotyping has it coming, so he hands us each the custard pie to administer for ourselves. The 'foul oath' stains every reader, for their own good. Stains all Rome.

If this is 'tough' knowledge for somebody to acquire, Perotti's title may turn out, after all, to provide the story with compact but exact programming (and I stand convicted of prejudice against Perotti: and Phaedrus . . .?). For 'Knowing somebody' (*NOSSE HOMINEM*) is all about the powerful knowledge here paraded in the person of Pompey the Great, within the Republican mythology of Roman valour realized by volunteering for monomachy against the unRoman, which is touted as mighty vindication of 'the honour of Roman rule' (v. 31, *laudem Romani imperi*). Summed up in the exchange of a crown and formal acclamation for a soldierly feat, valuation of this valour is set at a generalissimo's whole baggage-train—'finery, gold, and a great haul of silver' (v. 5).

The power that Pompey's oath puts into his recognition of the mess he makes of 'knowing' his trooper is his tribute to the power of that 'somebody', the power to break the stereotype which was backed by a whole regiment: he was 'saddled with the name of a dead-cert. fairy' (v. 3, *famam . . . certissimi*); an army's 'word points at' the trooper, straight and true (v. 6f., *rumor . . . | arguitur*); Pompey 'never credited' his 'somebody', not for a moment (v. 14, *nec credit*). Only when the voice of experience ('one of the more senior members of the generalissimo's staff', v. 22) suggested taking a chance on the nobody ('My own belief is that this man is better trusted to Fortune . . .', v. 23) did the top brass get 'brought under fire', *not* 'for foolhardiness', but for failing at 'knowing a person' (v. 25). Along with 'gasps from the whole onlooking army' (v. 27, *mirante exercitu*).

It's not difficult to see how the intimidating theatre of military discipline looms over the one-off oddball: 'frogmarched to camp HQ', he is brought up before the 'Great Commander-in-Chief', and his imperious 'orders' (*rapitur in praetorium . . . imperator . . . iubet*, vv. 7, 11, 13). In the sequel, what daring he must show even to present himself at that 'desk out front of the tribunal' where the entire team of staff officers is in conclave (v. 19). If the 'soldier's oath' was in the first place improvised 'foul play', then in the finale it is dignified as an extemporized twist to a formal congratulation for heroism above the call of duty, delivered on oath by (arguably) one of the very greatest leaders of men Rome ever produced (vv. 30–4). But no 'straight as they come' simplicity can handle our joker's sinister nighttime bushwhacking and bare-faced lying under oath (v. 12, *uir animi simplicis* ~ vv. 4, 10, *insidiatus nocte . . . in sinistram*). For this 'somebody' is, precisely, 'a human being' (*HOMINEM* in the 'title' . . .). How tough is it to combine the roles of 'soldier' and 'fairy' (vv. 1, 3)? Can a 'disgrace to the camp' be credited with 'nerve on that scale' (vv. 13–14, *dedecus castrorum . . . tantam audaciam*)? How tough is it to tell that 'the man who looked the part of a fairy was really a tower of might' (v. 18)? What are the limits of the human? This *is* the army, Mr Jones.

In the story which rubs in the inescapable logic that 'When the disgraceful thief is a hero, the hero must be a disgraceful thief', the 'somebody' who turns out to be a 'person' is recognized as 'soldier' (vv. 26, 30, 34), and crowned a 'hero' (vv. 30–1: cf. v. 24, *fortem uirum*). Ultimately, the Leader sees how tough (impossible) it is to read humanity: he is Great enough himself to underwrite the lesson of individual idiosyncrasy. The story clinches its final nexus of power and knowledge by acting out empathy: perform the oath, and you'll get the soldier's number instantly.

His big (Great) lie told the truth about him after all. 'Great' Pompey should have *weighed* the evidence more carefully ('Mr Big', *Magnus*, v. 1 ~ 'an enormous physical specimen', *uasti corporis*, v. 1 ~ 'the *great* haul of silver', *magno pondere*, v. 5) How could anyone of his stature rate this giant a featherweight ('no serious loss', v. 24, *iactura* leuis)? Real courage/manliness (*uirtus*) is a matter of 'might', not 'looking the part' (v. 18, *habitu* ~ *uiribus*).

Notice that, at least the way Perotti tells it, the fable dropped a hefty clue along the way about how easily truth gets 'dissipated': when the ~~hero~~'s oath 'spreads round' a handful of spit, this counters the word 'spread round' camp of his Great Muletrain Robbery (vv. 6, 10, *dissipat* | ~ *dissipat* |). Pompey's faithful imitation of the oath proves his eyes are working just fine, at the death.

Now, where did Phaedrus get this story from? Word of mouth, is a best guess. In a similar anecdote in Horace, a soldier of the great Late Republic general Lucullus—presumably on campaign in the 70s BCE in Asia, before replacement by Pompey—explains candidly to his commander that his courage ebbs as his purse fills (*Letters* 2. 2. 26–40):

Robbed of all his savings in his sleep one night, he stormed off and dislodged the royal garrison from their post, and was duly commended and rewarded for it; next time courage was at a premium, the canny roughneck told his officer: 'Someone'll go where you say who's jus' lost 'is belt 'n' braces'.

(*collecta uiatica . . . lassus dum noctu stertit, ad assem* | *perdiderat; . . . clarus ob id factum donis ornatur honestis; . . . uirtus, . . . grandia . . . meritorum praemia; . . . ibit eo quo uis qui zonam perdidit*)

The ancient commentators give circumstantial details which they could *sincerely* derive only from a putative literary source (Sallust, *Histories*?); but the story, involving camp-theft and the anti-heroic presentation of 'glorious' martial exploits, very likely owes its pattern and phlegmatic wit to initial circulation as 'regimental mythology'. In typically cavalier fashion, Phaedrus' grandest editor Louis Havet seized on the story of one Tritanus, a gladiator's son who rose to a barbarian challenge to the might of Pompey's army (Pliny, *Natural History* 7. 81):[5]

The enemy fighting him on challenge he overcame with his right arm—unarmed!—and grabbing him with just one finger carried him back to camp.

Writing about the same time as Phaedrus, Pliny says he took this from Pompey's friend and fellow-campaigner Varro ('in his [lost] compilation "Tales of Prodigious Strength"'). The prodigiously strong—voluminous—writer Varro did indeed march on each and every one of Pompey's expeditions over two decades, down to the First Triumvirate in 60/59 BCE.[6] But in the context of Phaedrus' collection, 'folklore' is the obvious inspiration. The tale is a naughty version of the traditional story-line of 'Hidden depths': heroic feats from a puny or delicate-looking character when no one dreamed he had it in him. It makes a 'foul' tilt at the physiognomic coding of high and mighty society.

Walter Headlam (on Herodas, *Mime* 2. 73) suggested that Phaedrus' story was 'the same in its essential points' as the tale hanging from the proverb 'Needing a haircut on Samos': a paroemiographer (= proverb-compiler) tells how a long-haired Samian boxer was jeered at the Olympics for his Ionian effeminacy, but to the surprise of all won the prize and 'became a proverb'. The Alexandrian scholar Eratosthenes also told how one 'Pythagoras' (a good Samian name), with long hair and purple robes, once silenced the catcalls by scratching from the boys' event and outclassing the adult field.[7]

But in Phaedrus, the refutation of prejudice is dramatized in military terms, brightly coloured from the Roman patriotic tradition, by means of a duel, the traditional 'Single combat to prove valour' of army folklore.[8] *This* 'David' is a felonious, treacherous, perjured ~~fairy~~ of a—marine. The humorous trade-off in gold against steel plays close enough to iconoclastic scoffing at gender coding, to make the fable good and vulgar.

We can appreciate how Pompey's camaraderie in joining the private's earthy ethos stamps the story (ignored, naturally, by all of our Pompey books) as the happy myth of a happy outfit. And we can leave it at that—a popular chief, in line with Mommsen's traditional assessment: 'A good officer, but otherwise of mediocre gifts of intellect and of heart'.[9] This was *exactly* how Sulla found young Pompey:

He had fought a successful battle against three enemy generals, he wrote; he would take it as a great honour if I could spare the time to visit his camp. The messenger—primed, it now occurs to me, by Pompeius himself—went on at great length about his general's personal courage: how *he had single-handed engaged a gigantic Gaulish cavalryman*, and led the attack to victory.

. . . His camp was a model of military discipline . . . Pompeius himself strode forward in front of the ranks, flushed and handsome, and hailed me loudly, in the ritual formula, as a triumphing general. His men roared their sudden approval, stamping the ground and hammering on their shields. . . .

'You must speak to the men, sir', Pompeius said. He was trembling with pleasure. When he raised his hand there was instant silence. He had them well trained.[10]

Horace and Phaedrus telling frontier tales of Lucullus and Pompey must mean more than this, however. These were the last times that Rome could possibly take the form of a citizen army of soldier mates, off in the wild slogging it out to win the empire. Already distorted into the long-term command of a professional army cohering around personal loyalty to their marshal, these regiments wound the world up until the Republic cracked apart in successive convulsions of civil war. Next in line would be Julius Caesar, who would make the crucial move from traditional scourge of barbarian Gaul to invader of his own country, with campaign-hardened troops ready to fight for (control of) Rome.[11] Julius would muck in with his Caesarian *commilitones*. After Actium, Caesar Augustus would bar the appellation (Suetonius, *Life of Augustus* 25. 1). From a (post-)Augustan perspective, therefore, Phaedrus' story comes to read as a nostalgic, or at any rate evocative, flashback to Rome before the Caesars, to the Republic's legions conquering in the footsteps of Alexander.

Under the superannuated Emperors Tiberius and physically

challenged Claudius or the boy Caesars Gaius and Nero, these glimpses of 'Greatness' in action, back when *imperator* still meant playing *dux* in the front line of that 'Roman empire' without an emperor (vv. 4, 19; 11; 31), would keep traditional discourse on Roman dignity and distinction alive as the fund of thinking over the new realities of autocracy. Standing garrisons arrayed across the provinces, with a centralized command-structure radiating from the palace, imply a shift in the definition of power. But if the militaristic ideology signified by the iconic charisma of a dashing Roman Alexander was obsolete, stories of the past kept it as indispensable as ever: soldier emperors alongside their 'buddies' kept *uirtus* as muscular masculinity intact as the bottom-line of Roman pride.[12]

In this sense, the hand-to-hand fighting showcased in Phaedrus' monomachy, with its dual vindication of (howsoever disguised) 'manliness' and/as superiority over uncivilized humanity, uses Pompey to tell tales on the Caesars. The wrinkle that a Greekling freedman from the palace should be the one harking back to olden times—to present a dubious patriot with the only kind of *crown* a Roman should ever have seen fit to tolerate, at the hands of the only kind of *imperator* Rome should have ever known . . .—only underlines the eternal coding of Pompey, since Caesar crossed the Rubicon in 49 BCE, as the Other of Julius Caesar.[13] Even especially when we picture young Pompeius back in the beyond, before his warring turned sick, he signifies 'not-Caesar', and *Magnus* is the sign of Rome-without-Emperors, a resistant, recalcitrant, recusant reproach to the future: ~~Caesar~~; and ~~Caesars~~.

vv. 1–6

The last Roman we shall meet in this book, the last Roman in our Phaedrus editions, and with some claim to be one of history's last Romans, besides, the Conqueror Cn. Pompeius Magnus was rehabilitated by Octavian once his sons were liquidated: a Cn. Pompeius was already suffect consul for 31 BCE, the year of Actium; Augustus himself contrived to die in a year dated by a consular Sex. Pompeius.[14] At the Emperor's funeral, Pompey's image attested Caesarian triumph (Dio, *Roman history* 56. 34. 2). One of Tiberius' special in-house (senate-house) jokes makes 'Pompey' signify dead ancient history (Suetonius, *Life of Tiberius* 57. 2):

Tiberius threatened to clap an equestrian Pompeius in irons; he assured him he'd stop being Pompeius and become a Pompeian—a bitter jibe doubling up the man's name and the long ago debacle of the party for a pasting (*ueterem . . . partium fortunam*).

Of course this would actually keep 'Pompey' live, and politi-cally active; and his image, paraded by descendants for the purpose, could be guaranteed still to wring tears from the People of Tiberius' Rome (Tacitus, *Annals* 3. 23). Mean-while, his terminal/inaugural role as the last non-Caesarian Republican gave him vast and continuing currency in the self-conceptualization of Rome. When Pompey's elder son took *Magnus* for *praenomen*, it was the last time that 'greatness' still measured itself by Alexander, before eclipse by the Latin rendering '*Caesar*'.

The label was given him soon after 80 BCE—by Sulla? by his troops in acclamation?; or as flattery from his staff? 'Greatness' rightly got Pompey stick, in his day: as when the tragic actor had to encore his script's line 'Through our misery art thou great' a thousand times (Cicero, *Letters to Atticus* 2. 19. 3, '*nostra miseria tu es magnus*').[15] But he survived, for real, in his literal shaping of the Roman world: 'He won many battles, sub-jugated many princes and kings both by war and by treaty . . ., and established and organized most of the nations of the conti-nent of Asia with their own laws and constitutions, so that even to this day they still use Pompey's laws' (Dio, *Roman History* 37. 20. 2). And, from day one, death in defeat made Pompey everything no Emperor can ever be: 'I am incapable of *not* feeling pain at his fall: I knew him as a person of integrity, decent and grave' (Cicero, *Letters to Atticus* 11. 6. 5). If losing absolved, even sanctified, Pompey, naturally, it also gets him stick for letting Caesar win, for not stopping the Caesars![16]

As noticed already, every available resource for variation is utilized in this narrative of confrontation.[17] The first pairing, of *Magnus* and *miles uasti corporis* (v. 1), decisively undermines the portrait of the private's standing in camp.[18] *We* couldn't be more surely informed, where Pompey can only guess (wrong) what sort of thief he should envisage. Most (Roman) readers would *still* subscribe to the incompatibility of heroism with the look of a fairy, prejudice or not. This is what happens to Pompey.

A big brute among legionaries must be really huge.[19] But this one's manner—voice and walk—were sure signs of effeminacy: 'the softies known by Greeks as κίναιδοι have a sort-of minced voice, . . . and move the body the way women do' (*Physiognomic writers* 2. 134 Förster).[20] Anything *but* a 'broken' voice is meant—some falsetto effect is intended—but the ethical over-tones are the important ones.[21] In the would-be highly stylized sociality of Graeco-Roman culture, deviance was elaborately coded and stigmatized: a sway at the hip could ruin a man's everything.[22]

In the army, we would expect aggressive suspicion of sexual preference for passive relations to police and purge every unit round the clock and the planet. From what (little) we *hear*, it seems that, despite long service and technical disability to marry, '*Nothomosexualität*' or any other construction of sexual relations between the troops, barely showed up; where sexual offences do get a mention, they announce drastic penalties for *stuprum cum masculo*, or celebrate the repulsion of lusting officers pulling rank.[23] Roman soldiers must do what their officers tell them—even endure humiliating beatings as if they were not men; but their *uirtus* must stay proof against sexual violation.[24] Isn't Phaedrus' story saying (it is) that 'It takes a *man* to make a killing'? The Campanian Badius' challenge to Quinctius Crispinus of Rome says it best: 'If you're a *man*, step this way' (Livy 25. 18. 11, '*si uir esset, congrederetur*').

Our larger-than-life villain doesn't just indulge in grand larceny—beyond the normal petty thieving of Horace's Lucullan story—his swag is so exaggerated, he'd have a job stashing, or even fencing, it away.[25] In the mountain of 'purple and gold' plus 'a (great) weight of silver and gold',[26] along with the vital military transport, 'mule-train, and all',[27] Pompey's soldier is stealing his general's stupendous version of 'kit' (*sarcinas . . . meas*, v. 34). The glorious feat of arms (the duel, *not* the heist), with Pompey's honour in the balance, will make him worth his weight in praise—he already has his reward, in advance![28]

vv. 6–14

Camp gossip fastforwards us into our first visit to the C-in-C's tent (*arguitur miles, rapitur in praetorium*).[29] 'Rumour' *sounds* still less reassuring than 'reputation' did (*famam*, v. 3). But rules are there to be broken (in narrative and on camp...aign).

Pompey's brief query establishes him as the popular general who does his men proud and expects no less in return.[30] *Commilito* is part of the affective colouring, for 'Isn't [the good ruler] alone empowered to address the troops as "buddies"?' (Dio Chrysostom, *Speeches* 1. 22, συστρατιώτας). The Roman legion was becoming a closed society, sealed from exterior ties and reach, a network for life.[31]

The private's instant response to his 'Commander' underlines his 'nerve' (Pompey's last word, *ausus*, and his last thought, *audaciam*, vv. 9, 14).[32] Phaedrus vigorously polarizes 'the hero, always straight as they come', against 'that disgrace to the camp' (vv. 12–13). Caught, the camp-thief faced the bastinado; short of that, any formal shaming before the regiment was (officially) a mighty deterrent.[33] But the tricksy 'pathic fairy' is merely removed from Pompey's eyesight—a passive lump of waste (*propelli*, v. 13 ~ *eici*, v. 20).[34]

So to the 'foul oath' (v. 33, *turpe . . . iusiurandum*), a curiosity of vulgarity without close parallel. A similar gesture comes from a(nother) 'barbarian': 'Vagises, the oldest of the ambassadors, laughed and showed the middle of his upturned hand: "From here," he said, "hairs will sprout before you shall see Seleucia"' (Plutarch, *Life of Crassus* 13. 2). Spitting *per se* was, ordinarily (you could say), normal behaviour (Aristippus in *Vatican Gnomology* 25); but in a solemn denial, up before Pompey the Great, there is shame(lessness) in the backwater flourish.[35] The spittle forms (we could pretend to know) part of a 'mock-blinding ritual'. Eyes are favourite guarantors of oaths, and this story underlines why this should be, for 'if ever I clapped eye or set finger on the stuff' (v. 12, *si uidi aut tetigi*) at once pretends to leave no loophole, by adding eye-witness to physical handling so as to make denial of all 'knowledge' into total—wide-eyed—innocence. 'Eyes that melt into tears' were a commonplace notion, but eyes 'turning to droplets' which you could smear away in your palm suggests a 'folk'-conception of the eye as 'made of water'. Some ancient scientists agreed. And the same logic could be found, in reverse, in a healing miracle starring Vespasian: 'He would restore the eyes, if he spat in them' (Suetonius, *Life of Vespasian* 7. 2). The catchy manual simulation also works into the equation the physical 'handling' under denial—and about to be proved in combat (*si . . . tetigi*, v. 12 ~ *fidens manu*, v. 15).[36]

VV. 15–16

From the bizarre initial situation, we slip, in no time at all, into a familiar and recurrent scenario, in which our weirdo can play truer than true, and beat the system at its own game.[37] The clash of organized Roman unit with savage border-tribe, hungry to prove its braves men by single combat, was a natural setting for Roman tales of individual valour, with schematic moves knitting together a discourse on bravery, plus lashings of distinctively Roman ethos. If historical, Phaedrus' monomachy would be the last *proper* instance known to us, in a distinguished line reaching back to how 'How Manlius Torquatus won his torc, and his honorary *cognomen*', in 367/361 BCE, and 'How Livy's definitive *Foundation of Rome* won its spurs, and rose to the occasion' (Livy 7. 9. 6–10. 14):[38]

Then an exceptional physical specimen of a Gaul . . . stepped forward and, in the loudest voice he could summon, he said: 'The bravest man Rome now has, come let him step forward and fight, so that the outcome of our duel may show which of the two nations is the better in war.' For a long time there was silence among the foremost Roman braves, as they both feared to refuse the contest, and were reluctant to go for this extra-dangerous hazard. Then Titus Manlius . . . left his post to set off for the dictator, and said, 'My commander, without the word from you, I should never fight out of formation.' Then the dictator said, 'A blessing on your courage and your respect for father and fatherland, Titus Manlius. Set off and, with the gods' help, show the invincibility of the name "Rome".' [After the duel] The dictator laid on presentation of a golden crown, and treated the fight to a wonderful tribute at a full meeting.

(*tum eximia corporis magnitudine . . . Gallus processit et quantum maxima uoce potuit, 'Quem nunc', inquit, 'Roma uirum fortissimum habet, procedat agedum ad pugnam, ut noster duorum euentus ostendat utra gens bello sit melior.' diu inter primores iuuenum Romanorum silentium fuit cum et abnuere certamen uererentur et praecipuam sortem periculi petere nollent; tum T. Manlius . . . ex statione ad dictatorem pergit, 'Iniussu tuo', inquit, 'imperator, extra ordinem numquam pugnauerim . . .'. tum dictator, 'Macte uirtute', inquit . . ., 'ac pietate in patrem patriamque, T. Manli, esto. perge et nomen Romanum inuictum iuuantibus dis praesta.'. . . dictator coronam auream addidit donum mirisque pro contione eam pugnam laudibus tulit.)*

These Roman tales vindicate the 'manli(us)ness' of the disciplined world of culture, taking on nature at its own game, and (they said) winning. In history (we presume) monomachy did serve, on occasion, as a significant battle prelude which might inspire or deflate a tribal horde; Romans would have to be more phlegmatic. The vaunting champion laid low is of course a story pattern spread far and wide: the initiative comes from Goliath (v. 16), who displays rippling muscles in whole-hearted self-possession (this is his destiny: ready to take on all-comers),[39] if not bloodcurdling weaponry, and a stream of threats, boasts and insults to match.[40]

VV. 17–21

'Muttering' from the Roman side matches the initial 'rumour' that first brought private to Pompey. Shame befalls the rest, so the [shameless] ᾿hero᾿ can make his dramatic entry, and save the day: οἱ δ' ἄρα πάντες ἀκὴν ἐγένοντο σιωπῇ· | αἴδεσθεν μὲν ἀνήνασθαι, δεῖσαν δ' ὑποδέχθαι· | ὀψὲ δὲ δὴ Μενέλαος ἀνίστατο . . . (Homer *Iliad* 7. 92–4, after *the* Hectoring: 'They all fell quite silent, | ashamed to decline, afraid to take it on. | In the end, up stood Menelaus . . .'), Manlius in Livy 7. 10. 1 (above) and esp. in Claudius Quadrigarius (cited by Gellius, *Nights of Athens* 9. 13), *Gallus inridere coepit atque linguam exertare. . . . [Manlius] processit neque passus est uirtutem Romanam ab Gallo turpiter spoliari*, etc (translated below).[41]

In this second confrontation, the screwball personifies the God of War, on his way to vindicate patriarchal masculinity for Rome: in a word, *uirtus*.[42] This time he comes up when every-one else is skulking, to face Pompey deliberating with advisers at his 'desk', on the front of the platform next to the *praetorium*. This is where the presentation will be made, too, before the ranks massed in the camp *forum* (vv. 30 f.). No soldier story without the officers muscling in on the glory.[43] The soldier's words, or rather, his word, should *sound* like deference as well as effeminacy; but his *'licet?'*, the request for leave to quit the ranks, should (somehow) ring out, loud and clear as a sergeant-major, for this is the classic point of Roman discipline on parade: as when Claudius Asellus accepts a challenge, 'only delaying to request of the consul whether he had leave to fight the enemy challenger out of formation; on his permission, he at once took up arms . . .' (Livy 23. 47. 1, *id modo moratus ut consulem percunctaretur liceretne extra ordinem in prouocantem hostem pugnare, permissu eius arma extemplo cepit . . .*; so too Crispinus, *tantum moratus dum imperatores consuleret permitterentne sibi extra ordinem in prouocantem hostem pugnare, permissu eorum arma cepit . . .*, 25. 18. 12). The vital point of principle (of *ordo*) was enshrined with proverbial status in the context of monomachy: Livy 7. 10. 2 (above: cf. Oakley (1998) ad loc.) already foreshadows the mirror-image reversal scheduled to arrive in the next generation, when another young Manlius will forget to ask *his* commander, namely his father Torquatus, will return in triumph from the duel, and . . . will pay with his head (Livy 8. 7). Hence the saying: 'the orders of a Manlius'.[44]

But Pompey *still* doesn't know what story he is in, he has no time for his private, dismisses him out of hand, engrossed in the dire prospect for morale, and the shame it brings Rome.[45] He can't know, as Phaedrus' readers must, that Roman heroism fizzled out in Livy's later books, in the Late Republic, leaving rich pickings for parody, satire, cynicism . . . If Pompey's day dates the mockery of military tradition, how much farther removed from the old ways are the subjects of Tiberius?

Shame is, however, the primordial stock-in-trade of the duellist, responding to the insults of a barbarian challenge, 'mockery and (Maori-style) sticking-in-out of the tongue: . . . Manlius would not brook Roman manliness being shamefully spoilt, and despoiled (*turpiter spoliari*)' (Claudius Quadrigarius (above); so too Crispinus, *ne impune insultare Campanum pateretur*, Livy 25. 18. 11). Grand Livy's 'prudishness and

concern for dignity' has him squirm at Torquatus' Gaul's foul
tonguing (Oakley (1998) on Livy 7. 10. 5) and, its correlative,
Torquatus' equally foul beheading of the Gaul (cue Bowdler:
Oakley cuts a note ad loc. on Livy's note that he has cut his
source's atrocity: *corpus ab omni alia uexatione intactum*, 7. 10.
11). The tactless and tasteless tactic of Phaedrus' low-down
anecdote, breaking rules of propriety to create fun, is to exult in
waving foulness our way—spitting in our eye, and carving up
our corpse. Disgust won't spoil this fight. Rather, gusto is spoil-
ing for the fight, and will be fighting for the spoil.

What the fight spoils, though, is Rome. For the story reads,
or can read, as putting paid to those old legends of *uirtus*, with
its undeniable visualization of the reality of heroism, the only
uir fortis there can ever have been, short of propaganda. For—
mustn't those Manlii of yore have been oddballs, too? They
must have been a match for giant savages, to stand a chance
(says the sceptic in us all), and if a psychopath is wanted, a
sociopath is no bad bet. If these Rambo hulks were let out of
camp, it *must* have been because they were expendable—accept-
able losses . . .?

VV. 22–7

The anonymous elder, cement common in all storytelling,[46]
talks horse-sense set out over three generous lines. As well as
leaking the sort of managerial calculation that governs the
performance of cannon-fodder wannabe heroes, outside uplift-
ing mythology, his cynical/pragmatic/manipulative counsel
puts into words (and shields from the ignominy) Pompey's
utterly wrong-headed misreading of his man. The story's satire
bites here: why (we shall wonder, *next time*) is it that the most
sensible advice always turns out to be such tosh? For example,
Augustus used to tell anyone in range of hearing, including
himself: 'A safe general beats a daring general' (Suetonius *Life
of Augustus* 25. 4: Euripides, *Phoenician Women* 599, Ἀσφαλὴς
γὰρ ἐστ' ἀμείνων ἢ θρασὺς στρατηλάτης).[47]

VV. 27–34

The army's 'amazement' amplifies and caps the responses that stake out the story, from 'repute' and 'rumour', through 'muttering' and 'counsel', toward Pompey's final shock of recognition. The duel serves, before all, as cockpit of manhood as pugilism: e.g. 'Wonder overtook both onlooking horsetamer Trojans and well-greaved Achaeans' (Homer, *Iliad* 3. 342 f., θάμβος δ' ἔχεν εἰσορόωντας | Τρῶας θ' ἱπποδάμους καὶ ἐϋκνήμιδας Ἀχαιούς), 'both armies looking on', Claudius Quadrigarius (quoted by Gellius 9. 13, *utroque exercitu inspectante*), and, yes, 'both armies looking on' (Valerius Maximus *Paradigms* 3. 2. 24, *inspectante utroque exercitu*), etc.[48] Where the monomachy is a prelude to pitched battle, the result is, 1 Samuel 18: 52, 'And the men of Israel and Judah arose and shouted and pursued the Philistines . . .'.

Indescribable speed, as well as cueing drama, finesses protracted narration: for duels, cf. Livy 23. 47. 5, *dicto prope citius*, De Vaux (1959) 457.[49] Pompey's heterodox private is (uniquely) a deviant David, who matches his Goliath in bulk.[50] Decapitation elsewhere follows the barbarian's downfall, as in 'David ran, and stood upon the Philistine, and took *his* sword, . . . and cut off his head therewith' (1 Samuel 18: 51), or 'when he overturned him, he hacked off the head, tore off the torc' (Claudius Quadrigarius, quoted by Gellius 9. 13: source for Livy 7's Torquatus, Oakley (1998) note ad loc.). The spot of savagery settles the score by literal cutting down to size.

The return for salutation completes the spectacle (*uictor . . . rediit*, v. 29 ~ Livy 23. 47. 7, *uictor in castra redit*, etc.; cf. 7. 10. 12, *Romani . . . ad dictatorem perducunt*, with Oakley (1998) ad loc.). 'The winner of a single combat which followed a challenge was allowed to take the *spolia* of his defeated opponent home'.[51] Formal encomium before the assembled troops turns the feat 'above and beyond the call of duty' into a story— to crown past exploits and decorations, as in Livy 7. 10. 14 (above: with Oakley (1998) ad loc.).[52] More tangibly, the encomium functioned performatively as official donation of (symbolic, but no less material) reward for merit: the terms for civic excellence were marked with *un*civil tokens, as a duellist took a (momentary ~~emperor~~'s) gilt crown for promoting the prowess of Rome (e.g. Livy 7 (above)).[53]

Pompey, however, must turn, not to his private's past glories, but to his privateer's recent crimes. The historical Pompey was proud of his early campaigns—'always serving under his own command'! At the critical moment of Caesar's invasion of Italy in 49 BCE, this pride was summed up in his last vaunt: 'Wherever I stamp on the ground in Italy, there will rise up forces of both infantry and cavalry.'[54] Swearing like a trooper, the story's Pompey does more than make his private's bare-faced and fraudulent foulness his own, by casting his citation in the form of a re-citation of the oath palmed off on him at the earlier eye-balling; he also gets down to the ~~hero~~'s level by dubbing his baggage-train his 'kit-bag' (*sarcinas . . . meas*, v. 34). For the men, kit meant heavy packs humped on a 'forked pole'. The footsloggers' jokey nickname, 'Marius' mules', came from their being 'yoked' to this pole.[55]

6(a)

6(b)

6
Talent-Spotting: *King Demetrius* meets the *Poet Menander* (5. 1)

Demetrius qui dictus est Phalereus
Athenas occupauit imperio improbo.
ut mos est uulgi, passim et certatim ruit,
'Feliciter!', succlamant; ipsi principes
illam osculantur qua sunt oppressi manum   5
tacite gementes tristem fortunae uicem;
quin etiam resides et sequentes otium,
ne defuisse noceat, repunt ultimi.
    in quis Menander nobilis comoediis,
quas ipsum ignorans legerat Demetrius   10
et admiratus fuerat ingenium uiri,
unguento delibutus, uestitu fluens,
ueniebat gressu delicato et languido.
    hunc ubi tyrannus uidit extremo agmine,
'Quisnam cinaedus ille in conspectum meum   15
audet uenire?' responderunt proximi,
'Hic est Menander scriptor'. mutatus statim,
'Homo', inquit, 'fieri non potest formosior!'

[QUOMODO SAEPE FALLATUR HOMINUM IUDICIUM][1]

The Demetrius known as 'the Phalerean'
has taken Athens over, in the grip of his nasty régime:
the rabble converges in typical fashion from all over,
    stampedes in a race for it—
up goes the cry, 'Hip-, hip-. . .'; the luminaries, too,
plant kisses upon the hand which has smothered them,   5
silently bemoaning the sad turn of fortune;
why, even the quietist lot, devotees of the contemplative life,
come crawling along at the back, just in case harm comes of
    being missed.

In among 'em was Menander, a celebrity thanks to his
     comedies.
These Demetrius had read, without ever getting to know
     their author in person,   10
and he'd been impressed by the man's talent . . .
Swimming in unguent and gliding along in his robes,
along came Menander, effete enervation written in his every
     step.
     Once the tyrant spotted him at the end of the queue,
he snapped, 'Who's that fairy there think he is   15
to have the nerve to offend my eyesight?' Replied his
     entourage,
'That's *him*—Menander the writer'. Instant transformation:
the tyrant went on, 'There can be no one to touch him for
     looks'.

[How people's judgement is often deceived]

Now for the legacy of Greece; we have left Roman names
behind us. The story for this chapter is Phaedrus' only sur-
viving tale set in (legendary) Hellenistic Greek history. In
book 4 he presented a brace of widely-circulated anecdotes
about the archaic lyric poet Simonides; 4. 23 stresses how
fame brings a writer friends from afar, wherever they may land
up, and with them a specially blessed buoyancy proof against
misfortune: 'All that's mine comes with me'; 4. 26 tells how
nobles who refused full payment for a victory poem because it
dwelt on blessing the gods, were crushed when their royal
house collapsed upon them, whereas the poet was saved by a
mysterious visitation that called him to the door at the crucial
moment. Put these together and you might recognize the con-
tours of another poet proudly struggling to juggle dependence
and independence, in the teeth of less-than-ideal patrons within
the orbit of an unstable court (Ch. 3). The confrontation of poet
and prince in 5. 1 repeats this very scenario, within a single
story.
     We might suppose that our fabulist in verse shares not that
many traits with the fabulous comic playwright Menander,
whose hundred and more scripts put him among the two or
three most widely read authors through each century of the
Roman Empire. And if the jump from Menander's Athens to

Phaedrus' Thracian origins (Ch. 3) may shrink for a fable's sake, the kaleidoscopic shifts of power among the princes who competed for a slice of Alexander's empire do not *automatically* double for the dynasty of Julio-Claudian Caesars. And yet . . .

The link provided between 5. 1 and the preceding editorial reflection which texts of Phaedrus distinguish from '4 *Epil.*', to stand for '5 *Praef.*' in the absence of any more plausible shift, speaks to the question of what Phaedrus may be hoping to get said with his Athens. He just returned to the subject of 'Aesop's name—the word "Aesop", his fame, what "Aesop" means, his significance' (|| *Aesopi nomen*, 5. *Praef.* 1). To tell us that Phaedrus long since paid him his due: at this stage of the game, Phaedrus merely utilizes 'Aesop' as a designer label, just the way that contemporary artists attribute their works to classic masters, so as to combat prejudice against living talent (vv. 1–9). This point fresh in mind, readers are plugged straight into Athens, with the bridge 'But now I'm headed for a fable of this sort of tenor' (v. 10, *sed iam ad fabellam talis exempli feror*). So blank a formulation that it invites us to seek *whatever* connection, weak or strong, we may find between the reflections on strategic naming we have just read, and the anecdote they prelude.

Certainly there is a comic twist in the tale, from the moment that the Greekling Phaedrus names the prince who will boss the story, and deliver its punch-line. For at once we plunge, inescapably, into a veritable reign of error. Phaedrus himself— it is pretty unlikely that he passes on a blunder made by a Greek predecessor—sets the scene by glossing his prince 'Demetrius' as 'the Phalerean', whereas the story to come squares, not with that astounding Athenian citizen and freedman's son, who somehow arose to serve as puppet governor of Athens, but with the dashing and meteoric Demetrius nicknamed 'The Besieger' (*Poliorcetes*) to distinguish him from the scrum of other Demetrii who popped up in the wreckage of Alexander's world empire. By a disconcerting coincidence, Phaedrus also sins in the scansion of the offending adjective 'the Phalerean': many an editor has tried to spare him the *distractio* involved in counting *Phalereus* | as the quadrisyllable *Phalereüs* |. To make matters worse, we owe the punch line (omitted by MSS PR[Vi]) to Perotti, and we are also left to gather, from Perotti's 'title',

something of what Phaedrus' lost *epimythium* may have proposed to bid us conclude from the story: 'How people's judgement is often deceived'. What a mess, all told! But well worth
bearing with. (That's *my* story, anyhow; but 'how often . . .'.)

The reflexive satirical bite latent in this notice of prevalent
human prejudice once again menaces readers alongside
characters (cf. 5. 5, in Ch. 4 *Appendix*). If Menander carries off
his walk-on part bathed in the lurid light that an untouchable
favourite can relish, (arguably) the tyrant shows adroit reflexes,
which allow him to about-turn on the instant, without the
slightest loss of composure. So whose side is the story on?
Where does it put *us*? Does this parading promenade in the eye
of the tiger show the prince as both cleancut and cultured—
another Pompey (Ch. 5)? Or is this the tyrant's turn to play the
flatterer (*vs.* Ch. 1)? And if he does, is he making a doomed
lunge to cover up boorish ignorance, and retrieve his good
name; or does he change his tune—but from virulent scorn to
sarcastic mock-appreciation? Beware of your implication in the
upshot of whatever decision you make on this.

And as the fable flips about on you, be sure to spare a
moment to think through what sort of a mess people now find
themselves in when they have supposed that the *Aesopeia* which
Phaedrus is versifying was the single book listed among the out-
put of Demetrius of Phaleron (Diogenes Laertius, *Lives of the
philosophers* 5. 80): what, the question now arises, could have
induced Phaedrus to retell this as *Demetrius' own story about
himself*, rather than about the Besieger?[2] And, while we're on
the subject of names and namesakes, names at stake and the
stakes of naming, we can fairly guess that Phaedrus won't have
known of the 'moderate' Athenian statesman Phaedrus actively
involved in political negotiations with Demetrius Poliorcetes in
the 290s.[3] But his blurring of Demetrii can but add further
resonance to his portrait of a city forced to crawl on its
knees before a petty tyrant. More than failure to get the story
('hisstory') straight, the moral, however unintended, would
clearly be to the effect that there's *very* little to choose between
one Demetrius and another. The Phalerean and the Poliorcete
were more similar figures than most, having lorded over Athens,
lived in magnificence, and ended their careers in spectacular
failure: the prince, 'besieged by Fortune' (Dio Chrysostom,

Speeches 64. 22, πολιορκούμενος), drank himself to death after defeat, surrender, and capture, by his rivals; the philosopher left for Egypt and exile (to become—if you can swallow it— head of the Alexandrian library). Similar tales could be told of the pair; and, for example, the legendary hetaera Lamia seems to switch Demetrii, too.[4]

For Phaedrus to put the name *Demetrius* in the window, and remind us (willy nilly) that it was a 'generic name', spelling temporary, partial, and precarious ascendancy, in a politics now eclipsed by the intrusion of Rome, is not to say anything that *remotely* concerns the rule of the Julio-Claudian Caesares Augusti, which in Phaedrus' day had achieved apparently per-manent, total, and secure domination, for a single genealogy of just two or three princes. Yet the narrative of the mortifying prostration of Athens the home of freedom is told as a routine, a processional of ritual abasement, which *precisely* prequels the parades showcased by imperial Roman historians to lacerate the humiliation of their city beneath the tyranny that more than recalled the deplorable ways of despised post-Alexandrian Greek decadence (Tacitus, *Annals* 1. 7. 1):

But at Rome there plunged into slavery consuls, senators, knights and all. The greater each person's public exposure, the more counter-feit and in a hurry they were, fixing their faces to prevent joy at the emperor's decease or an overdose of sadness at the emperor's honey-moon, as they blurred tears/happiness with laments/flattery.

(*at Romae ruere in servitium consules patres eques; quanto quis inlustrior tanto magis falsi ac festinantes uultuque composito ne laeti excessu principis neu tristiores primordio lacrimas gaudium, questus adulationem miscebant.*)

To put this more strongly, élite Romans had for generations lived with the notion that they were given Athens' tracks to follow, and must think their own destiny in terms of proximity to, and distance from, the Athenian precedent. Whether a Roman reader had personally been shipped off to study in Athens, or was transported there by books, was immaterial; all manner of theorizing, and not least political thought, clung to the cultural scene of its origination, and this has served as a ruse of oblique pertinence for fables of power anywhere in the West ever since. Witness the saddling of Roman *imperium* on the

Greek *tyrannus* in Phaedrus' Graeco-Roman parable (vv. 2, 14). For, *as fable*, 5. 1 is no record or trace of a historical incident from what we term 'Early Hellenistic' turmoil; rather, the story rehearses a collision between blatant power and apparent powerlessness, as a provocative type-scene which folds the writing and reading of the story into its burden.

If Phaedrus has found another shameful fairy he can use as cover for his own bid to step into the public eye, setting his low-down comic sketch to send up the posh classic, he has also again shown how hierarchies construct the very conditions for their own inversion (Ch. 5). For his own sake, and for all of us, Phaedrus is promulgating the noble lie which holds that great leaders want to be great readers. So when a Demetrius lines up the social pyramid, he puts the writer last in *his* books; but lovely Menander is top of *our* class, and writes inconsequential Demetrius into the wings. Instead of ruling the roost, the prince becomes bibliophily's latest convert—a full half of the story after the rest of us acknowledged that Menander is forever the master of comic relief (v. 9).[5] When the fable's ~~Caesar~~ finally commands our attention with his ʾwisecrackʾ, the tables turn on him (as in the *epimythium* behind 'How people's judgement is often deceived'), and it is the red-nosed master of ceremonies who winds up getting it, courtesy of the prettified satiric hero, Menander: the laughing stock who puts seriousness in the dock. So we can salute our prince—as the puppet of our study in irony. And, yes, ultimately, by all means, in Rome ~~Demetrius~~ is *all about* telling tales on Caesar: when Phaedrus was brushing up his anecdote, no royals in uniform were falling about trying to get a piece of his street cred. in the empire of books; but at the same time, historians of Julio-Claudian mortification a-plenty *were* busy chewing their nails trying to pen the original tableaux that inspired the definitive vision produced by their successor Tacitus . . .

VV. 1–8

In Rome, the encyclopaedic literary output of Demetrius of Phalerum (Cicero, *On the Laws* 3. 14, *Phalereus ille Demetrius*) made him a better-known figure[6] than his royal namesake, the dashing crown prince Demetrius Poliorcetes. Phaedrus has evidently himself intruded the (nickname) *Phalereus* into his inherited tale, for educated contemporaries would see at once that the story is impossible for the Peripatetic philosopher-*cum*-puppet ruler, but fits 'that vile name' of the Besieger.[7] The occasion imagined for the confrontation, which presumably originated as 'biographical' lore rather later in the Hellenistic period, would be *Poliorcetes*' entry to Athens in 307 BCE from Piraeus, to restore Athenian liberty, as it was put, in the name of his father King Antigonus. The retiring opposition was extremely illustrious, the ousted leader *Demetrius of Phalerum* having in his *dekaëtia* (decade) as Cassander's stooge-governor attempted to realize a modest version of the Platonic 'philosopher-king', on Peripatetic lines. The school was involved in his fall, but his profession saved its poet Menander (Diogenes Laertius, *Lives of the Philosophers* 5. 79). The pro-Antigonid party made the coup a 'sad' day for Athens (v. 6) by setting in motion a hitherto unequalled display of self-abasement. Meantime, faced with the Phalerean in our text, *we* can hardly deny Phaedrus' historical confusion.[8] There are no *sure* parallels for the *distractio* (pulling apart, of the diphthong into two syllables) in *Phalereüs*, between the trimeter of Accius with *faciet Peleüs* | and Pentadius' *Theseüs Hippolyto . . .*[9]

With Theophrastus, Epicurus, Zeno, and Menander and his comedian rivals all active in Athens (plus their legendary women, Lamia, Glycera, and the rest), Stilpon at Megara and Crates in Thebes, the generation took a large slice of exemplary and anecdotal traditions in the Greek world. All of Demetrius Poliorcetes' occupations of Athens were marked by a gush of ceremonial honours, as in 307 BCE, when the Besieger was about to land, and 'the people gave loud applause and yelled acclamation, addressing him as benefactor and messiah', but most of the excesses, such as the notorious ithyphallic hymn regaling 'that sun, with all his friends orbiting round him—an awesome vision', belong to the late 290s. Poliorcetes' ostentatious display, à la Alexander, would make him an important prototype for the public relations of Caesarism.[10]

Phaedrus means to get across the wholesale helplessness when the jackboot comes to town: in the initial keynote *imperio improbo* (v. 2: 'in the grip of his nasty régime'), as often,

alliterative phrasing[11] subtends semantic convergence, as if
imperium = *improbum*, and *improbum* = *imperium*; indeed, this is
what this fable treats as its fundamental axiom, to the bitter-
sweet end. Just as important, he means to treat this early
instance of the recurrent scene of the 'spontaneous' mass reception organized for the arrival of conquerors and governors in
the footsteps of Alexander as a cliché—a familiar routine, anywhere in the Roman world, not least in the cosmopolis itself.[12]
This is made explicit at the outset, with the phrase 'in typical
fashion' (v. 3, *ut mos est uulgi*); and then acted out in the sick
parody of a civic procession which has 'the rabble' in the
vanguard, 'stampeding', then 'the luminaries' (who *should*
come first: v. 4, *principes*), before finally 'the quietist lot . . .
come crawling along' to bring up the rear (vv. 7 f.: last, where
they mean to stay, *ultimi*). In the world of the *Diadochoi*,
submission to the potentate currently in the ascendant was
presented with rich pageantry as the acclamation of a 'god on
earth' (*deus praesens*), whose epiphany was to be the 'salvation'
of the polis.[13]

Picture *first* the general rush (down into degradation) in one
single mass movement (*ruit*), then waves of cheering as successive groups take up the cry (*succlamant*, v. 4).[14] At centre-stage,
taking responsibility for the city they represent, the leaders
submit to the (proverbial) degradation of kissing the oppres-
sor's right hand, (as if) in veneration (v. 5)—all the more
degrading for being proverbial.[15] The long-suffering Athenians
became experts at putting on a good show for Hellenistic over-
lords, dramatizing the takeover as a divine κατάβασις (descent
to earth).[16] Athens indeed kept its 'free' status precisely so that
the home of ἐλευθερία (freedom) could 'freely' acclaim each
merciful saviour. But, in Athens the home of free speech,
nobody needed telling that one and all had 'Joy in their Looks
and Gall in their Hearts', each and every time they were forced
to witness another 'sad day' in their history (v. 6).[17]

When the story gets to the end of the queue, Phaedrus goes
out of his way to deplore the slowcoaches sluggishly stirring
from sloth to meet the man of action of the moment; he makes
us read through Demetrian eyes: all bloated wordiness, these
sedentary slackers (*resides*), partisans who follow only—repose
(*sequentes otium*); they 'creep' along (*repunt*), shamefully craven

figures of negativity on legs (*ne defuisse noceat*). So much for the pride of Greece, hamming up tyrant ἀπάντησις (reception party).[18] When Tacitus presents Rome rushing to submit to its new owner Caesars, he rams home Phaedrus' first two themes, whether he dwells on the élite (as in *Annals* 1. 7, quoted above), or merges leaders and led, as in the *Histories* (1. 45. 1):

> You'd have believed this wasn't the senate of Rome, or the people of Rome: one and all stampeded to the camp, outstripping those closest to them and competing to outdo the runners ahead . . ., kissing and kissing Otho's hand; the more forced what they were doing, the more they did it . . .
>
> (*alium crederes senatum, alium populum: ruere cuncti in castra, anteire proximos, certare cum praecurrentibus . . . exosculari Othonis manum; quantoque magis falsa erant quae fiebant tanto plura facere . . .*)

On the other hand, the terrorized motivation of Phaedrus' slugs is the bottom-line of the whole scenario, essential to the topos and *the* rhetorical moment for cutting indictment of cowardliness: Tacitean Romans who had taken to their heels to avoid the pleas of a Tiberius victim 'started showing themselves again—scared of the very fact that they had been afraid' (*Annals* 4. 70, *ostentabantque se rursum, id ipsum pauentes, quod timuissent*); his 'senators and equestrians increased the throng going out of Rome to meet him, some for fear, plenty for adulation, the rest, gradually joined by everybody else, just in case others set out while they themselves stayed behind' (*Histories* 2. 87, *onerabant multitudinem obuii ex urbe senatores equitesque, quidam metu, multi per adulationem, ceteri ac paulatim omnes ne aliis proficiscentibus ipsi remanerent*); and his Neronian courtiers 'harboured a more grievous terror of what would happen if they went missing from the show' (*Annals* 16. 5, *grauior inerat metus si spectaculo defuissent* . . .). Livy's regal Rome had prequelled all this: 'others congregated, for fear that not to have come might catch them out' (1. 47. 9, *conuenere . . . alii metu ne non uenisse fraudi esset*). All this 'terror' underlines how the invader's takeover models for so much, for every return from home, each official parade, the whole business of state occasions, under the thumb of any tyrant anywhere, maybe even (how not?) Rome . . .

Readers can tell that Phaedrus' third lot of Athenians carry the sting in the tale: these creeps bring the scene-setting foil onto the point of the anecdote, for the last will be first. The jarring collision between the rising crescendo of scornful derision for the obeisance, and the acclamation of the star victor of many a dramatic competition, opens the rift which Demetrius will try to close with a change of tune, in a 'comic' twist of his own script (v. 9, *in quis . . . nobilis* is in tension with *repunt* etc.).

vv. 9–13

Menander's first datable play is the Ὀργή (*Anger*) of 321 BCE. When the Phalerean took over, Menander was hardly so estab-lished; by 307 the poet at 35 was in his heyday. Legend held that something—Peripatetic connections?—cost him victories to the more popular 'democratic' Philemon. By Phaedrus' time, the plays were perhaps the best known of all Greek drama in Italy, fêted in schools, translations, and (love-) poetry.[19]

'In among 'em' (*in quis*, v. 9),[20] flounces Menander, tied up in comically incompatible linguistic registers within a tight phrase: *nobilis* and *ignorans* knot into a *figura etymologica*, derived from the same root (known ~ unknowing); whereas *nobilis* and *comoediis* celebrate strongly ironic (comic?) tension ('noble' ~ 'farce'). 'Admiration-from-afar' will not fit the *Phalerean* Demetrius of history. But if Alexander could keep Homer beneath his pillow, why shouldn't the womanizer *Poliorcetes* have a plain-covered copy of Menander *Comedies* under his?[21]

Phaedrus makes Demetrius' radically incompatible Menanders, the myth and the man, clash as his parenthesis runs up against the resumed depiction of Athens on parade: *ingenium uiri, | unguento delibutus, uestitu fluens* (vv. 11–12, 'the man's talent, | swimming in unguent and gliding along in his robes').[22] The vigorous caricature of this fairy (*cinaedus*, v. 15) is as neat as the last (Ch. 5). The long hair of any loose-liver must be plastered with a pomade of myrrh ointment: too much for Poliorcetes, as for any Greek colonel, or Roman prince: cf. Suetonius, *Life of Vespasian*. 8. 3, 'Scorning with a shake of the head a stripling drenched with perfume, he scolded him, "I'd have preferred you to reek of garlic".' The wilful poet genius comes out precisely to defy the social control incarnate in the soldier's short back-and-sides. Fairies must dress the part: glad to wear excessive robes, too long, too many provocative folds; soft, flimsy, costly: cf. Fufius Calenus in Dio, *History of Rome* 46. 18. 2, 'the one that trails his robe right down to his ankles'. A race apart.[23]

Of course, the 'flowing robes' may have been meant to tie in with the long chiton worn by Menandrian actors: Tertullian, *Greek dress* 4, 'By all means, if anyone should trail a delicate robe in the dirt in a Menandrian flounce, let him hear behind him what the comic writer heard: "What a madman that is, ruining a gown".' But the point is rather that tradition will insist on foisting upon writers the foibles of their characters and the idiom of their productions. Most aesthetic delicacy translates as effeminacy; but his heavily heterosexual comic routines fastened on Menander the character of a womanizer.[24] (No paradox there.)

Phaedrus toys with cultural politics, as, apparently subservient, Menander flaunts untouchability. As anti-hero, Menander makes a good choice for fable, with its loathing of superficiality, stereotyping prejudice, complacent censoriousness; mixed up forever with 'tricksy slaves, cruel fathers, nasty madams, and sexy whores', Menander's comedy suits Aesop just fine.[25] But he also walks into a straight man's role, on the receiving end of Phaedrus' story.

vv. 14–18

The royal presence is visually affronted;[26] right-hand men point to the provocative personality before them.[27] So infamy meets fame, two sides of a sheet of paper; contradiction grounds transgression, and *force majeure* eats words: as clear-cut a proposition as could be imagined, about the sovereign power, in the long term, of the taxonomy of worth recognized by a society.[28]

The story has Menander's looks yield to ethopoeia, for the playwright of love must wear some brand of attractive exterior: 'Menander the fair' (Athenaeus, *Post-prandial society* 6. 248d, 8. 364d, ὁ καλός . . . Μένανδρος). Comic distortion was said to have given 'a cast to his eyes, an edge to his mind' (Suda *Lexikon s.n.*, στραβὸς τὰς ὄψεις, ὀξὺς δὲ τὸν νοῦν). Poliorcetes' looks would be a divine ruler's, but the Phalerean would show (at best) Aristotelian magnificence (Suda *Lexikon s.n.*, σφόδρα ἦν εὐπρεπής). The *volte face* comes to us unglossed: *homo* in the 'quip' *could* implicate that core subject of Menandrian philosophy, 'Man', and Menander's scripts *did* work with minimal verbal knockabout, but plenty of ironic empathy, both between characters and with the audience. His work regularly turned on a comeuppance for anyone who would read off persons by the stereotyping his scripts would deconstruct. Flattery is always as complicated a rhetoric as you are prepared to make it: in the mouth of a dictator, caught in the act of extorting the meaningless rigmaroles of felicitation that mean so bitterly to the tyrannized, salutation of 'good looks' must prompt all manner of extrapolation.[29]

7(a)   7(b)

7
Your Life in their Hands:
The *King* and *Dr Cobbler*
(1. 14)

Malus cum sutor inopia deperditus
medicinam ignoto facere coepisset loco
et uenditaret falso antidotum nomine
uerbosis acquisiuit sibi famam strophis.
hic cum iaceret morbo confectus graui   5
rex urbis, eius experiendi gratia
scyphum poposcit; fusa dein simulans aqua
miscere illius antidoto se toxicum,
combibere iussit ipsum posito praemio.
timore mortis ille tum confessus est   10
non artis ulla medicum se prudentia
uerum stupore uulgi factum nobilem.
   rex aduocata contione haec addidit:
'Quantae putatis esse uos dementiae
qui capita uestra non dubitatis credere   15
cui calceandos nemo commisit pedes?'
   Hoc pertinere uere ad illos dixerim
quorum stultitia quaestus impudentiae est.

There was once an incompetent cobbler and ruinous poverty
   had driven him
to take up practising medicine somewhere he wasn't known,
busy flogging—as he misnamed it—an 'antidote'.
What with his oratorical acrobatics he built up quite a name.
So it was when the King of the City came down in the grip 5
of some grave malady and, to put the man to the test,
had a goblet fetched. Next he made out he was mixing
   poison with his
'antidote'—actually it was water that was poured in—
and bade him drink, proffering a purse.

In fear for his life he then made a clean breast of it: 10
no learning in the art had made a doctor of him,
his reputation was all the doing of the common people and
    their gullibility.
   The King called a rally and this is what he observed:
'Just how crazy do you folk think you are,
not stopping to think twice before you trust a man to heal
    souls   15
that no one once credited to heel soles?'
   I'd say that this is a true comment on people
whose silliness keeps cheek in business.

The Roman anecdotes named their Caesars: *Tiberius Caesar*,
and *Divus Augustus* (Chs. 1–2). Or they named Caesars *avant la
lettre*, would-be Caesars, or minions of the Caesars: *Pompey*,
Sejanus, *Bathyllus*, and *Phaedrus* (Chs. 5; 3; 4; 3). If the latter
group could aim off, and hit the target obliquely, the Greek
anecdote could name a tyrant far from any hold on Rome, but
allow typology to bring him there all the same: *Demetrius* (Ch.
6). We already met fable at work, without proper names, but
using a familiar cultural institution and transferable scenario, in
a fictional world: the pig-ignorant theatre (Ch. 4, *Appendix*).
   The rest of the stories in this book will do without proper
names; yet they still trot out a line of kings, of one sort or
another. Just as anecdotal naming read as veil, alibi, foil, and
just as specified rulers figured in stories read as fables, so the
nameless, timeless, stereotypes of fable speak to the concrete
situation of any narra*tion*: circumstances tailor, and doctor,
stories to suit. There would be no point in ruling that any
particular fable was, or was not, about Phaedrus' Roman
Caesars, about kings and kingship in any shape or form, fundamentally about kingship or not at all. Certainly, kings construe
as general paradigms of authority; but that does not prevent a
storified king from pertaining to a particular palace régime in
the ken of teller and audience. Such is the logic of fable, that it
can pin but not be pinned down. And such, too, is the logic of
narrative *read as* fable.
   In this chapter, we look at a fable where a monarch stands for
wisdom backed with power (and vice versa). This king sees
what's what, delivers the story's deflating shaft of wit: he stands

in for the storyteller's authority. Just as we could retell 'Tiberius and the Flunkey' as 'The King and his Page' (Ch. 1), so this fable would become, at the drop of a name, 'Tiberius and Dr Cobbler'. In some sense, *this* narration of the story, a polished versification in post-Augustan Latin, carrying the signature of a freedman of Augustus, cannot avoid application by its reader to the circumstances of Rome under the first Caesars. They did not trade under the name of king, they lived the specifics of their 'principate'; yet monarchy was topicalized for discourse in their culture by their ascendancy. Just as the Roman royalty of legend acquired new pertinence to Augustus and Augustans, so too fictional kings could now speak to Roman realities, construe and comment on the Caesars (Ch. 8).[1] Phaedrus' king gets to do what no Emperor could: he calls on his people to face their incapacity to look after themselves, and recognize their need for his nannying; no quibbling. What else are kings for? And what king has ever delivered on anything of the sort?

But, all the same, 'The Quack Discomfited' is a prolific theme much cultivated by popular narrative such as Aesopic fable. 1. 14 elaborates this core theme under the influence of the Greek proverb 'Nothing above the [shoemaker's] last' (*CPG Appendix of proverbs* 3. 90, Μηδὲν ὑπὲρ τὸν καλάποδα). The polarity between 'head' and 'foot' as 'top to toe' suggested the interlocking of physical metaphors, as the cobbler who left his last to play physician is said, in exchange for his customers' *pedes*, 'feet', to take charge of their *capita*, in the combined senses of 'heads' and of 'lives'.

Both quack and cobbler are characters with suitably unheroic associations. They abrasively obtrude in this jest onto the fairy-tale setting of the king lying stricken in his palace by some 'mysterious ailment'. The equally mysterious stranger leech admitted to the royal bedside is unromantically realized in the shape of an itinerant 'medicine-man'. In place of fairytale cure, there follows exposure, engineered by the canny monarch. An eventful narrative, concisely recounted; probably—given its connection with the Greek proverb—from Phaedrus' usual Aesopic source.[2] Translation from Greek to Latin transferred its cultural relevance, from the Hellenistic microcosms of the mini-Alexanders to the post-Augustan world empire of the

Caesars; at *no* stage did the fable wear cultural specificity on its sleeve. Rather, its net spreads wherever it is intelligible for the doctor to stake a claim to be the true 'head' of state, on the ground that our lives are in their hands, so they hold a monopoly on vital wisdom; wherever a cobbler can figure the low cunning of discountenanced counter-culture, the down-trodden masses' hero who takes power along with humiliation in providing the footing which keeps the body politic on its feet, and up and running; wherever—and this seems to be pandemic—a single human can assume at least the rhetoric of commanding attention, and obedience, from one and all.

The next (and last) chapter will briefly document how the Aesopic fable rams it home that precious little specification is required to activate the general principles of autocratic power relations. In the animal kingdom, it is not that human beings are dispensable, but rather that beasts are brought in to name roles in simplified models of the structural dynamics of (puta-tively, any) human society.[3] So particular fables that have lions or apes for kings may aim off particular monarchs, especially when they are collected into a general fund of outline models; but it is always part of the potential latent in any fable that it can be told, and/or read, nevertheless, for oblique pertinence to a specific social-political scenario, while its characteristic generality does duty for screen, alibi, and advertisement (= 'The Fable of Fable': Ch. 3).

A narration may direct application to contemporary realities, as when Phaedrus refers to 'change of *princeps*' in the *pro-mythium* to the very next fabula, 1. 15. 1 (*in principatu commu-tando ciuium* . . .), where an ass asks his old minder: 'What difference does it make to me | who my owner is, so long as I only carry one pack at a time?' And it would leap to any post-Augustan mind that 1. 30 and 4. 6 interlock as rival conclusions to be drawn from the series of civil wars which handed Rome its Caesars: when one frog tells another that the bull-fight spells destruction for them, since the loser will stampede through their marsh, the Latin has them 'compete to be the *princeps*' (1. 30. 5, *de principatu* . . . *certarent*), the *promythium* told us 'The lower classes suffer the fall-out when the power merchants feud' (v. 1), and the wise amphibian will wind up thematizing 'pertinence' (v. 11, 'the loser will trample us with his unforgiving hooves, | and in that way their madness has life-and-death relevance to our heads': . . . *pertinet* ||). Then when the mice army runs from the host of weasels, the troops dashed into their holes, but the generals' insignia—horns tied on their heads so they could lead their mice-or-men—blocked their escape, the *epimythium* Romanizes the terms (4. 6. 11–13, *populum* . . . *magnitudo principum* . . . *minuta plebes*), an aside told us 'the story is painted in every pub' (v. 2), and the fatal insignia are pictured as a warped version of Roman 'standard' (v. 7, *signum quod sequerentur milites*). Finally, the constitutive tease of Aesopic relevance extends beyond any direct mention by name of regal power, in any shape or form; any fable, couched in whatever terms, may *enact* autocratic ways (see Ch. 8).

VV. 1–13

The 'bungling cobler' (L'Estrange (1692) no. 401) was a favourite grotesque in street lore and vulgar genres, but without a stake in Aesopic fable. The typical cobbler was self-employed, as here. To look at, he should be bald and stunted, with a limp, and skin paled by the indoor life. His reputation suffers from prejudice against the trades; but in particular, he was lumped in with the evil-smelling and carcass-tainted tanning yards tucked well away from the town-centre, beyond the city-gates. In the agora, the shoemaker's business involved as much craft as craftsmanship. 'Sewing' was a familiar image for machination, and in the image repertoire of 'high' and 'low' culture, cobblers have perhaps always been put down in the mire. The tradesman who served the public on his knees made an unpopular self-made man and a favourite ancestor in abuse. In Rome, the shoemaker bought his hides tanned, and traded in his quarter by Subura.[4]

In 1. 14, the king degrades his challenger for control of lives, the doctor, by returning him to the foot of the social hierarchy. The failed doctor was a failed shoemaker, with 'poverty' as a rationalizing motif to open a tale, with a change of occupation and/or scenery, familiar in fairytale, obsessed with rags and riches: e.g. Grimm, *KHM* 39, 'A shoemaker, by no fault of his own, had become so poor that . . .'; Lang (1962) 154, 'The

Cunning Shoemaker' (Sicilian story), 'Once upon a time there lived a shoemaker who could get no work to do, and was so poor that he and his wife nearly died of hunger . . .'. Such tales buy into the status quo, inculcating the axiom that 'poverty and deprivation . . . prepare the ground for evil'. Desperate scheming is deprecated as the doomed rival of established (establishment) 'wisdom'.[5]

Until very recent times, nothing prevented anyone with the nerve from setting up as physician. Many tales, of all kinds, are based on the motif, as in the success story 'Of a Charlatan who Cured Asses' (Poggio (1968) *Joke* 86):

Not long ago, there lived in Florence an enterprising ne'er-do-well who . . . after reading in a medical book the name and formula of certain pills that were good for a multitude of illnesses, conceived the bizarre idea of impersonating a doctor . . . He wandered through villages and towns as a practising physician. He offered the pills for all manner of sicknesses . . . One day someone who had lost his ass came and asked if the fellow if he had a remedy for missing donkeys . . .[6]

Aesopic fables particularly fête doctors: one at the funeral should've given his orders when they could have been of use; a patient who always got optimistic check-ups says he's all but dying of good symptoms; and a doctor who predicted imminent death is told that Hades is angry with doctors for keeping the sick from dying, but the patient says he stepped forward and told Hades that this was no doctor—that was just an empty insult (*AES* 114; 170; 317).[7] Because animals get sick, and recover or die, but lack human science, rhetoric, blarney (*logos*), they make very basic physicians: Babrius lines up three in a row (120–2), as Fox asks Dr Frog how he will cure anyone else when he can't save himself from being so pale; Polecat offers to tend sick Hen, but the patient will live if he pushes off; and, getting uncomfortably close to Phaedrus' shoemaker, Dr Wolf agrees to extract the thorn from Ass's foot, but gets his teeth kicked in: 'I deserve to suffer this way—why did I just start tending the lame | when I've never learned the first thing about anything but butchering?' (*AES* 289, 7, 187, 699).[8] In fact, a version of this fable could once be read in Phaedrus: restored as Zander (1921) no. 24, where Dr Lion gets a kicking from Horse, with the title 'Those who don't know their trade, betray themselves', and the *epimythium* 'So whoever you are listening to this, | be what you be and don't lie' (Rom 3. 2 = Wiss 3. 2, *Qui (que) artem ignorant, illi se produnt; Ideo quisquis haec audis | quod es esto et mentiri noli).*

Country districts were served by travelling medicine shows, invariably mentioned with scorn by (urban, élite) texts. Thus Lucian tells of one racked with coughing as he hawked his cough drug (*Apology* 7). A doctor from foreign parts didn't have to work for the element of mystique; and could simply be spat out again after disappointment. Phaedrus uses the (naturalized) Greek '*antidotum*' (v. 3) to inject his victim with fake hype, instead of directly damning him with the label '*pharmacopola*' (drug-seller); he lays the treatment on thick, branding his perversion of truth-in-language, then providing a sample, with the self-enacting 'verbose trope' of *uerbosis . . . strophis*, which is given an extra flourish by its bracketing of the verse (4).[9] The medicine is a 'Sovereign Antidote' (L'Estrange (1692) no. 401), supposedly competent against any poison (v. 8) and master of whatever royal ailment (v. 5): the panacea could, in other hands, be a reputable concept.[10]

At v. 5, scene-setting business formulaically marks the transition to the body of the narrative. L'Estrange (1692) no. 401 mistranslated: '*This physician* came in time to fall sick himself . . .' (with a comma after *graui,* |), and others have found the King's unremarked resuscitation from sickbed in vv. 5–6 to pulpit in v. 13 awkward. Stories can seem to have been specially invented to tell us that monarchs can get ill, so common is the story motif 'There was once on a time an Old King who was ill . . .' (Grimm, *KHM* 6, 44, 97 . . .). In beast terms (as we shall notice in Ch. 8), Aesopica abound with Sick *Lions*: 1. 21, 4. 14, *AES* 142, 258, 336, 585, 698). The foreign doctor who arrives to cure the King, for a king's ransom, is also a widespread story-line, most familiar from Romance like *All's well*, and in fairy-tale.[11]

However many centuries the Free Republic lasted, kings and queens were of course never dethroned from the lore and language of Roman schoolchildren, or from everyday expressions.[12] On the other hand, traditional narrative provided somewhere shy of specifics that could handle the myriad ramifications of the return with the Caesars of one-man rule in

Rome. On one side, no fable could really fasten teeth into the Principate; on the other, the easy relevance of these simplistic fictions to the latest Julio-Claudian news, the last crisis or the debacle on its way, could hand anyone who could read or listen a vast repertoire of power scenarios, each kitted out with ready-made, widely-shared, and neatly-processed reflections. With this material, Romans could think together the fixes that straddle or run all social life, and the mutant monarchy of their *Caesares*.

Because the cobbler's patent panacea fits anyplace, the rigmarole of the king's test of the doctor with a 'goblet' of pretend poison to try out on himself *simultaneously* offers us familiar folk-narrative, with a dash of irony in the king's offer of 'cash on the table' (v. 9, *posito praemio*), *and* doubles for the newly topical routines that were part and parcel of the arrival of Alexandrian idioms to attest the Emperors' greatness. Doctors from the Greek East worked the superpower palace with their panoply of advice and concoction, skulduggery and remedy; 'pregustation' (fore-tasting) came to Roman life, at court, alongside dodgy apples and deadly mushrooms, and handed Romans parts in what they had taken for fictions. When Phaedrus was choosing 'false doct'rin' for his first book of *Fabulae*, he was already telling tales tailored for the world of the Caesars—and only just ahead of time: if, in the tabloid version of imperial history, Augustus may have been finished off by his wife; if Tiberius' Dr Charicles only gave him a surreptitious check to see how much longer to give him, before ironman Macro had him smothered with his pillow; and if Caligula was chopped down in his prime—nevertheless, Sejanus was already cooking up poison for Tiberius' son and heir Drusus, administered by the eunuch Lygdus, and with Claudius and his son Britannicus the imperial exit would reach the heights of melodramatic intrigue (Tacitus, *Annals* 12. 66 f., 13. 14 f.):[13]

Claudius' wife Agrippina chose a select poison to befog the brain and delay death, and picked Mme Locust, with a recent conviction for poisoning and a long string of palace assignments OHMS under her belt. Her know-how prepared the venom; to be administered by Halotus from the eunuch ranks, expert waiter at feasts and food-taster. . . . Agrippina took fright and . . . called in Dr Xenophon, in cahoots with her as a precaution: he (it is supposed) pretended to rely on induced vomiting for treatment, and stuck a feather smeared with instant poison down his throat, knowing perfectly well that top crimes are begun with danger attached, but finished off with prize attached . . .

~

At the Saturnalia, when the others his age were horsing around one way or another, they drew lots to sort out who should be king, and Nero was the lucky one. [So he picked on Britannicus, who responded with a clever protest by innuendo at being pushed out of his rightful inheritance, the world state. This panicked the cuckoo Emperor:] Nero ordered a preparation of poison, with the assistance of Julius Pollio who saw to it that a poisoner with a record was brought in on the job, Locust, Underworld Megastar . . . Nero couldn't stand the drawn-out crime . . . so right next to his, Caesar's, chamber, venom was boiled up that was tried and tested for instant action. It was regarded as a custom for the royal children to sit with the other élite youngsters and eat under the eyes of their nearest and dearest, on a table reserved for them . . . When Britannicus was dining there, a picked servant would taste his food and drink; so that this routine would not be dropped or the crime betrayed by the pair of them dying, the following cunning plan was dreamed up: a drink was handed Britannicus, still harmless, but too hot, yet already through the tasting; then, after he rejected it as too hot, the poison was poured in, mixed in cold water . . .

Finally, notice that traditional storytellers rarely, and literary raconteurs never, hesitate to run down 'the people': Phaedrus here hams up the collapse of his phoney victim, with his run of parallel phrases, *timore mortis ~ non artis . . . prudentia ~ uerum stupore uulgi*.[14]

vv. 13–16

Short tales like this usually want an accredited figure to address an audience set within the narrative, and so indirectly impose closure on the narrator's wider circle. The King's heavy speech-formula draws attention to the *dictum* on its way; then chiasmus between *capita* and *pedes* maximizes the polarity that measures vertical distance in the social pyramid.[15]

The repressive *moral* 'Stick to your last' was a favourite in the Antiquity we can read about: Aristophanes, *Wasps* 1430 f., 'And then, a bystander said 'Each person should do the trade he

knows' (= *AES* 428, 'The Sybarite Charioteer', κἄπειτ' ἐπιστὰς
εἶπ' ἀνήρ . . . | Ἔρδοι τις ἦν ἕκαστος εἰδείη τέχνην). The graphic
proverb Ne supra crepidam sutor iudicaret was given at least two
origin stories: *CPG Appendix of Proverbs* 3. 90 names
'Myrrichos the cobbler', but the anecdote with Apelles rebuk-
ing a cobbler who criticized the master's canvas on a detail of
footwear, and then cavilled 'on a matter at shin-level' has
almost swept the board (Pliny, *Natural history* 35. 84).
Erasmus, *Adages* 228a was responsible for the widespread
version *Ne* ultra *crepidam* . . .[16]

vv. 17–18

Solemnly formulaic mortar marks off the moral from its narrative: Οὗτος ὁ λόγος ἁρμόττει πρὸς ἐκείνους οἱ . . . (*AES* 17, etc.,
Perry (1940) 411). Compilers of literary fables vary their
pro- and *epimythia* so far as is possible, but the staple fare is
still bald declaration of a stark proposition. Here, Phaedrus
avowedly treats his poem as a received fable, with its own
message, to which he adds his own support ('True enough, if
you ask me'). Most modern readers dislike the 'morals' so
much, they won't even read them. They come from a voice that
wants to be a machine, not a person; registration of another
item duly entered, and interred, in the compilation catalogue.
But if you weigh up this one, for a start, you'll see how the
question of its 'truth' is *destabilized* by the explicit mention.

As the narrative sets about asserting that its shameless victim
made fools of the people and lined his own pockets, we won't
necessarily stop, see that the quack didn't get away with his
shoddy shoes, presumably because *that* line of business wasn't
all hot air and cool hype, and wonder which of these kinds of
game the trade of *fabulist* resembles the more closely. So . . .
shall we *not* consider, too, whether Phaedrus' impudence isn't
his bread-and-butter, on our tab, in case the dumb clucks
might, all along, be . . . ourselves?[17]

8(a)

8(b)

8
Kings of Fable and
Fables of Kings

This final chapter will produce just one more 'name'—the Athenian tyrant Pisistratus from back in the Herodotean mists of late sixth century BCE proto-history—but only as a fictional frame, with Aesop as fabulist (§ 4 below: 1. 2). Otherwise, the sole humans here are two fellow-travellers to Apeland (§ 1: 4. 13). This is the place to take a look at kings in the (beast-)fables of Phaedrus (a look, not proper study), before a concluding moral reflection on Aesopic kingship *mentions* some fables not found in Phaedrus, and pontificates (a little) on royalty and rhetoric, write and wrong (§ 5).

The first two fables here can't be read as Phaedrus wrote them. The run of stories in book 4 between 4. 13 and 4. 16 is a mess in the *paradosis* (MS tradition). To work backwards, 4. 16 opens its tale of the creation of same-sex sexualities abruptly, as a twin narration (by Aesop?) with 4. 15, of which only the last two lines survive, enough, that is, to indicate an aetiology for something too unspeakable for monkish (?) scribes—a thing about 'pudenda and woman's tongue'. Of 4. 14, we have just the first six verses, running straight on from the three-line *promythium* which is all that is left of 4. 13, which has a title for 4. 14 ('On the Lion-King') prefixed to it. Both 4. 13 and 14 tell tales on kings and emperors of any persuasion—no-win cynical, then red as you please in tooth and claw—beyond anything the anecdotes we have looked at ever managed. On its own, their mangling would look like a combination of botched copying and desperately blotted or perished copy; immediately before 4. 15–16, suspicion swells, but it is not so easy to see the mutilation of 4. 13–14 as the result of intentional cutting. As we shall see, Aesopic fable has still worse to say about monarchs than all these fables come up with (§§ 3–5).

Fortunately, we have versions in the medieval prose paraphrases of Phaedrus (PhP) for both 4. 13 and 4. 14. These
stories are too 'good' to miss, so we must bear with the garbled
narration and modernized Latin which come between
Phaedrus' own writing and us. In §§ 1–2 below, I supplement
the fragments of classical Latin with a version cobbled together
from PhP, [in square brackets], as if it isn't daft to pick out the
most Phaedrian phrases and pretend the lost poem will flicker
through. (*Not* so daft as vainly printing out verse compositions,
for ridicule.[1])

In §§ 3–5, we shall get back to 'pure' Phaedrus again. First,
and last, for brutally told brutality; in between, for elaborate
narration, as mock-anecdotal framing makes a telling tale we all
know already into, not just the most poetically amphibious, but
the most politically ambivalent, and amiably virulent, of all
Aesopic fables.

1. POLICY IS THE BEST HONESTY: EMPEROR *APE* (4. 13)

Utilius homini nihil est quam recte loqui:
probanda cunctis est quidem sententia,
sed ad perniciem solet agi sinceritas.
    [Duo homines, unus fallax et alter uerax,
iter simul agebant, et cum ambularent,
uenerunt in prouinciam simiorum.
quos, ut uidit unus ex multitudine simiorum,
ipse qui prior esse uidebatur,
iussit eos teneri, et interrogat
quid de se homines dicerent,
iussitque omnes sibi similes
adstare ante se ordine longo, dextra
laeuaque, et sibi sedile parari;
sicut uiderat imperatorem aliquando,
taliter sibi adstare fecit. iubentur
ergo homines adduci in medio.
                              ait maior,
'Quis sum ego?' fallax dixit, 'Tu es imperator.'
iterum interrogat, 'et isti quos uides
ante me stare?' respondet, 'hi sunt comites tui.'
et quia mendacio laudatus est

cum turba sua, iubet illum munerari,
et quia adulatus est, omnes illos fefellit.
uerax autem apud se cogitabat,
'Si iste mendax, qui omnia mentitur, sic accepit,
ego, si uerum dixero, magis munerabor'.
   tunc ait maior simius, 'dic et tu, quis sum ego,
et hi quos ante me uides?' at ille, qui semper
ueritatem amabat et loqui uerum consueuerat,
respondet, 'tu es uere simius, et omnes
hi similes tui simii semper sunt.'
iubetur continuo lacerari dentibus
et unguibus, eo quod uerum dixisset.
   Malis hominibus, qui fallaciam et malitiam amant,
honestatem et ueritatem lacerant.]

'More profitable for a person can nothing be, than straight-
   talking'
— yes, everybody must agree with *that* tag.
But honesty does tend to head straight for perdition.
   [Two people, one into lies and one into truth,
were travelling along together, and, as they went on their way,
they came to the land of the apes.
Once one of the mass of apes caught sight of them,
the one who thought he outranked them all,
he ordered their arrest, and asked
what the men said about him,
And he ordered all his kind
to stand in front of him, in a long line, to right
and to left, and a throne to be readied for himself—
just the way he had once seen an emperor do.
That's the way he had them stand by him. And so
the men are ordered to be fetched out in public.
                     The big
     wheel said,
'Who am I?' and the liar said, 'You are the Emperor.'
He asked again, 'and these you see here
standing before me?'; came the reply, 'These are your
   courtiers.'
And because he was praised by the fibbing,
along with his troop, he ordered him a reward,
and because he had kowtowed to him, the liar fooled the
   whole lot.

Now the truthful one was thinking to himself,
'If that liar, who always tells fibs, got such a welcome,
I, once I've told the truth, will get still more of a reward.'
    Then the big wheel ape said, 'Say, too, you, who am I,
and these you see before me?' Well, he always
loved truthfulness, and was used to telling true, so he
replied, 'You are, truly, an ape, and the whole lot
of these mates of yours are forever apes.'
He is ordered torn apart right away, tooth
and claw, just because he'd told the truth.
    This is for villains who love trickery and villainy,
and tear apart honesty and truthfulness.]

This fable tells us how to ape an emperor.[2] In the terms we have already seen at work, we know first, that the king knows all there is to know, he favours and nails as he sees fit: Augustus, for a start, sorting ewe from goat (Ch. 2); second, that the king says what goes, declares what is true, and is less of a king if he tailors what he says to others' true opinions: so Demetrius, mincing words on mincing Menander (Ch. 7); third, that the king must be flattered / cannot be flattered enough: Tiberius taught this lesson, putting down the Flunkey (Ch. 1). So come to his kingdom and make like the other primates: kingship is the act you must not monkey around with, for the autocrat is the one who is aping the autocrat, and he needs no under-studies: remember Prince Piper's painful exit-line (Ch. 4).[3] The king, the parody king (they are *all* parodies), takes it all the way—'tooth and claw'.

2. JUST WHAT THE DR ORDERED: SICK *LION* (4. 14)

Cum se ferarum regem fecisset leo
et aequitatis uellet famam consequi,
a pristina deflexit consuetudine
atque inter illas tenui contentus cibo
sancta incorrupta iura reddebat fide   5
postquam labare coepit paenitentia,
[et mutare non posset naturam,
coepit singulas seducere in secretum,

fallacia quaerere an os sibi puteret.
uerum seu mendacium dicerent,
omnes tamen laniabantur, ut saturaretur.
haec cum multis fecisset, uocat simium ad se,
interrogabat si putidum haberet os.
ille uero cinnamomo suauius
olere dixit, quasi deorum altaria.
   leo erubuit laudatorem laedere,
sed, ut deciperet, quaesiuit fraudem, atque se
finxit languidum. continuo uenere
medici diligentissime perquirentes
quomodo sanarent Regem bestiarum:
tentatis uenis erat inenarrabilis
pulsus. suadetur sumere cibum
aliquem in quietem et qui leuaret
fastidium, ut regibus omnia licent.
   'Ignota est mihi caro', inquit, 'simii,
hanc uellem probare'. ut est locutus,
statim rapitur beneloquens simius,
offertur regi et statim laniatur.
   Et loqui poena est et tacere tormentum.]

When lion had made himself king of the animals
and wanted to gain renown for fairness,
he turned aside from his previous ways
and in their midst he made do on basic rations,
dispensing justice with his word for inviolate bond.   5
After regrets started him faltering,
[and he wasn't able to change his nature,
he started taking animals off one by one out of the way,
and tricked them by asking whether his mouth smelled bad.
Whether they told truth or lied,
all of them anyhow got butchered, so he could get his fill.
When he'd done this to lots of them, he called ape to him,
and asked if he had a smelly mouth.
Ape said, sweeter than frankincense
was the smell—just like the altars of the gods.
   Lion was too embarrassed to harm his panegyrist,
but, to catch him, looked for a ruse and made himself out
to be poorly. At once the doctors came,
looking intensively as they could for how to heal the king of
     the animals:

when his veins were examined, it could not be put in words
what his pulse was like. He was urged to take up a special
        diet
of some sort, for calm, the sort to ease his
pickiness—for nothing is denied any king.
    'Something I've never tried', he said, 'is ape-meat,
I'd like to give it a try'. Once he'd spoken,
immediately sweet-talking ape was seized,
offered to the king, and immediately butchered.
    Both things apply: speaking brings punishment; silence
        brings torture.]

This complex story must have looked rather different in
Phaedrus' classical Latin, and there are some desperate
moments in PhP: Ad 49, which supplies most of the text for
the first half of the supplement, simply packs up when ape
embarrasses lion;[4] Wiss 5. 2 (typically) soldiers on, through a
patch of nonsense, to provide us with the rest of the story;[5] Rom
3. 20 tries (as usual) to tidy up a version very like that in Wiss.[6]
But none of this prevents us telling that this is, word for word,
the most systematically damning indictment of dictatorship we
are ever likely to come across.

    To be sure, read immediately after, and as a sequel to, 4. 13,
the Lion-King must redouble those same axioms: being
Emperor is a matter of strategy presented as policy, in short, an
act; the king orchestrates the action, prescribes what is true and
adjudicates between different claims to speak truth; once more,
the king demands flattery, and no flattery can ever be enough;
and the king must wield his power over all and sundry, without
compunction or mercy, to exert comprehensive, regal, ascendancy. But this time there is more—more beastly atrocity, and
much more fiendish 'logic'.

    Lion here 'has made himself king': we are invited to chew
over the 'contract' which might be supposed to govern kingship, by picturing its aetiology.[7] A people where brute 'nature'
had reigned thought to institute the rule of law, and thought a
ruler was needed to implement and safeguard the social order.
Expectations ran high: this was a revolution in process. But the
iron law of nature (in Kipling, the leopard's spots) soon insists
that what made the leader of the revolution will prove incom-

patible with his new role. Not to make a meal of it, this king soon preys, as before his elevation, on the subjects he is meant to protect. Carnivorous creatures need a constant supply of dead meat: they must kill, or die. In § 3, we shall find this proposition about power close to the heart of Aesopic fable, as a brute tableau; but in 4. 14, the denunciation is hitched to an articulated analysis of discourse at court, celebration of the king by 'the *speaking animal*':

This fiction preserves of animality the primitive sanction of all 'social behaviour', to eat or be eaten, but keeps of man that which characterizes him essentially, language. . . . The speaking animal of fable is thus like the figure of an origin of language in the devouring of bodies, and the animal's discourse is the figure of this devouring. . . . In the fable, to eat (or to be eaten) figures the radical power of discourse in language: to eat the other is the 'monstrous' fiction of the power to speak (to) the other. . . . Power institutes itself as power only through and in the representation of language.[8]

Yes, this time *both* liar *and* truth-teller are butchered. Speech in the king's presence is on his terms: he commands an interview, one on one; his question then demands an answer. The dilemma this time entraps those who offend against truth, thus perjuring themselves and corrupting the social order the king is meant to protect (by falsely protesting that his breath doesn't stink), as well as those who insult royal majesty (by telling him his breath does stink). The fable bites, in full close-up, when we realize that this scene (which Kafka should have written) tells on autocracy by staining its *every* word with civil carnage: the predetermined outcome of the interrogation *ensures* that those slavering chops are once more stained with blood, set to stink over the next victim. What the king says and what he does are smeared together: mouth-and-jaw-muscles flex his power. Like the rest of us, he lives as he breathes—and *his* life's work of public service is indeed the lifeblood of the community . . .[9]

But lion's 'heads I win, tails you lose' dilemma fails to be, precisely, fool-proof. Ape's flattery is itself proof against direct repression, because his panegyric must be music to the king's ears, and cannot be construed by him as an insult, *whatever the intent* may have been (on the same lines as Hans Andersen's 'Emperor's New Clothes'). All the same, the tyrant *has* nevertheless got somewhere; his will has been flouted and his strategic control flawed, but his next target has been winkled out where he can be lined up (always good to know where your next meal is coming from), as if there was a rationale for this arbitrary carnage *beyond* the need to feed on underlings (as if he has it coming); and, finally, *we* are handing lion the chance to show us there is no escape in honeyed words. Make no mistake: under a king, we will *all* end up rotting his teeth, and he shall lick his lips if ever he wants to savour his memories of us.

As we saw in Chapter 7, the king is charged with protecting national health. In a clutch of fables, lion(-kings) fester, weaken, starve and age (or pretend to be on the way out), until they must try and trick some walking meal to step right into the jaws of their caves, or some doctor must find the right treatment.[10] Accordingly, when society's 'doctor', the king, plays patient, we know very well what is afoot. In getting ordinary physicians to sign over to him the blank prescription he wants, and, with it, blanket legitimation of any outrage he may care to perpetrate, the tyrant suborns the people to sanction their own depredation (§ 4 below).

Politics boils down to the recrudescence of savagery under the veil of culture. The king's table manners elide all civilized 'cooking' processes, moving straight from slaughter to rotten after-taste; and the bloody feast converts instantly to the immaterial savour left behind by the meat intake consumed, the polar opposite of the hyper-cultural smoke of incense and burnt offering (bones and skin) which somehow sustains gods— outside the exchange that defines mortality.[11] Human pre-eminence is locked into the slicing of flesh; no monarch can stand proud of the pecking order. So where sacrifice can supposedly bring us closer to the gods without infringing their superior status, the king's rank is the product of suspended disbelief, a collectively willed denial that the king's eminence is 'contractual'.

Slanted to the personal politics of the realm of marriage (cf. Ch. 2), a version of the story has settled into the West African folk repertoire of Sierra Leone, where 'The goat, the leopard, and the lion' was dictated in 1961 by Fanka Konteh (here abbreviated from Finnegan (1967) 325–7):

A goat was once the lover of the lion's wife. Now the leopard knew about this love. The leopard went to the lion, her husband. 'The goat is making love to your wife. That is what I have come to tell you. But I will make a chance to bring you the goat, for you to eat him. For he is your wife's lover.' The lion's wife met her lover, the goat. 'The leopard said that we are making love. Don't be afraid. Bring with you honey in a pot.' The lion sat. The leopard sat. The goat sat. The lion's wife sat opposite. The lion's wife was watching her husband. When she saw her husband about to spring on the goat, the wife fell down on to the ground. Her husband said, 'Oh, my wife is going to die. Leopard, do you know of any medicine?' The leopard said, 'No.' The goat said, 'Yes. The skin of someone spotted.' The lion cut off one of the leopard's legs. The goat put it in the honey. The woman ate it. She turned over. The lion said, 'Well? Should I give her more?' She ate it. She opened her eyes. 'Give me more.' The lion cut again. The goat put it in the honey. The woman ate. She got up and sat. The lion said, 'Is it better now?' The lion cut again. The goat put it in the honey. She ate it. She got up and sat on a chair. She said, 'Aha, if I could get some more of that, it would be fine, so I could be completely better.'

The lion was just about to say, 'Leopard, lend me some more'— before he had spoken, the leopard had run off. Then the wife said, 'Well, goat; escape!' When the lion failed to catch the leopard, he said, the lion, the male, 'I have still got the goat, I will go and cut from him. So my wife may be well and not die.' He went home. The wife said, 'The goat has run away too.' 'Then he is saved from trouble, for I came here to catch him. But since he has run away, all right.'

You see now how it is to tell on someone, to slander them. Well, the leopard uttered slander about the goat, but this slander ended up against himself. Thus slander is bad.

This story cooks up social implosion, as bodily cheating breeds verbal foul play, which in turn spawns bodily feigning and fake diagnosis. The 'king's' power is conned, massaged into savagery, as raw meat is helped down with honey in an over-determined perversion of basic cultural norms: the recipe folds allelophagy (tabu eating of each other) into doctoring (culture's intervention on the body), and this eliminates civilized cooking by wrapping up barbarous violence in the natural hyper-cuisine that beggars all our categories. No one is killed, but everything is poisoned, stained, regressive, in this 'spotted' world of story gone to the bad.[12] Raw data or cooked results, either way, every single subjected person is, necessarily, good as dead meat.

Now let's rub it in with a story, short and sour, about
(animal-)fable, rub it in that, if you ask Fable, talk of civiliza-
tion, as of any other aspiration, is rot: Aesop is where humans
get nailed to stereotypes of creaturality. Fables can only ever
know kings as but kings; lions, only lions—

3. THE PROTECTION RACKET: DICTATOR *KITE* (I. 31)

Qui se committit homini tutandum improbo,
auxilium dum requirit, exitium inuenit.
   columbae saepe cum fugissent miluum
et celeritate pennae uitassent necem,
consilium raptor uertit ad fallaciam   5
et genus inerme tali decepit dolo:
'Quare sollicitum potius aeuum ducitis
quam regem me creatis icto foedere
qui uos ab omni tutas praestem iniuria?'
illae credentes tradunt sese miluo,   10
qui regnum adeptus coepit uesci singulas
et exercere imperium saeuis unguibus.
   tunc de reliquis una, 'Merito plectimur,
[huic spiritum praedoni quae commisimus'.]

The one who entrusts himself to a villain for protection,
in finding a shield, gets himself killed.
   When the doves had escaped kite over and over
and evaded death through wing-speed,
the predator switched strategy to guile   5
and fooled the defenceless creatures with a trick like this:
'Why do you live your lives in trepidation, rather
than making me your king by formal treaty,
so I shall keep you safe from all harm?'
They delivered themselves over to kite in trust,   10
he took the throne, and set to eating them one by one
and wielding power with cruel talons.
   Then one of those left said, 'We deserve to get struck
       down
[for entrusting our souls to this bandit'.]

—Or, rather, a lion is a wolf; an eagle, a kite. The king turns on his own people, again; this time, Phaedrus chooses 'pastoral', not medical, care as the promise that the king trades on for his political 'contract'—just as emphatic a theme in the Aesopic repertoire.[13] But now the story is told, not on the king, but on us: naturally, the predator will behave like a predator,[14] that is why he picks himself for the role of scourge of our enemies; and that is why he is our self-inflicted exterminator.[15] These doves learn the hard way, usual in fable, from the outcome.[16]

But *we*, on the other hand, are telling ourselves *their* story. Telling tales is, paradigmatically, *the* human activity, where power-and/as-representation intertwine/s between narrative and narration. These 'speaking animals' play off the law of the jungle against their playing it off, on *our* behalf; they make available to us ways to think with nature as if it were politics; they provide our best arena for catching the manipulative core intrinsic to the nature of politics. And the idea of fabulation is to pressurize listeners. Fables come with a warning attached:[17]

The fable is structured as a double bind: to heed its call you must ignore its call, you must make the mistake the fable denounces. In order to read, you must not read. And you cannot choose not to read.

So fable is not, after all, just stuck telling us that kings will be kings; fable, however simply and starkly schematized it may be (and 1. 31 *is* the norm, not 4. 14), is a warning that can be heard before, all over again, we go join the doves; before, all over again, citizens put themselves in the wrong hands, and . . . croak.

4. ANARCHY LURES K.O.: TYRANT *PISISTRATUS*, AND KING *LOG* AND KING *WATERSNAKE* (1. 2)

> Athenae cum florerent aequis legibus,
> procax libertas ciuitatem miscuit
> frenumque soluit pristinum licentia.
> hic conspiratis factionum partibus
> arcem tyrannus occupat Pisistratus.   5
> cum tristem seruitutem flerent Attici,
> non quia crudelis ille sed quoniam grauis
> omnino insuetis, onus et coepissent queri,

Aesopus talem tum fabellam rettulit:
   'Ranae uagantes liberis paludibus   10
clamore magno regem petiere ab Ioue
qui dissolutos mores ui compesceret.
   pater deorum risit atque illis dedit
paruum tigillum, missum quod subito uadi
motu sonoque terruit pauidum genus.   15
hoc mersum limo cum iaceret diutius,
forte una tacite profert e stagno caput
et explorato rege cunctas euocat.
illae timore posito certatim annatant
lignumque supra turba petulans insilit.   20
quod cum inquinassent omni contumelia,
alium rogantes regem misere ad Iouem,
inutilis quoniam esset qui fuerat datus.
   tum misit illis hydrum qui dente aspero
corripere coepit singulas. frustra necem   25
fugitant inertes, uocem praecludit metus.
furtim igitur dant Mercurio mandata ad Iouem.
afflictis ut succurrat.
                tunc contra deus:
"Quia noluistis uestrum ferre", inquit, "bonum,
malum perferte."
                Vos quoque, o ciues,' ait,   30
'hoc sustinete, maius ne ueniat, malum.'

Athens once blossomed egalitarian,
but pushy freedom messed up politics,
anarchy kicked over the old traces.
So it was when feuding factions got into cahoots
and Pisistratus seized the acropolis as tyrant.   5
Grim enslavement made the people of Attica weep,
not because he was savage but since he felt heavy to folk
entirely unused to this sort of thing, and they were just
   complaining at the incubus,
when Aesop told a fable like this:
   'The frogs roaming through marshes in freedom   10
with an almighty clamour begged a king of Jupiter,
to keep down with force behaviour out of control.
   The father of the gods laughed and bestowed upon them
a wee bit of log, whose launch, and the pool's sudden
stir and splosh, terrified the timid creatures.   15

It lay there buried in slime for a good while,
when it so happened one frog stuck its head up out of the
    pond
and after giving the king a going-over called up the whole
    lot.
They set aside fear, made a race of swimming over,
and hopped up on log in one insolent mob.   20
Once they had fouled it with every insult going,
they sent to Jupiter begging another king
since the one that had been sent was useless.
    Then he sent them watersnake, who with grating fangs
set to grabbing them one by one. To no avail they ran   25
for their lives, clueless; fear clamped down on their vocal
    chords.
On the sly, therefore, they gave Mercury a message for
    Jupiter,
they were being persecuted—help!
                    Then god said back:
"Because you wouldn't stick the good you had,
you must stick with your bad."   29
             You, citizens, too,' he said,
'put up with this, so no worse one comes, bad as it may be.'

In this telling,[18] this unforgettable political fable takes the
theme of self-inflicted terror as the king wanted by his people
turns vicious on them, and puts it to elaborate work: frogs, not
kings, hold centre-stage. This time the nation prayed for a king
as a heaven-sent boon to save them from themselves. A big
splash and plenty of ripples worked for a while, but the novelty
palled; second time round, they got more than they bargained
for—the problem of misrule was taken out of their hands, and
solved for good. So kingship is not a sale-or-return 'contract',
but a surrender of autonomy. Frogs get stuck with whatever
turn power happens to take.

    The frame provided dumps Aesop down in Athens,[19] in terri-
tory only as familiar to Latinity as the text of Herodotus
Histories 1, which is to say, not particularly familiar, for the
tyranny or tyrannies of Pisistratus which bridged between
aristocratic and democratic Athens in the late sixth century BCE
found no niche in the repertoire of Roman culture.[20] But this

montage points, not to the exercise in thinking Greek politics which the story could stimulate, but to its potential for applicability to the circumstances surrounding any narration: *our* host is Phaedrus, whose guest (and projection) Aesop is; and in our reading, Phaedrus is now our guest, and we use him to speak (what is on) our minds. Or, at least, no one can *decide* whether we do or don't; and what is more, the important question (if there were any such) would ask what else any such decision would amount to but a power-play making waves: an intervention with political-theoretical repercussions (splosh!). Frogs, those squashy losers in fable, should always look before they leap (they never do, they are frogs).[21]

The frame needn't throw us off the scent: what hearing could *Julio-Claudian* frogs give *their* fabulist? For one thing, no satellites of divine Rome's imperial 'Jupiter' hopped over to beg on behalf of sadly democratic cities for a king, on approval or not; nor had this happened before Rome had its own resident human Jove.[22] For another, the story of the Caesars' seizure of Rome/Principate itself isn't hard to square with the idea that the citizens wished an emperor *on themselves* to escape anarchy, but must leave us with an absurd (funny?) contrast between Augustus Log and Tiberius Watersnake. Still, the story's carapace of 'liberty and license' pushes readers to dwell on the provisionality of dynastic succession in the minds of Roman citizens: there was a ceremonial, and so real enough, *interregnum* (transition between reigns) between Caesars when, in *some* sense, the senatorial representatives of the polity *did* each time reconsider, and reaffirm, the monarchy.[23] With the snuffing of Gaius, could it be said, Rome did ditch one king and 'send for' another? And, in good time, Rome would also dump its deposed Nero in a swamp, and bring back anarchy to the world state in 68/9 . . . But these frogs' most suggestive proposition must lie elsewhere, in the dichotomy pictured by the fable, between log and watersnake.

Log is an absolute ruler. Removed from all exchange, he exercises no power; so ultimately he can have none. Watersnake eats his subjects, they asked for it and he gives it to them, over and over, amen. That's final, no way back, the absolute end of (hi)story. This, mind, coming from a freedman of Augustus attached to the palace staff, taking his first plunge into literature, in the piece he put second in his début volume. Just imagine him telling the Principate this way (maybe to commend this way of thinking? Maybe to expose it? Maybe). What would be getting said? For example, that people should be relieved to realize that they are no worse off under their notional figurehead of state (any log coulda been a watersnake)? Or, that it's no good supposing that the Caesars would ever again be optional at Rome (a regular supply of victims is the tariff for over-achieving 'social order')? Whatever the point, this fable (as if oblique analogy was not itself, precisely, a salient trait of Tiberius' reign: Ch. 1) has gone out of its way to ensure that no one could pin it to Rome. Any more than any of us could ever keep it there, stuck in ancient history, millennia from our political lives, without telling tales on . . . ourselves.

5. AND OTHER *WOLVES* (ETC.)

Kings are a dime a dozen in Aesop: fox lures ape into a trap to show he isn't clever enough to be king (*AES* 81). Ape tells camel and elephant they can't stand for king: one never gets riled, the other is scared of pigs (*AES* 220). Wolf admires his king-sized shadow: lion eats him up (*AES* 260). When the mouse set free by lion gets to gnaw him free of the net (*AES* 150: in Babrius (*Fables* 107) and PhP (= Zander (1921) no. 6)),[24] kingship isn't mentioned; whereas, when sleeping lion starts up because mouse runs over him, not for fear, but in case mouse disgraces (himself in) his mane, Babrius has fox mock him as 'the overlord of all the beasts' (82. 5), though our Greek prose version does without this (*AES* 146); and kingship is mentioned in some, but not all, versions of 'the lion's share' fable (Phaedr. 1. 5, *AES* 339, 149);[25] in the Greek Aesopica, Zeus makes fox king of the animals, and to see if he's a changed beast, he sends a beetle out in front of the coach; fox jumps for it, so Zeus dethrones him (*AES* 107), but no royalty is invoked when the weasel bride can't resist a passing mouse at her wedding reception (*AES* 50 = Babrius *Fables* 32, and PhP (= Zander (1921) no. 26).[26] Surely no one is going to deny that kingship is on the line, between the lines, in Babrius' pithiest poem (*Fables* 90 = *AES* 341):

Lion went berserk. Fawn in the wood
spotted him, said: 'Poor us:
What won't he do now he's mad
— he was too much to take when he was sane?'

If we must gather all autocratic behaviour within the domain of
'kings' (and *vice versa*), crossing all demarcations, cultural,
linguistic, and (paradigmatically, in beast-fable) between
animal species, this still does not constitute of it a kingdom set
apart from the other structures of power. Rather, monarchy
extends the spectrum of schemata, marking the approximation
to one of its poles. For the absoluteness of any king must always
in practice be compromised, by all the exchanges, relations, and
negotiations which bring about, establish, or confirm its reality.
When logs are kings and kings are logs, cabbages can (must) be
just round the corner, and then what has fable (un)done with
kingship?

Phaedrus chose for the very first—emblematic—fable of his
collection, 'Wolf and Lamb', the most savagely crushing
presentation of the self-confuting dialectic of power supremacy.
In the terms I have been using, this lion is a wolf; the king is
a sadistic wolf in lion's clothing. No, wolf is not 'king' and
doesn't say he is; but that doesn't stop him behaving tyrannic-
ally: trying to fake a grievance as pretext for pouncing on the
innocent, wolf accuses lamb, first, of muddying the water: but
wolf is upstream; second, of insulting him six months back: but
this was before lamb was born; so, third and last, it must have
been lamb's father—(before an answer can come back; but there
is no answer to this; aggression drops all disguise in the end—in
the lamb's heart-rending end)—wolf carves up lamb.[27]

So what tales does this 'king' tell on the king? The king is . . .

There is nothing 'above' the king, nothing is upstream.

The king stands above time: he masters and dispenses (with)
time.

The king stands above social structure, kingship valorizes or
nullifies kinship, in social and natural orders alike.

As we watch, horrified, wolf trying to play hurt, aggrieved,
diminished, so he can implement his superior strength, this
melodrama of power-relations shows how, *as would-be lion, as
lion manqué, as the only sort of king he can be*, wolf must try to
talk himself down ('minorant'), until he can look as though he is

obliged to get even with lambkin—impossibly. For a wolf is a wolf; lions can only ever be wolves in denial, however they would set themselves at the absolute limit (physically strongest, spatially impregnable, temporally transcendent, genealogically aboriginal, politically supreme, best and holiest . . .). For the rest of us, when we are not talking as courtiers must, there *are* only wolves.

In terms of self-vindication, the lamb takes the high ground (as true 'minorant', putting the 'majorant' in his place), doesn't know he's born, is a child below the age of responsibility. The lamb is nothing other than a lamb, and we—we must (not) make the mistake that (this) fable denounces:[28]

If the wolf is the king, 'Sire', and 'Majesty', he does not have a majorant. He is an absolute position like an absolute monarch. Not only is there no third man, but it is impossible to conceive of one: *quo nihil maius cogitari potest* ['than whom nothing greater can be thought']. Therefore the lamb has won, and the wolf has no majorant. He is himself the maximum. . . . If you want to win, play the role of the minorant.

Fable makes a winsome lamb of every reader of *Roman Stories from Phaedrus*.

Here, at the end, ready to read away, we have fetched up on the river bank where, fed to the wolves, we are led to the laughter.

Telling tales on our every *Caesar*.

From us, and on us, the last laugh.[29]

NOTES

CHAPTER I

1. Cf. Cartault (1899) 164 f.
2. Cf. Douglas(s) (1923); the anti-Tacitus in Tacitus: Jerome (1912) 269 n. 1.
3. e.g. Tac. *Ann.* 2. 87. 2, Suet. *Tib.* 26. 2, Dio 57. 8. 1 f.; thus, he joked that naming months for Caesars would store up problems for No. 13! (ibid. 58. 18. 2)
4. Cf. Beard and Henderson (forthcoming), on Sen. *Apocol.*
5. Tiberius' 'Solitude and Anguish': Maranon (1956) 204–15. Peter Wiseman reminds me that an emperor granted solitude is good as dead (e.g. Suet. *Ner.* 47. 3, Tac. *Hist.* 3. 84. 4): emperors must line their hall with lackeys, cf. Phaedr. 4. 13 in Ch. 8.
6. Let's repress any insidious thought that the transmission super-script information that Phaedrus was *Augusti libertus* (Boldrini (1990) 41 f.) *might* be an intelligent inference from 2. 5.
7. Dancer: Dio 57. 11. 6; Actius the comic actor: Suet. *Tib.* 47. Veteran: ibid. 48. 2. Money: Tac. *Ann.* 2. 38. 5f.; Suet. *Tib.* 46. Rhodes: Suet. *Tib.* 11. 1. Affable: Dio 57. 11. 1. ~~Flattery~~: Tac. *Ann.* 2. 87. 2, cf. Suet. *Tib.* 27, with Lindsay ad loc., Ben Jonson, *Sejanus* 1. 375, 'We not endure these flatteries'. Togonius and Gallio: Tac. *Ann.* 6. 2. 5–3. 3. Funeral: Dio 57. 14. 2. Helikon: Philo *Leg. ad Gaium* 166 f., cf. Balsdon (1934) 131.
8. See the classic treatment of Plass (1988), esp. 62–4: Tiberius and the Flunkey is, precisely, a classic exercise of power through 'wit' = violation through expectancy generated by the power of Caesar.
9. e.g. Rosenbaum (1998) on the story of storying 'the man who stands at the dark heart of this century'.
10. Etruscus' father: Bradley (1994) 69 f. Story: Graves (1953) 195 f.
11. In (terroristic) Greek rhetorical parlance, the opening ἐπαγγελία rehearses the ψόγος περιεργίας, with τοποθεσία and εἰκονισμός to follow.
12. Cf. Henderson (1998*b*) 73–107.
13. *Our Mutual Friend*, discussed by Trotter (1988) 134.
14. Cf. Ter. *Eun.* 248 f., *est genus hominum qui esse primos se omnium rerum uolunt | nec sunt ... Natio*: Cic. *In Pis.* 55, *officiosissima natio candidatorum*, Pease on Cic. *De nat. deor.* 2. 74.

15. Erot. *Gloss.*, Nachmanson (1918) p. 26. 20, cf. Philem. fr. 59 Kock, Αἰγύπτιος θοἰμάτιον ἠρδαλωκέ μου, and Paus. 2. 31, 'Ardalos, sooty son of Hephaestus', Wilamowitz (1935–72) 5. 2. 19 n. 3. *-io*: Olcott (1898) 84. *Ardalio* has an insistent ghost life in the (sanitized) form *ardelio*, folk-etymologized from *ardeo* (blaze; Keller (1891) 130). The Vatican glossaries were largely responsible for the word's entrance into European literature in this form, cf. *OED* s.v. Georges (1888) 486 and Sonny (1898) 381 straightened this out. Before 1885 *ardelio* was rendered 'busy idler' (e.g. Sam Johnson in *The Adventurer*, Sat. 3 Feb. (1753), 'Throughout all the town, the busy triflers swarm, | fix'd without proof, and without int'rest warm'; cf. Büchmann (1895) 345 f., 'Geschäftig Müssiggänger'; Bréal then guessed that *Ardalio* was a character in Roman mime (1885), but this, the *locus communis*, is mistaken (*pace* Reich (1903), 1. 2, ch. 4: 'borrowed from Dorian farce'; cf. Bertschinger (1921) 29). Mud: Mayor on Juv. 3. 247, 'legs fat with mud', Hugill (1931). Abjection: *CGL*, Index s.v. *ardalio: acutus cum malignitate* ('mucker: sharp and malevolent'), and esp. *Gloss. Lab.* p. 1616, cited by Reich (1903) 1, 444, *ardalio*: πολυπράγμων ('mucker: busybody'). Matter out of place: Douglas (1966).

16. Scurrying: Mayor on Juv. 1. 86. *otium occupatum*: Sen. *De breu. uit.* 12, Holden on Cic. *De off.* 3. 1, McCartney (1927) 192; in Greek, διατριβὴ ἀργός (e.g. Ar. *Ran.* 1498, Luc. *Anach.* 32. For the 'panting', cf. Theophr. *Char.* 2. 9 (Flattery), 'able to fetch and carry goods from the woman's market without taking breath (ἀπνευστί). Ado: Cic. *De rep.* 1. 17, *numquam se plus agere quam nihil cum ageret*, Otto (1890) 9, s.v. *agere* § 1; the plural *multa agendo* chimes with Greek poetry's πόλλα πράσσω vs. prosaic πολυπραγμονέω (Wilamowitz on Eur. *Herc. fur.* 266); cf. Sen. *De tranq. an.* 13, *agit multa . . . multa agit*. Self and others: Sen. *De breu. uit.* 14. 3; *sibi molestus*: Sen. ibid. 12, *Epp.* 98. 8.

17. Proems should cultivate τὸ σχῆμα ἐπιεικές: Pease on Cic. *De div.* 1. 9, *si placet. Si tamen*: Schmalz (1908) 333.

18. Macr. *Sat.* 1. 2. 7, cf. *RLAC* 7 (1969) 129 f., Bieber (1906) 3 f. The contrast with the usual label for the fables, *fictae fabulae* (1. *Prol.* 7, 2. *Epil.* 13), is between beast-tale and realistic anecdote. Lancelot: Chaucer, *Nonnes Prestes tale*; cf. Hom. *Od.* 14. 192 f. (Odysseus' lies) τοιγὰρ ἐγώ τοι ταῦτα μάλ' ἀτρεκέως ἀγορεύσω ('So I shall tell you this tale quite without deviation'), Sen. *Apocol.* 1. 1, *nihil nec offensae nec gratiae dabitur. haec ita uera*, Cervantes, *Don Quixote* (1950) 345, 'Listen . . . and you will hear a true story . . .'.

19. The formula of πρόσεξις: Enn. *ap.* Hor. *Serm.* 1. 2. 37, *audire est operae pretium procedere recte*, cf. F. Marx (1922) 139, Bryant

(1898) 121. A vestige of public performance: Ar. *Eq.* 624, Plaut. *Amph.* 151, Fraenkel (1957) 81 f., Biese (1926) 16 f.; as in the historians, Hdt. 1. 177, Avenarius (1956) 127.

20. Nøjgaard (1967) 2. 28.

21. e.g. Hor. *Epod.* 4. 53, *otiosa Neapolis.* Stop-over: Hahn (1922) 14, 'Villa als Abstiegequartier'.

22. Quote: Graves (1953) 320. Villa: D'Arms (1970) 184 f.: quarrying has spoiled the site (= no. 22a, pp. 23–7). Marius: Plin. *Nat. hist.* 18. 32. Cornelia: Plut. *Mar.* 34. 3f. Lucullus: Van Ooteghem (1959) 188 f.; cf. Jolivet (1987) 878–85. Last hours: Tac. *Ann.* 6. 50. 3, Suet. *Tib.* 73, Lindsay ad loc., and on Suet. *Gai.* 13. Romulus: Furneaux on Tac. loc. cit., Stein (1949–59) 1. 398 n. 198 (but *RE* 13. 2 (1927) 1705. 25, '*Lucullanum castellum*', says Baiae).

23. So Tac. *Ann.* 6. 50. 1, *uilla cui L. Lucullus quondam dominus*, Suet. *Tib.* 73, *uilla Lucullana*; so, too, Messalina covets *hortos . . . a Lucullo coeptos*, Tac. *Ann.* 11. 1. 1, cf. Van Ooteghem (1959) 194 f., Keaveney (1992) 148 f. Marbling: Plin. *Nat. Hist.* 36. 6, 49. How much of the place's history need Phaedrus or his reader know? Badian (1973) 131 and others assume he was *there* '*at the time*'.

24. Fool Monte: Schoder (1971–2) 98, fig. 1, *RE* 15. 2 (1932) 2043 and Tafel, and photographs in Van Ooteghem (1959), figs. 22–5. Quotes: Hor. *Epp.* 2. 1. 253, Sen. *Epp.* 89. 21, cf. Sen. *Contr.* 8. 6. 2, Sen. *Epp.* 51. 11, Wistrand (1972) 218 f., Pease on Virg. *Aen.* 4. 187, de St. Denis (1935) 103, Purcell (1987) 196.

25. Fleet HQ: Susini (1969) 1. 707 f.; cf. Hubaux (1933) 135 f. for the *mons aerius* beneath which Virgil buried Misenus, *Aen.* 6. 234 f. Lucania: e.g. Hor. *Carm.* 3. 4. 28, *Sicula Palinurus unda.*
   Note that *respicit* is Gronov's correction (1663), for *perspicit* R^{Gu}, *prospicit* R^{Ro}; *despicit* Guyet (1663). Cf. Vollmer on Stat. *Silu.* 1. 3. 40.

26. Prefer *alticinctis* (*coniunctim*, cf. *CGL* 2. 226. 12, ἀνεσταλμένος· *alticinctus*) to *alti|cinctis* P, *alti cinctus* R^{Gu}, *alte cinctis* Saumaise (1698), as Hor. *Serm.* 2. 8. 10 (*metri causa*), Sen. *Epp.* 33. 2, 92. 25, Petron. 126. 5. The ironic *prosopopoea* deserves the compound (contrast 1. 6. 6, 2. 4. 3).

27. Gatekeeper: as first impression, and synecdoche: Petron. 28 f., 72 f. Dissolute: belts and morals, syntax and virtue, all tangled together in a web of metaphor policing 'manliness': Graver (1998) on Sen. *Epp.* 114. Arms free: Plaut. *Mil. glor.* 1179 f., Norden on Virg. *Aen.* 6. 301, and Schol. Luc. *Vit. auct.* 7, for the Greek ἐξ-ωμίς, 'off-the-shoulder'. Taut: *Script. physiogn.* 2. 135 Förster, *molles* κιναίδους *. . . qui tunicam circa lumbos tendunt*, Gell. 6. 12,

Poll. 4. 119. *Linteum is* a belt (*pace* Perry (1965); cf. Gail (1826), Excursus 16, 1. 536 f.): Suet. *Gai.* 26, *succinctos linteo*, Gaius *Inst.* 3. 9. 2, *nudus quaerat linteo cinctus*, Petron. 28. 8, *succinctus cingulo*, 95. 8, *anus .. sordidissimo praecincta linteo*. Finest Egyptian pets: Petron. 31. 3, Quintil. 1. 2. 7, Stat. *Silu.* 5. 5. 66; finest linen: Wild (1970) 44, Forbes (1955–64) 4. 37. Tufts on belt: cf. Schol. Aesch. *Pers.* 155, βαθύζωνοι δὲ αἱ Περσίδες διὰ τὸ κροσσωτὰς ζώνας ἔχειν, Dierks (1883) 9 n. 2. *OLD* omits this use of *cirrus*, cf. Nettleship (1889) s.v., Blümner (1875–8) 1. 201 f.). Winckelmann (himself playing just this role for Cardinal Albani): 'the privileged and responsible page who looked after the valuable secular and sacred sculptures and paintings in the atrium' ((1767) 2:236).

28. Phaedrus: *pace* e.g. DeLorenzi (1955) 83 f., Maiuri (1956) 32 f. Villa's walks: Plut. *Mar.* 34. 2. Greenery: D–S 5. 925, '*Viridarium*'.

29. *laetus* concretely of 'healthy' plant growth, cf. Virg. *Georg.* 1. 1, *laetas segetes*; *laetamen* is Romanure. *uiridis* regularly connotes 'verdant youth', Virg. *Aen.* 5. 295, *uiridi . . . iuuentute*, hence 'lively dotage', ibid. 6. 304, *uiridis . . . senectus*.

30. Massie (1990) 115 f.

31. Spraying: Plaut. *Stich.* 354, *consperge ante aedes*, Suet. *Gai.* 43. Housework: Plaut. *ap.* Gell. 18. 12. 4, Titin. *ap.* Charis., *CGL* 1. 204. (For the orthography *conspargere* PR^Gu, vs. 5. 5. 11, *dispersus*, cf. *CGL Suppl.* p. 181. 31, *dispersio sed consparsio*, Callebat (1967) 129).

32. *Come officium* is not secure, but may be accepted, *pace* Housman on Manil. 5. 635. Did a scribe take *cirri* (v. 13) as the boy's 'locks', and *come* here as *comae*? (*come officium iactitans* Rigault (1617), cf. Krischan (1954) 79–81: *iactans o. come. sed* PR^Vi, *iactans o. comae* Pithou (1596), *iactans o. comes* Wase (1668)).

33. Interwoven: D–S 3. 1. 285 and n. 29. Pleached: Sherwin-White on Plin. *Epp.* 2. 17. 17, cf. Grimal (1969) 262, Reid on Cic. *Acad. Pr.* 2. 10. Latin usage does not support the attempt of Vitr. 5. 11. 4 to distinguish materially between ξυστός (sc. δρόμος) and the neuter *xystum*.

34. *enimuero adsilit* is a mimetic touch: 'Il ne fait qu'un saut' (Schwabe (1806)). In the paradosis, the chiasmus seems to have fallen on its 'r's: *Caesaremque* PR^Gu; *Caesar remque* R^Vi, Pithou (1596); then an unmetrical explanation was inserted into the resultant muddle (cf. 1. 25. 6, 4. 24. 2): *ut putauit esse nescioquid boni* (v. 20) PR^GuVi, del. Rigault (1630); suppl. *is* (*ut . . .*) Brotier (1783), cf. Festa (1898) 261, *id* Pithou (1596), *al. al.*; cf. Rank (1910) 270 f. *Any* version of this 'v. 20' would spike the guns of v. 22.

35. *alacer gaudio*: *TLL* 1. 1474. 1 f. *Dux*: standard imperial antono-masia, Berlinger (1935) 88. Royalty = periphrasis, the distension of language: Headlam on Herod. 5. 68, ἡ Δάου τιμή, Basil. *Epp.* 328, τὴν τιμιότητά σου.
36. Massie (1990) 70.
37. *multo maiores alap(a)e mecum uenerunt* PR^GuRoVi is unmetrical nonsense, corr. Rigault (1617): *ueneunt* Pithou (1596). *Mecum*: e.g. Virg. *Aen.* 4. 115. *Maioris*: unparalleled in K–S 1. 457. *Alapa* onomatopoeic, hence the preserved internal surd, González-Haba (1969), cf. 'slap', *OED* s.v. Nisbet *pater* (1918) collects all the evidence (add Basil, loc. cit., Greg. Nyss. *In Christ. resurrect.* 3 *MPG* 46. 657). 'Apotropaic': cf. Havers (1911) on Petron. 38. 9, *?sub|alapa?*. Handshake: Duff (1958) pl. 4. ('M. Schuster, "Die römische Freilassungsohrfeige und der Firmungsbackenstreich", *Wien. Blatt. f. d. Freund. d. Ant.* 6 (1929) 12–15 is noticed in *Bursian* 240 (1933) 84; cf. Oberg (1996) 163 f.)
38. Legislation: Bradley (1994) 156 f.
39. Reid: *ap.* Nisbet (1918) 7 n. 2. Embarrassment: cf. Hor. *Serm.* 1. 9, with Henderson (1999a) 202–27. Tiberius: Scott (1932).

CHAPTER 2

1. Cf. Robbins (1986) 152–9, 'The butler did it'.
2. Tanner (1979) 15, and *passim*.
3. Ibid. 13.
4. Beard (1993) paradigmatically explores Roman declamation, as fictional scenario for fictional arguments, yet also the practice of practical arguments about practice (55): 'an arena for learning, practising, and recollecting what it is to *be and think Roman*' (56). She deconstructs the category of 'myth' to show how the stuff of Roman discourse is normally disqualified from consideration. So does Phaedrus.
5. Boone (1987), esp. 1–27, 'Wedlock as Deadlock and Beyond'. This is where anecdotes part company from soaps: 'It is important to realise that soap operas serve to affirm the primacy of the family not by presenting an ideal family, but by portraying a family in constant turmoil and appealing to the spectator to be understanding and tolerant of the many evils which go on within that family' (Modleski (1990) 194: no closure for momma, there's always the next instalment). Roman family conflict: Dixon (1997).
6. Beard (1993) 60: Roman Law as a 'culturally embedded way of thinking'.

7. Tanner (1979) 13.

8. Edwards (1993) 60, cf. 34–62, 'The law against adultery', Galinsky (1996) 130.

9. The (sub-)literary equivalent to the progymnasts' exercise of ἔκτασις: Babr. 95. 1–102, expanding the fable of the 'Hart without a Heart', cf. Keidel (1894) 264 f.; cf. *AES* 711 vs. 711a, 716 vs. 716a, Christoffersson (1904) 117 f. On the syllabus: Quintil. 1. 9. 1.

10. In v. 2, *exponam* P is not secure (cf. 4. 16. 2, *exposuit senex*): *ponam* NV, *adponam* Postgate (1919*a*).

11. 3. 7. 1, *breuiter proloquar* heralds the longest beast-fable, 4. 5. 2, *narratione . . . breui* an extended go at humans; cf. 2. *Prol.* 12, 1. 10. 3, *App* 12. 5, Christoffersson (1904) 112 f. This has been taken up: LaFontaine (1962) *Préface*, 'L'élégance [et] l'extrême brèveté qui rendent Phèdre recommandable'; and/or fêted: Nøjgaard (1967) 2. 22 f.

12. Ἐπικίνδυνον γάρ . . . is a common gnomic form, cf. Plut. *Camill.* 6. 4, Ἀλλὰ τοῖς τοιούτοις καὶ τὸ πιστεύειν σφόδρα καὶ τὸ λίαν ἀπιστεῖν ἐπισφαλές ἐστι, Sen. *De clem.* 1. 23. 2, *periculosum est . . . ostendere ciuitati quanto plures mali sint . . .* Proverb: Sen. *Epp.* 3. 4, *utrumque enim uitium est et omnibus credere et nulli*, Otto (1890) 97 s.v. *credere* §2; Greek versions: Plut. *Camill.* loc. cit., Hes. *Op.* 372, πίστιες ἄρ τοι ὁμῶς καὶ ἀπιστίαι ὤλεσαν ἄνδρας.

13. Dubbed συμπλοκή by progymnasts: e.g. Theon, *Rhet. Gr.* 2. 72 Spengel = *AES* Testimonia 103, p. 240: 'Croesus + The Camel wants Horns (but loses Ears)' (*AES* 117). L'Estrange (1692) was to reinvent this wheel, e.g. nos. 230–3.

14. Schissel (1912–13) 1. 94.

15. Cassandra a one-off fairy-tale figure: *TMI* M301. 0. 1, Frazer on Apollod. 3. 12. 5. Potiphar's wife: *TMI* K2111, Braun (1938) 44 f., Yohannan (1968), Tschiedel (1969), cf. Trenkner (1958) 64 f.

16. Cf. Beard (1993) 57, 'intentionally ignoring all the fruitless fantasy about lost Roman popular culture', and 'necessarily concerned with Roman cultural traditions *as they are preserved*—both wider and narrower than their Athenian counterparts: wider . . . in their ethnic range . . .; narrower in the sense that . . . the *privileged location* of literary presentation was not mass public gatherings of citizens, but private gatherings of the elite', and published gatherings full of posh scribble.

17. He need not *name* Hippolytus' 'stepmother'; the fifth foot anapaest in *ruit Ilium* enacts the 'fall' (v. 4): otherwise found only where the wordbreak is weakened, e.g. 3. 14. 11, *erit utilis* |

(Havet (1895) § 72). Reminiscent of the conceit of 'ruin at the caesura' in Virg. *Aen.* 2. 363, *urbs antiqua ruit*. The chiasmus *Cassandrae . . . Ilium* calls attention to the mimesis.

18. *Ergo . . .*: cf. *App* 3. 12, *ergo . . . (pace* Havet (1895), Perry (1965), there is no call to transpose vv. 5–6 after v. 50).

19. Esp. 4. 7, 4. 22; *App* 2?

20. At v. 6, *stulta praue* P: Tacke (1911) 24 plugs the case for *stulte praua* NV.

21. At v. 7, Guyet's correction (1663) *fabulosam ne uetustatem eleues* at least gets the gist: *fabulosa ne uetustatem leuem* P (*fabulusa* teste Finch (1971) 306), *ne uetustatem leuem*, R^{GuVi}, *ne uetustate eleuem*, R$^{corr.}$, *fabulosam ne uetustatem asseras*, NV; *fabulosam ne uetustatem levem*, Ellis (1895) 33, *fabulosa ne uetustas eleuet*, Toll (1781), *et al. al.* For the verb, cf. 4. 3. 5, *qui facere quae non possunt, uerbis elevant*, Bramble (1974) 69 n. 2.

22. Schönberger (1910) 59.

23. Swear: e.g. Luc. *Philops.* 22, ἄκουε τοίνυν, τοῦτο μὲν καὶ ἐπὶ μαρτύρων, ὃ πρὸ ἐτῶν πέντε εἶδον, Schissel (1912–13) 97). The limit for the ἀπομνημόνευμα, egomorphic αὐτοπάθεια: e.g. Luc. ibid. 33, ἐγὼ δὲ ὑμῖν καὶ ἄλλο διηγήσομαι αὐτὸς παθών, οὐ παρ' ἄλλου ἀκούσας, Schissel (1912–13) 96.

24. The juvenile *toga praetexta* (robe with purple hem) was formally exchanged at puberty for the 'plain' *toga pura*: Wilson (1924) 52 f., Sherwin-White on Plin. *Epp.* 1. 9. 2. Injection of symbolic capital is the *point*, as the storyteller himself 'prepares' to stain conjugal love and childish innocence, and cancel the perfect, all-Roman family's future. The son's age—Greek had a word for it (μελλέφηϐος)—will prove integral to the plot, as well as piling on the pathos.

25. Fictional parallels: Rohde (1960) 595 and n., Trenkner (1958) 94 and n. 2 (of varying relevance).

26. Also known as a 'stir': e.g. 'Be not avenged till you know the truth, for you might make a stir in the dark, and afterwards it should rue you both' (Rickert (1908) 46, 'The Wise Man and his Son').

27. So Thiele (1908) 368, developing Hartman (1890) 70.

28. Nicholas (1962) 75. The system of παραμονή, with *operae*: Calderini (1908) 279f., Brunt (1971) 380 and n. 1; ties of *pietas* between *patronus* and *libertus*: Gardner (1998) esp. 74–8, 'Tribulations of the freed slave': Veyne (1987) 82–8. Wishing ex-master dead: Cic. *ap.* Quintil. 6. 3. 48, *cum obuium libertum* [of his enemy] *interrogasset 'rectene omnia?' dicenti 'Recte', 'mortuus est!', inquit.*

29. How on earth . . .: Oberg (1996) 159–61. Bequests to loyal freed-

men customary: Duff (1958) 102 f., Meiggs (1960) 217 f. *Captatio*: e.g. Quintil. 6. 3. 92, . . . *unus ex amicis recentioribus sperans aliquid ex mutatione tabularum, falsam fabulam intulerat* . . . Core formula for propriety as the perquisite of property: blame it on 'Agency; the servant as the instrument of the plot', Robbins (1986) 131–65.

30. *Ventitare . . . domus*: e.g. Lys. *Or.* 1. 19, Οὗτος ὁ φοιτῶν εἴη πρὸς τὴν γυναῖκα, Tac. *Ann.* 11. 12. 3 (Messalina) *non furtim sed multo comitatu uentitare domum. Stupro . . . pollui . . . domus*: not impossibly echoing the strong, and traditional, slogans of Hor. *Carm.* 4. 5. 2, *nullis polluitur casta domus stupris*; cf. Heubner on Tac. *Hist.* 2. 56. 1.

31. Lys. *Or.* 1. 11, ἧκον μὲν ἀπροσδοκήτως ἐξ ἀγροῦ, Men. *Perik.* 174, δεσπότην ἂν ἐξ ἀγροῦ θᾶττον πάλιν | ἔλθῃ ταραχὴν οἵαν ποήσει παραφανείς, Hor. *Serm.* 1. 2. 127, *nec uereor ne dum futuo uir rure recurrat*, Prop. 2. 23. 18, *hodie uir mihi rure uenit*; cf. Trenkner (1958) 158 and n. 4, Splettstösser (1898) § 1.

32. Cf. Apul. *Met.* 9. 20, where four interlocking tales of adulterous wives, each featuring the Untimely Return, come to a climax (several: Schlam (1992) 77 f.; cf. Walters (1993) 172–9). Adultery mime in Antiquity: Reynolds (1946).

33. Baby: Aarne and Thompson (1928) no. 910B, Trenkner (1958) 42 and n. 1. Families sharing a bedroom: Ar. *Nub.* 1 f., Cic. *Pro Rosc. Am.* 64, Luke 11. 5 f., Walcot (1970) 80 f., Jeremias (1963) 157 f. Class determined which couples had separate quarters, which children had sleep-in slave chaperons, etc., while dogs-bodies regularly kipped at the foot of master's bed: Bradley (1991) 9 and n. 23, 91, George (1997) 316 f. Bedrooms in ancient stories spell mayhem, and often enough murder: Riggsby (1997) 39 f.

34. Parents preserve budding offspring from the dangers of puberty: Ellis on Cat. 68. 15, Mayor on Juv. 7. 239 f.

At v. 21, *inf(o)elix* NV is most likely Perotti's 'improvement' of *uxoris* P, after *uxoris*, v. 18 and immediately before *mater natum* P (v. 22: *natum mater* NV): the clutter of family roles is exactly the point.

35. Dixon (1988) 129–35.

36. Spontaneous anger palliating the crime: Paul. *Sent.* 2. 26. 5, etc. (Bonner (1969) 119). Fictions of 'jealous passion' (*irae furentis impetum*, v. 25), in Greek ζηλοτυπία: Fantham (1986). Folklore: Bolte and Polivka (1903–22) on *KHM* 56, 'Liebsten Roland', Österley (1871) on *Gesta Rom.* 18, 'St. Julian'.

At v. 26, *accedit* P is probable (cf. Alton (1922) 326): *uadit* NV may have arisen from an intermediary *uccdit* (so Havet (1895): *tccbernis* P at 4. 6. 2 is remarked by Zwierlein (1970) 93).

37. Cashes in: the financial metaphor in *repraesentauit*, v. 32, was a cliché of noble suicide, e.g. Charondas (hoist with his own law) Val. Max. 6. 5. *ext.* 4, '*idem* . . . *ego illam sanciam', ac protinus ferro quod habebat destricto incubuit . . . poenam tamen repraesentare maluit ne qua fraus iustitiae fieret . . .*; cf. Suet. *Claud.* 34, Berger (1953) 676, '*Repraesentare*'. Tragic suicide: *ferro incubuit*, v. 33, draws the samurai as the instrument of noble remorse, e.g. Val. Max. loc. cit.; cf. Heubner on Tac. *Hist.* 2. 49. 2, *in ferrum pectore incubuit*, Hirzel (1967) 39 and n. 2. Sleep: the wife's shaky alibi is given *en passant*, the first part of sleep being traditionally held to be deepest: v. 31, cf. Virg. *Aen.* 1. 470 (Rhesus' camp) *primo . . . prodita somno*. The mimetically alliterative pleonasm *sopita . . . somno* turns up everywhere, e.g. Virg. *Aen.* 1. 680; cf. Bowra (1929) 71, R. Müller (1952) 101. Holy: *sanctam . . . uxorem*, v. 30, the adjective regularly used by respectful husbands: Harrod (1909) 38, Friedländer (1908) 4, Appendix 15. The story is out to enshrine the dominant idea, chastity (Link (1910) 73).

At v. 30, *cubiculo* PNV is not seriously undermined by Rank (1910) 275, proposing *illum prope*.

38. *Postularunt* and *pertraxerunt*, vv. 34 f., are *voces propriae*; but the *Cuiri* is a topical detail used improbably, for 'the criminal jurisdiction of the Cviral court was very slight' (Parks (1945) 50, *RE* 3 (1940) 24 f., '*Cuiri*, Geschäftkreis'). Under Augustus the old property and testamentary court became 'the home of causes célèbres', its function here (Crook (1967) 79; on the new set-up: Austin on Quint. 12. 5. 6, Sherwin-White on Plin. *Epp.* 2. 14, 4. 24, Mooney on Suet. *Vesp.* 10). The phrase *quod bona possideat*, v. 38, just points the finger of *cui bono?*, rather than making technical reference to *bonorum possessio* (which would set the woman on the path to ownership by *usucapio*: Nicholas (1962) 243 f.). We, or at any rate I, need not puzzle out how a civil case might develop from a testamentary charge (Thiele (1908) 368, Volkmann (1935) 68 f.).

39. The poor 'woman', *mulier*, v. 34, becomes the virtuous 'lady', *femina*, by v. 39. Legion stories of such persecution and vindication: *TMI* K2112, 'Genoveva', Clouston (1886), Trenkner (1958) 59 f., Schlauch (1927) 95 f., Jackson (1961) 87 f.

40. See Beard (1993) esp. 60.

41. Sussmann on Calp. Flacc. 24, comparing the (relatively) real Fabius Eburnus (Val. Max. 6. 1. 5).

42. What if . . . you had to deal with the other man *before* dealing with the wife? (Ps.-Quintil. *Decl. min.* 249) Or . . . your armless father told you to kill mother for him? (Sen. *Contr.* 1. 4) Or . . . you

couldn't tell the masked adulterer, and you couldn't mistake the wife, so . . .? (Calp. Flacc. 49) Or . . .? Ubiquitous fascination with this sad topic: Mayor on Juv. 10. 315–17, Henderson (1999*c*).

43. The problem of Augustus' Law: Treggiari (1991) 264–75, esp. 274, Scafuro (1997) 220. Declamation: Bonner (1969) 119, Russell (1983) 33 f., esp. Aphthon. 54. 5, Sen. *Contr*. 1. 4, 9. 1, Ps.-Quintil. *Decl. min.* 244, 284, 347, Sussmann on Calp. Flacc. 49.

44. The poor 'woman', *mulier*, v. 34, becomes the virtuous 'lady', *femina*, by v. 39. Phaedrus presses this home, with the mimetic word-order and the ethos of *stant patroni fortiter* (cf. Hor. *Serm.* 1. 9. 38, *neque aut ualeo stare aut noui ciuilia iura*).

45. *Consultatio* (*ante sententiam*) plus *relatio*: *RE* 4. 1 (1900) 1142 f., Berger (1953) 412 f. The (gist of) the oath: *cum ueritate et legum obseruatione iudicium esse disposituros* (Justin. *Cod.* 3. 1. 14. *Praef.*, *RE* 10. 1 (1917) 1257).

   At v. 39, *A diuo Augusto tunc petierunt* Müller (1877): **A. D. A. T. PETIERE** P: *Pontificem maximum tum rogauerunt* NV, cf. Burmann (1727) ad loc., '*Agnoscas episcopi manum* (*sc.* Perotti)'; cf. his Christian interpolation at 3. 5. 10: *poenas persoluit cruce* P: *p. soluit sceleris* NV.

   At v. 40, | *quod* P matches | *quod* (v. 37): *quando* R^{Vi}NV.

46. Solomon's Judgement: 1 Kings 3: 16 f., Frazer (1919) 2. 570 f.; at Rome: Suet. *Claud.* 15, Kelly (1957), Millar (1977) 228–40.

47. The Good King's clemency: Goodenough (1938) 94 f., Adam (1970) 20 f.

48. Law spawned telling lore about Emperors: 'When litigants detained Augustus in court with one case after another, he exclaimed that he wouldn't be in Rome after this'; 'Domitian delivered law conscientiously and energetically . . . he annulled arrogant Centumviral votes' (Suet. *Aug.* 97. 3; *Dom.* 8. 1; cf. Parks (1945) 32 f.).

49. Imperial mercy: Gaudemet (1962), Waldstein (1964).

50. *Causa . . . mali* is a cliché Latin calque on the Greek compound ἀρχέκακος: cf. Hom. *Il.* 5. 63; Virg. *Aen.* 6. 93, Luc. 1. 84, 7. 408, etc. Verbal sandwiching traps *libertus* in his sin, cf. Ov. *Fast.* 2. 35, *mali purgamina causam*. The metaphors couple (marry, I suppose) vigilant thoroughness with sensitive expertise in research: *perscrutatus* ~ *subtiliter limasset* (*rimasset* Schoppe (1598) would replicate the 'scrutiny': cf. Guaglianone (1976)). *Limasset* involves, not the usual 'filing' to smooth a surface, but the test of metal purity by removal of surface layers, cf. Apul. *Met.* 8. 8, *ad limam consilii desiderium petitoris distulit*, Symm. *Epp.* 1. 60, *amicus limatae*

probitatis (Bücheler (1915–30) 3. 26 adds Non. 525 Lindsay, *limari: exquirere*; cf. Glick (1938) 92). The family-tree house image of torn up roots, in Greek πρόρριζον: Griessmair (1966) 78; *a radicibus | euertisset*: cf. Plaut. *Aul.* 248, Glick (1938) 84. The boy *must* have been an only (male) child.

51. In Renaissance emblems, this motto *Non temere credendum* went with the hieroglyph of an eye in the palm of a hand: Alciati in Gandelman (1991) 3. Cf. Publil. *Sent.* 156, *Difficilem habere oportet aurem ad crimina*, Walbank on Polyb. 18. 40. 2.

52. 'Eyes more trustworthy than ears': *CPG* Apostol. 18. 71, cf. Hdt. 1. 8. 2, Walbank on Heraclit. *ap.* Polyb. 12. 27. 1, Sirach. *Ecclesiast.* 16, Festugière (1971) on *Hist. monach. in Aegypt.* 1. 19 p. 14.

53. 'The bi-polar cliché *aut gratiae . . . aut odio suo* is (nice and) pompously obtrusive: cf. historians' *sine ira et studio* (Goodyear on Tac. *Ann.* 1. 1. 3, Russo on *Apocol.* 1. 1, Weyman (1908) 278 f.), Epicureans' χωρὶς ὀργῆς καὶ χάριτος (Dihle (1971) 27 f.), Stoics' *neque ira neque gratia teneri* (Pease on Cic. *De nat. deor.* 1. 45) . . .

CHAPTER 3

1. A sketch of the original collection of *Phaedri Fabulae*: Henderson (1999*b*).

2. Conte (1992), cf. Fowler (1997) 20 f.

3. Cf. Leibfried (1982) for author- and reader-positions in Fable.

4. e.g. the mighty Wimmel (1960) finds no room in 331 pages littered with *Stellen* for any mention of Phaedrus. Lamberti (1980) makes some useful remarks.

5. Pinder (1869) 265–9 did at least select 3. *Prol.* for (rudimentary) commentary, alongside 1. 2, 2. 5, 5. 7 (and 4. 5). Nøjgaard (1967) 2. 153 rates the composition paralogical. Havet (1895) ruinously partitioned it: 'the most vigilant critic he has ever had and the most egotistical he can ever possibly have' (Housman (1900) 467; on his scientism, and characteristic 'insane amount of erudition': Cerquiglini (1999) 50; countering Havet on 3 Prol.: Tacke (1911) 32 f.). Prinz (1906) also deplored the confection: Rank (1917) 272–8. Just try any poem of Callimachus . . .

6. Rank (1917) 278 f. brings out the self-reflexive sampling of Phaedrus' poetastry paraded in the style of 3. *Prol.*

7. Henderson (1997*a*) esp. 12 f. Sejanus: Aelius § 133 in *RE* 1 (1893) 529–31; for our (improbable) image: Studniczka (1909).

8. Ben Jonson, *Sejanus His Fall* 1. 212–19: Henderson (1998*a*) esp. 25–32.
9. Von Blanckenhagen and Alexander (1990) 2.
10. Oceans of ink on this *anti-testimonium* for Phaedrus: is his work ignored (Prinz (1906)), as too low-brow (Dadone (1954) 7), under a cloud (Isleib (1906) 9 n. 2), as Greek (Jannelli (1811) 39, Lana (1955) 157), or through unscrupulous flattery (Postgate (1919*b*) 23)? Or hasn't Seneca *heard* of him yet from exile on his Corsican crag? Or is this, instead, where Phaedrus got the idea from? (Nøjgaard (1967) 2. 155) Polybius might frown, and Phaedrus might grin, at the mention of 'native *Roman* wit' (*Romanis ingeniis*).
11. Veyne (1987) 82–8.
12. Wallace (1959) 286.
13. Wishart (1998) 4, 111.
14. Ibid. 103–6, 208–12.
15. Suet. *De gramm.* 17, with Kaster (1995) ad loc.; Christes (1979*a*) 83–6.
16. Suet. *De gramm.* 20, with Kaster (1995) ad loc., Duret (1983) 1539–43, Christes (1979*a*) 72–82.
17. Suet. *De gramm.* 21, with Kaster (1995) ad loc., Duret (1983) 1479 f., Christes (1979*a*) 86–91. He gets onto Ovid's list of writers, as a comedian (*Ex Pont.* 4. 16. 30).
18. Treggiari (1969) 110–25, 'The learned professions and the fine arts': Phaedrus at 125. Apollodorus: Suet. *Aug.* 89. 1; Theodoros: Suda s.v. *Theodoros*; Antiochus: *CIL* 6. 5884, *a bibliotheca Latina Apollinis*, Griffin (1976) 105; Pappus: *AE* (1960) 26, *supra omnes bibliothecas Augustorum ab Ti. Caesare usque ad Ti. Claudium Caesarem*, Kaster (1995) 211. Cf. Forbes (1955), Chantraine (1967) ch. 8, Forte (1972) 180–2.
19. Atticus helped put up a statue of this Phaedrus in Athens: Raubitschek (1949).
20. Suet. *Gai.* 55. 2f., Jos. *Ant. Jud.* 19. 256–8 (with Wiseman (1991) 99, Gagé (1969)): Bücheler (1915–30) 2, 485, Dellacorte (1939) 136 f.; Rank (1917) 272 f., *RE* 6 (1907) 1536, *Eutychus* § 3, cf. § 4. Cf. Gail (1826) 2, 287, Excursus 1, Bloomer (1997) 264 n. 19. Surely a charioteer would precisely be busy working on a public holiday (vv. 8 f.): Rose (1936) 357 and n. 48 . . . [!].
21. *RE* 6 (1907) 1536, *Eutychus* § 2. Jos. *Bell. Iud.* 2. 179 has Agrippa openly praying *at dinner*, 'May I soon see Tiberius dead and you [Gaius] master of the universe', before Eutychus told on him to Tiberius.
22. Read Phaedrus and see—esp. Jedrkiewicz (1990) esp. 126 f.

23. To the prefaces and postfaces, add esp. 4. 11, 4. 21, 5. 4, *App* 2, 3, 7, 8; 'diatribe': Thiele (1906).

24. The terms (if's) dictated in editorials: 1. *Prol.* 5, 2. *Prol.* 9, 12, 2. *Epil.* 8, 10, 12, 15, 4. *Prol.* 4, 15, 4. *Epil.* 7, 5. *Prol.* 1, 6; cf. Hor. *Carm.* 1. 1. 7, 11, 35 (*sublimi . . . uertice*, 'Axis | Bold as Love', as someone once put it). The 'longing' is echoed, switched over to the writer, at 4. *Prol.* 20: *illitteratum plausum nec desidero.*

25. Niedermeier (1919) esp. 28 memorably studied the structure of the *bios* of Phaedrus: name/origin/physis/paideusis/fate and fortune . . .

26. *Eutychus* as common εὔφημον: Friedländer (1908) 4, Appendix 39, cf. Suet. *Aug.* 96. 2, Artemid. 3. 38, Pease on Cic. *De div.* 1. 102. Fictitious: Kaplan (1990). A mockery: Rank (1917) 287. Other literary dedications to freedmen: Josephus, *Contra Apionem* (to Epaphroditus), Scribonius Largus, *Compositiones* (to Callistus), etc., Bloomer (1997) 271 n. 61.

27. Smart (1761) iv: i.e. *John* Gay (*Fables*, London 1727).

28. Cic. *De diu.* 1. 80, Tac. *Ann.* 16. 5. 3, *RE.* 4. 1 (1900) 67, Clodius § 16.

29. *cura ~ studium*: Hauser (1954) 46. The carefree poet: Nisbet and Hubbard on Hor. *Carm.* 1. 26. Leisure/work ~ freedom/ compulsion: Toner (1995) esp. 17–21.

30. Cf., too, Hor. *Epp.* 2. 1. 1–4, 220–8, Ov. *Tr.* 2. 237, etc.; Mart. 12. 4, *plura legant uacui.*

31. The poem overworks the trope of *anteoccupatio* (πρόληψις), putting hasty words into another mouth: *inquis*, v. 4, *fortasse dices*, v. 8, *dicet fors aliquis*, 51 (cf. 5. *Prol.* 9, *sed dicis*; thoughts get poisoned at v. 24, *quid credis illi . . .?*). This marks adversative discourse, as (if) getting to the nitty gritty past the politesse: Hor. *Serm.* 1. 3. 19 f., *nunc aliquis dicat mihi, 'quid tu? | nullane habes uitia?'*; Sen. *De otio* 1. 4, *dices mihi, 'quid ais, Seneca? deseris partes?'.*

32. *soluto pectore*, v. 9, is a vigorous *stylistic* raise on the stake of *liber animus*, v. 3 (von Sassen (1911) 45).

33. Treating the *wife* well was optional, so a reputation for doing so would earn brownie points (if it could be made to stick): Veyne (1987) 40, 'The harmonious union'. *uicem*, v. 14, names the social place someone occupies, and so their 'duty' (e.g. Tac. *Ann.* 4. 8. 5, *uestram meamque uicem explete*): *propositum . . . et uitae genus*, v. 15 amplifies this to a 'calling' (cf. v. 22, *hanc . . . uitam*; as in e.g. *uitae genus*: Sen. *De otio* 7. 1, *tria genera sunt uitae . . . unum uoluptati uacat, alterum contemplationi, tertium actioni . . .*).

At v. 15, note *et* Pithou (1596): *ut* PR^GuVi (cf. Havet (1900) 298), *aut* Gude (1698), *al. al.*

At v. 22, note *et laude inuicta uitam in hanc* Desbillons (1786): *e. l. inuita i. h. u.* P, *nec* (Heinsius *Epp.* 21 *ap.* Scheffer) *Pallade* (Bentley *ap.* Postgate (1919*a*)) *h. inuita i. u.* Postgate (1919*a*), *e. l. multa u. i. h.* Gude ((1698) cf. Housman (1900) 467), *et laudem quaerens u. i. h.*, La Penna (1963) 228 *al. al.*: Gail (1826) 2. 288 f., Excursus 2.

34. Lumby (1908) 11: noticed by van Hoogstraten (1701).

35. *neniae*, v. 10, is the right word for this writing: self-deprecating of frivolous short poems (4. 2. 3), it retains an onomatopoeic charge, of droning on and on (Heller (1939) 307 n. 1)—as in the catechism of vv. 11–14, but also in the whole intonation of 1–26, with its debouchement in Lucretian scorn at vv. 24–6, cf. Lucr. 2. 12 f., *noctes atque dies niti praestante labore | ad summas emergere opes rerumque potiri*; with vv. 21 and 26, cf. Hor. *Carm.* 3. 24. 51 f., 62–4, *eradenda cupidinis | praui sunt elementa . . ., scilicet improbae | crescunt diuitiae; tamen | curtae nescioquid semper abest rei.||*, *Serm.* 1. 1, Ov. *Fast.* 1. 194 f., *cuius non animo dulcia lucra forent. | tempore creuit amor, qui nunc est summus, habendi*, etc. etc.

36. Prop. 3. 5. 19 f., *me iuuet in prima coluisse Helicona iuuenta | Musarumque choris implicuisse manus*; Hor. *Epp.* 2. 2. 91 f., '*mirabile uisu | caelatumque nouem Musis opus*'; Pers. *Prol.* 1–6, *Heliconidas . . . remitto . . ., ipse semipaganus*; *ILS* 5213 (Eucharis the mime) *docta, erudita paene Musarum manu | quae modo nobilium ludos decoraui choro | et Graeca in scena prima populo apparui*, with Wiseman (1985) 30–2.

37. Mnemosyne and Zeus: West on Hes. *Theog.* 54, Cook (1914–40) 1. 104, Pease on Cic. *De nat. deor.* 3. 54, *Ioue . . . Mnemosyne procreatae nouem . . .*, esp. Diod. Sic. 4. 7. 1. Ov. *Met.* 6. 114 alludes to 'Mnemosyne fooled by Jupiter playing shepherd' in his catalogue of Arachne's themes. She appears nowhere else in Latin poetry. In v. 19, *artium* of 'those skilled in arts' is one of Phaedrus' rare poeticisms: Bell (1923) 71, von Sassen (1911) 43. For the *chorus* (v. 19): e.g. Mart. 12. 3. 8, *Pierio . . . choro*, *Carm. Priap.* 2. 7, *castas, Pierium chorum, sorores*. *Schola* appears first in Latin poetry at v. 20: if there had been any such thing as a 'College of Poets' at Rome, something Martial could refer to as *schola poetarum* (3. 32. 8, 4. 61. 3), a quasi-'guild' meeting in an *aedes Musarum* (*Schol.* on Hor. *Serm.* 1. 10. 38), Phaedrus would be sending himself up a treat; for cold water (without mention of Phaedrus): Crowther (1973), Horsfall (1976).

38. Justin. 6. 8. 9, (Epaminondas) *homini inter litteras nato*, cf. Cic.

De or. 3. 131, *nati in litteris*, Sen. *Ad Polyb.* 2. 5, *animum eius liberalibus disciplinis, quibus non innutritus tantum sed innatus est, sic esse fundatum ut . . .*; Quintil. 1. 10. 21, reports as a Greek proverb that *indoctos a Musis atque a Gratiis abesse.*

At v. 20, note: *in ipsa paene natus sim* Heumann (1713) 609 f.; *i. i. n. s. p(a)ene* P; *i. i. p. s. n.* Heinsius (1698), *s. i. i. n. Phoebi iam* Havet (1895), cf. Housman (1920) 122, rejecting *s. i. i. n. Paeanis* Postgate (1919*a*).

39. *Literally* born in Pieria: Schwabe (1884) vs. *metaphorically*: Wölfflin (1884); cf. Hillscher (1891) 33 f. vs. Jannelli (1811) 2–10. Piso: Dellacorte (1939); Thracian *libertus*: Treggiari (1969) 247. The most exciting biography for Phaedrus: DeLorenzi (1955), esp. ch. 3; Peters (1946) is far more sensible.

40. Henry (1873–8) 2. 64 f. on *Aen.* 2. 77. Similarly, the whole Livian project of Roman History, we could say, rests in *his* preliminary gesture: *utcumque erit, iuuabit tamen . . . (Praef.* 3)

41. 'Obviously . . .': Finkelpearl (1998) 85 f., cf. 82–109, 'Sinon: Fiction, Naïveté, and the Audience', exposing the irony that: 'It is the mark of a good poet (or novelist) to deceive and of the good reader to be deceived. . . . All artful narrators are "Sinons", but most especially so are those narrators whose form sets up the assumption in their willingly believing audiences that the story they narrate will be true.' (85, 108). 'Sinon says' = badge of fictional discourse as reader-trap (Hexter (1990)).

42. *breui*, v. 34 is the most succinct way to promise to be succinct (cf. *TLL.* 2. 2178. 1 f.).

43. γέλοιον: Perry (1952) 227 f., *Testimonia* 53; σπουδογέλοιον: 1. *Prol.* 3 f., LaFontaine 6. 1. 5, Gerhard (1909) 229 n. 6, Mayer (1969) 102 f.; general corrective: 2. *Prol.* 3; 3. *Prol.* 33–40 = Perry, ibid. 228, no. 57, cf. Christes (1979*b*) 213, Bradley (1987) 150–3; Jul. *Or.* 7. 207c = ibid., no. 58. Aesopica as 'La morale delle classi subalterni': La Penna (1961). On the *Life of Aesop* and Roman slavery, esp. Hopkins (1993), Jennings (2000). Slavery and the Roman imagination, and image-repertoire: Fitzgerald (2000).

44. Daube (1972) 53.

45. Bloomer (1997) 84; Lewis (1996) 3 argues for a broad sweep of 'mediation of oppositions' in cultural productivity.

46. Simple poetry: Herder. Philosophy: Lessing. See Noel (1975) 137; Patterson (1991) *passim*: Fable as 'functional ambiguity'. Texts on fable 'theory': Dithmar (1982) nos. 42–7 = all eight Phaedrian pro-/epi-logues.

47. Secondary construal of slavery: Christes (1979*b*) 208–19. Safe criticism: Ahl (1984), with not a(n open) squeak about fable—see

Bartsch (1994) 63–97, 'Oppositional innuendo: performance, allusion, and the audience', esp. 90, citing 3. *Prol.* 45–50, and 244 n. 59.

48. e.g. Hor. *Serm.* 1. 4. 6, *hinc omnis pendet Lucilius.*

49. Proverbial: *CPG App. Prov.* 4. 12, ὁδοῦ παρούσης τὴν ἀτραπὸν μὴ ζήτει, Enn. *ap.* Cic. *De diu.* 1. 132 (*superstitiosi uates*) *qui sibi semitam non sapiunt, alteri monstrant uiam.* Mart. 7. 61. 4, *et modo quae fuerat semita facta uia est*, Otto (1890) 370, s.v. *uia.* (*Semita* vs. *uia*: André (1950) 109, 113.) Callimachus: *Ait.* fr. 1. 25–8, τὰ μὴ πατέουσιν ἅμαξαι | τὰ στείβειν, ἑτέρων δ' ἴχνια μὴ καθ' ὁμά | δίφρον ἐλᾶν μηδ' οἶμον ἀνὰ πλατύν, ἀλλὰ κελεύθους | ἀτρίπτους, εἰ καὶ στεινοτέρην ἐλάσεις, *Epig.* 30. 1 f., οὐδὲ κελεύθῳ | χαίρω τίς πολλοὺς ἔ ὧδε καὶ ὧδε φέρει, Wimmel (1960) 103–7, esp. 106 f., esp. Prop. 2. 23. 1 f., *cui fugienda fuit indocti semita uulgi*, 3. 1. 14, *non datur ad Musas currere lata uia*, 17 f., *quod pace legas opus hoc de monte Sororum,* | *detulit intacta pagina nostra uia*, 3. 16. 30, *non iuuat in media nomen habere uia*, Manil. 2. 50, *omnis ad accessus Heliconos semita trita est*; Babr. 2. *Prol.* 9–12, 'when the door was first opened up by me, | in went others, and they bring forth | poems like the riddles of a cleverer muse, | though they have learned nothing more than I know'. Satire and ?poetry?: Hor. *Serm.* 1. 4. 39–63.

For v. 38, note: *ego porro illius semitam* Schoppe (1598), *e. i. p. semita* PR^Gu (but see Bährens (1918) 192), *i. p. e. semita* R^Vi, *e. i. pro semita* Johnson (1708) (scorned by Housman (1920) 124), *i. porro i. semitam e.* Havet (1895).

50. 'Led to' (Burmann (1727), Nisard cit. Rank (1911) 55, cf. 51–8 vs. 'relating to' (Jannelli (1811) 34, Vollmer (1919); cf. Zimmermann (1934) 477 f.: 'after imprisonment through Tiberius' reign, maybe Gaius', too . . .'). Suffering satirist (Aesop, Archilochus, Homer, Socrates): Compton (1990); cf. 'Juvenal's exile': *Vit. Iuv., uenit ergo Iuuenalis in suspicionem, quasi tempora figurate notasset.* Antidote: e.g. Ov. *Tr.* 4. 10. 117–20, *gratia, Musa, tibi: nam tu solacia praebes* | *tu curae requies, tu medicina uenis.* | *tu dux et comes, tu nos abducis ab Histro,* | *in medioque mihi das Helicone locum.* Who, when . . .: do the future verbs at vv. 45, 47, show that possible future misinterpretation is the point, not some past trauma? (Zimmermann (1934) 478) Is *alius* + abl. *Seiano* at v. 41? (Bertschinger (1921) 11: a colloquialism, cf. Hor. *Epp.* 2. 1. 240, Brutus and Cassius ap. Cic. *Fam.* 11. 2. 2, Causeret (1886) 64, LHS 11) Or is *Seiano* dative, so this is Tiberius, who was Sejanus' prosecutor, judge and jury? (Griset (1925) vs. Klotz (1925)). Schanz proposed to read *Seiani!* (vs. *RE* 19. 2. (1938) 1476. 8) Does *foret* = *esset*, not *fuisset*, at v. 41 show this is all in the realm of

the imaginary? (Nisard, *cit.* Rank (1911) 55: 'Tout cela est une belle histoire, ou plutôt serait le thème d'une belle histoire', cf. Bloomer (1997) 105 f., 272 n. 67), or does *foret* = *fuisset*, and attest the autobiographical? (Rank (1911) 58, (1917) 287 n. 1, cf. Prinz (1906), (1923) 63 f.) The opposite problem arises in the Tiberian text of Valerius Maximus, denouncing the foiled, or failed, would-be assassin of Tiberius at the top of his voice and in no uncertain terms: but omitting the name (9. 11. ext. 4: Wardle (1998) 3 f.).

51. Disclaimer: Bramble (1974) 190–204, e.g. Mart. 10. 33. 9f., *hunc seruare modum nostri nouere libelli, | parcere personis, dicere de uitiis,* Plin. *Epp.* 1. 10. 7, *insectatur uitia, non homines, nec castigat errantes, sed emendat.* At v. 47, *conscientia animi* (knowing you've done something, good or bad: Nettleship (1889) 420) is part of the build-up to the high-and-mighty lecture, *mens est . . . ipsam uitam et mores . . . hominum* (vv. 49 f.): cf. Hor. *Serm.* 2. 1. 60, *quisquis erit uitae scribam color, Ars poet.* 317 f., *respicere exemplar uitae morumque iubebo | doctum imitatorem,* 344, *simul et iucunda et idonea dicere uitae,* Pers. 5. 52, *mille hominum species,* Mart. 8. 33. 19 f., *at tu Romano lepidos sale tinge libellos: | agnoscat mores uita legatque suos.* Aesop the Phrygian is ushered in as ὁ βιωφελέστατος (*Aes. Vit.* 1), as if another Menander (cf. *Comparatio Menandri et Philistionis* 2. 8–9 Jäkel, Φιλιστίωνα . . . τὸν βιωφελῆ; ib. 1. 3 ὁ τοῦ βίου τὴν πρᾶξιν ἐπιδείξας σοφοῖς | Μένανδρος).

52. A new home for vv. 45–50 (George Eliot, *Impressions of Theophrastus Such*): 'Whether the motto (which is singularly apt and good) should be on the title-page or the fly-leaf, I leave you to judge' (letter to J. Blackwood 9. 4. 1879, cit. Haight (1954–78) 6. 130 n. 6).

53. Suspicion: Hor. *Serm.* 1. 4. 64 f. (Satire =) *suspectum genus hoc scribendi?*
     At v. 46, note: *rapiet* P: *rapiens* Postgate (1919a). *accusator . . . excusatum,* vv. 41 ~ 48!

54. This is satire's territory, always out to probe beyond conventional forms: e.g. Hor. *Serm.* 2. 7. 83, *quisnam igitur liber?,* Pers. 5. 72, *libertate opus est,* etc. etc.

55. Rogers (1935) 168 f. Speculation about 'the trial': De Lorenzi (1955) 97 f., Rank (1911) 51 f., Romano (1927).

56. Terror: Seager (1972) 178–214, Bird (1969). *Maiestas* trials: Levick (1976) 180–200, esp. 195. Rigged: e.g. Tac. *Ann.* 4. 28. 1, *reus pater, acusator filius* in senate: *iudex idem et testis dicebat.* Proverbial: Men. *Monost.* 404 Jäkel, κατηγορεῖν οὐκ ἔστι καὶ κρίνειν ὁμοῦ, Publil. *Sent.* 729, *ubi iudicat qui accusat, uis non lex ualet;* in

legend, App. Claudius got his client M. Claudius to seize Verginia as his abducted slave, and denounce Verginius to the magistrate, namely App. Claudius, who is smitten with her, *'id se iudicio compertum adferre probaturumque uel ipso Verginio iudice ad quem maior pars iniuriae eius pertineat'* (Liv. 3. 44. 10).

57. Wishart (1998) 34.

58. Virg. *Ecl.* 6. 1–12 brought the Callimachean negotiation with the Muse to solliciting the Roman grandee addressee, dedicatee, reader (Varus). Propertius made fun with the rigmarole, the moment he became famous, and grew a great addressee: *quod mihi si tantum, Maecenas, fata dedissent, | ut possem heroas ducere in arma manus . . . bella resque tui memorarem Caesaris . . sed . . .* (2. 1. 17–39). See Wimmel (1960) *passim*, or read any Latin poetry you like.

59. Ἀπόπεμψις: Wimmel (1960) 100 and n. 3.

60. e.g. Ov. *Am.* 3. 15. 7 f., *Mantua Vergilio gaudet, Verona Catullo; | Paelignae dicar gloria gentis ego* (cf. v. 61, . . . *gloria*).

61. *Iners* = non-*ars*: Lucil. 452, *ars in quo non erit ulla*, cf. Ov. *Ars* 3. 412, etc.

62. Cf. esp. Ov. *Rem.* 369 f., 389 f., *Tr.* 4. 10. 121–4.

63. *Latium*: Hor. *Epp.* 1. 19. 23 f., *Parios ego primus iambos | ostendi Latio; dum*: Hor. *Carm.* 3. 30. 7–9, *usque ego postera | crescam laude recens, dum Capitolium | scandet . . . pontifex.* With *laudis conscientiam*, cf. v. 47, *animi conscientiam*.

64. 2. *Epil.* 10, 4. 22. 1, 5. *Prol.* 9, *Inuidia mordax.* Cf. Nisbet and Hubbard on Hor. *Carm.* 2. 20. 4.

65. At v. 52, note *Scytha* Schoppe (1598): *Scythae* PR[Vi], *Schytae* R[Gu], *Scythes* Stowasser (1893).

At v. 53: *suo* P: *suis* Havet (1895). At v. 54: *propior* Pithou (1596): *proprior* PR[GuVi] (cf. 3. *Epil.* 10).

At v. 56: *suos* P: *deos* Rittershausen (1598), *duos* Burmann (1718).

66. Juv. 8. 45. This neat, and power-packed, rhetoric entirely eludes even the worthy Thiele (1906) 574.

67. Phrygian: *Aes. Vit.* 1, *CPG* Zenob. 5. 16, Μᾶλλον ὁ Φρύξ, Perry (1952) 215 f., Testimonia 4. Thracian: ibid. 216, no. 5.

68. Diog. Laert. 1. 103, *Gnom. Vat.* 15, cf. 16, Clem. Alex. *Strom.* 1. 16 *MPG* 8. 792a, Reuters on Anach. *Epp.* 1. 1 (p. 71), Jöel (1893–1901) 2. 358, 808. One of the 'Seven Sages': Ephorus *FGH* 70 fr. 42, *RE* 2. 2 (1923) 2244. 28; his legend: Armstrong (1948) 18, Oltramare (1926) 14; contact with Aesop: Diog. Laert. 1. 105 = *Aes. Vit.* 51, Heinze (1891–2) 463 f.

69. Androtion *ap.* Ael. *Var. Hist.* 8. 6. 'Why?': Graf (1987) 99–101:

101: 'No special reason . . . His fame as a poet made him—or kept him, if he really was a hero or god of the Pierian Thracians—a Thracian'.

70. See esp. the inspired lucubrations of Ross (1975) esp. 21–34; pairing of Apollo with *Calliope* as the source of inspiration (at Prop. 1. 2. 27 f., 2. 1. 3 f.) will also be Virgilian allusion to Gallus: ibid. 60.

71. Most obviously in the pastoral of Nemesianus, 1. 24–6, (praise of Meliboeus) *dignus quem carmine Phoebus, | Pan calamis, fidibus Linus aut Oeagrius Orpheus | concinerent*; cf. Ov. *Am.* 3. 9. 21–3, *quid mater profuit Orpheo? . . . | et Linon . . .*; Quintil. 1. 10. 9, *utrumque dis genitum*, Tac. *Dial.* 12, *apud illos dis genitos . . . Orphea et Linum ac si introspicere altius uelis, ipsum Apollinem.*

72. Nisbet and Hubbard on Hor. *Carm.* 1. 24. 13.

73. Aesop, too, dies an outcast's death, tossed over a cliff after a frame-up for theft. What became of Anacharsis is no more clear to me than whatever it was happened to Sinon in the end (last glimpsed 'gleefully fire-raising and dancing on the grave of Troy': Virg. *Aen.* 2. 329 f.).

74. The most sensitive discussion of 'The death of Orpheus' is Thompson (1993) esp. 90–115: 'Killing me softly (with his song)' and 'The text in tatters/the floating song'.

75. See Ross (1975) 93, 118, cf. *Culex* 278 f.

76. The cameo at vv. 625–31, however, sticks to a parade of Virgil plus Ovid's echo-text in *Metamorphoses* 11: *ille uocali genitus Camena, | cuius ad chordas modulante plectro | restitit torrens, . . . | Thracios sparsus iacuit per agros, | at caput tristi fluitauit Hebro*: cf. Henderson (1983) 104.

77. Nisbet and Hubbard on Hor. *Carm.* 1. 12. 9. The old model: e.g. Ov. *Met.* 11. 1 f., *carmine . . . siluasque ferarum | Threicius uates et saxa sequentia ducit.*

78. Harpalyce from Callimachus (?): Austin on *Aeneid* 1. 317, cf. O'Hara (1996) 124. *Hebrus* ~ ἕβρος· τράγος βάτης, Hesychius, Maass (1925) 465, Paschalis (1997) 64. Cf. Henry (1873–8), 1. 598.

79. This is very likely influenced by the self-righteous closure to Ovid's ἀπόπεμψις at Ov. *Am.* 1. 15. 40, *. . . cum suus ex merito quemque tuetur honos.*

Editors are divided at v. 61: *quoniam* P: *quom iam* Hare (1726) *quod iam* Freinsheim (1664). *debetur* P, cf. Krischan (1954) 84: *debentur* R^{Gu}, *dabitur* Scheffer (1663), *detur* Freinsheim (1664).

80. Most famously, Hor. *Carm.* 1. 1. 35 f., *quodsi me lyricis uatibus inseres | sublimi feriam sidera uertice.* ||, *both* returns to the initial address to | *Maecenas*, setting terms for the reading of the

collection of *Odes* as an *indirect* request for literary canonization, *and* latches onto each and every reader among us—onto YOU.

81. Dedication and proving: P. White (1974) 53, briskly considering Ov. *Fast.* 1. 19 f. alongside Phaedr. 3. *Prol.*; cf. Prop. 2. 13. 11 f., 14, *domina iudice tutus ero*, etc. etc. For *candor* (v. 63), cf. e.g. Ov. *Pont.* 2. 5. 5, von Sassen (1911) 23; Hor. *Epp* 1. 4. 1, *candide iudex*. The notion is picked up again in the *Epilogue* to the book (vv. 27, 30 *iudicio tuo . . . integritatis . . . sincerae*; cf. 4. *Prol.* 19 *dignum . . . iudicatis*).

CHAPTER 4

1. In the MSS, 5. 5 is separated from 5. 6–7 by what Brotier (1783) removed to be our '4. *Epil.*' (Henderson (1999*b*) 310–11, 316–17).

2. Bücheler (1915–30) 2. 454–8, '*Coniectanea V*': from Jahn (1841) 'Addenda', 138, *Titulus Amerinus = CIL* 11. 4424 = *ILS* 5239 = Bonaria (1956) 2. 54, no. 506 (53f.; no. 505 = Phaedr. 5. 7).

3. Bücheler (1915–30) 2. 454–8 tried to explain Princeps' ʾagnomenˀ *CAPPA* as (*inter alia*) a reference to his habit of wearing shoes sporting the *lunula*, called κάππα by Ioh. Antioch. fr. 33 *FHG* 4. 553 (Cf. Suda s.v. χλαμύς, Lau (1967) Fig. 31b, O'Connor (1905)). Weinreich (1944–8) 155 thought Princeps might have been tall, thin—and 'K'-shaped . . . (Or did *KAPPA* spell out the K(οινόν: 'Community') of union-registered Τεχνῖται? ('Craftsmen': cf. *RE*. 5.2² (1934) 2481. 5 f.).)

4. e.g. Perry (1965) 88 n. 1, Christes (1979*b*) 215.

5. Moorhouse (1971), on 'The [London] Palladium'.

6. Milligan (1971) 92 f.: his part, n.b., in the downfall of A. Hitler.

7. As noticed in Ch. 3, Pinder (1869) 277–9 picked this story for his selection of five from Phaedrus; Weinreich (1944–8) gives expert commentary, with translation ('Hans Fürst'), spoiled somewhat by the assumption that the drama which is the occasion for Princeps' mistake represents a Bathyllan pantomime (so too Reich (1903) 1. 439, Beare (1964) 267 f.). But we are told just that Princeps took a bow *ludorum . . . die*, v. 19.

8. Why we have stars—to think (spite) with: Dyer (1982) esp. 38–52, 'Stars as stars'.

9. The story acts out the compound steps in the 'moves' of spectatorship analysed by Goffman: see Bartsch (1994) 211 n. 23.

10. Massie (1989): Maecenas tells him back (324), 'It's abject, isn't it, my surrender to him?' Bathyllus as the key figure in Augustanized panto: Leppin (1996).

11. Luc. *Salt.* 63; erotic mythological melodrama as staple: ibid. 2, Sittl (1890) 246 f.; Jory (1996) 37, *RE* 18. 3 (1949) 847–9.

12. e.g. Juv. 3. 63 f., 6. 61–77, 7. 90–2, 8. 185–98.

13. Actors in the audience: Bartsch (1994), esp. 2,: 'Here alone the ruler acts as captive audience for the will of his gathered subjects.' L'Acteur-Roi: DuPont (1985), a searing dissection of *histrionalis fauor* and the Caesars, which however mentions Phaedrus only as testimony for the flute in 'La musique' (88).

14. Riots at the first games for *Diuus Augustus*, after a pantomime went on strike for higher pay: Dio 56. 47. 2, Slater (1994) 124; more riots in 15: Tac. *Ann.* 1. 77, Slater (1994) 125 f.; strengthened bar: *Tabula Larinas*, Slater (1994) 140 f.; exile in 23: Tac. *Ann.* 4. 14. 3, Suet. *Tib.* 37, 2, Dio 57. 21. 3, Bollinger (1969) 57. 'A type': Jory (1981) 152.

15. Recall in 37: Jory (1981) 152. Cremated: Suet. *Gai.* 27. 4, cf. Bollinger (1969) 37. Collapse of theatre: Bartsch (1994) 1 f.

16. Nero/Paris: Beacham (1991) 147f. Rearranging the logic of theatre: Bartsch (1994) esp. 2f.

17. Suet. *Tib.* 38, cf. Cic. *Ad Att.* 13. 12. 3; but this Attic 'moonwalk' calls for a leap *of the imagination* (we don't *know* this Callippides was an 'actor', not a runner).

18. DuPont (1985) 100; cf. 396. Veyne (1990) 400–1 barely notes our tale.

19. Cf. my arguments about the non-entities in Hor. *Serm.* 1. 7 masking the mythological imperatives of 'Brutus' faced with the word or beast *rex*, and Caesar: Henderson (1998*b*) 73–107.

20. So: '*given that* Prince *is* secure / inviolate / in one piece' (constative); 'co-variant with Prince being secure / inviolate / in one piece' (theoretical); '*if* so be Prince is secure / inviolate / in one piece' (conditional); etc. . . .

21. Manea (1994) 56, dubbing his country's petty tyrant 'the national clown'.

22. Fellini, cit. Manea (1994) 52 f., on 'Auguste the Fool', in cerebration of Chaplin's Hitler, and other clowns. Theorized: Canetti (1973)—*Masse und Macht*—is the classic study.

23. *Ad derisum stulta*: anticipating *stultum*, v. 30, *magno . . . risu*, v. 31, *illudens*, v. 33.

24. *uanus animus*, v. 1, is a(n enlightened, 'philosophical') target: in (Greek) ethics, κενοδοξία. *Aura captus friuola*, v. 2 rustles up a not unpicturesque adjective to vary a cliché: *friuolus* occurs in Republican Latin only at *Ad Her.* 4. 11. 6 (cf. Phaedr. 3. 6. 8, *aufer friuolam insolentiam* ~ *insolentem*, 5. 7. 2; for its origins, cf. Isid. *Orig.* 9. 7. 26, *friuola sunt proprie uasa fictilia quassa*, Callebat

(1967) 406, Goldberger (1931–2) 139 f.). Undisguised, or un-castrated, the cliché *popularis aura* (e.g. Hor. *Carm.* 3. 2. 20, Liv. 3. 33. 7, Virg. *Aen.* 6. 815, Luc. 1. 132, Büchmann (1895) 322) would not serve. It would set *political* alarm-bells ringing *far* too loudly, in even the most cavernous of unoccupied crania.

    Arripuit . . . sibi fiduciam, v. 2, is some more standard moral sermonizing fare: (συν)αρπάζω ('fasten on (a claim to possession, a lucky break, a chance find)': Cic. *De Sen.* 62, Posidon. *ap.* Cic. *De nat. deor.* 2. 18; Jaeger (1915) 545); + φιλαυτία. *Derisus*, v. 3: κατάγελως, is (how apt) first extant in post-Augustan Latin (cf. 1. 11. 2, another promythium, Sen. Rhet., Val. Max., *TLL.* 5. 1. 633. 66f.).

25. Εὔφημον: e.g. Suet. *Vesp.* 19. 2, *Favor archimimus*, Artemid. 3. 38, Friedländer (1908) 4, Appendix 39; cf. '*Phaedrus*' etc., ch. 3. Slave-name?: Kajanto (1965) 74f., 291.

    With *ducitur*, v. 3, cf. *reducto*, 25.

26. '*Luxussklaven*': cf. *CPG.* Apostol. 3. 71, Ἀράβιος αὐλητής, Forbes (1955) 329, Wille (1967) 311 f. Upstart aesthetes: Brecht (1930) 39 f., Wille (1967) 332 f.; cheeks: Frazer on Apollod. 1. 4. 2, Marsyas, Plut. *Alcib.* 2; monkeys: Ar. *Rhet.* 3. 12. 1413^a, McDermott (1938) 2, nos. 106 f., 184, 271, 349, 483, 540–2, Wille (1967) 333 f.; ego: *Com. inc.* fr. 733 Kock, Αὐτὸς αὐτὸν αὐλεῖ, Headlam on Herod. 2. 32; lecherous: Archil. fr. 183 Bergk *PMG*, Schol. Lycophr. *Alex.* 771); effete: *Gnom. Vat.* 173, Bompaire (1958) 454). Cynics sucked on them: Diog. *ap.* Diog. Laert. 6. 51, Philostr. *Vit. Apoll.* 5. 21, Reuters on Anachars. *Epp.* 6. 2. Delirium: Vernant (1991) 125 f. Energy: DuPont (1985) 88.

27. On this theme of modernity: Burns (1972).

28. Philonides: Crinag. *Anth. Pal.* 9. 542 = Gow and Page (1968) 1995 f.; *Sophe Theorobathylliana arbitrix imboliarum*: *ILS* 5263 (Belonging rather to the school?: Rotolo (1957) 89, on *Testimonia* 3). No mask: Dierks (1883) 9. 'You love': Luc. *Harmon.* 2. Colloquial *comparatiuus inutilis*: Caes. *Bell. Ciu.* 2. 19, *nullus fuit ciuis Romanus paulo notior quin*, Wölfflin (1933) 176. *Solitus*, v. 5: e.g. 4. 4. 1, *AES* 37, Mart. 9. 73, Fraenkel (1964) 1. 80.

29. 'Helpless': Massie (1990) 61. This is B. § 7 in *RE.* 3. 1 (1897) 137 f., Treggiari (1969) 140 f., e.g. Hor. *Epod.* 14. 9, Sen. *Contr.* 10. *Praef.* 8, Tac. *Ann.* 1. 54. '22 BCE': so Jerome *Chron.* 27, 2. 143 Schöne; = 23: Jory (1981) 148; panto riots in 22 (and 17) BCE: Friedländer (1908) 2. 101 f. Twinned with Pylades: Sen. *Contr.* 3. *Praef.* 10, Bonaria (1956) 2. 50–4, nos. 484–507; fused with him: Jory (1981) 148–50. More *Bathylli*: Juv. 6. 63, Friedländer (1908), 4. *Appendix* 39, D–S 4. 1. 3161 (more *Pylades*: e.g. Timoth. *Anth.*

Pal. 7. 412, §§ 3–5 in *RE* 23. 2 (1959) 2083–5; *Paris* after *Paris*: e.g. Mart. 11. 13, §§ 2–6 in *RE*. 18. 4. (1949) 1536 f.). '*Bathyllus*' was a hypocoristic love-name, from *Bathykles*, say ('Deep-fame'). Anacreon's Samian παιδικά: § 5 in *RE*. 3. 1 (1897) 137, a well-remembered figure, cf. Antipater of Sidon, *Anth. Pal.* 7. 30 with Gow and Page (1965) on vv. 278 f., Fraenkel (1957) 68 n. 2, Wilamowitz (1913) 109 n. 1; an aulete: Max. Tyr. *Or.* 37. 5; so a name for a Ganymede: Alciphr. *Epp.* 3. 68 Hercher. The etymology stayed live, cf. *IG.* 3. 1197, Βάθυλλος· ὁ καὶ Ὕψιστος, Pers. 5. 122 f., *fossor*, | . . . *Bathylli* |: as if 'Truly-Madly-Deepling', or 'How-Deep-is-your-lust?'

30. *Is forte*: to open an anecdote: e.g. Tac. *Hist.* 3. 25, *Iulius Mansuetus ex Hispania . . . filium domi liquerat. is mox adultus . . . oblatum forte patrem . . . scrutatur. non satis memini quibus*: out-and-out parodies of such niceties at Plaut. *Amph.* 254, Sen. *Apocol.* 2, esp. Luc. *Ver. hist.* 1. 18. *concidit casu*, v. 7, is a casual colloquial (!) 'adnomination'; *graui* is an *epitheton sollemne*, 'nasty spill' (Lucr. 5. 1333, Liv. 8. 7. 11, etc.).

31. *nec opinans*, v. 8: less stylish than *inopinans* (Pascucci on [Caes.] *Bell. Hisp.* 2. 1), more prosaic than *necopinus* (1. 9. 6; first in Ov., Bömer on *Met.* 1. 224).

    At v. 8, note: *nec opinans et* Pithou (1596): *n. opia sed* PR^Gu, *ne copia* R^Vi, *necopinus et* Nevelet (1610).

32. Pun on *tibia*, vv. 8–9: Lucr. 4. 585, *tibia . . . digitis pulsata*, du Méril (1834) 432 (The Medieval 'Alda'), *crebrosque ingressibus eius* (*sc.* the lame man) | *longa facit iambos tibia iuncta breui*. *Auloi* were in one tradition of boxwood, Ov. *Fast.* 6. 697, Plin. *Nat. hist.* 16. 172; but for animal *tibiae*, cf. Philit. fr. 16 Powell and Antip. *Anth. Plan.* 305 (= Gow and Page (1968) v. 487 with n.: fawn); Defradas on Plut. *Sept. sap. conu.* 5. 150e (an old riddle: ass), Hygin. *Fab.* 165 (stag); Philostr. *Vit. Apoll.* 5. 21 (gold, brass, or shin of stag, or of ass).

    The complementary 'double pipes' were distinguished as male/female (Hdt. 1. 17), right/left (Varr. *Res. rust.* 1. 2. 15, *RE*. 6.1² (1936) 809. 48f.), equal/unequal (Comotti (1989) 51). *Duae dextrae* might be played conjointly (in the opening of the *Palliata*: Weinreich (1944–8) 156). Did pipers need two-handed virtuosity (à la jazz reedman Roland Kirk)?

33. The fall *is* a bit problematic: in drama, Greek pipers sat in the orchestra (e.g. Luc. *Salt.* 2), whereas Roman *tibicines* trod the boards to be near the actor speaking (cf. Cic. *Pro Mur.* 26, *transit tibicinis Latini modo*, Polyb. 30. 14, Brink on Hor. *Ars. Poet.* 214). In a Bathyllan extravaganza, just about anything went? (Pipers

among the cast or chorus: Beazley (1955) 309 f., Walden (1894)
27–9.) It sounds as if Princeps was *on* the *pegma*, a machine used
to whisk actors on or off stage in marvellous fashion (Sen. *Epp.*
88. 22, *pegmata per se surgentia . . . et tabulata tacite in sublime
crescentia*, Claud. *De Manl. Theod. cos.* 17. 325, *mobile ponderibus
descendat pegma reductis*, Mayor on Juv. 4. 122, Beacham (1991)
180, *RE.* 19. 1 (1937) 66 f., 5. 2^2 (1934) 1418). *Pegma* can also
involve trapdoor τερατεία, Strab. 6. 2. 6, or manoeuverable
scaffold or float, Jos. *Bell. Iud.* 7. 5. 5, or any suspended basket,
Jos. *Ant. Iud.* 14. 15. 5). Princeps was joining 'the gods', cf. Liv.
39. 13. 13, *raptos a diis homines dici quos machinae illigatos ex
conspectu in abditos specus abripiant*, presumably by a lift to the
roof, cf. Juv. 4. 122, *et pegma et pueros inde ad uelaria raptos*
(Weinreich (1944–8) 156 somehow talked himself into supposing
a collapse of side-scenes.).

34. Accidents with stage-machines were not unknown: *Com. inc.* fr.
750 Kock, κράδης ῥαγείσης (= the hook for flying in gods: Crusius
(1889) 697 f., Sall. *Hist.* 2. 70 Maurenbrecher, a *transenna*). The
fall from the skybound platform during his spectacular exit *en
plein air* is Princeps' upmarket refinement on the mundane slip,
the flying young stage-performer's nightmare: e.g. Lucill. *Anth.
Pal.* 11. 254, Weinreich (1944–8) 88, 91.

35. Cf. Cic. *Verr.* 2. 5. 28, *alias inter manus e conuiuio tamquam e
proelio auferretur*, Liv. 3. 13. 3.

36. Liv. 2. 12; cf. Pavlovskis (1967).

37. v. 12: a neat, but faintly odd, expression: cf. Prop. 3. 24. 18,
uulneraque ad sanum coiere mea, Sen. *Epp.* 2. 3, *non uenit uulnus ad
cicatricem* (Mood (1907) 4).

38. Spectators' 'desire' (*pothos*) for the artiste: Mart. 11. 43. 4 (Paris),
Romani decus et dolor theatri, Weinreich (1940–1) 1. 14, 20. Did
the piper *define* the act?: Jerome *Chron.* 27, (Pylades) *primus
Romae chorum et fistulam sibi praecinere fecit*. Or did Bathyllus lean
specially on *his* assistant? Wagenvoort (1920) 101 f. and Weinreich
(1944–8) 156 try their best to contrast Pylades' elaborate sensa-
tionalism (M. Bieber (1961) 165 f., 232 f., Wille (1967) 178 f.) with
Bathyllan traditionalism, as revealed not least by his simple
orchestration. Ballet stars took the *entrechat* to extremes (Plut.
Quaest. conu. 7. 8. 711 f., 'next thing to a κόρδαξ'). Lift from a
tibicen's support was a traditional concept: Liv. 7. 2. 9, *canticum
egisse aliquanto magis uigente motu quia nihil uocis usus impediebat*
(Wille (1967) 169 f.: *auloi* gave real 'jumpers' a 'lift', cf. Philostr.
Gymn. 55, Paus. 5. 7. 10; whence *tibicen* = 'prop', Paul. Fest. 503
Lindsay, *tibicines in aedificiis dici existimantur a similitudine*

tibiis canentium, qui ut cantantes sustineant ita illi aedificiorum tecta).

39. When the Cynic sage Apollonius grills Canus, the best piper still blowing strong, 'What does a piper *do*?' and is told 'Everything the audience wants', this is provocation for a demolition-job which expertly fingers it as a bodily craft, no more no less: a good pair of hands, and keep time (Philostr. *Apollon.* 5. 21).

40. Edwards (1994) 84, DuPont (1985) esp. 92, 396. For the phrasing of v. 17, cf. Planc. (Cic). *Fam.* 10. 17. 2, (after illness) *cum primum posse ingredi coepit*, Plin. *Nat. hist.* 8. 45, *uix ingredi posse*, Dio 57. 17. 4 (gout) διὰ τὸ τοῦ ἀνθρώπου . . . στῆναι . . . δύνασθαι. The asyndetonic alliterative phrase *precibus pretio*, 'für Gelte und güte Worte', 'by hook or by crook', has its terms in this order in Ter. *Eun.* 1055, Ov. *Fast.* 2. 805 (vs. 806), Hor. *Epp.* 2. 2. 173 (reversed: Acc. fr. 664 Ribbeck; *CIL* 4. 400, cf. Wölfflin (1933) 231, 272). But certain restoration of vv. 17–18 is impossible:

> *et incipiebat posse Princeps ingredi:* | *eum adducit precibus pretio ut tantummodo* Henderson (1976): *& i. princeps adduci reû. ingredi (i.* R^GuVi) *a se* | *reducit* (*reduci* R^Vi? *reducit* according to Brotier (1783)) *pretio* (*pretio* R^Vi, *ptio* P) *pretibus* (P, see Zwierlein (1970) 93, Finch (1971) 307) *u. t.* PR^Vi, *e. ut i. p. P. i.* Bentley (1726), *adducit* Saumaise (1698); *et i. i. P. eum* | *adducit pretio precibus, ut t.* Pinder (1869) 277, *ut i. i. P., eum* | *adducit p. p. u. t.* Müller (1877), cf. Önnerfors (1987) 441 f. One of the most vexed cruces in the *Fables*: Havet (1895) ad loc., Postgate (1896) 9, Festa (1898) 267 f., Gail (1826) 2. 367 f., *Excursus* 31.

Taking a bow makes for something of a freak-show specimen: with v. 19, *ut tantummodo* | . . . *ostenderet sese*, cf. Suet. *Aug.* 43. 3, *adulescentulum . . . exhibuit, tantum ut ostenderet, quod erat bipedali minor*; with (its echo) *modo reducto*, v. 25, cf. Plin. *Nat. hist.* 7. 158, *Galena Copiola emboliaria annum agens CIV reducta est*, Cic. *Ad fam.* 7. 1. 2 (Aesopus et c.), *rediere.*

41. The classical stage-curtain appears at v. 24 for positively the last time. It was dropped into a groove at the outset (Hor. *Epp.* 2. 1. 189, *premitur*), raised at the close to obscure the stage (Cic. *Pro Cael.* 65, *tollitur*, Ov. *Met.* 3. 113, *educitur*, cf. Beare (1964) *Appendix* E, 'The Roman stage-curtain': the mechanics are obscure, but obviously operated smoothly and wowed Rome: Virg. *Georg.* 3. 24, Ov. *Met.* 10. 111 f.). Properly the *aulaeum* was used for tragedy, the pantomime *entr'actes* being played before side-screens, *siparia* (*RE*. 2 (1896) 2399 f. and 3. 1² (1927) 262); but full-blown Augustan pantomime would presumably use the whole theatre.

Thunder established divine presence (Hom. *Il.* 4. 167, Virg. *Aen.* 8. 352, Bailey on Lucr. 6. 96), so imitation peals were early devised for the stage: Soph. *Oed. Col.* 1604 f., Cook (1914–40) 2. 827 f.; βροντεῖον, cf. Poll. 4. 130, ὑπὸ τῇ σκηνῇ ὄπισθεν ἀσκοὶ ψήφων ἔμπλεοι διωγκουμένοι φέρονται κατὰ χαλκωμάτων. *Claudiana tonitrua* deafened Roman theatre: Fest. 50 Lindsay, *ut ludis post scaenam coniectus lapidum ita fieret ut ueri tonitrus similitudinem imitarentur* . . . (cf. Plaut. *Amph.* 1062, 1129 f., Beare (1964) 254; in ceremonial fantasy, cf. Sall. *Hist.* 2. 70, Dio 59. 28. 6. Drums have been in use more recently, cf. *Lear* 1514 f., 1693 f., Campbell (1923) 132 f.).

42. 'The gods spoke' (v. 24) doesn't sound much like a pantomime (*pace* Weinreich (1944–8) 158 f. 'A performance might begin with a sort of patriotic chant' doesn't fit the bill, either (Charlesworth (1943) 4). Intermezzo: Handley (1953) 58 n. 3, *RE.* 5 (1905) 2491. *Embolium*, Weinreich (1944–8) 157, Wiseman (1985) 27. Pastime: Theophr. *Char.* 27. 7, Cic. *Fam.* 9. 22. 1, Mooney on Suet. *Galb.* 13.

43. Choral celebration of Roman royalty: Plin. *Pan.* 54. 1, *et quis iam locus miserae adulationis manebat ignarus cum laudes imperatorum ludis etiam et commissionibus celebrarentur, saltarentur, frangerentur?* All-purpose: Cic. *Pro Marc.* 32, *nisi te, C. Caesar, saluo, salui esse non possumus*, Hor. *Epp.* 1. 16. 27, *tene magis saluum populus uelit an populum tu* . . . (For recovery from royal illness: Hor. *Carm.* 2. 17. 25 f.; a birthday: Box on Phil. *In Flacc.* 81; presence in the 'royal box': D–S 1. 18; etc.: Alföldi (1934) esp. 86 n. 4, Cuss (1971) 74 f., Sauter (1934) 4 f., Weinstock (1971) 169f. In 'ritual' use: *ILS* 541 (*Fratres Aruales*, of Caracalla), *te saluo et securi sumus*).

44. e.g. Havet (1895) § 157 tried to date these *ludi* by guessing the occasion of the chorus of v. 27. On Hor. *Carm.* 4. 2 and *reditus*: Du Quesnay (1995), at 148 t(r)ying it in(to) 5. 7; cf. Aldrete (1999) 137, 'Tiberius was praised in the theater . . . when his entrance was greeted with the chant of [5. 7. 27].

45. Applause on hind-legs: Nisbet and Hubbard on Hor. *Carm.* 1. 20. 3, Mooney on Suet. *Vesp.* 13.

46. In the musician/tyrant sketch of 68 here, *orbem temperat* actually puns between 'rules the world' and 'tunes the round instrument'; with *populus quondam uniuersus ludorum die et accepit in contumeliam eius et adsensu maximo*, ibid., cf. *ipso ludorum . . . die, magno . . . risu, populus . . . ab uniuersis*, vv. 19, 31, 34, 38. In the skit on the emperor's correct titulature, 53 here, we are shown theatre as a leading edge in negotiating the Principate (as ~~domination~~).

47. Performer: *Anth. Lat.* 2. 111 Bücheler and Riese, *ingressus scaenam populum saltator adorat*, Mart. 1. 3. 7, (to a declaimer) *audieris cum grande σοφῶς, dum basia iactas . . .*, Sittl (1890) 171, *RE.* Suppl. 5 (1931) 518. 45f., '*Kusshand*'. Ruler: Tac. *Hist.* 1. 36, *nec deerat Otho protendens manus, adorare uulgus, iacere oscula et omnia seruiliter pro dominatione*, Dio 64. 8. 1, Taylor (1927) 53 f., Brilliant (1963) 23 f. For religious *adoratio*: Vouillème (1887) 10, Bolkestein (1929) 22 f.; right hands were pressed to lips to end prayers: Plin. *Nat. hist.* 28. 25, Wagener (1912) 38. *basia*: the vigorous colloquial term betokens extravagant behaviour (Bertschinger (1921) 30).

48. Prostration: Ar. *Au.* 500, προκυλινδεῖσθαι. Genuflection was more usual (Sittl (1890) 157 f., Weinreich (1944–8) 160; προσκύνησις in religious ritual: Bolkestein (1929) 31). *Phaedrus* is hamming up his scorn for these *moeurs*.

49. *Fautores*, v. 29: for Roman claques, cf. Bartsch (1994) 210; Nero would raise an army of so-called *Augustiani*: Dio 61. 20. 4, Bartsch (1994) 8. *Repeti iubet*, v. 31: such audience interference appears to have been common, cf. Hor. *Epp.* 2. 1. 185 f., *si discordet eques media inter carmina poscunt | aut ursum aut pugiles; his nam plebecula gaudet*, Cic. *Ad Att.* 2. 19. 3 (resentment of *Pompeius Magnus*), *tragoedus . . . 'nostra miseria tu es magnus', miliens coactus est dicere*, Macrob. *Sat.* 2. 7. 13, Wille (1967) 22 (cf. a restart at the races: Ov. *Am.* 3. 2. 7, Vigneron (1968) 1. 199). For theatrical encores, *palin*: Liv. 7. 2, Cic. *Pro Sest.* 118 (at the races: Plut. *Sull.* 18. 6; recital: Cic. *Pro Arch.* 18). *Homo meus*: Petron. 62. 13, *miles . . . meus*, Mart. 5. 54. 1, Ps.-Quint. *Decl.* 12. 18, Grimm, *KHM* 45, 'my little tailor' (colloquialism: Bertschinger (1921) 39, Heraeus (1937) 119, Hofmann (1950) 137). *Variatio*: *Princeps tibicen*, v. 4; *is*, 6; *cuius*, 14; *princeps*, 17; *eum*, 18; *tibicine*, 20; *reducto*, 25; *tibicen*, 29; *homo meus*, 32; *hunc*, 34; *Princeps*, 36. Crowns awarded to victorious artistes: Suet. *Dom.* 4, Plaut. *Amph. prol.* 69, Baus (1940) 151 f.); but this would have to be some kind of extraordinary presentation (lifetime service award . . .).
   At v. 34, note: *hunc coronam existimat* Pithou (1596): *h. c. estimat* P (*aestimat* R^{Vi}), *h. choro ueniam aestimat* Havet (1895), *rogari populus huic coronam existimauit* Shackleton-Bailey (1978) 454 f.

50. Stratification: Slater (1994) 140, Bartsch (1994) 220 n. 66. Προεδρία: Beare (1964) *Appendix* A, 'Seats in the Greek and Roman theatres' 241 f., *RE.* 4. 2 (1901) 1755. 46, '*cuneus*'. *Equites*: saw and heard best (Cic. *De sen.* 48, Arr. *Epictet.* 1. 25. 24); gave artistes feedback (Hor. *Serm.* 1. 10. 76, Auson. *Lud. sept. sap.* 100); led demonstrations (Cic. *Ad Att.* 2. 19. 3); cf. Slater (1994) 129–32.

51. *Niueus*: itself hyperbolic 'whiter-than-white' jeering: Klein (1936) 61. *Fasciae*, v. 36: wool wraps for thigh or calf worn by valetudinarians and fops (Hor. *Serm*. 2. 3. 255, Suet. *Aug*. 82 and Petron. 40. 5, Mart. 10. 104. 7, cf. Wilson (1938) 73 f., D–S 2. 2. 981). The brilliant hue is foppish (Val. Max. 6. 2. 7, (Pompey) *candida fascia crus alligatum*, Cic. *Ad Att*. 2. 3. 1, *cretatae fasciae*, Amm. Marc. 17. 11. 4; purple *fasciolae*: Cic. *De har. resp*. 21). But *crure* here must refer to the broken *tibia* of v. 8, strapped-up after the removal of the splints (cf. 17, *pace* Shackleton Bailey on Cic. *Ad Att*. loc. cit.). Fracture-splints: Hippocr. *De fract*. 30, Phillips (1973) 95; bandaging: cf. Galen *De fasc*., e.g. Kühn 18a. 774. T*unicis*, v. 37: the plural might mean (one) *tunica* plus *subucula* (Varr. ap. Non. 870 Lindsay, Mooney on Suet. *Vit*. 2. 5, Wilson (1938) 76). But some wore several *tunicae* (Augustus four: Suet. *Aug*. 82). White is the proper colour for holiday dress (Blümner (1889) 710, *RLAC* 7 (1969) 399 *Farbe*, Wilson (1938); so on stage: Val. Max. 2. 4. 6). Costume: pipers wore the trailing *stola* (Hor. *Ars. Poet*. 214, *tibicen traxit* . . . *uagus per pulpitum uestem*, Frazer on Ov. *Fast*. 6. 651, D. Bieber (1920) *Tafel* 50). White shoes: for women: Ov. *Ars* 3. 271, Mart. 7. 33. 1, Apul. *Met*. 7. 8, *calceis femininis albis illis indutus*, Clem. Alex. Περὶ ὑποδέσεως 2. 11 *MPG* 8. 537; dyed shoes: Headlam on Herod. 7. 28, Mayor on Juv. 7. 192, Lau (1967) 100 n. 2). Also for the stage: Istr. ap. *Vit. Soph*. fr. 51 Muller *FHG* 1. 425, τὰς λευκὰς κρηπῖδας . . . ἃς ὑποδοῦνται οἵ τε ὑποκριταὶ καὶ οἱ χορευταί.

52. Palace-servants were, however, known to wear white livery: Suet. *Dom*. 12. 3, Weinreich (1944–8) 161. The rubric *d(iuina) d(omus)*: first under Tiberius, *CIL* 13. 4635, *pro perpetua salute diuinae domus* (cf. *CIL* 7. 11, cit. Ogilvie on Tac. *Agr*. 14. 1, Phil. *In Flacc*. 23, Jullian (1893) 129 f., Alföldi (1935) 86 n. 3). *Ab uniuersis*: this is the point of theatre as community factory (e.g. Macrob. 2. 7. 1, *uniuersitas populi ad solum Caesarem oculos* . . . *conuertit*); but the phrase also rings the changes on *populus*, v. 34; *omnibus*, 35. (*Uniuersus* is rare in imperial Latin: Cramer (1889) 341 f., Hofmann (1948) 287.)

For the expressive colloquialism *capite* . . . *protrusus foras*, v. 39: Men. *Sam*. 141, ἐκ τῆς οἰκίας | ἐπὶ τὴν κεφαλὴν εἰς κόρακας ὤσαν, Bompaire (1958) 408 n. 3. Audiences could get rough, stone a victim (*AES* 121, Pease (1907) 15), or look to rush the stage (Sen. *Epp*. 115. 15, *totus populus ad eiciendum et actorem et carmen consurrexit uno impetu* . . .). Short of that, a president was supposed to punish bad *performances* (Plaut. *Cist*. 78, Luc. *Pisc*. 33).

53. Cf. Walters (1993) 101–5.

54. Parmeno: mentioned by Aeschin. *In Timarch.* 157, ps.-Aristot. *Probl.* 27. 3, Pickard-Cambridge (1968) Index s.v., Völker (1877) 215 f. The tragic actor Theodorus: Pickard-Cambridge (1968), Index s.v.

55. So Plut. *Quaest. conv.* 5. 1; accepted by Pickard-Cambridge (1968) 171.

56. Parmeno: Hellad. *ap.* Phot. *Bibl.* 532 b35 Bekker, 'That: comic poets would name servants for their character, e.g. Parmeno, Pistos (Faithful) . . .', Ter. *Ad.* 168, *accede illuc Parmeno,* | *nimium istuc abisti*; cf. Ar. *Eccl.* 868, Men. *Sam.* 281, Plaut. *Bacch.* 649, Ter. *Eun.*, *Hec.*, Varr. *Men.* 385 Bücheler (Geller (1966) 73 f. takes Varro's title to refer to the proverb), Donat. on Ter. *Andr.* 1, Austin (1921) 81 f.,107 f. Stage-name: Völker (1899) 31 f.

57. The grounds would be that the Greek proverb means nothing in the Latin West, and the comic actor was at best a name.

58. Not least the apparent staging by the actor of his 'act' followed by a procession of attempts by his emulators.

59. For a similar problem (with *App* 16): Henderson (1977*a*).

60. Arm-pits were where daggers and *quails* are carried: LSJ s.v. μάλη. More or less anything portable could be found or hidden in the fold across anyone's front (*sinus*): to empty someone's pockets, this must be 'shaken out' (v. 19, Plaut. *Aul.* 645–7, *'di me perdant si ego tui quicquam abstuli . . .' 'agedum excutedum pallium' 'tuo arbitratu' 'ne inter tunicas habeas'*, Landgraf on Cic. *Rosc. Am.* 97, D'Agostino (1928).

61. Cf. Starnes (1956) 65a, *Nihil ad Parmenionis [sic] suem.* Did Weinreich (1944–8) 151 n. 2, recalling the tale from 'European literature', mean just Erasmus?

62. Ehrenburg (1962) 168: 'Tairov knew what art means and would not recognize a theatre based on imitating life'. Same goes for his storytelling, which imitates Phaedrus, very likely by imitating *Gil Blas*: 'Messieurs, . . . laissons là . . . les applaudissements du parterre; il en donne souvent aux acteurs fort mal à propos. Il applaudit même plus rarement au vrai qu'au faux, comme Phèdre nous l'apprend par une fable ingénieuse. Permettez-moi de vous la rapporter: la voici . . .' (Le bouffon, le paysan, le cochon de lait: Lesage (1955) 1. 165 f.).

63. Scheiber cites *TMI* J2232, whence he refers to Jacobs (1889*b*) no. 80, one of several bogus ascriptions to 'The Greek Aesop'; a Hungarian parallel; and the reference to *Gil Blas.*

64. See Stallybrass and White (1986) esp. 27–79, 'The fair, the pig, authorship'.

65. *Nobilis* may (or may not) be nominative singular in both cases:

diues et nobilis: *TLL* 5. 1. 1588. 58 f.; cf. 3. 5. 6, *diues et potens*. Cf. *ILS* 5213 (Eucharis), *quae modo nobilium ludos decoraui choro*.

66. Presumably the crowd whistles and shouts abuse, until a squad runs on to do their pleasure: cf. Luc. *De merc. cond.* 5, *Pisc.* 5.

67. *Mortales* unsupported by an adjective is a 'solemn' touch. (In morals at 1. 20. 2, 3. 10. 56, and the programmatic 2. *Prol.* 3 only; cf. Cramer (1889) 342 f.). The way the world tends to go: *solet . . . ad . . . agi*, vv. 1–3: *sed ad perniciem solet agi sinceritas*, 4. 13. 3; *sole(n)t*: 1. 17. 1, 3. 2. 1, 4. 13. 3.
      At v. 1, note: *PRAVO* NV (in title): *paruo* PR^{GuVi}, *prono* Havet (1895).
      At v. 2, note: *praeiudicio* Saumaise (1698): *pro iudicio* P (cf. Cic. *Tusc.* 2. 63, *eius iudicio stare nolim*, 5. 81, *suis stare iudiciis*, Quint. 5. 6. 5, *stare iureiurando*, Nisbet on Cic. *In Pis.* 77.

68. *AES* 563, in Apion cit. Gell 5. 14, Sen. *De ben.* 2. 19. 2; simpler versions: A. Marx (1889) 58–61, Dorson (1970), Brodeur (1924).

69. Never before . . .: cf. Amphis fr. 14 Kock, 'I say the fife is the smartest—' 'What's a fife?' 'A new discovery of mine, something the theatre has never before hosted.' For such performers, cf. Wesselski (1910–20), Gaheis (1927), Blümner (1918) 24 f., 50 f., nn. 188–93, Mayor on Juv. 14. 265, Burmann on Petron. 47. 9. Greek: e.g. *artifices*, v. 7, would translate τεχνῖται (Ar. *Rhet.* 3. 2. 10, Nettleship (1889) 294, reporting a boxer here by mistake).

70. *Scurra notus urbano sale*, v. 8: cf. Plaut. *Most.* 15, *tu urbanus scurra, deliciae popli,* | *rus mihi tu obiectas?*, *Trin.* 202, *urbani adsidui ciues quos scurras uocant*. *Urbanus sal* is a cliché of Roman show-biz: inverted by Mart. 11. 13. 1 (Paris), *Urbis delicias salesque Nili*; cf. Weinreich (1940–1) 1. 13 f.
      At v. 4, note: *diues quidam et nobilis* NV: *q. d. n.* P.

71. Hush: Cf. *Ad Herenn.* 4. 60 (quoted on 5. 7. 35–38), Curt. 10. 6. 3, *futuri expectatio inhibitis lacrimis silentium fecit*. Mass silence normally called for a crier (Plaut. *Poen. Prol.* 11), a trumpet fanfare (Liv. 2. 45. 12), or an imperious wave (Pers. 4. 7, Sittl (1890) 224 n. 8).

72. Cf. Crusius (1893) 105 f., Harrison (1922) 209, Fig. 42.

73. Mimicry as pandemonium: Auson. *Epigr.* 5; birds (the easiest?): Petron. 68. 3, Plut. *Ages.* 21. 5, Jahn (1843) Introd. 92, Blümner (1918) 6, 24, 50 n. 191, *RE* Suppl. 6 (1935) 1279–82, θαυματοποιοί; other impressions: Plut. *De aud. poet.* 18, Plat. *Rep.* 3. 396b. Pigs were used in acts (Petron. 47. 9), but the porkling's κοΐ, κοΐ stars only in our story (cf. Wackernagel (1869) 29, 66 f.). A diminutive pig is needed for the story, but *porcellus* is regularly a colloquial

hypocorism, like 'pourceau', or τὸ δελφάκιον (as in Plut. *Quaest. conv.* 5. 1, cf. Bertschinger (1921) 21 f.).

74. At v. 20, note: *lancibus* PR^{GuVi}: *laudibus* NV. Burmann (1727) thought this 'loading with plate' would be a painful end for the *scurra 'Tarpeiae uirginis modo'*! Gifts of salvers for winners: Mart. *Spect.* 29. 6, (to gladiators) *quod licuit lances donaque saepe dedit*, 10. 29. 1, Juv. 6. 204. *Onero / honoro*: Varr. *De ling. lat.* 5. 73, *honos ab onere*, Serv. on Virg. *Aen.* 1. 289, *oneratus aspirationem non habet quia ab onere uenit; honustus uero quia etiam ab honore descendit retinet aspirationem*, *TLL* 6. 3. 2942. 23 f.

75. e.g. Babr. 2 = *AES* 295, Bléry (1909) 137 f., Ribbeck (1885) 30 f. Aesop started off digging ditches (*Aes. Vit.* 4); the rustic Wise Man: *RE* 16.1 (1933) 1192 f., Myson § 1.
    At v. 22, note: *mehercules* NV: *mehercule* P (cf. 3. 5. 4, 3. 17. 8).

76. Cf. Henderson (1999*a*) 53–5 on Terence, *Adelphoe*; 115–16 on Horace, *Odes* 3. 22.

77. At v. 26, note: *derisuros non spectaturos scias* Heinsius (1698): *d. n. expectaturos sit et* P, *d. n. spectaturos sit et* R^{Gu}, *d. n. exspectaturos sit, et* R^{Vi}, *derisurus non secuturus sedet* N, *derisurus n. sequuturus* V; *derisuri non spectaturi sedent* Pithou (1596).

78. Gruntnote: Greek γρυλλίζω is odd for its liquids ('grunt, grunzen, grugnire, grogner', Wackernagel (1869) 66 f.). Latin *grunnio* appears to replace **gru(n)dyo* (cf. Alciphr. *Epp.* 3. 67, γρύζω, Ernout (1909) 383).

79. Phrase: Polyb. 30. 22. 2, κρότος . . . καὶ κραυγή, cf. Gudeman on Tac. *Dial.* 39. 6, Heubner on Tac. *Hist.* 3. 83. 1.

80. Perotti tried to iron out this pig's tale by writing *porco* (NV) for *uero* (P). The lively alliteration hereabouts—*porcellum . . . priore . . . nil compererant latens peruellit aurem uero . . . celauerat . . . dolore uocem naturae exprimit*, vv. 30–33—may have helped prompt Heinsius' (1698) emendation of *uero* to *uerri* (boar). Conceivably it was in the back of Phaedrus' mind, first.

81. *Aperto*, v. 37, retains verbal force (as in Virg. *Aen.* 6. 406, *at ramum hunc—aperit ramum qui ueste latebat—agnoscas*).
    At v. 37, note: *probans* P: *exprobrans* NV.
    Housman (1902) 340 used 38 on incautious editors of *Culex*. Now there's a fable about Latin poetry / criticism for you.

82. Thus the boos at v. 34 can only be lame. For *acclamo* of disapproval: Sen. *Epp.* 47. 13; the sense of 'acclaim' gradually predominated: Mooney on Suet. *Dom.* 13. 1, Austin on Quint. 12. 5. 1.

83. Darrieussecq (1998) 134: telling how another pig put the lie to human superiority. I could seem to be getting a thing about the swinishness of people (and it might be the other way round):

Henderson (1997*b*) esp. 111, (1999*a*) 114–44. 'Pigs seems to have borne the brunt of our age, fear, affection and desire for the "low".' (Stallybrass and White (1986) 44–9 'Thinking with pigs', at 44)

CHAPTER 5

1. Knowing the status of this irritant, provocation, of a 'title' isn't at all tough: this chapter's discussion will begin from this.
2. See esp. Boldrini (1990*b*), and MSS NV in *Textus Fontes* in my *References*. I shall treat Perotti's text *as if* it gives just what Phaedrus wrote.
3. See Henderson (1999*b*) 312, 317.
4. So Gleason (1995) 134.
5. Havet (1898) 177. Oakley (1985) 396 § 27: Solin. 1. 75, SHA 29 (Firmus) 4. 2, *RE* 7² (1939) 241.
6. *RE* Suppl. 6 (1935) 1175–7. Varro wrote a *Naval Diary* and *How to Convene the Senate* for Pompey in the 70s: Moatti (1997) Index and 337 n. 45. Posidonius, Theophanes, L. Voltacilius Pitholaus, also wrote up Pompey's campaigns, and life, at first hand (used by Strabo, Josephus, etc.: Leach (1978) 214–18). Investment in culture maximized the chances of memorialization on favourable terms: Anderson (1963) esp. 57–82.
7. Headlam: on Herodas 2. 73, exploring the proverb τὸν ἐν Σάμῳ κομήτην (ps.-Plut. *Prou.* 2. 8)—probably irrelevant to the material presented, and meaning just 'Straw to Ephraim', as in *CPG* Diogen. 4. 58, cf. Martin (1922) 281 f. Paroemiographer: Kock's n. on com. fr., 3. 749; Eratosthenes: *ap.* Diog. Laert. 8. 47, cf. *Anth. Plan.* 3. 16, 3. 35 (cf. Theaetet. *ap.* Diog. Laert. 8. 48 = Gow and Page (1965) 3368–71: a story-type, cf. Gardiner (1930) 41). The philosopher was even sometimes made the star of this story: Beaupère on Luc. *Vit. auct.* 2. For the (early 3rd cent. BCE) boxing champ Pythagoras: Knab (1934) 33.
8. *TMI* H1561. 2.
9. Mommsen (1894) 5. 273.
10. Green (1961) 221 f.
11. Henderson (1998*b*) 37–69.
12. For Roman Alexanders, and the full, infinitely suggestive, early imperial portrayal by Curtius: D. J. Spencer (1997).
13. About to liquidate Caesar, 'it is said that Cassius turned to face Pompey's image, and called on him as if he could hear'. (Plut. *Brut.* 17. 2, cf. *Caes.* 66. 2 f.)
14. Grenade (1950), Syme (1986) 255–69, 'The descendants of

Pompeius', with *Tables* 14, 17. For the coding of the Augustan settlement through a Pompeius' return to the fold: Henderson (1998*b*) 154 on Hor. *Carm.* 2. 7. Pompey: *RE* 21. 2 (1952) 2062–2211 § 31, esp. 2204. 19–37.

15. *Praenomen*: Weinstock (1971) 104. '*Caesar*': Henderson (1998*b*) esp. 202 f. Labelling: Plut. *Pomp.* 13. 4 f.; Liv. 30. 45. 6; Corbeill (1996) 80–2. Theatre: cf. Ch. 4.

16. By hot-head Lucan: Henderson (1998*b*) 165–211 (esp. 182 n. 55).

17. *Magni Pompei*, v. 1, *ducis*, 4, *Magnus*, 8, '*imperator*', 11, *uir animi simplicis*, 12, *ducem*, 19, *Magnus*, 21, *principis*, 22, *Magnus*, 26, *Pompeius*, 29 ~ *miles*, v. 1, *hic*, 4, *miles*, 7, '*commilito*', 8, *ille*, 9, *dedecus castrorum*, 13, *illum*, 14, *cinaedus habitu sed Mars uiribus*, 18, *hunc*, 23, *militi*, 26, '*miles* ', 30, *militis*, 34. At v. 1, note: *Pompei* D'Orville (1727*b*): *Pompeii* NV.

18. *Vasti corporis* is colloquial exaggeration, cf. 1. 5. 5, *ceruum uasti corporis* |, Apul. *Met.* 8. 15, *lupos uastis corporibus sarcinosos*, Gell. 9. 13. (For the descriptive genitive, cf. Headlam on Herod. 4. 16, LHS 68.) v. 3: real parallels for *famam traho* are lacking, but it suits a context where an *un*pleasant reputation is in question (*attraho* is rare in poetry, *TLL* 2. 1159. 11 f.).

19. Recruits had to top 5' 8": Veget. *Epit. rei. mil.* 1. 5, Watson (1969) 39. Praetorians were still loftier: Dosith. *Adr. Sent.* 2.

20. *Molles autem quos Graeci* κίναιδους *dicunt* . . . *uocem tamquam perfractam habent*, . . . *mouent corpus ut mulieres*, cf. Förster (1893) 2. 103 f., 'voice', 94 f., 'gait'.

21. *fracte* is a hapax (cf. κατεαγώς, *fractus* e.g. Sen. *De uit. beat.* 13. 4: Gleason (1995), 112, Richlin (1997) 94). Ethical overtones: Colson on Quintil. *Inst. orat.* 1. 10. 32, Austin on ibid. 12. 10. 12, Bramble (1974) 76 and n. 2, *TLL* 6. 1. 1252. 26–1253. 8. Any speech impediment spelled effeminacy: lisp, Plut. *Alcib.* 1. 4; stammer, Aeschin. *Parapr.* 2. 99, βάταλος, Headlam on Herod. 2. 75, βάτταρος, Housman on Juv. 6. 9, *psellus*.

22. Effeminacy by gait: Gleason (1995) 62–4, Corbeill (1996) 165 f., Sonin (1999) 128–36. *Ambulo* is often the verb for the mignon's parade (χαλαίβασις: Suet. Περὶ βλασφημιῶν Taillardat 52), e.g. Sen. *Epp.* 114. 4, *quomodo Maecenas uixerit notius est quam ut narrari nunc debeat quomodo ambulauerit*, Macrob. *Sat.* 2. 3. 16, *Cicero* . . . *cum Piso gener eius mollius incederet, filia autem concitatius, ait filiae*, '*ambula tamquam uir*'.

23. Drastic penalties: a capital offence for the passive partner, Dig. 48. 5. 9 *Pr.*; cf. Polyb. 6. 39. 9, where Walbank's note ad loc., 'Presumably the active partner was liable to the same penalty', is not at all a presumption we can safely share.

24. Sexually inviolate: Walters (1997) 37–40. For cases: Plut. *Sert.* 26. 1, and esp. Val. Max. 6. 1. 10–12: a 2nd cent. Cornelius was allowed suicide; a 4th cent. Laetorius who had solicited an attendant killed himself; and, most celebrated, C. Luscius, Marius' nephew, was killed by C. Plotius for soliciting him *de stupro*: Marius exonerated him as justified homicide: Plut. *Mar.* 14. 3 sets this (with a Trebonius for villain) on campaign against the Cimbri of 104 BCE. (Fantham (1991) 280 f.) Lengthy pleading for the *miles Marianus* exhausts the stock of *topoi* on Roman manhood: Quint. *Decl. mai.* 3, Walters (1993) 39–64, esp. 42–6, (1997) 43 n. 32.

25. Soldiers of Rome swore an oath not to steal: Polyb. 6. 33. 1; but they were often unreformed desperadoes: MacMullen (1984) 441. The camp-following served as blackmarket: Xen. *Hell.* 6. 2. 23, Luc. *De hist. conscr.* 16, Knorringa (1926) 65.

26. V. 5 conflates two cliché pairings, 'purple and gold' (Plaut. *Curc.* 342, ibid. 488, Ter. *Heaut.* 778, 893, Apul. *Met.* 2. 2, Archipoet. 29, *dant nobiles—dona nobilia | aurum uestes—et his similia*, Bell (1923) 182, Pease on Virg. *Aen.* 4. 134, Shackleton-Bailey on Cic. *Ad Att.* 11. 25. 3); plus 'a (great) weight of silver and gold' (a phrase from Ennius, it seems: Cic. *De rep.* 1. 27, *immensum argenti pondus atque auri*, Hor. *Serm.* 1. 1. 41, *immensum . . . argenti pondus et auri*, Virg. *Aen.* 1. 359, *ignotum argenti pondus et auri*).

27. After 'bushwhacks the general's baggage-animals' (v. 4), 'rustles the mules' (v. 6) is a humorous touch of hyperbole (*auertit*: rustle, Catull. 64. 5, Virg. *Aen.* 1. 472, Nisbet and Hubbard on Hor. *Carm.* 1. 10. 10). Mules vital: Sulla had a myriad for the siege of Athens, Plut. *Sull.* 12. 2, cf. Vigneron (1968) 1. 149, Kromayer and Veith (1928) 394, D–S 3. 1. 416 f., '*Impedimenta*'. Hence the standing joke of rating the Chief Munitions Officer a *mulio*: Mayor on Juv. 7. 199; ps.-Virg. *Catal.* 10: Ventidius Bassus; Syme (1958): Sabinus; Mooney on Suet. *Vesp.* 4. 3: Vespasian; E. Meyer (1913) 44 n. 2.

28. The Roman general's authority over booty was virtually complete (Shatzman (1972) 177 f.). The commander was the belly in *AES* 130, 'The belly and the feet', cf. Daube (1972) 133–40, West (1969) 119 (age-old matrix for 'Belly and limbs': Gombel (1934), Hale (1968), Nestle (1927)). Officers' offensively gross baggage: Plut. *Ant.* 48. 3, Vigneron (1968) 1. 157 n. 1.

29. Gossip: Curt. 6. 2. 15, *rumor, otiosi militis uitium*, Wedeck (1927) 97. The *praetorium*, facing onto the *uia principalis*, was (officially) the focal point of camp-life: Walbank on Polyb. 6. 33. 3, D–S 5. 1. 640 f.

30. *Quid ais?* attracts attention, directs a question, brings it to

life: Bertschinger (1921) 36, Hofmann (1950) 2. 43 f.; combined
with -*ne*: Ter. *Andr*. 616, Cic. *Ad Att*. 2. 8. 1; *tu* adds to the
vigorous effect. General: Combès (1966) 244 f., 'le portrait de
l'*Imperator*: la vie au camp'.

31. *Commilito*: Heraeus (1902) 275–7. Late Republican marshals
encouraged morale in this way: Plut. *Luc*. 28. 3, Suet. *Iul*. 67. 2,
blandiore nomine; so too imperial contenders: Suet. *Galb*. 19, Tac.
Hist. 1. 29, 37 (Otho); cf. Tac. *Agr*. 33. 2, Plin. *Epp*. 10. 53
(Trajan), MacMullen (1984) 444 (used by troops on dedications:
ibid. 442). Augustus thought he eliminated the address, Suet.
Aug. 25. 1, cf. Instinsky (1956) 262, Ogilvie on Liv. 2. 55. 6. The
tactic is a perennial: Shakespeare *Henry V* 3. 3. 5, 'I am a soldier, |
a name that in my thoughts becomes me best', Jorgenson (1956)
96 f. Sealed society: MacMullen (1984) 440 f., Henderson (1998*a*)
11, 17 f.

32. *Continuo* was a bluff word: Norden on Virg. *Aen*. 6. 426, *TLL* 4.
728. 17–19: in Livy only in a soldier's speech, 42. 34. 6. *Imperator*,
v. 11: the Caesars would take care to reserve this title of honour
conferred by acclamation from a general's troops, for the royal
family (Tac. *Ann*. 3. 74. 6, Kromayer and Veith (1928) 536 f.,
Combès (1966) *passim*).

33. Bastinado: Polyb. 6. 37. 9; shaming: MacMullen (1984) 449 f. For
dishonourable discharge (*ignominiosa missio*), cf. Lucil. 198 f.
Marx (Scipio at Numantia), *Praetor noster ad hoc*, '*quam spurcust
ore quod omnis* | *extra castra ut stercus foras eiecit ad unum*'.

34. Grottanelli (1983) reads the tale for its transgressive
'trickster/scapegoat/champion/saviour': 136f., 'Only the shameless pervert . . . has the courage to offer himself to the risk . . .
Power and impurity, pollution and salvation, go together because
they are all products of the same daring gestures.'

35. Curiosity: Sittl (1890) 140. If you never spit, you are ill: Ellis on
Cat. 23. 16; a freak: Solin. 1. 741; or a prim Persian: Dio Chrys.
Or. 13. 24, Ussher on Theophr. *Char*. 19. 4. Social semiotics of
(Greek) spitting: Sonin (1999) 178–97. Spit in popular superstition: as apotropaic (Gershenson (1969), Nicolson (1897) 35–7);
spit into the hand to add weight to a blow (McCartney (1934),
Lipscomb (1934), Knowlson (1910) 180); 'the juvenile practice of
making an oath mere terrible by spitting' (Opies (1967) 126 and n.
2, cf. Radfords (1961) 319, 'Finger wet, finger dry, | cut my throat
if I lie', said after wetting the finger with spittle; etc. (cf. Bergen
(1890), Crombie (1892), De Mensignac (1892), Dundes (1980)
esp. 111–13). Respectable soldiers swore by their standards: Tert.
Apol. 16, Watson (1969) 27 f.

36. Eyes in oaths: Aeschin. *De fals. leg.* 153, Sittl (1890) 139 n. 2, Tolle (1883) 10). No loophole: cf. Plaut. *Aul.* 640 f., *non hercle equidem quicquam sumpsi nec tetigi* . . . Commonplace melting: e.g. Hom. *Il.* 3. 176, Plaut. *Pseud.* 818, *oculi ut exstillent* (*exstillesco* is a *hapax* intensifying *exstillo*: *TLL* 5. 2. 1911. 19–22, 23–35). The eye made of water: Aristot. *De sens.* 2. 433ª12, Pease on Cic. *De nat. deor.* 2. 141, Magnus (1901) 75, 226, 454, 'Die Anatomie des Auges'. Healing miracle: cf. Tac. *Hist.* 4. 81, Weinreich (1909) 68, 112. Handling: spitting into the *left* hand leaves the traditionally potent right to perform the exsecration: Wagener (1912) 17.

37. *breue tempus* . . . *et*, v. 15: the formula articulates the story by smoothing away distraction, e.g. Virg. *Aen.* 9. 395, *nec longum in medio tempus cum* . . ., Liv. 40. 48. 4, *haud multum tempus intercessit cum* . . ., Weber (1904) 16, 'Nicht lange danach . . .'. (This Latin *et* is a distinctive idiom: e.g. Virg. *Georg.* 2. 80, Apul. *Met.* 8. 5, LHS 481 f., *TLL* 5. 2. 895. 25 f.)

38. Roman duels: Polyb. 6. 54. 4, Oakley (1985): *App* 10 = 396 § 28; (1998) note on Liv. 7. 9. 6; Feldherr (1998) 92–111. Last: e.g. Munda in 45 BCE was *civil* war, as is ps.-Quintil. *Decl. min.* 317 (= ibid. 396 f. §§ 30–1; Holford-Strevens adds [Jew vs. Roman] Jos. *Bell. Iud.* 6. 168–76: ibid. 410; Oakley (1998) on Liv. 7. 9. 6 adds Procop. *Bell.* 1. 13. 29–39). The other duels with Celts and Germans, from Manlius through *App* 10: Oakley (1985) 400 f. Torquatus: ibid. 393 f. § 6, (1998) n. on Liv. 7. 9. 6–10. 14.

39. All-comers: challenges to duels are open, Oakley (1998) on Liv. 7. 9. 8.

40. Ubiquitous 'Davids and Goliaths': Walker (1910) 53 f., De Vaux (1959), Dorson (1970). *Fidens manu*, v. 15: cf. Hom. *Il.* 16. 624, *Il. Lat.* 712. Initiative: Trojan [Hector] to Achaeans, Hom. *Il.* 7; the foe to Alexander, Diod. Sic. 17. 83. 5; Numanus to the 'Phrygians', Virg. *Aen.* 9. 590–620; cf. Keith (1923–4). Muscles: Gauls and Germans fought stripped to the waist: Heckenbach (1911) 122, Heubner on Tac. *Hist.* 2. 22. 1. Weaponry: De Vaux (1959) 495f. Stream: Glück (1964) 25 f., Fenik (1968), Index s.v. 'Threats and taunts', Miniconi (1951) Index, 177, De Vaux (1959) 497.
    At v. 16, note: *e Romanis* Orelli (1832): *de R*. V (N is unreadable), *de nostris* Jannelli (1811).

41. *Muttering: musso* is to mutter indistinctly on purpose, often in fear (as here, cf. Lucr. 6. 1179, Liv. 28. 40. 2, Amm. Marc. 24. 7. 5; *muttio* is to mutter when one should keep silent, as in 3. *Epil.* 34). *Musso* had long been associated with such contexts (Enn. *Ann.* 343 f.: whence Sall., Liv., Virg.: Wreschniok (1907) 33); the inten-

sitive *mussito* disappears from poetry after Plaut. and Ter., and is
rare in prose (once in Liv.: *TLL* 8. 1707. 20–30).
So the text is insecure, note: *mussitant* D'Orville *ap.* Beck
(1812) 218: *mussant* N (D'Orville (1727*a*) V; *et primi mussant*
Jannelli (1811), *p. quin mussant* L. Müller (1877), *p. iam m.*
Postgate (1919*a*), *p. ipsi mussant* LaPenna ((1963) 229), *et al. al.*
Dressler (1838) falsely reports *mussitant primi* from D'Orville
(1727*b*).

42. *Mars*: cf. Hom. *Il.* 11. 295, Cic. *Ad Att.* 15. 11. 1, Miniconi (1951)
197. *Virtus*: cf. Quint.. *Decl. mai.* 3. 2, where Marius' man fights
for 'Mars the father of the fatherland'.

43. *Pro tribunali*: Fest. 290 Lindsay, Nisbet on Cic. *In Pis.* 11; cf.
Brand (1968) 69 f.

44. Deference: Gell. 4. 1. 13, *tum ille ostentator uoce iam molli atque
demissa . . . inquit. Licet?*: Oakley (1985) 406 and n. 121; omitted for
Torquatus by Claudius Quadrigarius; supplied by Livy: Feldherr
(1998) 94, 96 n. 47. *Imperia Manliana*: Otto (1890) s.v., Oakley
(1998) on Liv. 8. 7. 22. Torquatus Junior: Oakley (1985) 394 § 8,
(1998) on Liv. 8. 7. 1–22. These and (Rome's/Livy's) other duels
go to make up a 'family' *of discourse*: Kraus (1998) 269 f.

45. *enimuero*, v. 20: plenty of feeling here, cf. Donat. on Ter. *Andr.*
206, *'enimuero' significationem habet nimium permoti atque irritati
animi* (*TLL* 5. 2. 592. 70 f.). *uirum*, v. 21: such pronominal use of
uir was an historian's stylism (Heubner on Tac. *Hist.* 3. 80. 2).
But the text is uncertain: at vv. 20–1, note: *enimuero eici | uirum
ut* Zell (1828): *e. eiici u. | u.* NV, *eum uero eiici | u.* Jannelli (1811).
On other conjectures: Ellis (1896) 161.
in re atroci, v. 21: another cliché of military exegesis (*TLL* 2.
1108).

46. In fable: 4. 2. 16 f., 4. 18. 8, Avian. 7. 14, *AES* 13, 290, 692 . . .

47. *ego* and *arbitror* (v. 23) convey measured counsel, cf. Liv. 29. 17.
3, *sed ego causam . . . differendam arbitror esse*. For the faded
metaphor, cf. Liv. 7. 12. 11, *placebat . . . fortunae se committere
contra hostem*, etc. *Iactura*, v. 24: for such calculations, cf. Liv. 5.
39. 12, 6. 19. 2, *TLL* 7. 1. 64. 11. Augustus' Euripides: cf. *Suppl.*
508, Bucher-Isler (1972) 59.

48. On the fabulation of the Roman duel as spectacle: Feldherr (1998)
esp. 100–11.

49. *Dicto celerius*: Plin. *Nat. Hist.* 36. 138. *Dicto citius* is more usual:
Otto (1890) s.v. *dicere* § 5, Weyman (1904) 379; in Greek, Eur.
Hipp. 1186, θᾶττον ἢ λόγος. For close relatives: *omnium spe celerius*
(Liv. 21. 6. 5, *TLL* 3. 754. 7–9); *dictum factum* (Otto (1890) s.v.
dicere § 6, Immerwahr (1966) 73 and n.); *celerius quam asparagi*

coquuntur' (Suet. *Aug.* 37); and 'before you can spit' (Gow on Theocr. 29. 27, πρὶν ἀποπτύσαι, etc. *RE* 18. 4. (1949) 1724. 61–5, παροιμία).

50. Size: e.g. Lang (1892) 125 f., 'Heart of ice' (Prince Mannikin *vs.* Prince Fadasse) 'The contrast between the two champions was so great that there was a shout of laughter from the whole assembly', Dorson (1970) (Gaelic version of Culloden and after), 'The Englishman was a big stalwart man and seemingly very strong. The Highlander was but a slip of a slender, sallow stripling'; so in ancient monomachy: e.g. Livy 7. 9. 8 (above), with Oakley (1998) ad loc., 1 Sam. 17. 4, 'Goliath of Gath, whose height was six cubits and a span', Vell. Pat. 1. 12. 4 (Scipio Aemilianus) *ex prouocatione ipse modicus uirium immanis magnitudinis hostem interemisset . . .*, Anderson on Tac. *Germ.* 4. 2. Decapitation: the mutilation is denied for Manlius by Liv. 7. 10. 11—as a barbarism: Friedrich (1956) 26, Deonna (1965) 17 and n. 10. The 'rolling of heads' in epic warfare (Miniconi (1951) Index, 172) took a full broadsword slash impossible with the Romans' 'Spanish' blade and its two-feet stabbing design (used—by anachronism—by Torquatus in Claud. Quad. *ap.* Gell. 9. 13/Liv. 7. 10. 5, cf. Walbank on Polyb. 6. 23. 6, Kromayer and Veith (1928) 325, Oakley (1998) on Liv. 7. 10. 5–9). Such a blow was the barbarian technique: Serv. on Virg. *Aen.* 9. 749, *sublatum alto consurgit in ensem: genus feriendi Gallicanum*, Zwicker (1905) 30, cf. Veget. *Epit. rei milit.* 1. 11, *non caesim sed punctim ferire discebant. nam caesim pugnantes non solum uicere sed etiam derisere Romani*, Ogilvie and Richmond on Tac. *Agr.* 36. 1; for the contrast in weaponry: Liv. 22. 46. 5, Walser (1951) 40.

51. Versnel (1970) 309 and n. 10: Gell. 2. 11. 3, *spolia . . . prouocatoria*, Plin. *Nat. Hist.* 7. 102, Oakley (1998) on Liv. 7. 10. 11.

52. Encomium: a tremendous idea, thought Polyb. (6. 39. 1), cf. MacMullen (1984) 449. *His . . . super*, v. 29: for the odd postposition, cf. 1. 27. 8, 2. 6. 11. *Super* for *de* belongs to less formal Latin (Callebat (1967) 237, Hofmann (1950) 163, LHS 281); but here the idea of the encomium as *capping* the triumph is in play.

53. Golden crown: as for the egregious, multi-crowned, L. Siccius Dentatus, Oakley (1985) 393 § 2; cf. Steiner (1906) 98, Oakley (1998) on Liv. 7. 10. 14. Ordinary *gregarii* were usually presented 'with necklaces, armbands, medals' (*torq. armil. phal*); the *corona* was usually reserved for higher ranks (an exception: *ILS* 2225), but inscriptional service-records rarely indicate to which stage each honour belongs: Watson (1969) 114 f. (So Steiner (1906) 31 f. may be over-rigid.) *Quia*, v. 31: a formal citation would use the

hoary preposition *ob* (Pearce (1970) 311–13: in the *Corp. Caes.*, *ob* appears only in one award- and two discharge-formulae, none by Caesar: Pascucci on *Bell. Hisp.* 26. 1, LHS 246). *Laudem Romani imperi*, v. 31: cf. Cic. *Pro Sest.* 98, *uel capitis periculo defendenda sunt . . . prouinciae, socii, imperii laus.* So Liv. 7 (above: *nomen Romanum inuictum praesta*), etc., Oakley (1985) 407, (1998) on Liv. 7. 10. 4.

54. Plut. *Pomp.* 22. 6, (to censor) 'πάσας . . . ἐστράτευμαι [στρατείας], καὶ πάσας ὑπ' ἐμαυτῷ αὐτοκράτορι'; Plut. *Pomp.* 57. 5; cf. Corbeill (1996) 176–89, 'Pompeius Imperator'.

55. *Furca*: Kromayer and Veith (1928) 426 f. *Muli Mariani*: Fest. 24, 148 Müller, Otto (1890) s.v., McCartney (1912) 54.

CHAPTER 6

1. This, Perotti's title (so Havet (1895): *QUOD S. F. H. I.* D'Orville (1727), *QUAM S. F. H. I.* Guaglianone (1969)) gives a hint of the epimythium missing from MS P.

2. So Bloomer (1997) 271 n. 59.

3. § 4, *RE* 19. 2 (1938) 1553–5.

4. Tales: Duris *ap.* Athen. 12. 542b (Phalerean) ~ Ael. *Var. Hist.* 9. 9 (with Perizonius ad loc.: Besieger); Lamia: Diog. Laert. 5. 76 ~ Plut. *Syncr. Demetr. et Ant.* 3. 2.

5. At his eponymous 'siege' of Rhodes, Poliorcetes spares a genuine Protogenes: he would 'rather burn the likeness of his father than such a great work of art' (Plut. *Demetr.* 22. 2 f., Gell. 15. 31).

6. Cf. Holden on Cic. *De off.* 1. 3, *Brut.* 37, *eruditissimus ille quidem, sed non tam armis institutus quam palaestra . . . suauis sicut fuit uideri maluit quam grauis.*

7. *Midsummer Night's Dream* 2. 2. 106 f.: T. Spencer (1954) 46.

8. As in many publications, e.g. Salac (1960), cf. Gail (1826) 2. 357, *Excursus* 27; 5. 1 is 'Demetrius of Phaleron, fr. 25' in Wehrli (1944–59) Vol. 1. 4.

   But at v. 1, note: *Demetrius qui dictus est Phalereus* (*Phaloreus* V) NV; *D. q. d. P.* PR[corr.], *D. q. d. P.* P (*D. rex q. d. est P.* R[Vi]) R[GuVi], *D. P. r. q. d. e.* Alton (1922) 325; *D. r. q. P. d. e.* Postgate (1919*a*) makes a metrical boob of his own (Housman (1920) 124). *rex* in R probably crept into the text from the (surely non-Phaedrian) 'title' *Demetrius rex et Menander poeta* PR[Vi], with *rex* from *tyrannus*, v. 14, as *poeta* from *scriptor*, v. 17.

9. *Scaen.*[2] fr. 668 Ribbeck; *Anth. Lat.* 234. 20. Phaedrus' blunder might encourage second thoughts on *Culex* 117, *Orpheüs Hebrum*

(but cf. Kenney OCT ad loc.; Birt (1898) 11 ff., esp. 15, was characteristically cavalier, but unconvincing: Neumann (1912) 28 f., Housman on Manil. 1. 350; the senarius *CE* 108. 3 Bücheler, *Trebius Basileüs coniunx quae scripsi dolens*, is lost). Transposition removes the only comparable metrical problem, 5. 10. 7, *latrans* | (So MS P): Gow's tentative defence, (1895), after jeers from Housman (1900) 467, led to his pained coinage of the phrase 'the cross-nibb'd pen' for his critic's style.

10. Plut. *Dem.* 9. 1, οἱ μὲν πολλοί . . . ἀνεκρότησαν καὶ βοῶντες . . . εὐεργέτην καὶ σωτῆρα προσαγορεύοντες . . . Excesses: Ferguson (1911) 60, 64 f., K. Scott (1928), Rosen (1967) 86–9; hymn—by Hermippus or Hermokles (Alfonsi (1963) 161 f.)—: Duris *FGH* 76 fr. 13, σεμνόν τι φαίνεθ᾽ οἱ φίλοι πάντες κύκλῳ | . . . ἥλιος ὁ ἐκεῖνος (K. Scott (1928) 229–32, Powell (1925) 173, Cuss (1971) 45 f.). Prototype: Weinstock (1971) 289 n. 8, Index *s.n.* As 'liberator of Athens' (*bis*), the Besieger's story was for ever: Habicht (1998) 91 f. on Pausanias; his portraiture: Ridgway (1990) 125–8 (Phalereus at Memphis (?): ibid. 132–4).

11. In Phaedrus confined mainly to such clichés, e.g. 1. 3. 9, 2. 1. 6.

12. e.g. Cic. *Ad Att.* 8. 16. 1, Weinstock (1971) 289 n. 9.

13. Acclamation: Weinstock (1971) 330; epiphany: *RE* Suppl. 4 (1924) 306 f.; salvation, Wendland (1904) 338.

14. Normally *succlamo* means 'interrupt (a public speech), protest' (= ὑποφώνεω; first in Brut. (Cic.) *Ad fam.* 11. 13a. 3: Gebhard (1891) 17 f.). Here the sense must be 'acclaim' (cf. Liv. 34. 50, Mooney on Suet. *Dom.* 13. 1). *Sub-* may suggest 'taking up' the cry.

   At v. 4, note: *succlamant* R^{GuVi}NV (*suo clammant* P, *sub clamant* P^{corr.}); *succlamans* Burmann (1698).

15. Cliché of degradation: Quint. *Decl. min.* 298, *caedentis manus oscularis et ferrum portas*, Tilley (1950) H85, 'A man kisseth those hands that he would see cut off', Pope (1950) 24, *Epist.* 1. 84, 'And licks the hand just rais'd to shed his blood' (cf. Bonner (1969) 10). The kiss on the (right) hand as submission: e.g. Hom. *Il.* 24. 478 (Priam) κύσε χεῖρας | . . . αἵ οἱ πολέας κτάνον υἷας, Luc. 2. 113 f., *spes una salutis* | *oscula pollutae fixisse trementia dextrae* (Wagener (1912) 18, cf. Deonna (1965) 78, Sittl (1890) 79). The hand kiss as glamorized veneration: Brilliant (1963) 14, in Pompeian and Herculanean painting, Theseus' hands are kissed by the children he has saved by despatching the Minotaur (cf. Index, 'Gestural situations').

16. Classic invitation for rhetorical flourish: e.g. Sen. *Suas.* 1. 1. 6, *occurrerunt uenienti ei* [= M. Antony] *Athenienses cum coniugibus et*

liberis et Dionuson salutaverunt, cf. Dio 48. 39. 2; first 'Romanized' for Flamininus 'the Liberator': Walbank on Polyb. 18. 46. 12.

17. Free Athens' shame: Plut. *Demetr.* 10 f., Athen. 6. 253a ('Athens the free': Aesch. *Pers.* 242, *Schröder* 25 f.; free speech: e.g. Eur. *Hippol.* 422). Translation from L'Estrange (1692) no. 447. 'Sad' cliché: cf. 1. 2. 5f., *arcem tyrannus occupat Pisistratus. | cum tristem seruitutem flerent Attici . . .*

18. For the (philosophical) life of political quietism (ἡσυχία): Chion of Heraclea *Epp.* 16, Boll (1920), Kretschmer (1938).

19. Ὀργή : Webster (1950) 107, *RE* 15. 1 (1931) 707–61 § 9; his first victory: 710. 18–40. 5. 1 = Körte and Thierfelder (1952) Testimonium 9 for the Life of Menander: 'wertlos', *RE* loc. cit. 35–52. Second fiddle: Gell. 17. 4. 1, Webster (1953) 103, McKeown on Ov. *Am.* 1. 15. 17–18. Speculation on Menandrian politics in Rome: MacKendrick (1954). Menander in Italian schools: Quint. 1. 8. 8; translations: Plin. *Epp.* 6. 21, *Anth. lat.* 2. 1 no. 97; (love-)poetry: Prop. 3. 21. 28, *librorumque tuos, docte Menandre, sales,* Ov. Am. 1. 15. 17–18 with McKeown's note; in general: Fantham (1984).

20. Ablative plural with -o/a stem as a low-brow form (cf. 3. 13. 11, App 9. 2): Heinze on Hor. *Carm.* 1. 26. 3, Bertschinger (1921) 7 n. 2, LHS 840.

21. In legend, the philosopher Demetrius sits with the poet Menander at Theophrastus' feet: Diog. Laert. 5. 79, 5. 36. The anecdotal motif of admiration-from-afar: 4. 23. 19–24, *hic litterarum quidam studio deditus, | Simonidis qui saepe uersus legerat | eratque absentis admirator maximus, | sermone ab ipso cognitum cupidissime | ad se recepit,* Nep. *Aristid.* 1. 4, *cui ille respondit se ignorare Aristiden, sed sibi non placere* (inverted).

22. For the punctuation at vv. 9–11, *comoediis, . . . uiri:* Tacke (1911) 50 and n. 3. In *admiratus fuerat* (v. 11), the 'double' pluperfect is more colloquialism (Bertschinger (1921) 14, 16). *uiri* (v. 11) is a storyteller's quasi-pronominal idiom, in oblique cases: Mackail on Virg. *Aen.* 1. 91.

23. Κόμη: *RLAC* 4. 632, Gerhard (1909) 192 f. Pomade of myrrh ointment: Tit. *ap.* Macrob. *Sat.* 3. 16. 15, *unguentis delibuti, scortis stipati* (myrrh: Fuf. Calen. *ap.* Dio 46. 18. 2, Virg. *Aen.* 12. 100, Gerhard (1909) 190 f., Headlam-Knox on Herod. 2. 76). Hair and social control: Hallpike (1978) esp. 141.

    Flowing robes: e.g. Aristipp. *Epp. Socr.* 9. 1 f., ἀλειφόμενός τινι τῶν εὐωδεστάτων μύρων καὶ σύρων ἐσθῆτας μαλακάς, *RLAC* 4. 630; soft: Gerhard (1909) 143 f.; light-weight: Nicostr. Com. 9 Kock 2. 222; over-expensive: Gerhard (1909) 149.

Note that at v. 12, MS P has *v. afluens*, for *uestitu fluens*: only glossary specialists have believed in the existence of the verb (e.g. Havet (1896) 147, Souter (1927) 270, Nettleship (1889) 78; cf. *TLL* 1.1250).

24. Tert. *loc. cit.* did *not* derive from reading 5.1, *pace* Geffcken (1909) 117. For the costume: Plut. *Qu. conu.* 1.2. 615d, Webster (1953) 119. Writers' characters ~ writers' characters: cf. Ar. *Thesm.* 167, ὅμοια γὰρ ποιεῖν ἀνάγκη τῇ φύσει, Roggwiller (1926) 18 f.; e.g. Ar. *Ach.* 411 f. (Euripides), *Thesm.* 136 f. (Agathon), etc.). Aesthete ~ effeminate: Gerhard (1909) 147 f. Menander the philanderer: e.g. Ov. *Tr.* 2. 369 f.; his usual partner Glycera: Schepers (1926).

25. Ov. *Am.* 1. 15. 17 f.: the name 'Men-ander' even stakes a claim to be 'a man meant to stay around' (*dum . . . uiuent . . ., Menandros erit*, cf. Manil. 5. 474–6, *in cuncta suam produxit saecula uitam, | doctior urbe sua linguae sub flore Menander, | qui uitae ostendit uitam chartisque sacrauit*).

26. vv. 15–16: For the affront to royal eyes, cf. Hdt. 1. 99 (Persian), 'Défense de cracher', Aesch. *Suppl.* 949 (tyrant to herald) 'Out of my sight', cf. Jos. *Bell. Iud.* 2. 148, ὡς μὴ τὰς αὐγὰς ὑβρίζειν τοῦ θεοῦ, Deonna (1965) 166.

   At v. 15–16, note: *conspectum meum* NV: *conspectu meo* PR^Ro; *uenire* PN^Jannelli (1811)V: *conspectu meo | a. uenari* J. Chauvin ap. Havet (1895), *conspectu meo | a. ceuere* Gow (1895); but the common phrase *in conspectum uenio* is apt, not inept, after *ueniebat*, v. 14 (Mood (1907) 9, Krischan (1954) 94).

27. *Hic est*, v. 17: so e.g. Pers. 1. 28, *pulchrum est digito monstrari et dicier hic est . . .*; in Greek, οὗτός ἐστι . . . (e.g. Plin. *Epp.* 9. 23. 5); or οὗτος ἐκεῖνος. For good or ill: Luc. *Rhet. praec.* 25, Gudeman on Tac. *Dial.* 7. 4, Bramble (1974) 100 and n.1, Sittl (1890) 51 f., Otto (1890) s.v. *digitus* § 8.

28. Esp. Walters (1993) 146–52.

29. It used to be claimed that Menander's squint was rendered in portraits for a time: Studniczka (1918) esp. 30 f., cf. Bieber (1961) 89 f., Schefold (1997²), esp. 216–21, figs. 111–14, Ashmole (1973); but cf. *RE*. 15. 1 (1931) 71. 23–60, Lefkowitz (1981) 14. Divine looks: Plut. *Dem.* 2, Nock (1928) 31 n. 50, L'Orange (1947) 39 f., 58, Weinstock (1971) 25 n. 2; portraits: Smith (1988) 64 and pl. 4. Peripatetic magnificence: MacKendrick (1954) 28, Ferguson (1911) 40 and n. 4; portraits (?): McDowall (1904) pl. 4, and 93 f. Deconstruct: see esp. Ter. *Eun. Prol. Formosus* (v. 18) is one of those Latin epithets in *-osus*—always unstable, and liable to capsize from aesthetic warmth into denigratory invective (Ernout (1949)).

Note that v. 18 is fully preserved only in V: PR^{Vi} also lack 5. 2. 1–2 (in N, Jannelli (1811) could read only *f..m.s*, D'Orville (1727) only *f..m*).

CHAPTER 7

1. On the kings of Livy 1: Henderson (1998*b*) 318.
2. Yet 1. 14 is second only to the 'parabolic' fable 1. 2 in length within Book 1. It is the first piece without an animal participant, and the first absent from Phaedrus' Late Antique paraphrases (and from LaFontaine. The fragmentary MS D passes from 1. 13. 12, where the main paradosis adds a spurious or misplaced epimythium, to 1. 17, but we cannot know why). Severe confinement of the Aesopic genre to the beast-fable is a postclassical phenomenon (cf. Bieber (1906) 3 f., Zander (1897) 15 f. Of the 'human' stories of Phaedrus which are also extant in the Greek prose collections (2. 2, 2. 3, 4. 1, 4. 10, 4. 12, 4. 18), only the canine 2. 3 survived beyond the 'Augustana' into later recensions).
3. Cf. Marin (1978).
4. *Malus . . . sutor*, v. 1: bad at his job; a bad man: the one goes with, leads to, the other. Cobbler bald and stunted: Headlam (1922) Introd. 48–51, Helm (1906) 76; limp: Tac. *Ann.* 15. 34. 3; pallor: Otto (1890) s.v. *sutor*. Greek portraits: Burford (1972) Plates 3–7. Prejudice: Lau (1967) 31 f.; yards: MacMullen (1974) 71 and notes, Lau (1967) 59, 179. Terminology had lagged behind urban specialization, e.g. Theophr. *Char.* 16. 6, ἐκδοῦναι τῷ σκυτοδέψῃ ἐπιρράψαι, Bryant (1899) 67, Forbes (1955–64) 5. 49 f. Craft: the tag κέρδων was settled on the haggling vendor of luxury footwear, in recognition of his 'foxiness': Macrob. 2. 4. 30, Meyer (1913) 6 n., Lau (1967) 216 f. 'Sewing': Brotherton (1926) 46. High/low: Stallybrass and White (1986) esp. 2–6; (modern European) shoemakers as suspected/subversive radicals: Hobsbawm and Scott (1980), Stallybrass (1997). Self-made: Luc. *Gall.* 14; ancestor, Anytos: Xen. *Apol.* 29 f., Vitellius: Suet. *Vit.* 2, Varus: Porph. on Hor. *Serm.* 1. 3. 130. Rome: Lau (1967) 62 f.; Subura: Brewster (1917) 53 f.
5. Motif: Propp (1968) 35. 'Poverty and deprivation': Lüthi (1970) 64: proverbial, cf. *malesuada fames*, Virg. *Aen.* 6. 276, οἱ δι' ἔνδειαν ὥσπερ οἱ ἀπορώτατοι ἀναγκάζονται ἀδικεῖν, Xen. *Mem.* 4. 2. 38, Bolkestein (1939) 329, Hemelrijk (1925) 77. Poverty teaches scheming: Secund. 17, Τί ἐστι Πενία; . . . Ἐπινοιῶν διδάσκαλος, W. Meyer (1915) 63 f., Tribukait (1889) 5.

6. 'The next day, after following his instructions, the peasant set out to find his ass. But along the way the action of the pills forced him to seek immediate relief for his bowels, so dashing from the road into the bushes he accidentally came upon his missing ass grazing there. He praised the physician's art and pills to the heavens. After this peasants flocked to the latter day Aesculapius in droves, for they had heard that here was a doctor who even had a remedy for recovering lost property.' Now you must've lost *your* ass . . .

7. Cf. Christoffersson (1904) 69 f.

8. Aarne and Thompson (1928) no. 47; cf. *AES* 392: Dr Wolf asks which bits of his patient Ass hurt, 'The bits you touch'; 599, Dr Crow offers to cure Eagle's sore eyes, but blinds him, eats the chicks and pecks him all over; Pilpay, 'The ignorant physician' (Rhys (1971) 174–9). For sick Lion remedies, see *Appendix*.

9. Setting up: Gil (1969) 73, Capel (1900) 69; cf. Ussery (1971) 18 f., Oliver (1972) 55 f., *TMI* K1955. More tales of instantly qualified doctors: e.g. *Gnom. Vat.* 226, Diog. Laert. 6. 62, 68, Grimm, *KHM* 98, cf. Jöpgen (1966) 59, 113, 125. Medicine shows: Dio Chrys. *Or.* 9. 4, Cic. *Pro Cluent.* 40, *pharmacopola circumforaneus*, Vercoutre (1880). Scorned: Teles. p. 26 Hense, Diog. Laert. 6. 42, Cat. *ap.* Gell. 1. 15. 9, Galen *De fasc.* 18a. 770 Kühn. Foreign doctor: Reuters on *Epist. Anach.* 1. 12, Gomme and Sandbach on Men. *Asp.* 374. *Antidotum*: first extant under Tiberius, cf. Cels. 5. 23, *TLL* 2. 168. 74. In Greek ἡ ἀντίδοτος is usual, sc. δόσις, but cf. LSJ s.v. (For the Latin phrase *medicinam . . . facere*, v. 2, cf. 1. 9. 8, *periculosam fecit medicinam*, *TLL* 8. 538. 34–7.) *Falso . . . nomine*, v. 3: cf. McCartney (1918–19) 349 f., Pfeiffer (1938) 9 n. 2. *Verbosis . . . strophis*, v. 4: the bracketing of the verse by the phrase throws it into relief. *Strophis* is first extant here in Latin, borrowed (they say) from the wrestling world long before (Aesch. *Suppl.* 623, δημηγόρους δ᾽ ἤκουσεν εὐπιθεῖς στροφάς, LSJ s.v.; cf. Sen. *Epp.* 26. 5, Bertschinger (1921) 28).

10. Panacea: Cels. 5. 23, Plin. *Nat. Hist.* 25. 30 f., Galen *De theriac.* 14. 270 Kühn, Capel (1900) 24 f.

11. Awkward: note that editors (e.g. Havet (1895)) posit a lacuna after v. 5 (cf. Thiele (1908) 356, Perry (1965) note ad loc., Gail (1826) 1. 515, *Excursus* 9); but for *hic*, cf. 1. 11. 6, 2. 8. 5, 5. 10. 6. *All's well*: Lawrence (1931) 55 f.; Märchen: Busk (1874) 54, 'The pot of marjoram', ibid. 136, 'A yard of nose'; Dawkins and Halliday (1916) 237 (a gipsy tale), *TMI* K1825.

12. For the game βασιλίνδα, cf. Hor. *Epp.* 1. 1. 59 f., *rex eris . . . | si recte facies*, Becq De Fouquières (1873) 63 f.; for Märchen:

Petron. 77. 6, Apul. *Met.* 4. 28. 1; everyday expressions: e.g. Pers.
2. 37, Petron. 57. 4, Von Wyss (1899) 51.

13. 'Goblet': originally, and often in Greek poetry, σκύφος is a rustic
tankard (Eumaeus' in Hom. *Od.* 14. 112, cf. Jebb on Phocyll. fr.
17); *scyphus* is a symposium goblet (Krause (1854) 343 f., Nisbet
and Hubbard on Hor. *Carm.* 1. 27. 1). 'Poison' is another
Hellenism long naturalized in Latin: τοξικόν in the general sense
of 'poison' is first extant in Strab. 3. 4. 18, but Latin *toxicum*
guarantees the usage much earlier: Plaut. *Merc.* 772, Bertschinger
(1921) 29. Originally the adjective, sc. φάρμακον, referred to
barbarian poison-tipped arrows (cf. Capel (1900) 1 f., Gow and
Scholfield on Nicand. *Alexiph.* 208, Scott (1923–4), and esp.
Lewin (1923)). Poison was traditionally taken in solution (*CGL* 3.
597. 46, *antidotum: confectio potionalis*, cf. Mayor on Juv. 1. 70).
Cash: contrast Helena's offer of her life as surety to the King of
France in *All's Well* (2. 1. 176 f.). *Praegustatio*: e.g. Apul. *Met.* 10.
26, Dio 60. 34. 2, Mayor on Juv. 1. 70. Antidotes were taken
before drinking (Juv. 14. 249, Capel (1900) 44). Augustus: Tac.
Ann. 1. 5; Tiberius: 6. 50; Drusus: 4. 8; on Claudius and
Britannicus: Henderson (1998*b*) 288–90.

At v. 8, note: *miscere illius antidoto se toxicum* Gude (1698): *m.
anthidoto i. s. t.* P, *i. m. anthidoto s. t.* R^Vi, *m. a. sese i. t.* L. Müller
(1875) 618. (*i. s. m. a. t.* Postgate (1919*a*): *contra metrum*,
Housman (1920) 124; *a. m. i. s. t.* Pithou (1596): scotched by
Müller (1877) *Preface* 12.)

At v. 9, note: *combibere* Burmann (1718), *bibere* PR^Gu, *hoc bibere*
Pithou (1596), *ebibere* Richter (1713) 64.

14. Running down the folk: Boas (1969). Hams up: cf. Curt. 7. 4. 8f.,
magicae artis . . . magis professione quam scientia celeber.

15. Heavy formula: Austin on Virg. *Aen.* 2. 593, *haec insuper addidit
ore:* |. *Head ~ feet* polarity: Ar. *Plut.* 650, ἐκ τῶν ποδῶν ἐς τὴν
κεφαλήν, Otto (1889) 309, Küspert (1902) 25.

At v. 13, note: *addidit* P, cf. Krischan (1954) 88; *edidit* Gronov.

16. Moral: cf. Von Prittwitz-Gaffron (1911) 34 f., Tribukait (1889)
17 f. Proverb: Otto (1890) s.v. *crepida*, Lau (1967) 198. Erasmus:
Tilley (1950) C480.

17. The subjunctive *dixerim*, v. 17, is a 'polite potential', cf. Cic. *Pro
Mur.* 60, *uerissime dixerim peccare te nihil*, LHS 333, Fraenkel on
Aesch. *Agam.* 838, λέγοιμ' ἄν. Truth: cf. 3. 4. 5, *App* 5. 22.

CHAPTER 8

1. 4. 13 is Zander (1921) no. 17; 4. 14 is ibid. no. 25 (both far from his best). The game of writing '*nouae fabulae*' is still played by Postgate (1919*a*), who takes a wild crack at 4. 14.
2. Note: the text is almost exactly that of Ad 51, with Rom 4. 8 all but discounted. The traditional folk-etymology *similis | simius* features (twice) in both: cf. Enn. ap. Cic. *de nat. deor.* 1. 97, '*simia quam similis turpissuma bestia nobis*'—*at mores in utroque dissimiles*, McDermott (1938) 144 and n. 191; and, agreeably enough, they also ham up the liar's identification of the courtiers, as *primicerii, campiductores, militares officii*. For later versions: Janson (1954) 40, 200 f., Welleski (1925) 197f., 204, Bolte and Polivka (1903–22) 2. 473 on *KHM* 107, 'Der beiden Wanderer'.
3. 'The royal ape' was proverbial in Greek: *CPG* Diogenian. 6. 98, Πίθηκος ἐν πορφύρᾳ, cf. Amm. Marc. 17. 11. 1, *simia purpurata*, Tilley (1950) 265, 'An ape's an ape, a varlet's a varlet, | though he be clad in silk or scarlet', Bieber (1906) 37, McDermott (1938) 117.
4. The *epimythium* (*Quia l. p. e. e. t. t.*) follows at once on *Leo uero erubuit laudatorem; cum sederet, mutauit fidem.* (cf. Rom. Vindobon. (*Cod. Ms. Lat.* 303), no. 57 (Hervieux (1894) 2. 444), (. . . *sed ut eam lederet, fidem irrumpens* . . .).
5. Where Wiss, as deciphered by Hervieux ((1894) 2. 188), helplessly deciphers his Phaedrian version as reading *potius clini uberi passim ullique genus*, Rom Vindob. (*Cod. Ms Lat.* 303), no. 57 comes up with *diligentissime . . . bestiarum.* (At least we know the answer to the question, 'Can we heal "The Lion-King" (text)?')
6. But note the misreading in Rom: *Leo uero erubuit laudatorem; sed ut deciperet, inuitauit fidem.*; in straightening out what the doctors must have been at, Rom also has them 'inspect the veins, but find the pulse *healthy*' (*pulsum sanum ut uiderunt*); this way, the prescription must take a (sinister) new twist. (Did Phaedrus' text write *sane* here? At any rate, Wiss rightly takes the pulse of this story and pronounes it *inenarrabilis.*)
7. At least, in Wiss 5. 2 he does (*Cum se ferarum rege[m] fecisset fortissimus leo*); Ad 49 and Rom 3. 20 have 'the animals make lion king' (*Cum sibi ferae regem fortissimum leonem fecissent; Cum sibi fere regem fecissent fortissimum leonem*). PhP obviously introduced a reason for the king-making, and for the selection of king, in their one-word supplement 'bravest', or . . . 'strongest' (*fortissimus*), depending on whether we want him to stand for right or might;

this equivocation is telling us something (everything) about Caesars.

8. Marin (1988) 95, in his classic discussion of LaFontaine's 'The Crow and the Fox' on the trail of the 'king's discourse' (= 1. 2: from Phaedr. 1. 13). LaFontaine demoted Phaedr. 1. 1 to be his 1. 10, emphatically promoting (non-Phaedrian, but in PhP; *AES* 373) 'Cicada and Ant' to focus programmatically on the hard-working song-and-dance act of . . . producing his *fables*: 'Eh bien! dansez maintenant'; Phaedr. 1. 2 gets relegated to 1. 3: with 'Maître Corbeau, sur un arbre perché', LaFontaine puts courtly rhetoric before politics.

9. The fable is based on Greek sayings, and folklore: 'Don't mention lion's bad breath', Perry (1952) 284, *Aesopi prouerbia* 128, Καὶ τίς λέγει τῷ λέοντι ὅτι ὄζει τὸ στόμα σοῦ; 'Sick lions eat monkey', Timoth. Gaz. 51 Bodenheimer and Rabinowitz 46, McDermott (1939) 47, Janson (1952) 82 and n. 35, 230 and n. 51, Wellmann (1930) 72, White (1954) 11; 'Vegetarian diet tames lion', Max. Tyr. *Or.* 2. 3, A. Marx (1889) 66 f., Babr. 101, 'When nice lion who was no lion was king . . .' (*AES* 334); cf. 'Once carnivores were vegetarian', Basil. *De struct. hom.* 2. 3. 4 *MPG* 30. 44d, 'Lion and Vulture before the Fall', Ar. *Pol.* 3. 13, Gatz (1967) 171 f., Kipling (1895) 1–28, 'How Fear Came'.

10. 'Sick lion' fables: esp. *AES* 258, When the animals came to visit lion, sick in his cage, wolf denounced fox for not paying his respects to their king, so fox protests he has been rushing round to consult the doctors for a cure—which turns out to be 'Skin a wolf alive and wrap the hide round you while it's still warm' (Fox observes: 'Masters need pushing toward love not hate') = Aarne and Thompson (1928) no. 50; Phaedr. 1. 21; *AES* 142 (Babr. 103), Fox reads signs of one-way traffic going in; *AES* 366 (Babr. 95), Fox delivers stag on a plate; cf. 585, 698.

11. (Lévi-Straussian) reading of a 'logic' of social existence structured around the alignment of 'codes' such as the political, alimentary, sacrificial, sensory . . .: esp. essays in Detienne and Vernant (1989).

12. Detienne (1979) 47, 54f.; Lévi-Strauss (1973).

13. Wolf taken on by Shepherd: *CPG* Diogenian. 5. 96, λύκος ὄιν ποιμαίνει, *AES* 234, cf. 153, 209, 234, 267, 342, 366. Owl to protect Doves from Hawk/Stork to protect Goose from Hawk . . .!: 588, 570.

14. Aesopic raptor birds are merciless killers of their prey, from Hesiod's 'Hawk and Nightingale' on: *Op.* 202–12, cf. *AES* 4, Daly (1962), Dalfen (1994), Hubbard (1995).

15. At v. 2, note: *auxilium* Ad 22, Wiss 3. 8, Rom 2. 2: *auxilia* P.
16. For later versions: Jacobs (1889*a*) 239. The formulaic finale 'I suffer what I deserve/what is just': Perry (1940) 404 and n. 42. Note that v. 14 is omitted by P, where v. 13 is followed, as last line in book 1, by an *incipit* in capitals. v. 14 here is the supplement of Havet (1895), from *qui nostrum spiritum tali credidimus inimico* Ad 22, *qui nos predoni commisimus* Wiss 3. 8, *qui nos tali commisimus* Rom 2. 2; cf. Vandaele (1897) 2.
17. Keenan (1995) 141, setting out deconstruction's compelling version of fable.
18. For myriad other versions: Jacobs (1889*a*) 51, 238, Aarne and Thompson (1928) no. Add. 277.
   At vv. 7–8, note: *grauis* | *omnino* PR^GuRo, *graue* Pithou (1596), *grauest* L. Müller (1875), *omne* Heinsius (1698), all with the comma after, not before, *onus*.
   At v. 28, note: *deus* P, *Tonans* Postgate (1919*a*), *Iupiter* Ad 21, *altitonans* Wiss 3. 7, Rom 2. 1.
19. As in Phaedr. 4. 5 (cf. Perry (1952) 224 f., Testimonia 39); but Aesop does not rub shoulders with *history* in fable collections.
20. § 3 in *RE* 19. 1 (1937) 156–91, esp. 158 f.; how long his régime lasted: Cic. *De nat. deor.* 3. 82; 'Scipio' theorizes how Napoleons come about: *ex hac nimia licentia . . . quam illi solam libertatem putant, aut ille ut ex stirpe quadam exsistere et quasi nasci tyrannum . . .*; when the popular leader is given a position of authority, and a bodyguard, *ut Athenis Pisistratus, postremo, a quibus producti sunt, exsistunt eorum ipsorum tyranni*: Cic. *De rep.* 1. 67 f., after Hdt. 1. 59–64: award of 'club-carriers' led to the first tyranny, when Pisistratus did not revolutionize Athens, but ἐπί τε τοῖσι κατεστεῶ -σι ἔνεμε τὴν πόλιν κοσμέων καλῶς τε καὶ εὖ; this (1. 60. 1) is when the factions conspired (as in Phaedrus' frame), and the father of history decided . . . not to mention that Aesop's road was not taken.
   We must try not to think the consequences of Aesop's counterfactual advice through: if Athens were content to be Athens (but that wouldn't be Athens), then that nice log Pisistratus could have been finessed; but given that he had them where he wanted, they should not have interrupted and exacerbated his, and his son's, tyranny, but instead spared themselves watersnakedom; but, in that case, tyrannicide would not have happened, nor democracy, nor—(well, what *does* go if 'Athens' goes?).
21. Look > leap: *AES* 43; cf. Phaedr. 1. 6, 1. 30, *AES* 69, 138, 141.
22. See Braund (1984): emperors made, unmade, replaced hosts of 'client kings'—but not on request from free peoples.

23. Cf. Beard and Henderson (forthcoming).
24. = Aarne and Thompson (1928) no. 75, cf. A. Marx (1889) 127 f.
25. Cf. Gorskyi (1888), Jacobs (1889*a*) 73 n. 1, 232, Aarne and Thompson (1928) no. 51.
26. Cf. Hako (1956) esp. 341, Zander (1897) 6, Keller (1876) 12, 'La donna', *et sim.*
27. In PhP, this brute of an opener is dethroned by the Cock who finds a Pearl on the dung-heap (= Phaedr. 3. 12, *AES* 503; relegated to 1. 20 in LaFontaine). Here is 'The Fable of (de-politicized) Fable': Speckenbach (1978) (cf. Gerhard (1909) 113).
28. Serres (1979) esp. 263–7; cf. Marin (1997) 55–84, 'The reason of the strongest is always best' (LaFontaine 1. 10), exploring this fable as an 'elementary structure of ethical signification' played out 'beyond good and evil': esp. 61, 'How is a story about power moralized as a discourse of justice? Or contrariwise, how is justice factualized as power?' Also on Phaedr. 1. 1: Grilli (1906); parallels and derivatives: Jacobs (1889*a*) 139; in visual images: Rozmovits (1995). On the implied jurisprudence: Oberg (1996) 151–3.
29. This closing thought is dedicated to R. W. Lamb, bookman and Phaedrus fan (cf. Lamb (1995)).

REFERENCES

Conspectuses of editions of Phaedrus: Gail (1826) *Preface* § 4, Hervieux (1883) 1. 199 f., Havet (1895) 10–12, Lamb (1995). Recent surveys of scholarship: Currie (1978), von Albrecht (1997) 2, 1002–7, Conte (1994) 433–5, 'A marginal poet'.

Abbreviations for Phaedriana: (i) *Textus fontes*:

P: *Codex Pithoeanus, Pierpont Morgan M. 906*: ninth-century Carolingian miniscule written as if prose, with titles added: the first edition was Pithou (1596).

R: *Codex (Sancti Remigii) Remensis*, destroyed by fire at Rheims Abbey in 1774. Collations:
R^{Gu}: Gude (1698);
R^{Ri}: J. Sirmond in Rigault (1617, 1630);
R^{Ro}: D. Roche, discovered in the Bibliothèque de l'Université, Paris, by Chatelain (1887);
R^{Vi}: Dom. J. C. Vincent (1774) 'Notice sur le ms de Phèdre qui est dans le Bibliothèque de l'Abbaye de Saint-Reims', *Almanach de Reims*: known through the marginalia made by de Xivrey (1830), in a school edition (1743), *Phaedri Augusti Liberti Fabularum Aesopiarum Libri Quinque*, published by Widow Brocas, Paris.

D: *P. Danielis Schedae, Vatican Codex Reg. Lat. 1616*, a ninth/tenth-century parchment fragment from St Benoît-sur-Loire, with 1. 11. 2–13. 12, 1. 17. 1–21. 10 written in verses, and titles independent of PR.

N: *Codex Neapolitanus IV F 58, Codex Perottinus. c.*1465–70. Disastrously waterlogged and progressively deteriorating, multiply collated. This is the autograph anthology of Perotti, Bishop of Siponto: *Nicolai Perotti Epitome fabellarum Esopi Auieni et Phaedri ad Pyrrhum Perottum fratris filium adulescentem suauissimum* (cf. D'Orville (1927): of the 157 poems (one written out twice), 32 are fables known from books '2 to 5' (i.e. 2. 6-*Epil*; 3. 1–8, 10–19; 4. 21–3, 25–6; 5. 1–5; for his proem, Perotti appropriated 3. *Prol.* 30, 31–7, 4. *Prol.* 15–19, 5. *Prol.* 8–9); 32 are the otherwise lost Phaedriana we call the *Appendix Perottina* (*App*: including two fragments; but 8 of these pieces are represented, in diluted form, from the prose paraphrasts); 36 are fables from Avianus' collection of forty-two; 57 are miscellaneous poems. The ingredients are thoroughly jumbled, though some signs of corresponsion with the order in PR survive (in the sequences 3. 4–7, and 5. 2–4; conspectus in Havet (1895) 287). Perotti deliberately 'streamlined' his texts, taken from a lost codex more complete than PR. As can be proved by comparison between poems common to PR and NV, *App* is incorrigibly inaccurate (and metrically abused). See esp. Boldrini (1990), for both *App* and Perotti.

V: *Codex Vat. Lat. (Urbin.) 368*: a sloppy but well-preserved late fifteenth-century copy of N, possibly at one remove: Boldrini (1990) 32–55.

PhP: Three mediaeval prose paraphrases of Phaedrus, viz.:

Ad.: *Ademari Cabannensis Codex (Leidensis) Voss. Lat. oct. 15, fol. cxva–cciiib. c.*1000–10: penned in St Martial Monastery at Limoges, probably by the monk and future historian Adhémar. Sixty-seven fables, charmingly illustrated, no book divisions or editorial comment.

Wiss: *Codex Wissemburgensis nunc Guelferbytanus* (Wolfenbüttel) *Gudianus Lat. 48, fol. 60b–82a*: tenth century *Liber Ysopi*, in Lombard script, from the Monastery of SS Peter and Paul of Weissembourg.

Prologue: *Epistula Magistro Rufo Aesopus*, 58 fables, the remains of another prologue in two versions, and a mutilation of Phaedr. 2. *Epil.* as its closing piece. Set out in five books (no connection with Phaedr.1–5 as preserved in PR). Heavily corrected in the eleventh century, painfully illiterate.

Rom: *Romuli Fabulae*, the collective name for a numerous group of related mediaeval Latin Aesopica, named for the pseudonymous editor responsible for the prologue (in later collections, Romulus is identified as *Romae Imperator*). The MSS of *Rom 'Vulgaris'*, the earliest from the tenth century, give texts of, or selections from, a core canon of: *Prol.*: 'To Tyberinus'; 81 fables; a derivative of Phaedr. 2. *Epil.* as an epilogue; a new non-Phaedrian, *Epil.* Full and near-full versions are generally organized in four books. Later, derivative, Romuluses show omissions and deviation from the standard ordering.

(ii) Others:

AES: Perry (1952, 1965), tabulation of fables.

App: *Appendix Perottina* (fables preserved only in Perotti's compilation, MSS NV, see (i) above).

PhP: Three mediaeval prose paraphrases of Phaedrus, garbling many pieces otherwise lost, but also mixing in non-Phaedrian fables, see (i) above).

Standard works of reference are abbreviated as follows:

AE   *L'Année Épigraphique: Révue des Publications Épigraphiques relatives à l'Antiquité romaine* (1888–), Paris.

CE   *Carmina Latina Epigraphica*, ed. F. Bücheler and A. Riese (rev. E. Lommatiszch) (1895–1926 = 1982) = *Anthologia Latina siue Poesis Latinae Supplementum, Pars Posterior*, Leipzig and Stuttgart, vols. 1–3.

CGL   G. Götz ed. (1888–1923) *Corpus Glossariorum Latinorum*, Leipzig, vols. 1–7.

CIL   *Corpus Inscriptionum Latinarum* (1863–91), Berlin, vols. 1–15.

CPG   *Corpus Paroemiographorum Graecorum*, ed. E. L. von Leutsch and F. G. Schneidewin (1839–51 = 1961), Göttingen and Hildesheim, vols. 1–2.

D–S   C. Darembourg and E. Saglio eds. (1877–1919), *Dictionnaire des Antiquités grecques et romaines d'après les Textes et les Monuments*, Paris, vols. 1–10.

FGH   *Die Fragmente der griechischen Historiker*, ed. F. Jacoby (1923–30; 1940–58), Berlin; Leiden, vols. 1–3.

FHG   *Fragmenta Historicorum Graecorum*, ed. C. Müller (1841–70), Paris, vols. 1–5.

ILS   *Inscriptiones Latinae Selectae*, ed. H. Dessau (1892–1916 = 1954–5), Berlin, vols. 1–3.

KHM   *Kinderundhausmärchen*, Grimm's fairy tales: see Bolte and Polivka (1903–22).

K–S   R. Kühner revised by C. Stegmann (1955³) *Ausführliche Grammatik der lateinischen Sprache: Satzlehre*, Hannover/Darmstadt.

LHS   M. Leumann, J. B. Hofmann, revised by A. Szantyr (1965) *Lateinische Grammatik: Syntax und Stilistik*, Munich, vols. 1–2.

LSJ   H. J. Liddell and R. Scott eds., revised by H. S. Jones (1940⁹) *A Greek–English Lexikon*, Oxford.

MPG   J.-P. Migne ed. *Patrologiae Cursus Completus, Series Graeca* (1857–94), vols. 1–161, Paris.

MPL   J.-P. Migne ed. *Patrologiae Cursus Completus, Series Latina* (1857–66), vols. 1–221, Paris.

OED   *Oxford English Dictionary* (1933), Oxford, vols. 1–12.

OLD   *The Oxford Latin Dictionary*, ed. P. G. W. Glare (1968–82), Oxford.

RE   *Real-Encyclopädie der classischen Altertumswissenschaft*, ed. A. Fr. von Pauly, revised by G. Wissowa (1893–), Stuttgart.

RLAC   *Real-Lexikon für Antike und Christentum: Sachwörterbuch zur Auseinandersetzung des Christentums mit der antiken Welt*, ed. T. Klauser (1950–91), Stuttgart, vols. 1–15.

TLL   *Thesaurus Linguae Latinae* (1900–), Leipzig and Stuttgart.

TMI   S. Thompson, *Motif-Index of Folk-Literature, a Classification of Narrative Elements in Folktales, Ballads, Myths, Fables, Mediaeval Romances, Exempla, Fabliaux, Jest Books, and Local Legends* (1955–8), Copenhagen, vols. 1–5.

NB. **Scholarship on Phaedrus is** in bold. *Standard commentaries on classical texts are* not *included in the* References.

Aarne, A., and S. Thompson (1928) *The Types of the Folktale. A Classification and Bibliography* (= *Folklore Fellows Communications* 74), Helsinki.

Adam, T. (1970) *Clementia Principis, der Einfluss hellenistischer Fürstenspiegel auf den Versuch einer rechtlichen Fundierung des Principats durch Seneca* (= *Kieler Historische Studien* 11), Kiel.

Ahl, F. M. (1984) 'The art of safe criticism in Greece and Rome', *American Journal of Philology* 105. 174–208.

Albrecht, M. von (1997) *A History of Roman Literature*, Leiden, vols. 1–2.

Aldrete, G. S. (1999) *Gestures and Acclamations in Ancient Rome*, Baltimore.

Alföldi, A. (1934) 'Die Ausgestaltung des monarchischen Zeremoniells am römischen Kaiserhofe', *Mitteilungen des Deutschen Archölogischen Instituts (Römische Abteilung)* 49. 1–118.

Alföldi, A. (1935) 'Insignien und Tracht der römischen Kaiser', *Mitteilungen des Deutschen Archölogischen Instituts (Römische Abteilung)* 50. 1–171.

Alfonsi, L. (1963) 'Sull' "itifallo" di Ermippo (?)', *Rheinisches Museum* 106. 161–4.

Alton, E. H. (1922) (review of Postgate (1919)) *Hermathena* 19. 321–9.

Anderson, W. S. (1963) *Pompey, his Friends, and the Literature of the First Century B. C.*, University of California Publications in Classical Philology 19. 1.

André, J. (1950) 'Les nom latins du chemin et de la rue', *Révue des Études Latines* 28. 104–34.

Armstrong, A. McC. (1948) 'Anacharsis the Scythian', *Greece & Rome* 17. 18–23.

Ashmole, B. (1973) 'Menander: an inscribed bust', *American Journal of Archaeology* 77. 61.

Austin, J. C. (1921) *The Significant Name in Terence* (= *University of Illinois Studies in Language and Literature* 7. 4), Urbana.

Avenarius, G. (1956) *Lukians Schrift zur Geschichtsschreibung*, Meisenheim-am-Glan.

Badian, E. (1973) 'Marius' villas: the testimony of the slave and the knave', *Journal of Roman Studies* 63. 121–32.

Bährens, W. A. (1918) 'Berichtigung', *Glotta* 9. 192.

Balsdon, J. P. V. D. (1934) *The Emperor Gaius*, Oxford.

Bartsch, S. (1994) *Actors in the Audience. Theatricality and Doublespeak from Nero to Hadrian*, Cambridge, Mass.

Baus, K. (1940) *Der Kranz* (= *Theophaneia* 2), Bonn.

Beacham, R. C. (1991) *The Roman Theatre and its Audience*, London.

Beard, M. (1993) 'Looking (harder) for Roman myth: Dumézil, declamation and the problems of definition', in F. Graf, ed. (1993) *Mythos in mythenloser Gesellschaft. Das Paradigma Roms* (= *Colloquium Rauricum* 3), Stuttgart, 44–64.

Beard, M., and J. Henderson (forthcoming), Seneca, *Apocolocyntosis*.

Beare, W. (1964) *The Roman Stage*, London.

Beazley, J. D. (1955) 'Hydria-Fragments in Corinth', *Hesperia* 24. 305–19.

Beck, C. D. (1812) '*De Longi Pastoralium et Phaedri Fabularum Recens Inuentis Supplementis*', *Acta Seminarii Regii et Societatis Philologicae Lipsiensis* 2. 187–31.

Becq De Fouquières, L. (1873) *Les Jeux des Anciens*, Paris.

Bell, A. J. (1923) *The Latin Dual and Poetic Diction. Studies in Numbers and Figures*, Toronto.

Bentley, R., ed. (1726) *P. Terentii Afri Comoediae, Phaedri Fabulae Aesopiae, P. Syri et Aliorum Veterum Sententiae*, Cambridge.

Bergen, F. (1890) 'Some saliva charms', *Journal of American Folklore* 3. 51–9.

Berger, A. (1953) *Encyclopedic Dictionary of Roman Law*, (= *Transactions of the American Philosophical Society* 43. 2. 331–809), Philadelphia.

Berlinger, L. (1935) *Beiträge zur inoffiziellen Titulatur der römischen Kaiser*, Breslau.

Bertschinger, J. (1921) *Volkstümliche Elemente in der Sprache des Phädrus*, Bern.

Bieber, D. (1906) *Studien zur Geschichte der Fabel in den ersten Jahrzehnten der Kaiserzeit*, Munich.

Bieber, M. (1961²) *The History of the Greek and Roman Theater*, Princeton, NJ.

Biese, Y. M. (1926) 'Bemerkungen zu einem *topos* in den Prooimien der antiken Geschichtsschreiber', in *Commentationes Philologicae in Honorem J. A. Heikel*, Helsinki, 12–23.

Bird, H. W. (1969) 'L. Aelius Seianus and his political significance', *Latomus* 28. 61–98.

Birt, T. (1898) *Sprach man* avrum *oder* aurum*? (= Rheinisches Museum Erganzungsheft*), Frankfurt.

Blanckenhagen, P. von, and C. Alexander (1990) *The Augustan Villa at Boscotrecase (= Deutsches Archäologisches Institut Rom, Sonderschriften* 8), Mainz.

Bléry, H. (1909) *Rusticité et Urbanité romaines*, Paris.

Bloomer, W. M. (1997) *Latinity and Literary Society at Rome*, Philadelphia.

Blümner, H. (1875–8) *Technologie und Terminologie der Gewerbe und Künste bei den Griechen und Römern*, Leipzig, vols. 1–2.

——(1889) 'Über die Farbenbezeichnungen bei den römischen Dichtern 2', *Philologus* 48. 706–22.

——(1918) *Fahrendes Volk im Alterthum, Sitzungsberichte der bayerischen Akademie der Wissenschaft, philosophische-historische Klasse, München, Abhandlung* 6.

Boas, F. (1969) Vox Populi. *Essays on the History of an Idea*, Baltimore.

Boldrini, S. (1990*a*) *Note sulla Tradizione manoscritta di Fedro (i tre codici di étà carolingia), Bollettino dei Classici, Supplement* 9.

——(1990*b*) *Fedro e Perotti. Ricerche di storia della tradizione*, Urbino.

Bolkestein, H. (1929) *Theophrastus Charakter der* Deisidaimonia *als religionsgeschichtliche Urkunde (=Religions-Geschichtliches Versuchen und Vorarbeiten* 21. 2), Giessen.

——(1939 = 1979) *Wohltätigkeit und Armenpflege im vorchristlichen Altertum*, Utrecht/New York.

Boll, F. (1920) *Vita contemplatiua, Sitzungsberichte der Heidelberger Akademie der Wissenschaften, philosophische-historische Klasse, Heidelberg, Abhandlung* 8.

Bollinger, T. (1969) Theatralis Licentia. *Die Publikumsdemonstrationen an den öffentlichen Spielen im Rom der früheren Kaiserzeit und ihre Bedeutung im politischen Leben*, Winterthur.

Bolte, J. and G. Polivka (1903–22) *Anmerkungen zu den Kinderundhausmärchen der Brüder Grimm*, Leipzig, vols. 1–5.

Bompaire, J. (1958) *Lucien, Écrivain. Imitation et Création (= Bibliothèque des Écoles Françaises d'Athènes et de Rome* 190), Paris.

Bonaria, M. ed. (1956) *Mimorum Romanorum Fragmenta*, Genoa, vols. 1–2.

Bonner, S. F. (1969² = 1949) *Roman Declamation in the Late Republic and Early Empire*, Liverpool.

Boone, J. A. (1987) *Tradition Counter Tradition: Love and the Form of Fiction*, Chicago.

Bowra, C. M. (1929) 'Some Ennian phrases in the *Aeneid*', *Classical Quarterly* 23. 65–75.

Bradley, K. (1987) *Slaves and Masters in the Roman Empire: A Study in Social Control*, Oxford.

—— (1991) *Discovering the Roman Family: Studies in Roman Social History*, Oxford.

—— (1994) *Slavery and Society at Rome*, Cambridge.

Bramble, J. C. (1974) *Persius and the Programmatic Satire*, Cambridge.

Brand, C. E. (1968) *Roman Military Law*, Austin, Tex.

Braun, N. (1938) *History of Romance in Graeco-Oriental Literature*, Oxford.

Braund, D. (1984) *Rome and the Friendly King: The Character of Client Kingship*, Beckenham.

Bréal, M. (1885) 'Ardelio', *Révue de Philologie* 7. 137.

Brecht, F. J. (1930) *Motiv- und Typengeschichte des griechischen Spottepigramms* (= *Philologus Supplementband* 22. 2), Leipzig.

Brewster, E. H. (1917) *Roman Craftsmen and Tradesmen of the Early Empire*, Menasha, Wis.

Brilliant, R. (1963) *Gesture and Rank in Roman Art* (= *Memoirs of the Connecticut Academy of Arts and Sciences* 14. 2), New Haven.

Brodeur, A. G. (1924) 'The fable of the grateful lion', *Publications of the Modern Language Association* 39. 485–524.

Brotherton, B. (1926) *The Vocabulary of Intrigue in Roman Comedy*, Chicago.

Brotier, G., ed. (1783), *Phaedri Augusti Liberti Fabularum Aesopiarum Libri Quinque*, Paris.

Brunt, P. A. (1971) *Italian Manpower*, Oxford.

Bryant, A. A. (1898) 'Some Plautine words and word groups', *Harvard Studies in Classical Philology* 9. 121–5.

—— (1899) 'Greek shoes in the classical period', *Harvard Studies in Classical Philology* 10. 57–102.

Bücheler, F. (1915–30 = 1965) *Kleine Schriften*, Leipzig/Osnabruck, vols. 1–3.

Bucher-Isler, B. (1972) *Norm und Individualität in den Biographien Plutarchs*, Zurich.

Büchmann, G. (1895[18]) *Geflügelte Worte. Der Citatenschatz des deutsches Volkes*, Berlin.

Burford, A. (1972) *Craftsmen in Greek and Roman Society*, London.

Burmann, P. ed. (1698[1], 1718[2], 1727[3]) *Phaedri Augusti Liberti Fabularum Aesopiarum Libri Quinque*, Amsterdam/The Hague/Leyden.

Burns, E. (1972) *Theatricality*, London.

Busk, R. H. (1874) *Folklore of Rome*, London.

Calderini, A. (1908) *La Manomissione e la Condicione dei Liberti in Grecia*, Milan.

Callebat, L. (1967) Sermo Cotidianus *dans les Métamorphoses d'Apulée*, Paris.

Campbell, L. B. (1923) *Scenes and Machines on the English Stage*, Cambridge.

Canetti, E. (1973) *Crowds and Power*, Harmondsworth.

Capel, W. C. K. (1900) *De Veneficiis apud Romanos*, Leyden.

Carlyle, T. (1932) *Sartor resartus*, London.

Cartault, A. (1899) *Études sur les Satires d'Horace*, Paris.

Causeret, C. (1886) *De Phaedri Sermone Grammaticales Obseruationes*, Paris.

Cerquiglini, B. (1999) *In Praise of the Variant. A Critical History of Philology*, Baltimore.

Cervantes, M. de S. (1950) *Don Quixote*, Harmondsworth.

Chantraine, H. (1967) *Freigelassene und Sklaven im Dienst der römischen Kaiser. Studien zu ihrer Nomenklatur*, Wiesbaden.

Charlesworth, M. P. (1943) '*Pietas* and *Victoria*: the Emperor and the Citizen', *Journal of Roman Studies* 33. 1–10.

Chatelain, E. (1887) 'Un nouveau document sur le *Codex Remensis* de Phèdre', *RPh* 11. 81–8.

Christes, J. (1979a) *Sklaven und Freigelassene als Grammatiker und Philologen im antiken Rom*, Wiesbaden.

——(1979b) 'Reflexe erlebter Unfreiheit in den Sentenzen des Publilius Syrus und den Fabeln des Phaedrus. Zur Problematik ihrer Verifizierung', *Hermes* 107. 199–220.

Christoffersson, H. (1904) *Studia de Fontibus Fabularum Babrianarum*, Lund.

Clouston, W. A. (1886) 'The innocent persecuted wife, Asiatic and European versions of Chaucer's "Man at Law's Tale"', *Chaucer Society Second Series* 20. 367–414.

Combès, R. (1966) *Imperator*, Paris.

Comotti, G. (1989) *Music in Greek and Roman Culture*, Baltimore.

Compton, T. (1990) 'The trial of the satirist: poetic *Vitae* (Aesop, Archilochus, Homer) as background for Plato's *Apology*', *American Journal of Philology* 111. 330–47.

Conte, G. B. (1992) 'Proems in the middle', in F. Dunn and T. Cole, eds. (1992) *Beginnings in Classical Literature*, Cambridge, Mass. (= *Yale Classical Studies* 29), 147–59.

——(1994) *Latin Literature: A History*, Baltimore.

Cook, A. B. (1914–40) *Zeus. A Study in Ancient Religion*, Cambridge, vols. 1–3.

Corbeill, A. (1996) *Controlling Laughter. Political Humor in the Late Roman Republic*, Princeton, NJ.

Cramer, F. (1889) 'Was heisst "Leute"?', *Archiv für Lateinische Lexicographie* 6. 341–76.

Crombie, J. E. (1892) 'The saliva superstition', in J. and A. Nutt, eds. (1892) *Papers and Transactions of the International Folk-Lore Congress 1891*, London, 249–58.

Crook, J. (1967) *The Law and Life of Rome*, London.

Crowther, N. B. (1973) 'The *Collegium Poetarum* at Rome: fact and conjecture', *Latomus* 32. 575–80.

Crusius, O. (1893) 'Sphinx und Silen', in *Festschrift für J. Overbeck* (1893), Leipzig, 102–8.

Currie, H. MacL. (1978) 'Phaedrus the fabulist', *Aufstieg und Niedergang der Römisches Welt* II. 32. 1. 497–513.

Cuss, D. (1971) *Imperial Cult and Honorary Terms in the New Testament*, Freiburg.

Dadone, M. (1954) 'Appunti sulla Fortuna di Fedro 1. Fedro e Seneca', *Rivista di Studi Classici* 2. 3–12.

D'Agostino, V. (1928) 'De uerbi "excutiendi" apud nonnullos argentei aeui scriptores usu atque significatione', *Bollettino di Filologia Classica* 35. 153–6.

Dalfen, J. (1994) 'Die ὕβρις der Nachtigall. Zur der Fabel bei Hesiod (*Erga* 202–218) und zur griechischen Fabel im allgemein', *Wiener Studien* 107. 157–77.

Daly, L. W. (1962) 'Hesiod's fable', *Transactions of the American Philological Association* 92. 45–51.

D'Arms, J. H. (1970) *Romans on the Bay of Naples*, Harvard.

Darrieussecq, M. (1998) *Pig Tales*, London.

Daube, D. (1972) *Civil Disobedience in Antiquity*, Edinburgh.

Dawkins, R. M. and W. R. Halliday (1916) *Modern Greek in Asia Minor*, Cambridge.

Dellacorte, F. (1939) 'Phaedriana', *Rivista di Filologia e di Istruzione Classica* 17. 136–44.

DeLorenzi, A. (1955) *Fedro. Poesia e Personalità*, Florence.

Denis, E. de St. (1935) *La Rôle de la Mer dans la Poésie latine*, Paris.

Deonna, W. (1965) *Le Symbolisme de l'Oeil*, Paris.

Desbillons, F. J. (1786) *Phaedri Augusti Liberti Fabularum Aesopiarum Libri V*, Mannheim.

Detienne, M. (1979) *Dionysos Slain*, Baltimore.

Detienne, M., and J.-P. Vernant, eds. (1989) *The Cuisine of Sacrifice among the Greeks*, Chicago..

Dierks, E. (1883) *De Tragicorum Histrionum Habitu apud Graecos*, Göttingen.

Dihle, A. (1971) '*Sine ira et studio*', *Rheinisches Museum* 114. 27–43.

Dithmar, R. (1982) *Texte zur Theorie der Fabeln, Parabeln und Gleichnisse*, Munich.

Dixon, S. (1988) *The Roman Mother*, London.

254   References

Dixon, S. (1997) 'Conflict in the Roman family', in Rawson and
    Weaver (1997) 149–67.
Dorson, R. M. (1970) 'Esthetic form in British and American folk
    narrative', in J. Mandel and B. A. Rosenburg, eds. (1970) *Medieval
    Literature and Folklore Studies: Essays in Honor of F. L. Utley*, New
    Brunswick, NJ, 305–21.
D'Orville, J. P. (1727*a*) *Nicolai Perotti Epitome Fabularum Aesopi
    Auieni et Phaedri*, Parma (= *Codex D'Orville 524*, Bodleian Library,
    Oxford: transcription of Ms N, cf. Garzya (1957).
——(1727*b*) Notes in Burmann (1727).
Douglas, M. (1966) *Purity and Danger: An Analysis of Concepts of
    Pollution and Taboo*, London.
Douglas(s), (G.) Norman (1923) *Siren Land*, London.
Dressler, C. T. (1838) *Phaedri Augusti Liberti Fabularum Aesopiarum
    Libri V*, Bautzen.
Duff, A. M. (1958²) *Freedmen in the Early Roman Empire*, London.
Dundes, A. (1980) 'Wet and dry, the evil eye', in *idem* (1980) *Inter-
    preting Folklore*, Bloomington, Ind., 93–133.
DuPont, F. (1985) *L'Acteur-Roi, ou Le Théâtre dans la Rome antique*,
    Paris.
Du Quesnay, I. M. Le M. (1995) 'Horace, *Odes* 4. 5: *Pro Reditu
    Imperatoris Caesaris Divi Filii Augusti*', in S. J. Harrison, ed. (1995)
    Homage to Horace: A Bimillenary Celebration, Oxford, 128–87.
Duret, L. (1983) 'Dans l'ombre des plus grands I: Poètes et prosateurs
    mal connus de l'époque augustéenne', *Aufstieg und Niedergang der
    Römisches Welt* II. 30. 3. 1447–561.
Dyer, R. (1982) *Stars*, London.
Edwards, C. (1993) *The Politics of Immorality in Ancient Rome*,
    Cambridge.
——(1994) 'Beware of imitations: theatre and the subversion of
    imperial identity', in J. Elsner and J. Masters, eds. (1994) *Reflections
    of Nero: Culture, History and Representation*, London, 83–97.
Ellis, R. (1895) *The Fables of Phaedrus. An Inaugural Lecture*, Oxford.
——(1896) 'Havet's *Fables of Phaeder*', *Classical Review* 10. 159–63.
Ehrenburg, I. (1962) *First Years of Revolution 1918–21*, vol. 2 of *Men,
    Years, Life*, London.
Ernout, A. (1909) *Les Éléments dialectaux du Vocabulaire latin*, Paris.
—— (1949) *Les Adjectifs latins en -osus et en -ulentus* (= *Collection
    Linguistique publiée par la Société de Linguistique de Paris 54*), Paris.
Fantham, E. (1984) 'Roman experience of Menander in the Late
    Republic and Early Empire', *Transactions of the American Philo-
    logical Association* 114. 299–309.
——(1986) '*ZHLOTYPIA*: A brief excursion into sex, violence, and
    literary history', *Phoenix* 40. 45–57.

——(1991) '*Stuprum*: public attitudes and penalties for sexual offences in republican Rome', *Échos du Monde Classique* 35. 267–91.

Feldherr, A. (1998) *Spectacle and Society in Livy's History*, Berkeley and Los Angeles.

Fenik, B. (1968) *Typical Battlescenes in the* Iliad, *Hermes Einzelschriften* 21.

Ferguson, W. S. (1911) *Hellenistic Athens*, London.

Festa, N. (1898) 'Note al testo di Fedro', *Studi Italiani di Filologia Classica* 6. 257–70.

Festugière, J., ed. (1971) *Historia Monachorum in Aegypto*, Brussels.

Finch, C. E. (1971) 'The Morgan Manuscript of Phaedrus', *American Journal of Philology* 92. 301–7.

Finkelpearl, E. D. (1998) *Metamorphosis of Language in Apuleius. A Study of Allusion in the Novel*, Ann Arbor.

Finnegan, R. (1967) *Limba Stories & Storytelling*, Oxford.

Fitzgerald, W. (2000) *Slavery and the Roman Literary Imagination*, Cambridge.

Förster, R., ed. (1893) *Scriptores Physiognomonici*, Leipzig, vols. 1–2.

Forbes, C. A. (1955) 'The education and training of slaves in antiquity', *Transactions of the American Philological Association* 86. 321–60.

Forbes, J. (1955–64) *Studies in Ancient Technology*, Leyden, vols. 1–9.

Forte, B. (1972) *Rome and the Romans as the Greeks saw them, Papers and Monographs of the American Academy in Rome* 24.

Fowler, D. (1997) 'Second thoughts on closure', in D. H. Roberts, F. M. Dunn, and D. Fowler, eds. (1997), *Classical Closure: Reading the End in Greek and Latin Literature*, Princeton, NJ, 3–22.

Fraenkel, E. (1957) *Horace*, Oxford.

——(1964) *Kleine Beiträge zur klassischen Philologie*, Rome, vols. 1–2.

Frazer, J. G. (1919) *Folklore in the Old Testament. Studies in Comparative Religion*, London, vols. 1–3.

Freinsheim, J. (1664) *Phaedri Augusti Liberti Fabularum Aesopiarum Libri V*, Argentorati.

Friedländer, L. (1908[7]) *Roman Life and Manners Under the Early Empire*, translated by L. A. Magnus and A. B. Gough, London, vols. 1–4.

——(1919–22) *Darstellungen aus der Sittengeschichte Roms in der Zeit von August bis zum Ausgang der Antonine*, revised by G. Wissowa, Leipzig, vols. 1–5.

Friedrich, W.-H. (1956) *Verwendung und Tod in der* Ilias, *homerische Darstellungsweisen, Abhandlungen der Akademie der Wissenschaft in Göttingen, philologische-historische Klasse* 38.

Gagé, J. (1969) 'L'Étendard d'Eutyche: sur un mot de Cassius Chaeréa, le meurtrier de Caligula', *Collection Latomus* 102. 275–83.

Gaheis, A. (1927) *Gaukler im Altertum*, Munich. [*Not seen*]

256   *References*

Gail, J. B., ed. (1826) *Phaedri Augusti Liberti Fabularum Aesopiarum Libri Quinque*, Paris, vols. 1–2.

Galinsky, K. (1996) *Augustan Culture. An Interpretive Introduction*, Princeton, NJ.

Gandelman, C. (1991) *Reading Pictures, Viewing Texts*, Bloomington, Ind.

Gardiner, E. N. (1930) *Athletics of the Ancient World*, Oxford.

Gardner, J. F. (1998) *Family and* Familia *in Roman Law and Life*, Oxford.

Garzya, A. (1957) 'Nicolo Perotti's *Version of the Enchiridion of Epictetus*, Edited by R. P. Oliver', *Orpheus* 5. 156–7.

Gatz, B. (1967) *Weltalter, goldene Zeit und sinnverwandte Vorstellungen* (= *Spudasmata* 16), Hildesheim.

Gaudemet, J. (1962) *Indulgentia Principis* (= *Conferenze romanistiche* 6), Trieste.

Gebhard, E. (1891) *De D. Innii Bruti Genere Dicendi*, Jena.

Geffcken, J. ed. (1909) *Kynika und Verwandtes*, Heidelberg.

Geller, H. (1966) *Varros Menippea* Parmeno, Cologne.

George, M. (1997) 'Repopulating the Roman House', in Rawson and Weaver (1997) 299–319.

Georges, K. E. (1888) '*Ardalio*', *Archiv für Lateinische Lexicographie* 5. 486.

Gerhard, G. A. (1909) *Phoinix von Kolophon. Die gnomisches Poesie der Hellenistischenzeit*, Leipzig.

Gershenson, D. E. (1969) 'Averting βασκανία in Theocritus: a compliment', *California Studies in Classical Antiquity* 2. 145–55.

Gil, L. (1969) *Therapeia. La Medicine Popularen el Mundo Classico*, Madrid.

Gleason, M. (1995) *Making Men. Sophists and Self-Presentation in Ancient Rome*, Princeton, NJ.

Glick, M. K. (1938) *Studies in Colloquial Exaggeration in Roman Comedy*, Chicago.

Glück, J. J. (1964) 'Reviling and monomachy as battle preludes in ancient warfare', *Acta Classica* 7. 25–31.

Goldberger, W. (1931–2) 'Kraftausdrücke im Vulgärlatein', *Glotta* 20. 101–50.

Gombel, A. (1934) *Die Fabel vom Magen und die Gliedern*, Halle.

Goodenough, E. R. (1938) *The Good King in the Politics of Philo Judaeus*, Yale.

González-Haba, M. (1969) 'Petron. 38, 9 *est tamen subalapa*', *Glotta* 47. 253–64.

Gorskyi, K. (1888) *Die Fabel vom Löwen-Antheil in ihrer geschichtlichen Entwicklung*, Berlin.

Gow, A. S. F., and D. L. Page, eds. (1965) *Hellenistic Epigrams*,

Cambridge, vols. 1–2.

—— (1968) *The Greek Anthology: The Garland of Philip*, Cambridge, vols. 1–2.

Gow, J., ed. (1905) *Phaedri Augusti Liberti Fabularum Aesopiarum Libri*, in Postgate (1894–1905), vol. 2. 47–67.

Graf, F. (1987) 'Orpheus: a poet among men', in J. Bremmer, ed., *Interpretations of Greek Mythology*, London, 80–106.

Graver, M. (1998) 'The manhandling of Maecenas: Senecan abstractions of masculinity', *AJPh* 119: 607–32.

Graves, R. (1953² = 1934) *I, Claudius*, Harmondsworth.

Green, P. (1961) *The Sword of Pleasure*, Harmondsworth.

Grenade, P. (1950) 'Le mythe de Pompée et les Pompéiens', *Révue des Études Anciennes* 52. 28–63.

Griessmair, E. (1966) *Das Motiv der Mors Immatura in den griechischen metrischen Grabinschriften*, Innsbruck.

Griffin, J. (1976) 'Augustan poetry and the life of luxury', *Journal of Roman Studies* 66. 87–105.

Grilli, A. (1906) *La favola Latina Prima di Fedro. Saggio Critico*, Imola. [*Not seen*]

Grimal, P. (1969²) *Les Jardins Romains*, Paris.

Griset, E. (1925) *Per la Cronologia ed il Significato delle Favole di Fedro*, Turin. [*Not seen*]

Gronov, J. F. (1663) Annotations in Scheffer (1663).

Grottanelli, C. (1983) 'Tricksters, scapegoats, champions, saviors', *History of Religions* 23. 117–39.

Guaglianone, A., ed. (1969) *Phaedri Augusti Liberti Liber Fabularum*, Turin.

—— (1976) 'Nota a Fedro', *Annali della Facoltà di Lettere e Filosofia, Università di Macerata* 9. 367–73.

Gude, M. (1698) Notes in Burmann (1698).

Guyet, F. (1663) Annotations in Scheffer (1663).

Habicht, C. (1998²) *Pausanias's Guide to Ancient Athens*, Berkeley and Los Angeles.

Hahn, G. (1922) *Der Villenbesitz zur Zeit der Republik*, Bonn.

Haight, G. S. ed. (1954–78) *The George Eliot Letters*, New Haven, vols. 1–9.

Hako, M. (1956) *Das Wiesel in der europäischen Volksüberlieferung* (= *Folklore Fellows Communications* 167), Helsinki.

Hale, D. G. (1968) 'Intestine sedition and the fable of the belly', *Comparative Literature Studies* 5. 377–88.

Hallpike, C. V. R. (1978) 'Social hair', in T. Polhemus, ed., *Social Aspects of the Human Body*, Harmondsworth, 134–46.

Handley, E. W. (1953) 'XOPOU in the *Plutus*', *Classical Quarterly* 3. 55–61.

258   *References*

Hare, F. (1726) *Epistola Critica ad Eruditissimum V. H. B., S. E. I. In qua omnes doctiss.* *Bentleii in Phaedrum notae atque emendationes expenduntur*, London: *ad calcem* in Burmann (1727).

Harrison, J. E. (1922²) *Prolegomena to the Study of Greek Religion*, Cambridge.

Harrod, S. G. (1909) *Latin Terms for Endearment and of Family Relationship. A Lexicographical Study Based on* CIL *VI*, Princeton, NJ.

Hartman, J. J. (1890) *De Phaedri Fabulis Commentatio*, Leyden.

Hauser, M. (1954) *Der römische Begriff* Cura, Basle.

Havers, W. (1911) 'Lat. *est sub alapa*: Petron. *Cen. Trin.* C. 38', *Indogermanische Forschungen* 28. 189–90.

Havet, L., ed. (1895) *Phaedri Augusti Liberti Fabulae Aesopiae*, Paris (Havet § = *Disquisitiones Criticae, ad calcem*).

—— (1896) 'Quelques passages de Phèdre', *Révue de Philologie* 20. 146–8.

—— (1898) 'Phaeder, *Append. Perott.* 8', *Révue de Philologie* 22. 177–8.

Havet, L., (1900) 'Quelques passages de Phèdre', *Révue de Philologie* 24. 293–315.

Headlam, W. ed. (1922) *Herodas, the Mimes and Fragments*, Cambridge.

Heckenbach, J. (1911) *De Nuditate Sacra Sacrisque Vinculis*, Giessen.

Heinsius, N. (1698) Annotations in Burmann (1698).

Heinze, R. (1891–2) 'Anacharsis', *Philologus* 50. 458–68.

Heller, J. L. (1939) 'Festus on *Nenia*', *Transactions of the American Philological Association* 70. 357–67.

Helm, R. (1906) *Lukien und Menippus*, Leipzig.

Hemelrijk, J. (1925) *Penia und Ploutos*, Utrecht.

Henderson, J. (1976) *'Anecdote and Satire in Phaedrus: Discussion and Commentary'*, unpublished D.Phil. dissertation, Oxford University.

—— (1977) 'The homing instinct: Phaedrus, *Appendix* 16', *Proceedings of the Cambridge Philological Society* 23. 17–31.

—— (1983) 'Poetic technique and rhetorical amplification: Seneca *Medea* 579–669', *Ramus* 12 (= A. J. Boyle (ed.) *Seneca Tragicus*, Berwick, Vic.), 94–113.

—— (1997a) *Figuring out Roman Nobility: Juvenal's Eighth Satire*, Exeter.

—— (1997b) 'The name of the tree: recounting *Odyssey* 24. 340–2', *Journal of Hellenic Studies* 117. 87–116.

—— (1998a) *A Roman Life: Rutilius Gallicus on Paper and in Stone*, Exeter.

—— (1998b) *Fighting for Rome*, Cambridge.

——(1999a) *Writing Down Rome*, Oxford.

——(1999b) 'Phaedrus' Fables: *the original corpus*', *Mnemosyne* 52. 308–29.

——(1999c) 'Smashing bodies: the Corinthian Tydeus-Ismene Vase', in J. I. Porter, ed. (1999) *Constructions of the Classical Body*, Ann Arbor, 19–49.

Henry, J. (1873–8) *Aeneidea*, London and Dublin, vols. 1–2.

Heraeus, W. (1902) 'Die römische Soldatensprache', *Archiv für Lateinische Lexicographie* 12. 255–80.

——(1937) *Kleine Schriften* (= *Indogermanische Bibliothek* 17), Heidelberg.

Hervieux, R. ed. (1883–9, 1894^2 = 1970) *Les Fabulistes latins depuis le siècle d'Auguste jusqu'à la fin du moyen âge*, (2: *Phèdre*), vols. 1–5, Paris/Hildesheim.

Heumann, C. A. (1713) *'Phaedri Fabularum Aesopiarum Libri V cum Adnotationibus J. G. Walchii & c.'*, in *Neue Bibliothec oder Nachricht und Urtheile von neuen Büchern* 27. 603–14.

Hexter, R. (1990) 'What was the Trojan Horse made of?', *Yale Journal of Criticism* 3. 109–31.

Hillscher, A. (1891) *Hominum Litteratorum Graecorum ante Tiberii Mortem in Urbe Roma Commoratorum Historiae Criticae*, Leipzig.

Hirzel, R. (1967^2 = 1907–8) *Der Selbstmord*, Darmstadt/Leipzig.

Hobsbawm, E., and J. Scott (1980) 'Political shoemakers', *Past and Present* 89. 86–114.

Hofmann, J. B. (1948) 'Die lateinischen Totalitätsausdrücke', in *Mélanges de Philologie, de Littérature et d'Histoire ancienne offerts à J. Marouzeau*, Paris, 283–90.

——(1950^3) *Die lateinische Umgangssprache*, Heidelberg.

Hoogstraten, D. van (1701) *Phaedri Augusti Liberti Fabularum Aesopiarum Libri Quinque*, Amsterdam.

Hopkins, K. (1993) 'Novel evidence for Roman slavery', *Past and Present* 138. 3–27.

Horsfall, N. (1976) 'The *Collegium Poetarum*', *BICS* 23. 79–95.

Housman, A. E. (1900) 'Corpus Poetarum Latinorum, Fasc. III, ed. J. P. Postgate, London 1895', *Classical Review* 14. 465–9.

——(1902) 'Remarks on the *Culex*', *Classical Review* 16. 339–46.

——(1920) Postgate's 'Phaedri Fabulae Aesopiae', *Classical Review* 34. 121–4.

Hubaux, J. (1933) 'Misène', *L'Antiquité Classique* 135–64.

Hubbard, T. K. (1995) 'Hesiod's fable of the hawk and the nightingale', *Greek, Roman and Byzantine Studies* 36. 161–71.

Hugill, W. M. (1931) 'The condition of the streets in ancient Athens and in ancient Rome', *Classical World* 24. 162–4.

Idries Shah (1974) *Thinkers of the East*, Harmondsworth.

Immerwahr, H. R. (1966) *Form and Thought in Herodotus* (= *American Philological Monographs* 23), Cleveland, Ohio.

Instinsky, H. U. (1956) 'Wandlungen des römischen Kaisertums', *Gymnasium* 63. 260–8.

Isleib, W. (1906) *De Senecae Dialogo XI⁰ qui est Ad Polybium De Consolatione*, Marburg.

Jackson, K. H. (1961) *The International Popular Tale and Early Welsh Tradition*, Cardiff.

Jacobs, J. ed. (1889a) *Caxton's Aesop, the Fables of Aesop as First Printed by William Caxton in 1484*, London, vols. 1–2.

—— (1889b) *The Fables of Aesop*, London.

Jäger, W. (1915) 'Ein stilgeschichtliche Studie zum Philipperbriefe', *Hermes* 50. 536–53.

Jahn, O. (1841) *Specimen Epigraphicum in Memoriam Olai Kellermanni*, Kiel.

Jahn, O. ed. (1843 = 1967) *A. Persi Flacci Saturarum Liber cum Scholiis Antiquis*, Leipzig and Hildesheim.

Jannelli, C. (1811) *Phaedri Fabulae ex Codice Perottino Ms. Regiae Bibliothecae Neapolitanae Emendatae, Suppletae et Commentario Instructae*, Naples.

Janson, H. W. (1954) *Apes and Apelore in the Middle Ages and Renaissance* (= *Studies of the Warburg Institute* 20), London.

Jedrkiewicz, S. (1990) 'Fedro e la Verità', *Quaderni Urbinati di Cultura Classsica* 63. 121–8.

Jennings, V. J. (2000) 'Representing Aesops', unpublished Ph.D. dissertation, University of Cambridge.

Jeremias, J. (1963⁶) *The Parables of Jesus*, London.

Jerome, T. S. (1912) 'The Tacitean Tiberius. A study in historiographic method', *Classical Philology* 7. 265–92.

Jöel, K. (1893–1901) *Der echte und der xenophontische Sokrates*, Berlin, vols. 1–2.

Jöpgen, U. (1966) *Wortspiele bei Martial*, Bonn.

Johnson, T. (1701¹, 1708²) *Phaedri Augusti Liberti Fabularum Aesopiarum Libri V*, London.

Jolivet, V. (1987) 'Xerxes Togatus: Lucullus en Campanie', *Mélanges d'Archéologie et d'Histoire de l'École Française à Rome* 99. 875–904.

Jorgenson, P. A. (1956) *Shakespeare's Military World*, Berkeley, Calif.

Jory, E. J. (1981) 'The literary evidence for the beginnings of imperial pantomime', *Bulletin of the Institute of Classical Studies* 28. 147–61.

—— (1996) 'The drama of the dance: prolegomena to an iconography of imperial pantomime', in W. J. Slater, ed. (1996) *Roman Theater and Society* (= *E. Togo Salmon Papers* 1), Ann Arbor, 1–27.

Jullian, C. (1893) '*Deus noster Caesar*. A propos de Scribonius Largus', *Révue de Philologie* 17. 129–31.

Kajanto, I. (1965) *Latin* Cognomina (= *Societatis Scientiarum Fennicae Commentationes Humanarum Litterarum* 36), Helsinki.

Kaplan, M. (1990) *Greek and the Imperial Court from Tiberius to Nero*, New York.

Kaster, R. A., ed. (1995) *Suetonius De grammaticis et rhetoribus*, Oxford.

Keaveney, A. (1992) *Lucullus. A Life*, London.

Keenan, T. (1995) 'Fables of responsibility', in A. Gelley, ed., *Unruly Examples. On the Rhetoric of Exemplarity*, Stanford, Calif., 121–41.

Keidel, G. C. (1894) 'Die Eselherz-(Hirschherz, Eberherz)-Fabel', *Zeitschrift für vergleichende Litteraturgeschichte* 7. 264–7.

Keith, A. L. (1923–4) 'The taunt in Homer and Vergil', *Classical Journal* 19. 554–60.

Keller, O. (1876) *Über die Bedeutung einiger Thiernamen*, Graz.

——(1891) *Lateinische Volksetymologie und Verwandtes*, Leipzig.

Kelly, J. M. (1957) *Princeps Iudex* (= *Forschungen zur Recht* 9), Weimar.

Kipling, R. (1895) *The Second Jungle Book*, London.

Klein, H. W. (1936) *Die volkstümlichen Sprichwörtlichen Vergleiche in Lateinischen und romanistischen Sprachen*, Tübingen.

Klotz, A. (1925) (review of Griset (1925)), *Berliner Philologische Wochenschrift* 827–9.

Knab, R. (1934) *Die Periodoniken*, Giessen.

Knorringa, H. (1926) Emporos. *Data on Trade and Trader in Greek Literature from Homer to Aristotle*, Utrecht.

Knowlson, T. S. (1910) *The Origins of Popular Superstitions and Customs*, London.

Körte, A., and A. Thierfelder, eds. (1952²) *Menandri quae Supersunt*, Leipzig.

Kraus, C. S. (1998) 'Repetition and empire in the *Ab Urbe Condita*', in P. Knox and C. Foss, eds., *Style and Tradition. Studies in Honor of W. Clausen*, Stuttgart, 264–83.

Krause, J. H. (1854) *Angeiologie. Die Gefässe der alten Völker imbesondere der Griechen und Römer*, Halle.

Kretschmer, M. (1938) *Otium, Studia Litterarum, Philosophie und Βίος Θεωρητικός im Leben und Denken Ciceros*, Leipzig and Würzburg.

Krischan, J. (1954) 'Zu Phaedrus II', *Wiener Studien* 67. 77–98.

Kromayer, J. and G. Veith (1928) *Heerwesen und Kriegsführung der Griechen und Römer*, Munich.

Küspert, O. (1902) *Über Bedeutung und Gebrauch des Wörtes* caput *im alteren Latein*, Erlangen.

LaFontaine, J. de (1962) *Fables choisies mises en vers*, ed. G. Couton, Paris.

Lamb, R. W. (1995) Annales Phaedriani: *Rough Notes Towards a Bibliography of Phaedrus*, Lowestoft.

Lamberti, G. (1980) 'La Poetica del *lusus* in Fedro', *Rendiconti dell'Istituto Lombardo* 114. 95–115.

Lana, I. (1955) *L. Annaeus Seneca*, Turin.

Lang, A. (1892) *The Green Fairy Book*, London.

——(1962 = 1897) *The Pink Fairy Book*, London.

La Penna, A. (1961) 'La morale delle favole esopiche come morale delle classi subalterne nell'Antichità', *Società* 4. 438–537.

——(1963) '*Marginalia Aesopica*', in *Lanx Satura N. Terzaghi oblata. Miscellanea Philologica*, Genoa, 227–36.

Lau, O. (1967) *Schuster und Schusterhandwerk in der griechisch-römischen Literatur und Kunst*, Bonn.

Lawrence, W. W. (1931) *Shakespeare's Problem Comedies*, New York.

Leach, J. (1978) *Pompey the Great*, London.

Lefkowitz, M. R. (1981) *The Lives of the Greek Poets*, London.

Leibfried, E. (1982) 'Autorposition, Leserbild. Zerstreute Bemerkungen zu unterschiedlichen Problemen', in P. Hasubek, ed., *Die Fabel. Theorie, Geschichte und Rezeption einer Gattung*, Berlin, 13–26.

Leppin, H. (1996) 'Tacitus und die Anfänge des kaiserzeitlichen Pantomimus', *Rheinisches Museum* 139. 33–40.

Lesage, A.-R. (1955) *Histoire de Gil Blas de Santillane*, Paris, vols. 1–2.

L'Estrange, Sir R. (1692) *The Fables of Aesop and Other Eminent Mythologists*, London.

Levick, B. (1976) *Tiberius the Politician*, London.

Lévi-Strauss, C. (1973) *Introduction to a Science of Mythology*, vols. 1–4. vol. 2, *From Honey to Ashes*, London.

Lewin, L. (1923) *Die Pfeilgift, nach eigenen toxikologischen und ethnologischen Untersuchungen*, Leipzig.

Lewis, J. E. (1996) *The English Fable. Aesop and Literary Culture, 1651–1740*, Cambridge.

Link, W. (1910) *De Vocis 'Sanctus' Usu Pagano Quaestiones Selectae*, Regimonti.

Lipscomb, H. C. (1934) 'Additional note' [to McCartney (1934)], *Classical World* 28. 24.

L'Orange, H. P. (1947) *Apotheosis in Ancient Portraiture* (= *Institut for sammenlignende Kulturforskning, Series B Skrifter* 14), Oslo.

Lumby, J. R. ed. (1908) *More's Utopia, translated by Raphe Robynson (1716)*, Cambridge.

Lüthi, M. (1970) *Once Upon a Time. On the Nature of Fairy Tales*, Bloomington, Ind.

Maass, E. (1925) '*Eunouchos* und verwandtes', *Rheinisches Museum* 74. 432–76.

References 263

McCartney, E. S. (1912) *Figurative Uses of Animal Names in Latin and their Application to Military Devices*, Pennsylvania.

—— (1918–19) 'Puns and plays on proper names', *Classical Journal* 14. 343–58.

—— (1927) 'Modifiers that reflect the etymology of the words modified', *Classical Philology* 22. 184–200.

—— (1934) 'On spitting into the hands as a superstitious act', *Classical World* 27. 99–100.

McDermott, W. C. (1938) *The Ape in Antiquity*, Baltimore.

McDowall, K. A. (1904) 'Some Greek portraits', *Journal of Hellenic Studies* 24. 81–98.

MacKendrick, P. (1954) 'Demetrius of Phalerum, Cato and the *Adelphoe*', *Rivista di Filologia e di Istruzione Classica* 32. 18–35.

MacMullen, R. (1974) *Roman Social Relations 50 B.C. to A.D. 284*, New Haven.

—— (1984) 'The legion as a society', *Historia* 33. 440–56.

Magnus, H. (1901) *Die Augenheilkunde der Alten*, Breslau.

Maiuri, A. (1956) 'Fedro a Miseno', *La Parola del Passato* 11. 32–7.

Manea, N. (1994) *On Clowns: The Dictator and the Artist*, London.

Marin, L. (1978) 'L'Animal-fable Ésope', *Critique* 34. 775–82.

—— (1988) *Portrait of the King*, Basingstoke.

—— (1997) *Food for Thought*, Baltimore.

Martin, D. E. (1922) *The Antiquity of Proverbs*, New York.

Maranon, G. (1956) *Tiberius. A Study in Resentment*, London.

Marx, A. (1889) *Griechische Märchen vom dankbaren Tieren und Verwandtes*, Stuttgart.

Marx, F. (1922) *Molossische und bakcheische Wortformen in der Verskunst der Griechen und Römer, Abhandlungen der Deutschen Akademie der Wissenschaften zu Berlin, Klasse für Sprachen, Literatur und Kunst* 37. 1.

Massie, A. (1989) *Augustus: A Novel*, London.

—— (1990) *Tiberius: The Memoirs of the Emperor*, London.

Mayer, G. R. (1969) *Die Funktion mythologischer Namen und Anspielungen in LaFontaines Fabeln (= Romanistisches Versuchen und Vorarbeiten* 28), Bonn.

Meiggs, R. (1960) *Roman Ostia*, Oxford.

Mensignac, C. de (1892) *Recherches ethnographiques sur la Salive*, Bordeaux. [*Not seen*]

Méril, E. du (1834) *Poésies inédites du Moyen-Âge, précédées d'une Histoire de la Fable antique*, Paris.

Meyer, E. (1913) *Der Emporkömmling. Ein Beitrag zur antiken Ethologie*, Giessen.

Meyer, W. (1915) *Laudes Inopiae*, Göttingen.

Millar, F. (1977) *The Emperor in the Roman World*, London.

Milligan, S. (1971) *Adolf Hitler: My Part in his Downfall*, London.

Miniconi, R.-J. (1951) *Thèmes guérriers de la poèsie Épique gréco-romaine*, Paris.

Moatti, C. (1997) *Raison de Rome. Naissance de l'esprit critique à la fin de la République*, Paris.

Modleski, T. (1990) 'The search for tomorrow in today's soap operas', in T. Bennett, ed., *Popular Fiction: Technology, Ideology, Production, Reading*, London, 189–207.

Mommsen, T. (1894) *A History of Rome*, London, vols. 1–5.

Mood, J. R. (1907) *Some Figurative Uses of* Venire *and* Ire, Baltimore.

Moorhouse, G. (1971) 'The Palladium', *Nova* (January) London, 31.

Müller, L. ed. (1867¹, 1877², . . .) *Phaedri Augusti Liberti Fabularum Aesopiarum Libri Quinque*, Leipzig.

—— (1875) 'Metrisches zu Phaedrus', *Rheinisches Museum* 30. 618–19.

Müller, R. (1952) *Motivkatalog der römischen Elegie*, Zurich.

Nachmanson, E., ed. (1918) *Erotian*, Glossarium, Göteborg.

Nestle, W. (1927) 'Die Fabel des Menenius Agrippa', *Klio* 21. 350–60.

Nettleship, H. (1889) *Contributions to Latin Lexicography*, Oxford.

Nevelet, I. N. (1610) *Mythologia Aesopica*, Frankfurt.

Neumann, P. (1912) *De Vocum Graecarum apud Poetas Latinos ab Hadriani Temporibus ad Claudiani Aetatem Usu*, Bratislava.

Nicholas, B. (1962) *An Introduction to Roman Law*, Oxford.

Nicolson, F. W. (1897) 'The saliva superstition in classical literature', *Harvard Studies in Classical Philology* 8. 23–40.

Niedermeier, L. (1919) *Untersuchungen über die antike poetische Autobiographie*, Munich.

Nisbet, R. G. (1918) 'The *festuca* and *alapa* of manumission', *Journal of Roman Studies* 8. 1–14.

Nock, A. D. (1928) 'Notes on ruler-cult, I–IV', *Journal of Hellenic Studies* 48. 21–43.

Nøjgaard, M. (1967) *La Fable antique, vol. 2. Les grands fabulistes*, Copenhagen.

Noel, T. (1975) *Theories of the Fable in the Eighteenth Century*, New York.

Oakley, S. P. (1985) 'Single combat in the Roman Republic', *Classical Quarterly* 35. 392–410.

—— (1998) *A Commentary on Livy Books VI–X*, vol. 2, Oxford.

Oberg, E. (1996) 'Römische Rechtspflege bei Phaedrus', *Rheinisches Museum* 139. 146–65.

O'Connor, C. J. (1905) 'The *lunula*' worn on the Roman shoe', *Transactions of the American Philological Association* 36, *Transactions* 61–2.

O'Hara, J. J. (1996) *True Names. Vergil and the Alexandrian Tradition of Etymological Wordplay*, Ann Arbor, Mich.

Olcott, G. N. (1898) *Word Formation in the Latin Inscriptions*, Rome.
Oliver, P. (1972) *The Story of the Blues*, Harmondsworth.
Oltramare, A. (1926) *Les Origines de la Diatribe romaine*, Geneva.
Önnerfors, A. (1987) 'Textkritisches und Sprachliches zu Phaedrus',
  Hermes 115. 429–53.
Opie, I. and P. (1967) *The Lore and Language of Schoolchildren*,
  Oxford.
Orelli, J. G. (1832) *Phaedri Augusti Liberti Fabularum Aesopiarum
  Libri V*, Turin.
Österley, H. ed. (1871) *Gesta Romanorum, mit Nachweisungen*, Berlin.
Otto, A. (1889) 'Der menschliche Körper und seine Teile im Sprich-
  wört', *Archiv für Lateinische Lexicographie* 6. 309–40.
——(1890 = 1971) *Die Sprichwörter und sprichwörtlichen Redensarten
  der Römer*, Leipzig and Hildesheim.
Parks, E. P. (1945) *The Roman Rhetorical Schools as a Preparation for
  the Courts Under the Early Empire*, Baltimore.
Paschalis, M. (1997) *Virgil's Aeneid. Semantic Relations and Proper
  Names*, Oxford.
Patterson, A. (1991) *Fables of Power: Aesopian Writing and Political
  History*, Durham, NC.
Pavlovskis, Z. (1967) '*Vir fortis sine manibus* and the handless maiden',
  Classica & Mediaevalia 28. 86–113.
Pearce, T. E. V. (1970) 'Notes on Cicero, *In Pisonem*', *Classical
  Quarterly* 20. 309–21.
Pease, A. S. (1907) 'Notes on stoning among the Greeks and Romans',
  Transactions of the American Philological Association 38. 5–18.
Perry, B. E. (1940) 'The origin of the epimythium', *Transactions of the
  American Philological Association* 71. 391–419.
——(1952) Aesopica. *A series of texts relating to Aesop or ascribed to
  him or closely connected with the literary tradition that bears his name*,
  1, Illinois.
——ed. (1965) *Babrius and Phaedrus*, Cambridge, Mass., and London.
Peters, W. A. M. (1946) *Phaedrus. Een Studie over Persoon, Werk en
  Taal van den romeinschen Fabeldichter*, Nijmegen.
Pfeiffer, R. (1938) *Die Netzfischer des Aischylos und der Inachos des
  Sophokles, Sitzungsberichte der bayerischen Akademie der Wissen-
  schaft, philosophische-historische Klasse, München*, 9. 2.
Phillips, E. D. (1973) *Greek Medicine*, London.
Pickard-Cambridge, A. (1968²) *The Dramatic Festivals of Athens*,
  Oxford.
Pinder, N. (1869) *Selections from the Less Known Latin Poets:
  Phaedrus*, Oxford, 263–79.
Pithou, P., ed. (1596) *Phaedri Augusti Liberti Fabularum Aesopiarum
  Libri Quinque Nunc Primum in Lucem Editi*, Troyes.

Plass, P. (1988) *Wit and the Writing of History. The Rhetoric of Historiography in Imperial Rome*, Madison, Wis.

Poggio Bracciolini, G. F. (1968) *The Facetiae*, New York.

Pope, A. (1950) *An Essay on Man*, London.

Postgate, J. P., ed. (1894–1905) *Corpus Poetarum Latinorum*, London, vols. 1–2.

—— (1896) (unread paper: 'emendations of the text of Phaedrus'), *Proceedings of the Cambridge Philological Society* 43. 9–10.

—— (1919*a*) *Phaedri Fabulae Aesopiae*, Oxford.

Postgate, J. P., (1919*b*) 'Phaedrus and Seneca', *Classical Review* 23. 19–24.

Powell, J. U. (1925) *Collectanea Alexandrina Poetarum Graecorum Aetatis Ptolemaicae*, Oxford.

Prinz, K. (1906) *Der Prolog zum dritten Buche von Phaedrus Fabeln, Jahresbuch des Gymnasiums der königliches katholisches theresianischen Akademie in Wien*. [*Not seen*]

—— (1923) 'Zur Chronologie und Deutung der Fabeln des Phaedrus', *Wiener Studien* 43. 62–70.

Prittwitz-Gaffron, E. von (1911) *Das Sprichwort im griechischen Epigramm*, Giessen.

Propp, V. (1968) *Morphology of the Folktale*, Austin, Tex.

Purcell, N. (1987) 'Town in country and country in town', in E. B. MacDougall, ed., *Ancient Roman Villa Gardens*, Washington, 187–203.

Radford, E. and M. (1961) *Encyclopedia of Superstitions*, New York.

Rank, L. (1910) '*Observatiunculae ad Phaedrum*', *Mnemosyne* 38. 261–77.

—— (1911) '*Observatiunculae ad Phaedrum, 2.*', *Mnemosyne* 39. 51–67.

—— (1917) '*Noua Phaedriana, 2*', *Mnemosyne* 45. 272–309.

Raubitschek, A. E. (1949) 'Phaidros and his Roman pupils', *Hesperia* 18. 96–103.

Rawson, B. and P. Weaver, eds. (1997) *The Roman Family in Italy: Status, Sentiment, Space*, Oxford.

Reich, H. (1903) *Der Mimus*, Berlin, vols. 1–3.

Reynolds, R. W. (1943) (1946) 'The adultery mime', *Classical Quarterly* 40. 76–84.

Rhys, E., ed. (1971 = 1913) *Aesop's and Other Fables*, London.

Ribbeck, O. (1885) *Agroikos. Eine ethologische Studien, Sitzungsberichte der Heidelberger Akademie der Wissenschaften, philosophische-historische Klasse, Heidelberg*, 10. 1.

Richlin, A. (1997) 'Gender and rhetoric: producing manhood in the schools', in W. J. Dominik, ed., *Roman Eloquence: Rhetoric in Society and Literature*, London, 90–110.

Richter, G. (1713) *Specimen Animaduersionum Criticarum*, Jena.

Rickert, E., ed. (1908) *The Babees Book: Medieval Manners for the Young*, London.

Ridgway, B. S. (1990) *Hellenistic Sculpture, vol. 1. The Styles of Ca. 331–200 B.C.*, Bristol.

Rigault, N., ed. (1599¹, 1617², 1630³, . . .) *Phaedri Augusti Liberti Fabularum Aesopiarum Libri Quinque*, Paris.

Riggsby, A. M. (1997) '"Public" and "private" in Roman culture: the case of the *cubiculum*', *Journal of Roman Archaeology* 10. 36–56.

Rittershausen, C., ed. (1598) *Phaedri Augusti Liberti Fabularum Aesopiarum Libri Quinque*, Leyden.

Robbins, B. (1986) *The Servant's Hand. English Fiction from Below*, Durham, NC.

Rogers, R. S. (1935) *Criminal Trials and Criminal Legislation under Tiberius*, Connecticut.

Roggwiller, A. E. (1926) *Philosophie Dichtung Kunst und Religion in der attischen Komödie*, Zurich.

Rohde, E. (1960³ = 1914) *Der griechische Roman und seine Vorläufer*, Leipzig and Hildesheim.

Romano, B. (1927) 'Phaedrus *fabulae* III. *prol. vv.* 33–50', *Bollettino di Filologia Classica* 33. 309–14.

Rose, H. J. (1936) *A Handbook of Latin Literature*, London.

Rosen, K. (1967) 'Political Documents in Hieronymus of Cardia, 323–302 B.C.', *Acta Classica* 10. 41–94.

Rosenbaum, R. (1998) *Explaining Hitler. The Search for the Origin of his Evil*, Basingstoke.

Ross, D. O. (1975) *Backgrounds to Augustan Poetry. Gallus, Elegy and Rome*, Cambridge.

Rotolo, V. (1957) *Il Pantomimo*, Palermo.

Rozmovits, L. (1995) 'The Wolf and the Lamb: an image and its afterlife', *Art History* 18. 97–111.

Russell, D. (1983) *Greek Declamation*, Cambridge.

Salac, A. (1960) '*Ad Menandri iuuenilia*', *Eunomia* 4. 38–40.

Sassen, H. von (1911) *De Phaedri Sermone*, Marburg.

Saumaise, C. (1698) Annotations (via Gude) in Burmann (1698).

Sauter, F. (1934) *Kaiserkult bei Martial* (= *Tübinger Beiträge zur Altertumswissenschaft* 21), Tübingen.

Scafuro, A. C. (1997) *The Forensic Stage. Settling Disputes in Graeco-Roman New Comedy*, Cambridge.

Scheffer, J., ed. (1663) *Phaedri Augusti Liberti Fabularum Aesopiarum Libri Quinque*, Uppsala.

Schefold, K. (1997²) *Die Bildnisse der antiken Dichter, Redner und Denker*, Basel.

Scheiber, A. (1966) 'Alte Geschichte im neuen Gewande', *Fabula* 8. 1087–9.

Schepers, M. A. (1926) '*De Glycera Menandri Amoribus*', *Mnemosyne* 54. 258–62.

Schissel Von Fleschenberg, O. (1912–13) *Rhetorische Forschungen*. *1. Novellenkranze Lukians, Band 2. Die griechische Novelle*, Halle.

Schlam, C. C. (1992) *The Metamorphoses of Apuleius. On making an Ass of Oneself*, London.

Schlauch, M. (1927) *Chaucer's Constance and Accused Queens*, New York.

Schmalz, J. H. (1908) '*Si tamen*', *Glotta* 1. 333–9.

Schoder, R. V. (1971–2) 'Virgil's poetic use of the Cumae area', *Classical Journal* 67. 97–109.

Schönberger, H. (1910) *Beispiele aus der Geschichte, eine rhetorische Kunstmittel im Ciceros Reden*, Augsburg.

Schoppe, C. (1598) Annotations in Rittershausen (1598).

Schröder, O. (1914) *De Laudibus Athenarum a Poetis Tragicis et ab Oratoribus Epidicticis Excultis*, Göttingen.

Schwabe, J. G. S., ed. (1781^1, 1806^2) *Phaedri Augusti Liberti Fabularum Aesopiarum Libri Quinque*, Halle and Brunswig, vols. 1–2.

——(1884) 'Phaedrus doch in Pierien geboren', *Rheinisches Museum* 39. 476–7.

Scott, J. A. (1923–4) 'The use of poisoned arrows in the Odyssey', *Classical Journal* 19. 240–1.

Scott, K. (1928) 'The deification of Demetrius Poliorcetes', *American Journal of Philology* 49. 137–66, 217–39.

——(1932) 'The "*diritas*" of Tiberius', *American Journal of Philology*. 53. 139–51.

Seager, R. (1972) *Tiberius*, London.

Serres, M. (1979) 'The algebra of literature', in J. V. Harari, ed., *Textual Strategies. Perspectives in Post-Structuralist Criticism*, Ithaca, NY, 260–76.

Shackleton-Bailey, D. R. (1978) '*Phaedriana*', *American Journal of Philology* 99. 451–5.

Shatzman, I. (1972) 'The Roman general's authority over booty', *Historia* 21. 177–205.

Sittl, K. (1890) *Die Gebärden der Griechen und Römer*, Leipzig.

Slater, W. J. (1994) 'Pantomime riots', *Classical Antiquity* 13. 120–44.

Smart, C. (1761) *Poetical Translation of the Fables of Phaedrus*, London.

Smith, R. R. R. (1988) *Hellenistic Royal Portraits*, Oxford.

Sonin, J. (1999) 'The Verbalisation of Non-Verbal Communication in Classical Greek Texts', unpublished Ph.D. dissertation, University of Cambridge.

Sonny, A. (1898) '*Ardalio*', *Archiv für Lateinische Lexicographie* 10. 381–2.

Souter, A. (1927) '*Miscellanea Latina*', in *Raccolta di Scritti in Onore di F. Ramorino*, Milan, 270–88.

Speckenbach, K. (1978) 'Die Fabel von der Fabel. Zur Überlieferungsgeschichte zum Wirkungsgeschichte der Fabel von Hahn und Perle', *FMS* 12. 178–229.

Spencer, D. J. (1997) 'The Roman Alexander: Studies in Curtius Rufus', unpublished Ph.D. dissertation, University of Cambridge.

Spencer, T. (1954) 'Three Shakespearian Notes', *Modern Language Review* 49. 46–51.

Splettstösser, W. (1898) *Der heimkehrende Gatte und sein Weib in der Weltlitteratur*, Berlin.

Stallybrass, P. (1997) 'Footnotes', in D. Hillman and C. Mazzio, eds., *The Body in Parts: Fantasies of Corporeality in Early Modern Europe*, New York, 313–25.

Stallybrass, P., and A. White (1986) *The Politics and Poetics of Transgression*, London.

Starnes, D. T., ed. (1956) *Proverbes or Adagies gathered out of the Chiliades of Erasmus, by R. Taverner* (1569), Miami, Fla.

Stein, E. (1949–59) *Histoire du bas-empire*, Paris, vols. 1–2.

Steiner, P. (1906) 'Die *dona militaria*', *Bonner Jarhrbücher* 114. 1–98.

Stowasser, J. M. (1893) *Phaedri Fabulae*, Leyden.

Studniczka, F. (1909) *L. Aelius Sejanus: eine ikonographische Vermutung vorgelegt zum Winckelmannsfeste des archaeologischen Seminars der Universität Leipzig am VIII. December MDCCCCIX*, Leipzig.

——(1918) 'Das Bildnis Menanders', *Neue Jahrbücher für klassische Altertum, Geschichte und deutsche Litteratur und für Pädagogik* 41. 1–31.

Susini, G. (1969) 'Phaedrus II, 4, 10', *Collection Latomus* 101. 707–9.

Syme, R. (1958) 'Sabinus the muleteer', *Latomus* 17. 73–80.

——(1986) *The Augustan Aristocracy*, Oxford.

Tacke, A. H. W. (1911) *Phaedriana*, Berlin.

Tanner, T. (1979) *Adultery in the Novel: Contract and Transgression*, Baltimore.

Taylor, L. R. (1927) 'The "*Proskynesis*" and the Hellenistic ruler cult', *Journal of Hellenic Studies* 47. 53–62.

Thiele, G. (1906) 'Phädrus-Studien. 1', *Hermes* 41. 562–92.

——(1908) 'Phädrus-Studien. 2', *Hermes* 43. 337–72.

Thompson, J. A. S. (1993) 'Ovid's Orpheus: Studies in *Metamorphoses* 10–11', unpublished Ph.D. dissertation, University of Cambridge.

Tilley, M. P. (1950) *A Dictionary of the Proverbs of England in the Sixteenth and Seventeenth Centuries*, Ann Arbor, Mich.

Toll, J. (1781) Annotations in Schwabe (1781).

Tolle, K. (1883) *Das Betheuern und Beschwören in der altromanischen Poesie mit besonderer Berücksichtigung der französischen*, Göttingen.

Toner, J. P. (1995) *Leisure and Ancient Rome*, Cambridge.

Treggiari, S. (1969) *Roman Freedmen During the Late Republic*, Oxford.

Treggiari, S. (1991) *Roman Marriage. Iusti Coniuges From the Time of Cicero to the Time of Ulpian*, Oxford.

Trenkner, S. (1958) *The Greek Novella in the Classical Period*, Cambridge.

Tribukait, P. (1889) *De Prouerbiis Vulgaribusque Aliis Locutionibus apud Bucolicos Graecos Obuiis*, Regimonti.

Trotter, D. (1988) *Circulation: Defoe, Dickens, and the Economies of the Novel*, Basingstoke.

Tschiedel, H. J. (1969) *Phaedra und Hippolytos, Variationen eines tragischen Konflictes*, Erlangen.

Ussery, H. E. (1971) *Chaucer's Physician: Medicine and Literature in Fourteenth Century England*, New Orleans.

Vandaele, H. (1897) *Qua mente Phaeder Fabellas scripserit*, Paris.

Van Ooteghem, J. (1959) *L. Licinius Lucullus*, Gembloux.

Vaux, R. de (1959) 'Les combats singuliers dans l'Ancien Testament' in *Biblica* 40. 495–508.

Vercoutre, A. (1880) 'La médicine publique dans l'antiquité classique', *Révue d'Archéologie* 39. 99–110, 309–21, 348–62.

Vernant, J.-P. (1991) 'Death in the eyes: Gorgo, figure of the *Other*', in *Mortals and Immortals: Collected Essays*, Princeton, NJ, 111–38.

Versnel, H. (1970) *Triumphus*, Leyden.

Veyne, P. (1987) *A History of Private Life. Vol. 1, From Pagan Rome to Byzantium*, Cambridge, Mass.

——(1990) *Bread and Circuses. Historical Sociology and Political Pluralism*, London.

Vigneron, P. (1968) *Le Cheval dans L'Antiquité*, Nancy, vols. 1–2.

Völker, F. (1877) *De Graecarum fabularum actoribus*, Halle.

——(1899) *Berühmte Schauspieler im griechischen Altertum*, Hamburg.

Volkmann, H. (1935) *Zur Rechtsprechung im Prinzipat des Augustus*, Munich.

Vollmer, F. (1919) 'Lesungen und Deutungen III, § 11. Zur Chronologie und Deutung der Fabeln des Phaedrus', *Sitzungsberichte der bayerischen Akademie der Wissenschaft, philosophische-historische Klasse, München*, 5. 9–24.

Vouillème, E. (1887) *Quomodo Veteres Adiurauerint*, Halle.

Wackernagel, W. (1869²) *Voces Variae Animantium. Ein Beitrag zur Naturkunde und zur Geschichte der Sprache*, Basel.

Wagener, A. P. (1912) *Popular Associations of Right and Left in Roman Literature*, Baltimore.

Wagenvoort, H. (1920) 'Pantomimus und Tragödie im augusteischen

Zeitalter', *Neue Jahrbücher für klassische Altertum, Geschichte und deutsche Litteratur und für Pädagogik* 45. 101–13.

Walcot, P. (1970) *Greek Peasants, Ancient and Modern*, Manchester.

Walden, J. W. H. (1894) 'Stage-terms in Heliodorus', *Harvard Studies in Classical Philology* 5. 1–43.

Waldstein, J. W. (1964) *Untersuchungen zum römischen Begnadigungsrecht*, Abolitio, Indulgentia, Venia (= *Commentationes Aenipontanae* 18), Innsbruck.

Walker, T. (1910) *Die altfranzösischen Dichtungen vom Helden im Kloster*, Tübingen.

Wallace, L. (1959) *Ben-Hur*, London.

Walser, G. (1951) *Rom, das Reich, und die fremden Völker in der Geschichtsschreibung der frühen Kaiserzeit*, Baden-Baden.

Walters, J. (1993) 'Ancient Concepts of Manhood and their Relation with Other Markers of Social Status', unpublished Ph.D. dissertation, University of Cambridge.

——(1997) 'Invading the Roman body: manliness and impenetrability in Roman thought', in J. P. Hallett and M. B. Skinner, eds., *Roman Sexualities*, Princeton, NJ, 29–43.

Wardle, D. (1998) *Valerius Maximus*, Memorable Deeds and Sayings. *Book I*, Oxford.

Wase, C., ed. (1668) *Phaedri Augusti Liberti Fabularum Aesopiarum Libri Quinque*, London.

Watson, G. R. (1969) *The Roman Soldier*, London.

Weber, L. F. (1904) *Märchen und Schwank*, Kiel.

Webster, T. B. L. (1950) *Studies in Menander*, Manchester.

——(1953) *Studies in Later Greek Comedy*, Manchester.

Wedeck, H. E. (1927) 'A note on army conditions, ancient and modern', *Classical World* 20. 97–8.

Wehrli, F. R. (1944–59) *Die Schule des Aristoteles*, Basle, vols. 1–10.

Weinreich, O. (1909) *Antike Heilungwunder*, Giessen.

——(1940–1) *Martials Grabepigramm auf den Pantomimen Paris (XI. 13)*, *Sitzungsberichte der Heidelberger Akademie der Wissenschaften, philosophische-historische Klasse, Heidelberg*, 31. 1.

——(1944–8) *Epigramm Studien. 1: Epigramm und Pantomimus*, *Sitzungsberichte der Heidelberger Akademie der Wissenschaften, philosophische-historische Klasse, Heidelberg*, 34. 1.

Weinstock, S. (1971) *Divus Iulius*, Oxford.

Welleski, A. (1925) *Märchen des Mittelalters*, Berlin.

Wellmann, M. (1930) *Der Physiologus. Eine religionsgeschichtlich-naturwissenschaftliche Untersuchung, Philologus Supplementband* 22. 1.

Wendland, P. (1904) 'Σωτήρ. Eine religionsgeschichtliche Untersuchung', *Zeitschrift für die Neutestamentliche Wissenschaft unde die Kunde der älteren Kirche* 5. 335–53.

272   *References*

Wesselski, A. (1910–20) *Narren Gaukler und Volksliebinge*, Berlin, vols. 1–5. [*Not seen*]

West, M. L. (1969) 'Near Eastern material in Hellenistic and Greek Literature', *Harvard Studies in Classical Philology* 73. 113–34.

Weyman, C. (1904) 'Zu den Sprichwörtern und sprichwörtlichen Redensarten der Römer', *Archiv für Lateinische Lexicographie* 13. 379–406.

——(1908) '*Sine ira et studio*', *Archiv für Lateinische Lexicographie* 15. 278–9.

White, P. (1974) 'The presentation and dedication of the *Siluae* and the *Epigrams*', *Journal of Roman Studies* 64. 40–61.

White, T. H. (1954) *The Book of Beasts*, London.

Wilamowitz-Möllendorf, U. von (1913) *Sappho und Simonides*, Berlin.

——(1935–72) *Kleine Schriften*, Berlin, vols. 1–6.

Wild, J. P. (1970) *Textile Manufacture in the Northern Provinces*, Cambridge.

Wille, G. (1967) *Musica Romana. Die Bedeutung der Musik in Leben der Römer*, Amsterdam.

Wilson, L. M. (1924) *The Roman Toga*, Baltimore.

——(1938) *The Clothing of the Romans*, Baltimore.

Wimmel, W. (1960) *Kallimachos in Rom. Die Nachfolge seines apologetischen Dichtens in der Augusteerzeit, Hermes Einzelschriften* 16.

Winckelmann, J. J. (1767) *Monumenti Antichi Inediti, vols. 1–2*, Rome.

Wiseman, T. P. (1985) *Catullus and his World. A Reappraisal*, Cambridge.

——(1991) *Death of an Emperor. Flavius Josephus*, Exeter.

Wishart, D. (1998) *Sejanus*, London.

Wistrand, E. (1972) 'Aussichtstürme in römischen Villen', in *Opera Selecta* (= *Skrifter utgivna av Svenska Institutes i Rom* 10), 218–20.

Wölfflin, E. (1884) 'Die Epoden des Archilochus', *Rheinisches Museum* 39. 156–7.

——(1933) *Ausgewählte Schriften*, Leipzig.

Wreschniok, R. (1907) *De Cicerone Lucretioque Ennii Imitatoribus*, Bratislava.

Wyss, W. von (1899) *Die Sprichwörter bei den römischen Komikern*, Zurich.

Xivrey, J. Berger de (1830) *Phaedri Augusti Liberti Fabularum Aesopiarum Libros Quinque . . . edidit*, Paris.

Yohannan, J. D. (1968) *Joseph and Potiphar's Wife in World Literature*, New York.

Zander, C. (1897) *De Generibus et Libris Paraphrasium Phaedrianarum* (= *Acta Universitatis Lundensis* 33), Lund.

——(1921) *Phaedrus Solutus vel Phaedri Fabulae Nouae XXX*, (*Skrifter utgivna av humanistiska Vetenskapssamfundet i Lund* 3), Lund.

Zell, K. (1828) *Phaedri Augusti Liberti Fabularum Aesopiarum Libri V*, Stuttgart.

Zimmermann, R. C. W. (1934) 'Mitteilungen zu Phädrus', *Berliner Philologische Wochenschrift* 476–80.

Zwicker, J. (1905) *De Vocabulis et Rebus Gallicis siue Transpadanis apud Vergilium*, Leipzig.

Zwierlein, O. (1970) 'Der codex Pithoeanus des Phaedrus in der Pierpont Morgan Library', *Rheinisches Museum* 113. 91–3.

INDEX OF CHIEF PASSAGES
DISCUSSED IN THE TEXT AND NOTES

GENERAL INDEX

1. CITATIONS

2. GENERAL

Sejanus ix, 57–92, esp. 65–6,
  205 n. 7
shoes, white/dyed 118, 222
  n. 51
silver and gold, great weight of
  141, 228 n. 26
Simonides 152
Sinon 62, 80, 209 n. 41
slave:
  as fabulist 65, 81, 209 n. 43
  manumission ritual 30
  out to impress master 15–16,
    25–26
  sex-object 23–4
Socrates, fabulist manqué 74–5,
  79
soldier queen 131–48
spit 142, 229 n. 35
"subject" (victim, subversive,
  anti-hero, etc.) 2–3, 189–91
  see Aesop, ape: flatterer,
  cobbler, doctor, doves,
  flunkey, freedman, frogs,
  lamb, liar, Menander,
  Phaedrus, rustic, soldier
  queen, truth-teller, widow
subjunctive, polite potential 239
  n. 17
suicide, tragic 203 n. 37

telling tales:
  accident 111, 218 n. 34
  acting acting 127
  admirer from afar 160
  adultery/revenge 39, 50, 202
    nn. 32, 36
  anteoccupatio 207 n. 31
  setting in army camp 133–5,
    142, 144–5, 228 nn. 25, 27–
    29, 229 nn. 30, 32–3
  autopathy/autopsy 44, 110,
    201 n. 23
  belief 37
  "before you could say . . ."
    231–2 n. 49

blindness 52
brevity/dilation 37, 41, 200
  nn. 9, 11
celebrity/spite 100
chance 110, 217 n. 30
climactic rhythm 26, 45
combining stories 42, 200
  n. 13
"as crowds do" 158, 173
"David and Goliath" 137,
  143–4, 230 n. 40, 232 n. 50
declamation 44, 48–51, 199
  n. 4, 204 n. 43
derision 26, 107–8, 123, 126,
  156
voice of experience 135, 146
premature expulsion 142
expulsion as finale 89–90,
  101, 107, 111, 123, 222
  n. 52
fame/humiliation 111–12,
  116–18, 123, 161
public gaze 113, 118, 147
getting ahead (of yourself)
  27–8
habit/normality 110, 112, 224
  n. 67
hidden depths 137
histor(icalit)y 11–14, 70, 105,
  138–9, 156, 159, 167–8,
  171–2
inevitability 98–9
interior focalization 111–12
scene of judgement 37, 49
light (of reason)/blindness 46,
  52
non-verbal mimesis 134
muttering 144, 230 n. 41
"my character" 221 n. 49
night time/murk 46, 52–3
on oath 201 n. 23
parade of submission 158
pay-off 29, 196 n. 19, 232
  n. 52
pride/fall 98–9, 112, 118

3. LATIN LITERATURE

centrepiece prologue 60–1
Dichterweihe 62–3, 73–4, 90
disclaimer of malice 82–3,
    87–90, 211 n. 51

poetic self-deprecation as
    captatio 84–5, 212 n. 58
poetry as way of life 66–8, 75,
    207 n. 33

4. LATIN AND GREEK WORDS

acclamo 225 n. 82
afluo 236 n. 23
alapa 30, 199 n. 37
alius (+ ablative) 210 n. 50
alticinctus 197 n. 26
alueolus 25
ambulo 227 n. 22
antidotum 171, 238 n. 9
ardalos, ardalio (not *ardelio*) 20,
    196 n. 15
arripio 216 n. 24
artes 208 n. 37
auerto 228 n. 27
popularis aura 216 n. 24

caput 167
carmen 73
causa mali 204 n. 50
chorus (*Pierium*) 208 n. 37
cinaedus 141, 160, 227 n. 20
cirrus 198 nn. 27, 32
commilito 138, 142, 229 n. 31
conscientia animi 211 n. 51
continuo 229 n. 32

de/grunnio 126, 225 n. 78
derisus 216 n. 24
diuina domus 222 n. 52

eleuo 201 n. 21
enimuero 231 n. 45
exstillesco 230 n. 36

famam traho 227 n. 18
formosus 236 n. 29
fracte 226 n. 21
friuolus 215 n. 24

hic est 236 n. 27

in-ers 212 n. 61

kappa 214 n. 3

laetus 198 n. 29
licet? 145, 231 n. 44
limo 204 n. 50
linteum 198 n. 27

magnus/Magnus 136, 140
Menander 236 n. 25
mortales 224 n. 67
mulio 228 n. 27
multa ago 196 n. 16
musso/muttio 230 n. 41

natio 20
neniae 208 n. 35
necopinans 217 n. 31
paulo notior 216 n. 28

ob 233 n. 53
onero/honoro 225 n. 74
orbis 220 n. 46

Parmeno 121, 223 n. 56
pegma 218 n. 33
Phalereüs 157, 233–4 n. 9
porcellus 224–5 n. 73
precibus pretio 219 n. 40
princeps/Princeps 114, 216
    n. 25

quid ais? 229 n. 30
quis (not *quibus*) 235 n. 20